Praise for *Don't Ever Get Famous*

"Not concerned with 'creating a literary mafia or codifying a poetics,' as Anne Waldman has put it, New York's downtown poets of the '60s and '70s largely await discovery. This collection of essays does a fine job of showing how varied and complex their achievements were. It might just get them famous after all."

—Peter Nicholls

"Daniel Kane has assembled a much-needed collection of essays that re-situates a wide-ranging movement that not only changed writing, but the landscape of writing, as well. . . . Writers like Bernadette Mayer, Clark Coolidge, Amiri Baraka, Anne Waldman, and others will no longer be overlooked or misapprehended in the rush to solidify the mythology of the New York writing scene."

—Marcella Durand

"*Don't Ever Get Famous* re-draws the map of New York poetry during the 1960s and 1970s. Essays in this landmark volume complicate the 'New York School' label and reveal a wide diversity of writers and cultural traditions that converged in the Lower East Side during a politically volatile time. By collecting these superb essays by poets and critics, Daniel Kane has taken the door off its hinges and let the wind from the East River blow afresh through the house of poetry."

—Michael Davidson

"Here it is, the missing years, the whited-out parts, the lost connections. How did we get from O'Hara/Ginsberg to Language/Slam? We've got Daniel Kane and the contributors included herein to thank for filling in the blanks, for digging way deep and bringing to light the poets who, in doing it all for art, changed the landscape of poetry."

—Bob Holman

Don't Ever Get Famous

Essays on New York Writing
after the New York School

Edited by
Daniel Kane

Dalkey Archive Press
Champaign · London

"Anne Waldman: Standing Corporeally in One's Time" by Rachel Blau DuPlessis originally
appeared in *Jacket Magazine*. *"Angel Hair* Magazine, the Second-Generation New York School,
and the Poetics of Sociability" by Daniel Kane originally appeared in *Contemporary Literature*.

Library of Congress Cataloging-in-Publication Data:

Don't ever get famous: essays on New York Writing after the New York School / edited by
Daniel Kane. – 1st ed.
    p. m.
   ISBN-13: 978-1-56478-460-5 (acid-free paper)
   ISBN-10: 1-56478-460-6 (acid-free paper)
   1. American poetry—New York (State)—New York—History and criticism. 2. American
poetry—20th century—History and criticism. 3. Poets, American—New York (State)—
New York. 4. New York (N.Y.)—Intellectual life—20th century. 5. New York (N.Y.)—In
literature. I. Kane Daniel, 1968-
   PS255.N5D66 2007
   811'.5409—dc22

                                                                    2006016861

Support for this volume has been provided by:
Rachel Blau DuPlessis; Kim McGalliard; Lauren Kane; University of Glasgow American
Studies Research Fund; Columbia University, English Department Graduate Studies Research
Fund; Eric Homberger; University of East Anglia Research Fund; Capricorn Farms,
Purveyors of Top Quality Boer Goats.

Partially funded by a grant from the Illinois Arts Council, a state agency.

Dalkey Archive Press is a nonprofit organization whose mission is to promote international
cultural understanding and provide a forum for dialogue for the literary arts.

www.dalkeyarchive.com

Printed on permanent/durable acid-free paper, bound in the United States of America,
and distributed throughout North America and Europe.

This book is dedicated to Lorenzo Thomas, 1944-2005.

Many thanks to great friend and scholar Stephen Cope,
who helped me conceive of this book in the first place.

Contents

Introduction

DANIEL KANE

"Work your ass off to change the language," Bernadette Mayer counseled her students nearly thirty years ago, "and don't ever get famous." It was partly facetious advice, although in retrospect, it seems curiously portentous as well. Although many poets affiliated with what is now known as the New York School have received a good deal of attention in both popular and academic circles, few of them have been drawn from the ranks of those who followed the first wave of New York poets (those gathered in Donald Allen's groundbreaking, but limited, anthologies). Indeed, as much as has been written on Frank O'Hara, John Ashbery, Barbara Guest, Kenneth Koch, James Schuyler, and other so-called New York School writers, an equally minimal amount of critical attention has been paid to the poets based geographically in downtown New York who started to surface in the sixties and seventies. I refer here not just to poets of the "second-generation" New York School like Ron Padgett and Ted Berrigan, but to other writers as well; *Umbra* poets Lorenzo Thomas, Calvin Hernton, Ishmael Reed, and David Henderson; Deep Image poets Jerome Rothenberg, George Economou, and Robert Kelly; and writers affiliated with Downtown performance and conceptual-art communities like Hannah Weiner, Vito Acconci, Bernadette Mayer, et al.

This collection of essays begins the work of correcting the historical record by taking a recuperative and critical approach to the poetry of New York writers of the '60s and '70s. Readers will note that the essays focus almost entirely on "Downtown" or Lower East Side-based poets. Of course, there were certainly plenty of *other* kinds of New York poets during the period under discussion who are not considered here, as there were plenty of "mainstream" poets too who did not affiliate themselves with the *idea* of Downtown in either its geographical, political, or cultural-literary sense. Yet the Downtown scene of the '60s and '70s was affiliated with some of the major manifestations of the political counterculture and the artistic avant-garde. Ted Berrigan wrote for the counterculture magazine *The East Village Other*; the Poetry Project at St. Mark's Church featured performances by proto-punk Patti Smith and held fundraisers for draft resisters; Downtown poets were intimately connected to the anti-war movement; members of the Velvet Underground socialized with poets including Lewis Warsh and Anne Waldman; what was to become known as the Black Arts movement was partly initiated and complicated through the auspices of *Umbra* magazine. Considering the cultural and political ferment associated with the artistic renaissance on New York's Lower East Side, it seems the time has come for a collection covering a very specific slice of "New York writing."

In my earlier book *All Poets Welcome: The Lower East Side Poetry Scene in the 1960s*, I wished to include the poets affiliated with the Downtown scene within the overall history of contemporary American poetry. I found myself attempting to evoke a cultural and social environment for the writers under discussion as much as, if not more than, I was reading and analyzing the poetry itself. Writing *All Poets Welcome* partly satisfied my desire for a cultural history of poets I felt had been unfairly excised from literary history, as it made me hungry for a more direct and critical engagement with the innovative writing coming out of the Lower East Side scene. Thus, I have invited a variety of different scholars and poets to weigh in on the literature of this period.

Contributors seek to recognize the significant and, until now, relatively ignored texts that were produced in New York City in the 1960s and early 1970s. There are a number of reasons why contributors to this book believe it is important to concentrate on Downtown poets of the 1960s and '70s. For one, our most recent assertively avant-garde grouping—and by that I refer generally to the language writing phenomenon—has become relatively familiar and institutionally-entrenched. At the same time, performance poetry, representing the populist end of the spectrum, is by now popularly acknowledged via corporate sponsorship, mainstream media, and poetry slam competitions from Albuquerque to the Lower East Side to Kalamazoo. Yet at present, a neglected interval obtains between what is immediately contemporary and what scholarship has defined as the golden age of the 1950s and early 1960s. Thus, we have critical and popular work on poets of the 1950s, including Terence Diggory's and Stephen Paul Miller's *The Scene of My Selves: New Work on New York School Poets*; Martin Duberman's *Black Mountain: An Exploration in Community*; Michael Davidson's *The San Francisco Renaissance: Poetics and Community at Mid-Century*; David Lehman's *The Last Avant-Garde: The Making of the New York School of Poets*, and the virtual cottage industry attendant to the Beat mythos. Books on language and spoken-word communities of the '80s and '90s are also available in relative abundance, including Bob Perelman's *The Marginalization of Poetry: Language Writing and Literary History*, Christopher Beach's *Artifice & Indeterminacy: An Anthology of New Poetics* and *Poetic Culture: Contemporary American Poetry Between Community and Institution*, Maria Damon's *The Dark End of the Street: Margins in American Vanguard Poetry*, Anne Vickery's *Leaving Lines of Gender: A Feminist Genealogy of Language Writing*, and Mark Wallace's and Steven Marks's *Telling it Slant: Avant-Garde Poetics of the 1990s*, to name a few. Yet whatever happened to New York poetry in the 1960s and '70s, much of which directly influenced and impacted the poetries of today? *Don't Ever Get Famous* aspires to fill in this gap. While the neglect of significant poets and poetic scenes that impels us to write here is not unique to New York City culture, nevertheless what is specific to New York is the very magnitude of what has been overlooked.

New York's poetry scene in the 1960s and 1970s was far from merely transitional. No magic leap occurred from the "New American Poetry" to "Language" writing; from Beat performance poetry to Poetry Slams, from late Harlem Renaissance to the Black Arts Movement. The essays in this book argue that the barely-analyzed period of New York in the 1960s and '70s was foundational to our current poetry environment. The establishment of the Poetry Project at St. Mark's Church allowed an otherwise marginal poetry a means of dissemination by way of readings, lectures, performances, workshops and the like (many of which were attended, and later given, by poets central to contemporary innovative poetry); writers affiliated with *Umbra* magazine informed the Black Arts Movement, which evolved in the 1960s into an international phenomenon even as Umbra poets poets themselves maintained a cosmopolitan stance in distinction to their Black Nationalist peers; procedural techniques and poetics theory developed by poets including Bernadette Mayer and Clark Coolidge partly inspired Charles Bernstein, Bruce Andrews, Lyn Hejinian, Ron Silliman, and other writers; overlapping spaces of "black" and "white" poetries were created; a vibrant and practically unprecedented magazine culture informed the writing at the time. The current maps of 20th-century poetry generally fail to take these phenomena into account. We redraw the lines here.

This collection is not solely celebratory or commemorative—while focusing our attention on the texts themselves, we also examine these decades' poets and their respective communities with an emphasis on cultural, sociological, and historical contexts as well as strictly literary or aesthetic ones. The tones and positions of these essays are as various as the poetry under discussion—equally chatty, erudite, critical, interrogatory, fun, and written by academics as well as academically unaffiliated poets, the work in this book is aimed at a relatively broad spectrum of readers. While scholars of poetry will benefit from the rigorously argued essays included here, we also recognize that basic introductory articles on especially underrepresented writers including Lewis Warsh, Joe Ceravolo, and Lee Harwood are useful for both "expert" and newcomer alike.

I have arranged these articles in a broadly thematic fashion, sandwiched between two essays that, at first glance, may surprise some readers by their very presence in such a book. The first essay is Andrew Epstein's "'Against the Speech of Friends': Amiri Baraka Sings the White Friend Blues"; the final essay is Andrea Brady's "The Other Poet: Wieners, O'Hara, Olson" (which focuses on John Wieners's poetry). Baraka and Wieners, both of whom were introduced to a wider reading public via Donald Allen's *The New American Poetry*, were contemporaries of O'Hara, Ashbery and other New York based writers, and formed lasting links with the younger writers affiliated with the 1960s and '70s scenes. However, neither of them are generally considered to be specifically "New York" writers. That said, while Baraka and Wieners worked to transcend regional and generational limits to connect to ever-shifting poetic communities, they continued to refer to New York as a foundational and influential site for the production of innovative poetry, as they influenced and were influenced by O'Hara and the New York School generally. Thus, I place these essays at the beginning and end of this book precisely because Baraka and Wieners figure in as impressive and exciting literary and social models to the mostly younger poets that form the primary basis of study here. Importantly, Baraka and Wieners represent *alternative* "elders"—I was not interested to begin and end this volume with articles on the predictable influence that Ashbery, Koch, Schuyler, Guest, and other first-generation New York School writers had on succeeding generations. Rather, the very fluidity of position-takings represented by Wieners and Baraka is evoked in Epstein's and Brady's work in order to expand our notions of what constitutes both Downtown New York writing as a geographical and historical fact and "The New York School" as stable literary / aesthetic sign.

Epstein and Brady recognize that the poets' output is crucial to our understanding of the variousness and importance of the Lower East Side poetic community. Linking Baraka to figures including Frank O'Hara,

Ralph Waldo Emerson, Ted Berrigan, Ron Padgett, and Lorenzo Thomas, Epstein sets the stage for a concern that drives practically all the essays in this book—how a poet negotiates his or her status as an independent producer of literary work with the facts of writing in and out of community. As Epstein writes, Baraka was a "bridge between different factions" of Black Mountain, Beat and New York School coteries. Baraka worked to productively complicate the kinds of facile classifications that would lump poets under loosely-defined literary camps. To begin this book with an essay that in some fundamental way shows how Amiri Baraka *informed* New York School aesthetics (as opposed to being merely *influenced* by such aesthetics) is to question the very terms most scholars use in discussing the New York School grouping and its literary and historical lineage. Working against a predominantly white, European model of inherited influence that helps define mainstream characterizations of the New York School, Epstein shows how Baraka "came to embody an exciting experiment in collaboration, friendship, and intertextuality across traditional boundaries of race, at a moment when American writers had both the opportunity and the desire to establish productive alliances in a space outside the officially sanctioned discourses of American identity and community."

In the same spirit, I end the book with Andrea Brady's fascinating article *The Other Poet: Wieners, O'Hara, Olson*. It is certainly true that Wieners lived only occasionally in lower Manhattan, returned again and again to Boston during his peripatetic years, and ultimately resided on Boston's terrifically-named Joy Street during his last decades. Yet Wieners's influence on Frank O'Hara, while generally acknowledged, is rarely discussed; his influence on succeeding New York poets is practically ignored. Brady quotes trenchantly from Wieners's poems to show how Wieners was very much enamored with the values he associated specifically with New York City: "He remembered his 'private residence on / West 8th' as a 'shrine of devotion to Manhattan / Gotham shows mad weirdos and high-jinx'; but 'Nothing like it is now on Beacon Hill' ('Biding in the Gloom,' *Selected* 274), and Boston is 'nothing to match New York's / excitement'" ('Home-Duty,' *Selected* 247). Brady explores Wieners's "similarities to and differences from O'Hara and Olson," and finds Wieners synthesizing the glamour and surface pleasures of much of O'Hara poetry with the vatic drive we find in Olson. Yet Brady is careful to show Wieners emerging from under the shadow of these "influences"; "As a chronicler of the ups and downs of the early gay rights movement, as an aficionado of the culture industry, as an incisive critic of state institutions and social perceptions of mental illness, and as an artificer whose syntax and diction expressed the profoundest states of alienation, his poetry stands alone."

The greater part of this volume is concerned with poets for whom the Lower East Side in the 1960s and '70s was to prove crucial to their development. These essays examine individual oeuvres, important literary magazines, and associated coteries.

Jed Rasula's essay "*Deep Image*" provides us with a succinct chronology of perhaps one of the more amorphous and least-understood groups of poets affiliated with the Lower East Side scene. Rasula historicizes this group in its appropriate context. Beginning with a brief discussion of Pierre Reverdy, that most beloved of New York School influences (recall O'Hara's final lines from his poem "A Step Away from Them": "My heart is in my / pocket, it is *Poems* by Pierre Reverdy"), Rasula takes us on a journey that is far, far away from anything conventionally resembling the New York School. Rasula revisits the term "deep image" in a manner so far unprecedented. The critical writings of figures as various as Gaston Bachelard, Sergei Eisenstein, Jack Spicer, Noam Chomsky, and Ludwig Wittgenstein are called to mind in order to frame a little-known literary phenomenon. Deep Image is situated by Rasula firmly within the Lower East Side-based milieu of poets Jerome Rothenberg, David Antin, Robert Kelly, and others, most of whom participated in editing magazines like *Trobar*, *Poems from the Floating World*, and *Some/thing*. Reading the poetry of, among others, Robert Creeley and David Antin, Rasula illustrates how poetry identified with the deep image involved a solicitous posture toward poetic vision, a petition to the unconscious, and a potentially social aspect tending towards radicalism. Perhaps most compellingly, Rasula identifies the work of deep image poets as partly responsible for the "linguistic turn" in American poetry, thus providing us with a bridge originating with Kelly, Rothenberg and Antin, spanning to the language poets of the late twentieth century.

Essays following Rasula's revisioning of literary history focus on one of the most important phenomena of the '60s and '70s generation—the small-circulation little magazine. Jon Panish examines *Umbra* magazine in order to explore how its cosmopolitan approach to racial identity productively defines it apart from the later, more nationalist Black Arts movement; Harry Thorne re-reads Ted Berrigan's *C: A Journal of Poetry* to argue that Berrigan was a far more heterodox writer and editor than the limited "New York School" tag allowed for; I analyze how Lewis Warsh's and Anne Waldman's *Angel Hair* magazine and books worked to determine an avant-garde reception independent of literary taxonomy and academic discourse; and Linda Russo discusses Hannah Weiner's and Bernadette Mayer's poetry within the context of the mimeographed magazines *The World* and *0-9* in order to make new links between the poets' work, a developing, non-essentialist feminism, and the nascence of Language writing.

Rather than merely considering *Umbra* as a stepping-stone to the more well-known Black Arts groupings initiated in part by Amiri Baraka, Panish argues that *Umbra* magazine offered a more cosmopolitan and, in hindsight, more "useful" model for racial consciousness vis a vis poetry and community than those models produced by the Black Arts groups. Though Panish shows how race is as central to Umbra's mission (the first issue of the magazine states that "the experience of being Negro" is its primary "orientation") as it is to the Black Arts movement, he argues that Umbra's approach to race "is plural and flexible in ways that the development of mid-1960s nationalism did not allow." Following David Lionel Smith's general model, Panish makes "a distinction between the Black Arts movement's 'black aesthetic' and Umbra's 'black aesthetics; as Smith argues, 'the former suggests a single principle, while the latter leaves open multiple possibilities. The former is closed and prescriptive, the latter, open and descriptive.'" Because of Umbra poets' approach to race, Panish suggests that it is more accurate (and useful) to view them "as having anticipated the complex and pluralist notion of blackness that is a hallmark of contemporary cosmopolitan conceptions of art than as immediate precursors to the cultural nationalism of the Black Arts movement." Panish shows how, in "both the composition of the group (black and white members) and the selection of poets and poems (not only black and white poets but poets constructing different black identities) presented in the magazine, the example of Umbra demonstrates an understanding of the complexity of racial identity and, more important, racial expression in art that clearly sets it apart from the subsequent period of Black Arts, the black aesthetic, and black cultural nationalism in general. As such, Umbra may represent a more useful and usable example for contemporary black avant-gardists than the subsequent Black Arts groups."

In Harry Thorne's "'The New York School is a Joke': The Disruptive Poetics of *C: A Journal of Poetry*," literary history is once again productively realigned. In this case, Thorne illustrates how Berrigan was by no means attached to a coherent and uniform "New York School" aesthetic. Showing how earlier critics have selectively focused on Berrigan's loosely-defined "New York School" tendencies, Thorne redirects our attention to the fact that Berrigan was interested in a far more unorthodox vision of poetic community and aesthetics than has so far been made evident. We learn that C's "anti-establishment ethos was channeled into an editorial strategy that eschewed the codification of a poetics in favor of contrast and idiosyncrasy," and as a result any contemporary tendency to position Berrigan and *C* as mere extensions of a "New York School" world emblematized by O'Hara and Ashbery is thankfully corrected.

In my essay on *Angel Hair*, I revisit *Angel Hair* magazine and related publications to demonstrate the profound influence so-called "second-generation" New York School writers have had on contemporary American poetry overall. I argue throughout the article that we can infer what I call a "poetics of sociability" in second-generation work, and indeed, that failing to recognize the initial communal impulses behind these texts is to miss much of what is important about the writing. By analyzing the nature of second-generation sociability in contrast to earlier formations and by reading selections from *The Angel Hair Anthology*, I take a look back into the construction of the second generation as it manifested itself through the primary mode of dissemination—the small-circulation, community-based little magazine typical of what we now refer to as "the '60s" avant-garde scene.

Linda Russo's work serves, as so much of the work in this book does, to question academic tendencies towards facile classification. Focusing on Bernadette Mayer's and Hannah Weiner's output against the backdrop of the Lower East Side scene generally, Russo discovers a nascent feminism working actively to undermine homosocial poetic formations typical of the times. Russo also illustrates how Mayer and Weiner were in many ways ahead of the game, in that "their innovations have a foundation in an engagement with both conceptual art and performative and performance-oriented texts." We learn how, in collaboration with other contributors, "Mayer and Weiner created spaces contiguous to the Lower East Side poetic community that allowed for an exploration of writing's potential as an investigative and performative medium." Tracing how Mayer and Weiner questioned and enriched the social and ideological context of the Poetry Project, Russo shows how writing affiliated with the second generation is often far more complex and politically dissident than it is generally given credit for.

The importance of Bernadette Mayer's work to contemporary American poetry, as well as the remarkable shift from a male-dominated poetic community to one informed by innovative feminist consciousness, is explored further in subsequent essays. In "Faulting Description: Clark Coolidge, Bernadette Mayer and the Site of Scientific Authority," Lytle Shaw focuses on how Coolidge and Mayer produced works that fed off the interrelationships between scientific authority and language. He illustrates how such a focus distinguishes these two writers from most of their peers in American poetry, and moves on to connect Mayer and Coolidge to the Postminimalist artists of their generation. Shaw reads Mayer's and Coolidge's work in terms of how it led in part to a fractured reception in which the two poets were claimed at once by the New York School and by the Language writers, emphasizing nevertheless how their work could be "read persuasively by neither of the main interpretive paradigms that came into play in the receptions of the two schools." Importantly for this book as a whole, Shaw shows how Coolidge and Mayer interrogate the very notion of stable geographic space as a source for poetry. According to Shaw, Mayer's and Coolidge's poetry results in "displacing and complicating any immediate relation between self and site."

In her essay "Anne Waldman: Standing Corporeally in One's Time," Rachel Blau DuPlessis counters the prevailing conception of New York School-affiliated writing as politically disengaged by focusing on Anne Waldman's monumental long poem *Iovis*. DuPlessis discusses how Waldman "tries to place herself corporeally into gender materials and relationships and, in her long poem (among other works), she investigates the damage and attraction of the gender sites we know." DuPlessis is committed to this work because, as she puts it, "To the avant-garde, many feminisms have been inadequately mobile, uninterested in merriness, multiplicity of means, and chiaroscuro, too wedded to a monochromatic representation of the world of gender, too clear about univocal critiques and desires for healing or wholeness, too willing to buy a piece of power, or to engage in mono-dimensional naming rather than creating fissure and palimpsests." DuPlessis asks rhetorically if a feminist poetics of innovation might make some dynamic syntheses of the politics *and* aesthetics surrounding gender questions, and answers her own question wonderfully by showing how, in *Iovis*, Waldman has confronted this seam between politics and the aesthetic with her long poem.

Maintaining a focus on women's writing in relationship to influence, community, and gender, Bob Perelman in his essay "'fucking / me across the decades like we / poets like': Embodied Poetic Transmission" analyses Alice Notley's assertion of poetic inheritance. Perelman discusses Notley's talk *Doctor Williams' Heiresses* as a significant moment in the characterization of contemporary literary histories. For Perelman, the talk can be read as a declaration of difference between the second-generation New York School and Language Writing, between what he terms "writing that foregrounds the fact of the poet writing in real time and writing that foregrounds textuality." Perelman illustrates his point in part by practically cross-examining a number of claims of organic poetic transmission and influence (i.e., Neal Cassady sleeping with someone who slept with someone who slept with Walt Whitman). Perelman also refers to O'Hara's *Personism* and Eliot's *Tradition and the Individual Talent* in order to "suggest how thoroughly interlaced the notions of poet and poetry are. They seem so tightly bound up in fact that neither will serve well any longer as a useful binary term." Perelman uses these anecdotes to question Notley's organic take on poetic inheritance: "It strikes me that [Notley's] fronting of private knowledge, contact, inheritance, membership in a select order of poetic authenticity was something distinct from the various practices of some writers in the audience at 80 Langton that were coalescing into what became known as Language Writing. Williams was as crucial a figure for Language Writers as for Notley, but the admiration was for a more textual poet."

The remainder of this volume is taken up by introductory articles on relatively underrepresented writers. Poet Ange Mlinko examines the career of Charles North in terms of his position on the margins of the second-generation New York School; Nick Selby traces British poet Lee Harwood's poetic development through Harwood's engagement with and involvement in the New York poetry scene; Paul Stephens and Patrick Masterson collaborate on an essay that serves as a critical thematic introduction to Joe Ceravolo's diverse body of work; Gary Lenhart considers Lewis Warsh's oeuvre against the background of the shifting communities to which Warsh belonged, the poetry that surrounded him, and his imaginative response toward the events and ambiance of his experience; and Umbra poet and critic Lorenzo Thomas illustrates the literary and social contexts that informed his friend Ron Padgett's early poetry and poetics.

I would of course have liked there to be more work on more poets. It is practically scandalous, for example, that there are no essays here that read the work of Diane Wakoski; Kenward Elmslie; Michael Brownstein; Eileen Myles; Kathleen Fraser; David Shapiro; Joe Brainard; and dozens of other writers. (Readers would do well to consult Steve Clay's and Rodney Phillips's *A Secret Location on the Lower East Side*, Ron Padgett's and David Shapiro's *An Anthology of New York Poets*, Lewis Warsh's and Anne Waldman's *The Angel Hair Anthology*, and Allen De Loach's *The East Side Scene* for a more comprehensive understanding of individuals who constituted the various poetic communities discussed here). I say this partly in an effort to deflect the usual accusations of ignoring important poets. I worked as best as I could here under the typical space restraints, and could only edit what I received in response to my call for papers. I acknowledge ruefully that I wish this book was ten times as long and considered ten times as many poets.

Finally, we focus on New York poets of this era not solely for reasons of literary taxonomy—indeed, we wish to trouble rather than codify assumptions about the stylistic, social, and/or cultural consistency of the works often gathered under the "New York School" rubric. It is our aim to show how the New York scene was a fertile—even a model—arena for the study of a broad range of issues attendant to the writing of the time, writing that went beyond limited definitions attendant to the New York School tag. While Bernadette Mayer counseled her fellow poets to never "get famous," we nevertheless hope that this book will undermine her imperative at least slightly. If we do not succeed in catapulting the poets gathered here to stardom, we will at least settle for providing them with the due they have so long deserved as major, innovative poets.

Don't Ever Get Famous

"Against the Speech of Friends":
Amiri Baraka Sings the "White Friend Blues"

ANDREW EPSTEIN

> True jazz is an art of individual assertion within and against
> the group. Each true jazz moment . . . springs from a contest
> in which each artist challenges all the rest; each solo flight, or
> improvisation, represents . . . a definition of his identity.
>
> —Ralph Ellison

"I think / I know now / what a poem is," Amiri Baraka writes at the end of his pivotal 1960 poem "Betancourt." "A / turning away . . . from what / it was / had moved / us . . ." (*Transbluesency* 41). This statement about the supreme importance of *turning away*—and its centrality to Baraka's definition of poetry itself—speaks volumes about his poetics and the course of his volatile, controversial career. The compulsion to resist stasis and conformity at every turn, and to embrace continual motion and change instead underlies Baraka's constant, controversial reinvention of himself, his restless, experimental poems, and his intense ambivalence towards friendship and community. Baraka's poetry is driven by an ongoing, often discordant dialogue with his friends and fellow writers, as the poetic self insists on its eccentric individuality and struggles against various forms of affiliation and influence—racial, literary, and social.[1] But at the same time, his work thrives on the stimulation and provocation of the postwar New York poetry and arts community, a collective avant-garde movement made up of like-minded creative souls dedicated to resisting the status quo and inventing new aesthetic and social forms.

In its negotiation of these conflicting impulses, Baraka's work stands as a particularly cogent example of a larger paradox—that at the heart of experimental American poetry pulses a commitment to individualism and dynamic movement that is sharply at odds with an equally profound devotion to avant-garde collaboration and community. This tense dialectic between a deep-seated aversion to conformity and a poetics of friendship actually energizes postwar American poetry and poetics, drives the creation, the meaning, and the form of important poems, and frames many of the key interrelationships which make up its poetic communities. For

Baraka, as for poets of the New York School like his close friend Frank O'Hara, the problem of friendship becomes a crucial topos, a gnawing burden, and a fertile literary question that sparks countless poems. The friction between individualism and camaraderie not only fuels Baraka's writing, but also shapes the complex literary and personal relationships he shares with members of the postwar avant-garde—friendships fraught with a mixture of affiliation and resistance, collaborative frisson and anxious sibling rivalry.

To a greater extent than is often acknowledged, in the late 1950s and early 1960s, Baraka stood at the very center of the social and artistic universe that came to be known as the "New American Poetry" (thanks to Donald Allen's groundbreaking 1960 Grove Press anthology, which included Baraka's work).[2] Baraka arrived in Greenwich Village in 1957, and although he was seven to ten years younger than many of the leading figures of a postwar avant-garde that had been operating for years, he entered that scene as a dynamic young turk and quickly became an indispensable, unusual figure, one who could be equally at home with his elders from the Black Mountain, Beat, and New York School camps. By co-editing the influential small journals *Yugen* and *The Floating Bear*, Baraka established himself as an important catalyst—as a promoter, editor, critic, and poet—while at the same time building close relationships with many of the poets themselves. Socially, aesthetically, and as an editorial impresario, Baraka served as a kind of bridge between different factions, drawing from and moving within several of these overlapping groups as a kind of "Pan-New-American Poet." The series of apartments Baraka shared with his wife Hettie Jones on West 20th St., East 14th St., and Cooper Square became famous as latter-day literary salons—magnets for members of the New York poetry community eager to engage in socializing, debauchery, and artistic activity. Baraka was also involved with his peers in the just emerging second generation of the New York School, including his exact contemporary Ted Berrigan, appearing in each other's journals and admiring one another's work. In his *Autobiography*, Baraka recalls learning of the work of Berrigan and Lorenzo Thomas: "[Thomas's] work appeared about the same time that Ted Berrigan and Ron Padgett and Joe Brainard, the Oklahoma free association semi-surrealists began to appear. I was especially impressed by Thomas and Berrigan, and very curious about Thomas because he was black" (*Autobiography* 268). Baraka even dedicated a celebratory poem entitled "The Rare Birds" to Ted Berrigan, in which he connects his fellow New York poet to other "rare birds" who "brook no obscurity, merely plunging deeper / for light"—filling the poem with symbols of artistic independence and courage like Charlie Parker, Langston Hughes, Pablo Picasso, William Carlos Williams, John Coltrane, and, implicitly Berrigan himself (Waldman 174).[3]

These facts suggest that during a crucial eight year period as the 1950s turned into the 1960s, Baraka came to embody an exciting experiment in collaboration, friendship, and intertextuality across traditional boundaries of race, at a moment when American writers had both the opportunity and the desire to establish productive alliances in a space outside the officially sanctioned discourses of American identity and community. The moment, however, was an unfortunately brief one. Few, if any, major African-American writers have ever been as thoroughly enmeshed in a community of white writers, lovers and friends as Baraka, and few have so dramatically extricated themselves from this kind of interracial dialogue. Baraka was utterly immersed in the bohemian world of Greenwich Village in the heady days when integration seemed both "hip" and possible, where his wife, closest friends, and influences were white. However, pressured by the increasingly urgent racial politics of the time to reconsider and rediscover his connection to African-American culture, Baraka found himself painfully caught between black and white cultures, communities, and identities.[4]

Critics of Baraka's work have dutifully discussed his early affiliation with white bohemia in postwar New York. But it is most often viewed as a brief and unsatisfying stepping stone on the way to his triumphant arrival at a militant, politicized Black Arts stance, rather than as the source of Baraka's most enduring work and as one of the most exciting moments of cross-racial dialogue in recent American literature.[5] Baraka's relationship with the white avant-garde community is not, as most accounts have it, a simple case of a young, confused African-American poet desperately searching for his "true" voice, eventually triumphing by shedding his white friends and their way of writing and at last arriving at a more political and "blacker" art. The major, book-length studies of Baraka—such as those by Werner Sollors, Kimberly W. Benston, and William J. Harris—which are excellent in many ways, tend to treat his oeuvre, following Baraka's own commentary on his career, as one big conversion narrative: we follow the questing poet on a journey of progressive enlightenment, a clear movement from "whiteness" to "blackness" to "Third World, internationalist Marxist-Leninism" (after 1974). They chart the growth from a detached, passive, overly "white," and obscure

"Beat" poetics to an activist "black" aesthetic in which the poet finds his "real" identity at last.

However, Baraka's powerful, agonized pre-Black Arts writings suggest a much messier, more interesting story. His so-called "Beat period" is much more than a misguided, temporary stop along the way to his being what he referred to as "even blacker" (*Home* 10). If we dismiss Baraka's earlier days, as he himself did in 1968, as "just whiteness," we risk overlooking the extent of his impact on white poets and vice versa—a fascinating and fertile cross-racial conversation that Aldon Nielsen rightly argues is "a turning point in the history of racial politics in American writing" (*Black Magic* 1, Nielsen, *Writing* 216). "Probably never before Baraka," Nielsen observes, "had any black poet been so instrumental in the early careers of white poets, so integral a player in the development of the emerging poetics of his time" (216). Our study of postwar American poetry, and of the "New York School" of poetry in particular, should be attuned to the overlapping spaces of "black" and "white" poetries; it should be especially sensitive to cross-racial affiliations, influences, and friendships and how they complicate poetic communities in general, and this highly significant community in particular.[6]

Considering Baraka as a figure enmeshed in and central to the postwar avant-garde complicates stable, reductive visions of phenomena like the "New York School," reminding us that literary history must attend to the messy complexities of actual poetic communities and friendships which often disturb the tidy rubrics that have been established and grown entrenched. To delve into Baraka's relations with the white avant-garde and his friendship with poets like O'Hara, to closely analyze the writing which emerges out of such dialogues, is to confront the failings of our typical maps of twentieth-century poetry—which so often would cordon off O'Hara the "New York School" poet from Baraka the African-American poet. Given that Baraka, like O'Hara, is preoccupied with the philosophical and poetic problem of friendship, its pleasures and dangers, it is particularly important that we understand his work's complex navigation of avant-garde community.

The fact remains that many of Baraka's best, and most famous, works absolutely depend on his thorny relations with his white avant-garde companions for their subject matter, their emotional force, and their aesthetic complexity. Like Frank O'Hara, Jack Spicer and other postwar avant-gardists, Baraka envisions poetry to be a form of contentious position-taking in the literary field—or, to paraphrase Ralph Ellison's famous definition of jazz in the epigraph above, a contest in which each person challenges all the rest by riffing within and against the group. From his older friend O'Hara, Baraka learns that poetry itself can be an arena in which to grapple with friendship and its discontents, even to play off the writing of one's friends, leading Baraka, like O'Hara, to address his fellow poets (often by name) in poem after poem, to praise, critique, and goad them.

Baraka's turbulent writings about friendship and his immersion within the downtown poetry community are laden with great pain, urgency, and indecision. As such, they actually demonstrate the limitations of the poetics of "sociability" "often celebrated as a key feature of the New York School, and to a lesser extent, the Beat, San Francisco and Black Mountain poetics of the postwar period (Kane 178). Like O'Hara, Baraka writes as much about friendship's discontents, mysteries, and burdens as he does its pleasures. In a 1964 interview, Baraka drew attention to the source of the bitter tensions in his recent work: "I'm trying to work with complications of feelings, love and hate at the same time" (*Conversations* 8). This is a key insight into one of Baraka's most fruitful periods, in which he repeatedly dramatizes these "complications of feelings," his struggles with what he both loves and hates. However, critics have glossed over the strength and sources of this ambivalence and its crucial importance to Baraka's most successful writings. They also tend to simplify Baraka's actually quite varied and nuanced associations with white poets and to neglect the importance of his misgivings about the notion of a communal avant-garde project. In doing so, readers also tend to overlook Baraka's profound interest in philosophical questions about the conflict between friendship and autonomy.

But the struggle is everywhere: when the poet in *The Dead Lecturer* speaks as "Joseph to his Brothers" or screams "choke my friends" (*Transbluesency* 70, 99), when a character in *The System of Dante's Hell* sings the "white friend blues" (86), when Ray secretly sobs and cradles the head of the beaten white homosexual boy in *The Toilet*, when Walker Vessels in *The Slave* murders his erstwhile white friend Bradford Easley, or when Baraka alludes to his friendship with O'Hara by writing "I've loved about all the people I can. Frank, for oblique lust, his mind" or announces his desire "To begin, aside from aesthetes, homosexuals, smart boys from Maryland" (*System* 15, 29). At the heart of *The System of Dante's Hell*, one of Baraka's most tormented works, he writes "YOU LOVE THESE DEMONS AND WILL NOT LEAVE THEM" (59). This painful combination of attraction and repulsion, this self-dividing need to leave behind what one cherishes, is at the root of the turmoil, the tremendous ambivalence that surges through so many of his works.

It is undeniable that the increasingly tense race relations of the early 1960s, along with heated debates about the compatibility of art and politics, drove a wedge between Baraka and his friends. His growing identification with the African-American struggle for freedom and self-determination against oppression, and the righteous anger and impatience for change fostered by Malcolm X, forced Baraka to reject his earlier skeptical outlook, which, like the New York School's prevailing ethos, had depended on a wariness of partisan commitment, ideology, and dogma.

While racial tensions and ideological differences certainly play a major role in Baraka's conflicted feelings about the avant-garde and the idea of a poetic community, they are also rooted in his deeply Emersonian belief in the virtues of nonconformity and his antipathy to fixity. In "How You Sound??," his statement on poetics for *The New American Poetry* (1960), Baraka fired off a vigorous declaration of poetic independence that reads like a postwar bohemian riff on Emerson's "Self-Reliance" and "The American Scholar": "I *must* be completely free to do just what I want, in the poem. . . . The only 'recognizable tradition' a poet need follow is himself . . . & with that, say, all those things out of tradition he can use, adapt, work over, into something for himself. To broaden his *own* voice with. (You have to start and finish there . . . your own voice . . . how you sound)" (424-25). Above all, Baraka insists, an artist must remain independent from the herd and free from any imposed conventions or restrictions; what matters most is your own distinctive, idiosyncratic "sound" or signature. Although critics have not made much of the connection, Baraka's aggressive nonconformity, and the poetics of turning away it fosters, can usefully be seen—as he himself argued in 1963—as an outgrowth of a "continuing tradition" he implicitly connects to American writers like Emerson and Twain: a "stance . . . of *self-reliance*, Puddn'head Wilson style" (*Moderns* xvi). Indeed, Baraka's poetics, and his inveterate commitment to radical individualism, spring from a pragmatist idiom that begins with Emerson and passes through William James, the modernist poets William Carlos Williams, Wallace Stevens, and Gertrude Stein, and black thinkers and writers like W. E. B. Du Bois, Alain Locke, Sterling A. Brown, and Ralph Ellison, to postwar poets who greatly influenced Baraka like Robert Duncan and O'Hara.[7]

This intellectual orientation helps explain why Baraka, in the early 1960s, became concerned that his own writing too closely resembled the writings of his friends. Baraka recalls that this recognition led him to begin "writing defensively" in a very conscious way: "I was trying to get away from the influence of people like Creeley and Olson" (*Conversations* 91). For an innate nonconformist like Baraka, the idea of following another's lead was deeply troubling. "The imitator is the most pitiful phenomenon since he is like a man who eats garbage," Baraka bluntly put it in an essay, echoing Emerson's similar warning that "imitation is suicide" in "Self-Reliance" (*Home* 176, *Essays* 259).

However, while Baraka is wholly committed to this kind of staunch artistic and personal independence, he also insists on the importance of fomenting alternative, subterranean communities and literary movements which seek to counter the oppressive hyper-conformity and homogeneity of the Cold War 1950s. In his uncomfortable yoking together of these twin impulses, Baraka exemplifies the dissonant contradiction felt by many progressive intellectuals, musicians, artists, and writers—a contradiction which resulted from the fact that two of the most pressing imperatives driving such figures in the decades following World War II were in reality diametrically opposed. The first imperative declared that any serious artist or writer must be a free-thinking individual at all costs, independent and idiosyncratic, committed to ceaseless mobility and disdainful of absolutes and ideology. For example, such gestures abound within the pages of Donald Allen's *The New American Poetry*, where one encounters Frank O'Hara imagining an individualistic poet as liberating hero, "one alone will speak of being / born in pain / and he will be the wings of an extraordinary liberty" (264), and finds the nonconformist chant "I go separately" as a thrice-repeated refrain of Barbara Guest's "Santa Fe Trail" (217). The second commandment urged such innovative outsiders to join together with like-minded iconoclasts, experimenters, and "hipsters" into collective alliances and communities; their shared project would be to oppose hegemonic political, social, and literary forces and to dramatically renovate stale, outdated aesthetic forms. For instance, in the poem "One Night Stand," one of Baraka's own contributions to the *New American Poetry*, he portrays this united "we," literalizing the military underpinnings of the avant-garde as a concept and imagining himself as one member of a communal, bohemian assault on a fortified old city that smacks of the *ancien regime*:

> We roared through the old gates! Iron doors hanging
> all grey, with bricks mossed over and gone into chips

dogs walked through . . .
The old houses dusty seeming & old men watching us slyly
as we come in: all of us laughing too loud.

We *are* foreign seeming persons. Hats flopped so the sun
can't scald our beards; odd shoes, bags of books & chicken.
We have come a long way, & are uncertain which of the masks

is cool. (Allen 360-1)

The barely submerged conflict between these dual motives—in a sense, a dialectic oscillating within the dominant discourses of the day—propels Baraka's writing. As the rest of this essay will illustrate, Baraka's writings again and again reflect a tug-of-war between the compulsion to be an idiosyncratic nonconformist and the desire to be an avant-garde team player.

This helps explain why, despite our general sense that Baraka was a leading figure of vanguard rebellion, he is actually so deeply ambivalent, even skeptical, about the avant-garde itself and writes about that ambivalence repeatedly. For all their vaunted excitement about collaborative ventures, the poets in and around the New York School are less than wholehearted in their commitment to working as a group, or, in fact, to any joint purpose. As dyed-in-the-wool individualists and skeptics, these poets are never fully devoted to any group effort to reject and overturn rigid literary orthodoxies. As Baraka self-deprecatingly puts it in "One Night Stand," at the very moment these eccentric, "foreign-seeming" bohemians are storming the castle, they remain ironically "uncertain which of the masks / is cool," suggesting a wariness of turning rebellion into fashion or a pose, an ambivalence towards the idea of rebelling under a common banner.

Such discomfort became apparent in Baraka's writing as he began to find the notion of aesthetic "schools" repellent, even when a given school's raison d'être was a joint resistance to conformity. For example, in a revealing, little-known piece he published in *Kulchur* in 1961 called "Milneburg Joys (or, Against 'Hipness' As Such)," Baraka harshly critiques his own New York bohemian scene. This caustic essay refers ironically to the downtown community as "Milneburg," in a nod to A. A. Milne, the author of *Winnie-the-Pooh*, a book that also inspired the title of Baraka's journal, *The Floating Bear* (Sollors 276 n.26). For Baraka, the world of

Pooh seems to have epitomized the youthful energy, the innocence and sense of adventure in the Village poetry milieu. But, increasingly, it also suggested that world's unreality and naïve detachment from political exigencies, and the essay positions Baraka himself as the scourge of that insulated, complacent community.

In the essay, Baraka asks "What do we do now? New York, March 1961. The world here, almost as we have made it" (41). By 1961, the Beats have been ensconced in *Time* magazine, "'hipness' as such" has become fashionable, the rebels have been anthologized in Donald Allen's *The New American Poetry*, the beatnik has become the ridiculous caricature Maynard G. Krebs on the TV sitcom "The Many Loves of Dobie Gillis," and the avant-garde, inching towards "success," has reached a crossroads. Now that the young iconoclasts have established themselves as a force of dissent, and of considerable marketability, Baraka wonders, what next? What about forcing *real* change—political, social, aesthetic? Is this all there is?

Baraka's angry piece deliberately punctures the aura of the avant-garde collective, exposing the enforced homogeneity and "party-line" aesthetics at its heart. He implies that all the clamor about the bold new forms, strategies, and influences at the heart of the postwar avant-garde—the open-field poetics of Olson's "Projective Verse," the "spontaneous bop prosody" of the Beats, the obsession with process and spontaneity in Action Painting and the New York School, the critique of establishment, bourgeois values—all threaten to turn into so much cant as they are adopted by more and more followers and become solidified into a program. At about the same time that he wrote the Milenburg essay, Baraka was summing up his weariness with the clichés of the day in a parallel passage in *The System of Dante's Hell*:

> Blues. I Got. Abstract Expressionism blues. Existentialism blues. I Got. More blues, than you can shake your hiney at . . . Got poetry blues all thru my shoes. I Got. Yeah, the po-E-try blues. And then there's little things like "The Modern Jazz Blues." Bigot blues . . . White friend blues. Adultery blues . . . I had the Kafka blues . . . and give it up. So much I give up. (85-87)

Here Baraka sings the blues about the Greenwich Village coffeehouse and Cedar Bar scene he shares with his white companions like Frank O'Hara, Gilbert Sorrentino, Allen Ginsberg, and Diane di Prima, a scene he feels is dominated by an increasingly stale haze of Jackson Pollock and Clement Greenberg, Sartre and Kierkegaard, Kafka and bebop, fashionably irreverent poetry and rampant adultery. In the Milneburg essay, he laments the emergence of derivative hangers-on, "cheaters, imitators, weaklings" who had begun to appear on the scene (42). (Baraka later recalled that he wrote the essay to attack those who thought "talking the prevailing talk, or walking the prevailing walk" was "all there was to it") (*Autobiography* 261-2). "All one need do is learn code words," he complains. It is this shared, insider language that Baraka rejects: "I repudiate the cult of *Opinion*." Perfectly happy deciding as a group who is to be deemed sufficiently "hip," this mutual admiration society lacks any sense of critical self-regard. But Baraka sarcastically objects, unwilling to equate companionship with identification or unity: "But I refuse to come to terms with 'my friends' in this *cold* manner. We have gotten drunk together and cursed the same evils . . . does this not mean then that our minds are of like valence? Bullshit." "Why did we leave that other world in the first place," he wonders at the essay's close, "if the same undifferentiated vagueness is to be cannonized [*sic*] once again" (43).

At a moment when a sense of a collective avant-garde enterprise seemed to be solidifying—when *The New American Poetry* had turned a slew of diverse poets into an umbrella organization of like-minded writers, gathered under what Baraka called in his *Autobiography* "the broad banner of our objective and subjective 'united front' of poetry," when the Beats had successfully created the impression they were a band of unified outsiders, when journals like Baraka's *Floating Bear* were circulated only to a small circle of *cognoscenti* familiar with its "code words," when the new journal *Locus Solus* had begun to shore up the identity of the nascent New York School—Baraka seems to wonder: have he and his friends merely succeeded in knocking off one orthodoxy only to install another? (232). This fear leads him to recoil from that federation of poets and artists who constitute the "Milneburg" of the postwar avant-garde—and from the friendships and social alliances that underlie it—because it threatens to absorb the distinctive identities of its members, to breed *undifferentiated* mediocrity and unoriginality (232).

Instead of being zealous warriors in the avant-garde crusade, as our standard narratives of the period tend to indicate, postwar poets like Baraka and O'Hara point out its contradictions and limitations at every turn.[8] These writers are highly sensitive to the spaces where individualism crashes into the communal, movement ethos of the avant-garde. They cling to the notion, difficult as it may be in practice, that the strongest writers and thinkers are those who manage to fend off all forms of assimilation, who take flight from pressures that would have us conform, blend in, or, worst of all, stop moving. This mandate not only demands a skepticism towards literary movements and avant-garde cant, but it also leads Baraka to use his writing as a vehicle to work through a complex, troubling set of attitudes about close friendship and community itself.

This helps explain why, in his early phase, Baraka presents a self that is so dramatically unstable, uncertain, and as he puts it in one poem, "constantly changing disguises" ("Short Speech to My Friends," *Transbluesency* 73). When he asks "What is hell?" at the end of *The System of Dante's Hell*, the answer given is "your definitions," because, for Baraka, such demarcations limit and entrap the self (153). To escape the hell of fixity, Baraka projects a precarious, self-erasing, tormented, and protean subjectivity in experimental poems that are part of a ceaseless and multivalent project of "turning"; they rely on jagged, twisting syntax, ambiguity, and wordplay in order to wriggle free from all forms of closure, static representations of self or community, and settled political stances. Baraka's poetry exemplifies the kind of cross-racial avant-garde poetics that Nathaniel Mackey has traced as a general practice within experimental poetry: such writing attempts to open "presumably closed orders of identity and signification, accent fissure, fracture, incongruity, the rickety, imperfect fit between word and world" (19). This kind of poetry "worries resolute identity and demarcation, resolute boundary lines, resolute definition" (20). Wary of viewing African-American identity and culture in simplistic, resolute terms, Baraka's early work adamantly refuses to accept what Mackey calls "the reification of fixed identities that has been the bane of socially marginalized groups" (20). However, he seems to find as much torment and confusion as liberation in this refusal.

For Baraka, the project of evading the hell of fixed, pigeon-holed identity often takes the form of an effort to forget, even to destroy, the self. In his poems we meet a persona constantly in transition, in the process of transforming into someone else, being killed or dissolved or razed only to be recreated. In Emerson's great essay "Circles," he describes the urgent need to forget, erase, and abandon one's already-defined self in a way that prefigures Baraka's writing:

> The one thing which we seek with insatiable desire is to forget ourselves, to be surprised out of our propriety, to lose our sempiternal

memory, and to do something without knowing how or why; in short,
to draw a new circle. (*Essays* 414)

As Richard Poirier notes, for Emerson and the pragmatist writers who
follow him, "you are free only when you are getting out of whatever
closet you are in, including your idea of yourself" (*Poetry* 73). This is
a necessary but exceedingly difficult process: "Along the way," Poirier
says, "much has to be abandoned—sons and lovers, thoughts one had
deemed precious, ideas of oneself more precious still" (*Poetry* 69). If any
contemporary poet can be said to have taken up the task of Emersonian
abandonment, to have *actually given up* friends, daughters, and lovers, his
own precious thoughts, and ideas of his own identity, and thus taken the
trope to its furthest, and most literal, point, it is Amiri Baraka.

Perhaps it is not surprising that such a kinetic and fiercely independent
self finds the idea of sustaining harmonious friendships or assimilating
into a group identity deeply suspect, if not untenable. But impelled by his
conviction that, for better or worse, "I am and was and will be a social
animal," Baraka's work, often with shattering drama and personal emo-
tion, continues to compulsively represent friendship in order to weigh its
puzzles and satisfactions (*System* 153). In his poems, prose, and plays of
the early 1960s, Baraka begins to acknowledge that despite the bracing
oxygen of companionship, collaborative exchange, and avant-garde com-
munity, he must forcefully turn away from his closest allies, their writing,
and even the very idea of permanent friendships.

In his play *The Toilet* (1961), Baraka transforms these mixed feelings
towards his white friends—his stinging confusion about whether to go on
living and writing within the white New York poetry community or to
embrace African-American solidarity—into a drama that stages the clash
between individualism and the pressures of the social.[9] The play explores
what happens when a sensitive and intelligent protagonist encounters a
violent gang. In Baraka's own estimation, *The Toilet* is a tale of noncon-
formity and its costs: he explained in an introduction to the play that it is
about "a boy's inability (because he is a victim) to explain that he is some-
thing stranger than the rest," and who suffers because of the close-minded
"social order" to which he belongs.[10] The short play, which is based on an
actual incident from Baraka's teenage years, features a confrontation in a
high school bathroom between a group of African-American boys (led by
tough guy Ora Matthews) and James Karolis, a white boy. Through much
of the play, the kids are waiting for their leader, the "short, intelligent,

manic" Ray, who they call Foots, to arrive. Ray (a stand-in for Baraka himself) is supposed to fight Karolis, because the white boy has sent a love letter to Ray "telling him he thought he was 'beautiful' . . . and that he wanted to blow him" (*Baptism* 56). When Ray finally appears, he is very obviously reluctant to fight Karolis (who the others have already begun to batter) but he is pressured by the other boys.

The play's considerable irony and tension stem from this: it is clear to the audience and reader, though not to the gang members, that Ray has already been intimate—across supposedly indelible lines of race and sexual orientation—with Karolis and is painfully caught between his need to impress the thugs who follow him and his tender feelings for Karolis. Finally Karolis, exasperated, challenges Ray to fight, saying "You have to fight me. I sent you a note, remember. That note saying I loved you. (*The others howl at this.*) The note saying you were beautiful. (*Tries to smile*). Remember that note, Ray?" When Ray refuses to respond, and begins to fight, Karolis presses harder on the splitting seams of Ray's identity:

> KAROLIS: Did I call you Ray in that letter . . . or Foots? (*Trying to laugh.*) Foots! (*Shouts*). I'm going to break your fucking neck. That's right. That's who I want to kill. Foots! . . . Are you Ray or Foots, huh? . . . I'll fight you. Right here in this same place where you said your name was Ray . . . Ray, you said your name was. You said Ray. Right here in this filthy toilet. You said Ray. (*He is choking Foots and screaming. Foots struggles and is punching Karolis in the back and stomach, but he cannot get out of the hold*). You put your hand on me and said Ray! (59)

By insisting on the disjunction between the two names, Karolis exposes the gap between Foots, the gang leader who conforms to the group's expectations, and Ray, the sensitive, smart, homosexual young man who is a nonconformist, who is "stranger than the rest" but cannot reveal it.[11] Baraka will often attempt to kill off one part of himself in his writing, and in this case, Karolis tries to murder the Foots that is imprisoning Ray, or, if you will, the Amiri cloaking LeRoi. Hiding his true feelings because of the fierce (and homophobic) social pressure to conform, Ray refuses to engage, or even to deny, Karolis's questions. When the two boys begin to fight, Karolis quickly gains the advantage, and the other boys, led by Ora, jump in to save Foots and, as a mob, pummel the white boy senseless. Lying bloodied on the floor, Karolis says "No, no, his name is Ray, not Foots. You stupid bastards. I love somebody you don't even know"

(*Baptism* 60). The boys drag the beaten Foots out of the bathroom, leaving Karolis alone, crumpled in a heap.

The final stage directions create a crucial tableau:

> *At this point, the door is pushed open slightly, then it opens completely and Foots comes in. He stares at Karolis' body for a second, looks quickly over his shoulder, then runs and kneels before the body, weeping and cradling the head in his arms.* (62)

The play's conclusion surely stresses human compassion over violence, interracial connection over racial hatred, and same-sex affection over close-minded bigotry. As such, *The Toilet* epitomizes Baraka's equivocal feelings in the early 1960s about his relations with the white bohemian community of Greenwich Village, about his own identity, friendship, and race, and is a good example of the aesthetically rich and ambiguous works those feelings sparked. Like the central figures in other Baraka works of the period like "The Heretics" and *Dutchman*, the protagonist is caught between the seductive but de-legitimizing "white" world and the angry "black" gang, and fits comfortably into neither.[12] For Werner Sollors, Baraka's plays of this period all critique their main characters' lack of ethnic solidarity: works like *Dutchman*, *The Slave*, and *The Toilet* condemn their "sensitive protagonists" for their "central weakness": "their lack of group identification is viewed as alienation from ethnic roots" (102). However, if this play is meant to condemn Ray's failure to identify with his "blackness," as Sollors suggests, why would Baraka portray a group of African-Americans summarily brutalizing his play's sympathetic white and gay character in a release of sickening power and violence, and why is the African-American hero subsequently plagued by such remorse and indecision? In my eyes, Baraka's plays of the early 1960s express a deep wariness about the group identification Sollors discusses and are far more ambivalent than critical.

In addition to conveying such mixed feelings about racial unity, *The Toilet* also forces us to assess why Baraka attempts a kind of failed exorcism of the homosexual and sensitive intellectual. It is important to note that in Baraka's writing of this period, homosexuality actually becomes a site of tremendous ambivalence. In many of his early writings, Baraka alludes to his own bisexual experimentation and homoerotic desires, only to be wracked with a mixture of attraction and self-lacerating repulsion towards such desires and acts. Again and again, homosexuality is linked to things Baraka values most highly yet increasingly feels oppressed by and forced to renounce—poetry, the avant-garde, downtown bohemia, white culture, and intellectualism.[13] The central conflict and resolution of *The Toilet* suggest Baraka's bitterly divided attitudes about both homosexuality and interracial relationships, two of the main ingredients in his experience of the New York poetry scene—in short, his devastating need to relinquish and destroy everything he loves.

Perhaps uncomfortable with the play's expression of these mixed feelings, Baraka later disavowed *The Toilet*'s ending. Asked about his earlier work in the midst of his Black Nationalist phase in 1971, Baraka explained that

> some of it is very painful to me. When I look at it now, I can see some of my real hangups at that time. I was working my way through things I didn't understand—for instance, the ending of *The Toilet* where there is a sort of coming together of the black boy and the white boy. When I first wrote the play, it ended with everybody leaving. I tacked the other ending on; the kind of social milieu that I was in dictated that kind of rapprochement. It actually did not evolve from the spirit of the play. I've never changed it, of course, because I feel that now that would only be cute. I think you should admit where you were even if it's painful, but you should also understand your development and growth. (*Conversations* 91)[14]

Baraka's revisionist claim that the final gesture of connection "did not evolve from the spirit of the play" and was merely a false concession seems dubious given the overwhelming emphasis throughout the play on the secret relationship between Ray and Karolis. In any case, these comments make clear that the creation of *The Toilet*, and the meaning of the play, stem from Baraka's increasingly strained relationships with white avant-garde poets, and, more generally, from his complicated navigation of the problem of friendship that the Lower East Side poetry world presented to him. Growing out of "where I was at that time," his "social situation," at a moment when he was "working through things I didn't understand," *The Toilet* is powerful *because* of its author's confusion and ambivalence, and the ambiguity with which he treats its central conflicts—not marred by them (*Conversations* 189). The play arises from the questions plaguing Baraka: should he brutally reject his white friends and lovers, turn away from the Village poetry scene, and relinquish his sensitive and poetic side in favor of strident and committed political action, here symbolized by a thuggish, intolerant African-American mob? Or should he espouse nonviolence and strive for reconciliation and friendship across racial lines?

I take Ray's gesture of love for the white homosexual Karolis to be an important metaphor for Baraka's conflicted feelings towards his white friends—and perhaps most specifically, one of his closest white gay friends, Frank O'Hara. This becomes even clearer when the play is viewed in the larger context of Baraka's work. The haunting, bathroom-beating incident from Baraka's childhood that *The Toilet* recreates also appears in an important earlier poem, "Look For You Yesterday, Here You Come Today." In the midst of that scattered, collage-like poem, Baraka moves from the Karolis brawl to a subtle allusion to Frank O'Hara—a movement that illuminates the lingering personal guilt that *The Toilet* attempts to work through and the connection between that play's central conflict and O'Hara himself. He writes:

> An avalanche of words
> could cheer me up. Words from Great Sages.
> Was James Karolis a great sage??
>   Why did I let Ora Matthews beat him up
> in the bathroom? Haven't I learned my lesson.
>
> I would take up painting
> if I cd think of a way to do it
> better than Leonardo. Than Bosch.
> Than Hogarth. Than Kline.
>
> Frank walked off stage, singing
> "My silence is as important as Jack's incessant yatter." (T 18)

Baraka's intriguing reference to "Frank" and "Jack" has thus far escaped notice by critics. He is alluding to a notorious incident involving O'Hara and Jack Kerouac: in March 1959, O'Hara gave a poetry reading with his good friend Gregory Corso in New York, in an event that represented the fragile coming together of "Beat" and "New York School" poetries, a congruence Baraka was also a part of. The evening turned unpleasant when Corso's teasing, homophobic onstage remarks gave way to a drunken, jealous Kerouac's heckling of O'Hara. At one point, Kerouac shouted out "you're ruining American poetry, O'Hara," to which O'Hara, not missing a beat, acidly replied: "That's more than you ever did for it." Finally O'Hara simply gave up and left the stage, explaining "This may seem uninteresting but it's no more uninteresting than Jack Kerouac's wanting to read."[15]

Why does Baraka move so quickly, in the poem "Look for You Yesterday," from the memory of the Karolis beating, to a statement about artistic originality and individualism, to an allusion to the O'Hara incident? For one thing, Kerouac's homophobic attack on O'Hara mirrors Ora Matthews's assault on the homosexual Karolis. Apparently, Baraka still feels guilty about failing to stop either attack, suggesting the two are parallel. "Haven't I learned my lesson," he asks, and then immediately goes on to recount the Kerouac-O'Hara fight, thus implying that the answer is no. Furthermore, Baraka celebrates O'Hara's proud stand against his aggressor (as he walks off stage "singing" his witty defiance) and implicitly links the "great sage" Karolis with his current friend O'Hara, a latter-day exemplar of artistic individualism and nonconforming homosexuality.

The connection between "Look For You Yesterday" and the play makes it even more likely that the rapprochement between the black Baraka character Ray and the white homosexual Karolis in *The Toilet* parallels the friendship between Baraka and O'Hara. Because Baraka's later comments make it clear that the play "actually invokes my own social situation at the time," and because of the linkage already made in "Look For You Yesterday," we can safely see Karolis as in some ways a stand-in for O'Hara. This congruence seems particularly germane if we recall that O'Hara's friendship with Baraka was complicated by a powerful romantic, sexual attraction that may or may not have been reciprocated. O'Hara's biographer Brad Gooch relates that "O'Hara's relationship with Jones was always a matter of conjecture to those around them and O'Hara did little to allay the confusion" (337). He goes on to quote Kenneth Koch's recollection of O'Hara's initial excitement upon meeting Baraka:

> He said he'd met this marvelous young poet who was black and good-looking and very interesting. "And not only that," he said, "he's gay." . . . I don't know whether LeRoi yielded to Frank's almost irresistible charms or not . . . So I assumed that LeRoi was gay for a while, but that's before I got to know him. I don't know whether Frank was serious or not. Maybe he was just optimistic. (337)

At the very least, we can assume that the relationship between O'Hara and Baraka was flirtatious and intense, and that O'Hara—who was both notoriously attracted to black men and had a knack for falling for his ostensibly straight friends—probably propositioned Baraka. Gooch mentions that Diane di Prima, who was sleeping with the married Baraka, "was also privy to signs of the light flirting [between Baraka and O'Hara] that went on at the time. According to di Prima, 'When Roi and I were in the thick of our affair, I said to him, 'Let's run away together to Mexico.' He said, 'You're the second person who asked me to do that this week.' I said, 'Who was the other one?' He said, 'Frank'" (Gooch 370). If this is true, O'Hara's romantic invitation to Baraka would parallel Karolis's expression of love for Ray in the letter that forces Ray into the uncomfortable position of having to renounce his affection for the white friend/lover—further suggesting that the play dramatizes Baraka's vexing friendship with O'Hara as a metaphor for the larger questions underlying his alliances with the white avant-garde. The play reveals a writer caught in a titanic struggle with what he loves and detests at the same time; like so many of his works, *The Toilet* conveys the distress Baraka feels about the two communities that were exerting overwhelming, competing claims on his writing and his very soul—the white New York poets and the radical black nationalists.[16]

Like *The Toilet*, many (if not all) of the poems in *The Dead Lecturer* (1964), Baraka's second, and to many eyes, best book of poetry, are born out of these conflicts that were erupting between himself and his friends. Indeed, in the early 1960s, his most creative and frenetic period of activity, Baraka's agonizing ambivalence about his alliances with his comrades in the white avant-garde becomes even more palpable and central to his writing. Even the titles of his poems—"Joseph to His Brothers," "[Robert] Duncan spoke of a process," "A Short Speech to My Friends," "A Poem for Speculative Hipsters," "A Poem for Democrats," "I don't love you," "Will They Cry When You're Gone, You Bet"—reveal the extent to which his poems are preoccupied with addressing his fellow writers and his relationships with them. As Baraka has explained, "again and again [the poems] speak of this separation, this sense of being in contradiction with my friends and peers" (*Autobiography* 255-56). If the book merely delineated the poet's denunciation of his white companions, their politics and their aesthetics, it would be a rather simple affair, and perhaps make for uninteresting poetry. However, as in the other works I have been discussing, the brilliance and emotional charge comes from the indecision and ambiguity within the poet himself, his attitudes, and his language. While I will focus only on a few examples, such moments are multiplied throughout the book.

In these poems, Baraka creates a running dialogue with his friends, those people he admits he genuinely loves but needs to leave, about the changes he is experiencing. In the poem with the telling title "Joseph To His Brothers," Baraka immediately draws a distinction between "them" and "me"—"They characterize / their lives, and I / fill up / with mine" (*Transbluesency* 70). Whereas his friends are detached and passive, talking about their lives abstractly, Baraka wishes to live actively and passionately, to "fill up with what I have, with what / I see (or need." The resonances with the Biblical story of Joseph and his brothers are notable: Baraka alludes to the story of the most-loved son of Jacob and his difficult relationship with his brothers as a way of exploring the problems of poetic siblinghood.

By drawing on the metaphor of brotherhood to figure the bond of friendship, Baraka suggests both the closeness and the rivalrous emotions underlying his relationships with the white poets. He deliberately links himself with Joseph, the poet-like interpreter of dreams, whose father gives him a coat of many colors, eliciting the jealous resentment and hatred of his more prosaic brothers, who decide to sell him into slavery rather than murder him. Years later, now a powerful advisor to the Pharaoh of Egypt because of his dream-reading abilities, Joseph reveals himself to his brothers, saying "I am Joseph your brother, whom ye sold into Egypt." (Genesis 45:4). Unlike the tale of Cain and Abel, however, the biblical story of fraternal rivalry Baraka chooses ends with reconciliation, not murder. By drawing on this figure who is sold into slavery by his brothers (obviously rich in metaphoric associations regarding his racial heritage), only to be eventually reunited with them, Baraka hints that reconciliation or understanding is still a viable possibility.

In the poem, Baraka does not yet demand a breaking off of communications between himself and his brothers, insisting instead that they listen to him and his changing ideas: "The story is a long one. Why / I am here like this. Why you / should listen, now, so late, and / weary at the night." In "Joseph to His Brothers," Baraka uses the poem to reveal himself to O'Hara and Ginsberg, Creeley and Olson, Corso and Wieners, saying, with dire forewarning and a powerful demand for recognition: "I am Joseph your brother, whom ye sold into Egypt."

In "Green Lantern's Solo," Baraka takes another individualistic flight away from the group melody, explaining that "I break and run, or hang back and hide" (*Transbluesency* 102). The poem opens with a reference to "the field"—which for Baraka is associated with the projectivist notion of the poem as an open field—noting that it has now "drawn in / as if to close, and die, in the old man's eyes / as if to shut itself." For Baraka, it seems that Olson's open field poetics—so important to the New American Poetry—have become constricting, as has the cultural "field" of the Lower East Side, the ground zero of postwar avant-garde art and poetry and the home of Olson (temporarily), along with O'Hara, Ginsberg, Paul Blackburn, Joel Oppenheimer, Fielding Dawson, Baraka himself, and so many other writers and artists. The time has come, Baraka implies, to go solo—both enacting his philosophical commitment to individualism and literally foreshadowing his imminent departure from downtown up to Harlem. The bohemian community he depicts is decidedly unpleasant and stifling, where one is "surrounded / in dim rooms by the smelly ghosts of wounded intellectuals." He then goes on to wickedly critique a series of unnamed friends for their hypocrisy and detachment from life ("my friend, the lyric poet, / who has never had an orgasm. My friend, / the social critic, who has never known society") and their pomposity ("my friend" who acts "as if he was the slow intellect who thought up God"). Throughout the poem, Baraka attacks a moribund intellectual scene in radical decline, "their lives, dwindled, rusted, corrupted / away" (*Transbluesency* 103). In contrast, he holds up the Green Lantern's heroic independence, his ability to go it alone. At the same time, he remains aware of the impossibility of total autonomy—he admits no one is "completely free" or "completely innocent," conceding this is a state "no thing I know can claim." But the poem still ends by attacking the dangerous tendency towards dogma, towards absolutism, while invoking an Emersonian wariness of instructors who bully their disciples: "No man except a charlatan / could be called 'Teacher,' as / big birds will run off from their young / if they follow too closely."

In the end Baraka critiques those "naïve fools" who

> can not but yearn
> for the One Mind, or Right, or call it some God, a thing beyond
> themselves, some thing toward which all life is fixed, some static
> irreducible, constantly correcting, dogmatic economy
> of the soul. (T 104-05)

Baraka satirizes those absolutists, those dogmatists, whose desire for stability, for unity, leads them to foolishly imagine that life has a fixed end, foundation, or static meaning. His comic book alter ego, the Green Lantern, fights against such fixity by playing his solo, by at least trying to remain independent and aversive to conformity.

Ironically, Baraka would soon reject the skeptical stance so forcefully laid out here in favor of a much more doctrinaire and absolutist world-view: an essentialist belief that race, and later economic class, are *the* thing toward which "all life is fixed." And the man who felt that only a "charlatan" could be called "teacher" was soon to dub himself "Imamu Amiri Baraka"—which means "spiritual leader and blessed prince/warrior chief."

A final example, *"Duncan spoke of a process,"* may help sum up the struggle at the heart of Baraka's work that I have been exploring, as it presents the conflict rather starkly. Picking up on the title's reference to Robert Duncan's ideas about "process," Baraka begins "And what I have learned of it, to repeat, repeated / as a day will repeat / its color, the tired sounds / run off its bones" (*Transbluesency* 92). As can be seen in earlier poems like "The Dance," Baraka learned much from Duncan's view of experience as "dance" and motion. But here he seems to have wearied of the ideas he finds himself mouthing without inspiration (underscored by the triple repetition of "repeat"). He admits that his attraction to ideas like Duncan's is due, in part, to a sense of fellowship—"What / was only love," Baraka writes, "or in those cold rooms, / opinion." Thus, he seems to be guilty of adopting what he calls in the essay "Milneburg Joys" the hip "code words" of the group (42). The poem, like that essay, takes pains to say "I repudiate the cult of *Opinion.*" But despite his rejection of derivativeness, Baraka still worries how *empty* he would be without the work of his friends, which, he implies, "filled me / as no one will. As, even / I cannot fill / myself."

This duality, this balancing act between the speaker's companions and his autonomous individuality, persists through the poem's open-ended conclusion:

> I see what I love most and will not
> leave what futile lies
> I have. I am where there is
> nothing, save myself. And go out to

> what is most beautiful. What some noncombatant Greek
> or soft Italian prince
> would sing, "Noble Friends."
>
>   Noble Selves. And which one
> is truly to rule here? And
> what country is this?

In effect, with this conclusion Baraka crystallizes the dilemma of friendship and self-reliance so central to his work. The "noncombatant," "soft," and literary side of Baraka clings to his "noble" friendships. The other, more combative side clings to his "noble selves." Which of the two is "most beautiful" remains ambiguous. Baraka even structures these lines so that "selves" rings like an echo of "friends," highlighting the blurry relationship between the two.

And which one is to rule here, he wonders, "friends" or "selves"? Are they mutually exclusive or can they be reconciled? "What country is this?" he asks, as if intending to stress how central to American literature and thinking such questions are. Is "America" a country founded on principles of democratic community and togetherness? Or on self-reliant individualism, a go-it-alone frontier spirit that resists group thought, numbing conformity, and received ideas? Can it be *both*? The poem ends on a note of irresolution, unable to choose between our selves and our friends.

Baraka's feelings about these issues were soon to be much less wracked with ambivalence and uncertainty, and his writings more resolute. Immediately after the assassination of Malcolm X in February 1965, Baraka finally did what he had known for some time he would have to do: he made a clean break with his white friends and his wife and family. In "I don't love you," another direct address to his erstwhile companions in the white avant-garde, Baraka portrays a figurative and literal escape from Greenwich Village as a geographical and symbolic space, and celebrates his release from all bonds to his white friends and lovers, and to white culture itself:

> The dont's of this white hell.
> The crashed eyes of dead friends,
> standing at the bar eyes focused on actual ugliness.
> I don't love you.
> Who is to say what that will mean.

I don't love you expressed the train,
moves, and uptown days later we look up
and breathe much easier

I don't love you (*Black Magic* 55)

Following this rupture, the dramatic social, cultural, and political pressures of the times seem to have driven Baraka towards a more direct and instrumental poetry of communal African-American identity and empowerment. Since the 1960s, his reputation as a very public, radical political figure, as a fiercely ideological writer, has often obscured the experimental poet who loathed conformity, doctrinaire positions, and all forms of definitive closure, who embraced uncertainty and flux, and who declared "a position / for myself: to move" (*Dead Lecturer* 71). Ross Posnock isolates the dilemma faced by African-American intellectuals like Baraka who are torn between being "race men" (spokespersons for their people) and pragmatists who distrust essentialism and espouse pluralism, a dilemma that seems to have weighed heavily on Baraka in the 1960s: "how to reconcile a philosophy that refuses the primacy of identity with the politics of racial group advocacy." There are simply no easy resolutions to this nagging conundrum. But in the later 1960s, Baraka's response was to largely jettison the former and champion the latter, rather than trying to continue to juggle the two.

The anger and political conviction of Baraka's later work can at times be potent, and his innovative use of black vernacular and emphasis on the musical, performative dimension of poetry have been extremely influential. (His later poems function as scores for his dynamic performances). But largely missing from his later work is the fraught struggle over the nature of his own identity and the energetic dialogue carried on in writing with his white companions. Reading Baraka as a poet adjacent to and in conversation with the New York School of poets and other literary communities, who writes incessantly about his ambivalent relation to those collectives, gives us a better understanding of both this perennially controversial writer, and those poetic groupings that have become such convenient, misleading markers for literary history. Baraka's works of the early 1960s represent a fascinating chapter in the history of American poetry, a moment when innovative poetry was inspired by the possibilities and tribulations of integration and cross-racial colloquy. Rather than being solely a paean to the intimate coterie ethos of the postwar avant-garde, Baraka's writing also suggests the limits and burdens of community and a poetics of sociability, as it repeatedly stages the irresolvable face-off between American individualism and friendship. Writing within the knotty center of the New York poetry universe in the 1960s, Baraka arrives at a vision of poetry as a continual and painful process of turning away from and returning to group affiliations and forms of assimilation. In the coda Baraka added to *The System of Dante's Hell* in 1965, almost five years after he wrote that disturbed, unsettled book, he stated "the world is clearer to me now, and many of its features, more easily definable" (153). But to find his way to that sense of "home," to arrive at that certitude about his own identity and his interracial friendships with his avant-garde companions, Baraka had to abandon much, had to turn away once and for all from that which had moved him.

WORKS CITED

Albrecht, James. "Saying Yes and Saying No: Individualist Ethics in Ellison, Burke, and Emerson"*PMLA* 114 (1999): 46-63.

Allen, Donald M., ed. *The New American Poetry: 1945-1960*. New York: Grove, 1960.

Altieri, Charles. *Enlarging the Temple: New Directions in American Poetry of the 1960s*. Lewisburg, PA: Bucknell UP, 1979.

Baraka, Amiri. *The Autobiography of LeRoi Jones*. Chicago: Lawrence Hill Books, 1984.

—. *The Baptism and The Toilet*. New York, Grove, 1967.

—. *Black Magic: Collected Poetry, 1961-1967*. Indianapolis: Bobbs-Merrill, 1969.

—. *Conversations with Amiri Baraka*. Ed. Charlie Reilly. Jackson: UP of Mississippi, 1994.

—. *The Dead Lecturer*. New York: Grove, 1994.

—. *Home: Social Essays*. Hopewell, NJ: Ecco Press, 1966.

—. "Milneburg Joys (or, Against 'Hipness' as Such)." *Kulchur* 1.3 (1961): 41-43.

—, ed. *The Moderns*. New York: Corinth Books, 1963.

—. *The System of Dante's Hell* New York: Grove, 1965.

—. *Transbluesency: The Selected Poems of Amiri Baraka/LeRoi Jones (1961-1995)*. Ed. Paul Vangelisti. New York: Marsilio, 1995.

Benston, Kimberly W. *Baraka: The Renegade and the Mask*. New Haven: Yale UP, 1976.

—, ed. *Imamu Amiri Baraka (LeRoi Jones): A Collection of Critical Essays*. Englewood

Cliffs, NJ: Prentice-Hall, 1978.

Breslin, James, E. B. *From Modern to Contemporary: American Poetry, 1945-1965.* Chicago: U of Chicago P, 1984.

Davidson, Michael. *The San Francisco Renaissance: Poetics and Community at Mid-Century.* Cambridge: Cambridge UP, 1989.

Dickstein, Morris. *The Revival of Pragmatism: New Essays on Social Thought, Law, and Culture.* Durham: Duke University Press, 1998.

Ellison, Ralph. *The Collected Essays of Ralph Ellison.* Ed. John F. Callahan. New York: Modern Library, 1995.

Emerson, Ralph Waldo. *Essays and Lectures.* New York: Library of America, 1983.

Epstein, Andrew. *Beautiful Enemies: Friendship and Postwar American Poetry.* New York: Oxford University Press, 2006.

Golding, Alan. *From Outlaw to Classic: Canons in American Poetry.* Madison: U of Wisconsin P, 1995.

—. "*The New American Poetry* Revisited, Again." *Contemporary Literature* 39.2 (1998): 180-211.

Gooch, Brad. *City Poet: The Life and Times of Frank O'Hara.* New York: Knopf, 1993.

Harris, William J. *The Poetry and Poetics of Amiri Baraka: The Jazz Aesthetic.* Columbia: U of Missouri P, 1985.

Hudson, Theodore R. *From LeRoi Jones to Amiri Baraka: The Literary Works.* Durham: Duke UP, 1973.

Kane, Daniel. *All Poets Welcome: The Lower East Side Poetry Scene in the 1960s.* Berkeley: U of California P, 2003.

Lehman, David. *The Last Avant-Garde: The Making of the New York School of Poets.* New York: Doubleday, 1998.

LeSueur, Joe. *Digressions on Some Poems By Frank O'Hara.* Farrar, Straus and Giroux, 2003.

Mackey, Nathaniel. *Discrepant Engagement: Dissonance, Cross-Culturality, and Experimental Writing.* Cambridge: Cambridge UP, 1993.

Nielsen, Aldon N. *Writing Between the Lines: Race and Intertextuality.* Athens: U of Georgia P, 1994.

—. *Black Chant: Languages of African-American Postmodernism.* Cambridge: Cambridge UP, 1997.

O'Hara, Frank. *The Collected Poems of Frank O'Hara.* Ed. Donald Allen. Berkeley: U of California P, 1971.

Perkins, David. *A History of Modern Poetry: Modernism and After.* Cambridge: Belknap/Harvard UP, 1987.

Perloff, Marjorie. *The Dance of the Intellect: Studies in the Poetry of the Pound Tradition.* Cambridge: Cambridge UP, 1985.

—. *Frank O'Hara: Poet Among Painters.* Austin: U of Texas P, 1977.

Poirier, Richard. *Poetry and Pragmatism.* Cambridge: Harvard UP, 1992.

Posnock, Ross. *Color and Culture: Black Writers and the Making of the Modern Intellectual.* Cambridge: Harvard UP, 1998.

Sanders, Mark A. *Afro-Modernist Aesthetics and the Poetry of Sterling A. Brown.* Athens: U of Georgia P, 1999.

Shelley, Percy Bysshe. *Shelley's Poetry and Prose.* Ed. Donald H. Reiman and Sharon B. Powers. New York: Norton, 1977.

Sollors, Werner. *Amiri Baraka/LeRoi Jones: The Quest for a "Populist Modernism."* New York: Columbia UP, 1978.

Waldman, Anne, ed. *Nice to See You: Homage to Ted Berrigan.* Minneapolis: Coffee House Press, 1991.

West, Cornel. *The American Evasion of Philosophy: A Genealogy of Pragmatism.* Madison: U of Wisconsin P, 1989.

Deep Image

JED RASULA

> An image is a stop the mind makes between uncertainties.
> —Djuna Barnes, *Nightwood* 111

In his journal of literary Cubism, *Nord-Sud*, in an issue containing poems by Philippe Soupault, Louis Aragon, and Tristan Tzara, Pierre Reverdy published a few pages of reflections on the image. "L'Image" was one in a series spanning the run of *Nord-Sud*; other topics included emotion, space, syntax, tradition, and cinematography.

> L'Image est une creation pure de l'esprit.
>
> Elle ne peut naître d'une comparaison mais du rapprochement de deux réalités plus ou moins éloignées.
>
> Plus les rapports des deux réalités rapprochées seront lointains et justes, plus l'image sera forte—plus elle aura de puissance emotive et de réalité poétique. {The Image is a pure creation of the mind. It cannot be born from a comparison but by bringing together two more or less distant realities. Insofar as the relationship between the two realities is distant and exact—the greater will be its emotional power and poetic reality.} ("L'Image" 3)

This is only the beginning of Reverdy's ruminations, but it's what André Breton chose to cite in the first manifesto of Surrealism, accompanied by enigmatic remarks about the author from whom Breton had become estranged. In 1952, he looked back on Reverdy with respect: "Once you knew him, nothing seemed as important as his theses on the image in poetry"—which, with his other pieces in *Nord-Sud*, "put forth several lasting principles and major themes on the subject of poetic creation" (*Conversations* 30, 22). For the adventure of Surrealism, Reverdy's dicta offered a salutary provocation, foremost of which is the suggestion that the image is a pure creation of the mind. Mind (l'esprit), not *eye*. Furthermore, "poetic reality" demands that the bipolar forces conjoined in the image maintain their separation. There is no blending or merging, but rather a sustained tension in the electromagnetic sense. "It is, as it were," wrote Breton, "from the fortuitous juxtaposition of the two terms that a particular light has sprung, *the light of the image*" (*Manifestoes of Surrealism* 37).

As it happened, the lyric effusions of Surrealist poetry rarely lived up to the incandescence of the image. In fact, despite the constant risk of pictorial anecdotalism, it was in the visual arts that the *deep image* of Surrealism was memorably achieved—albeit not strictly in optic terms, but in the tactile provocations of Meret Oppenheim's fur-covered teacup, or Man Ray's clothing iron studded with nails. By 1950, in buttoned-down Cold War America, with its tweed-suited academy poets confident that a return to form was the order of the day, Surrealism seemed decidedly "pre-War," outdated. For young poets made uncomfortable by the spirit of conformism—David Antin and Jerome Rothenberg—the European avant-garde was news that stayed news. For Robert Bly and James Wright, too, it seemed absurdly premature to assume pre-war vanguard provocations had been meaningfully assimilated. The Midwest of Bly and Wright converged with the metropolis of Antin and Rothenberg in a commitment to translation as *recovery* of an untapped potential for English language poetry, rendering in a distinctively American idiom the enigmatic volatility of the subconscious and the pre-rational, manifested in work by poets like Federico García Lorca, Pablo Neruda, César Vallejo, Georg Trakl, André Breton, and Vicente Aleixandre. From about 1961-1965, "deep image" served simultaneously as spiritual intoxicant and technical device; it was a way of embracing foreign poetry as a revitalizing tactic, attaining "more of the joy of the unconscious" as Bly put it ("On English and American Poetry" 47). In contrast to what Robert Kelly disdainfully thought of as the aridity of "craft" ("Letter to Kenneth Irby" 24), deep image incited "a fertility of critical examination" ("Letter to the Editor" 25). "To strip to the least," Kelly later recalled the fundamental initiative, "& the least was: image" (*Statement* [6]).

Because discussions of deep image have been consistently riddled with error, it's necessary to begin with a succinct chronology. Although the first mention of the term was in 1960, its subsequent association with Robert Bly makes it imperative to consider his magazine *The Fifties* (later *The Sixties*) instrumental to the dissemination of the concept, if not the term. Jerome Rothenberg, who had appeared in *The Fifties* #3 with translations of Paul Celan as well as his own work, published the first declaration of deep image in his little magazine *Poems from the Floating World* #2 in 1960. He regarded the magazine as "an on-going anthology of the deep image"

(Alpert 100), and the third issue in 1961 was offered under the portfolio title "The Deep Image: Ancient and Modern," followed by "The Deep Image is the Threatened Image" in the fourth issue. Two more key statements appeared in Robert Kelly's magazine *Trobar* in 1961: Kelly's "Notes on the Poetry of Deep Image" in the second issue, and Rothenberg's "Why *Deep* Image" in the third. Kelly's "Notes" had been privately circulated in late 1960, precipitating Rothenberg's lengthy correspondence with Robert Creeley on deep image, published in *Kulchur* in 1962. Also in 1962, the New York journal *Nomad* featured a cluster of deep image work by Rothenberg, Kelly, George Economou and Armand Schwerner, including further position statements by Rothenberg and Kelly. The topic of deep image had become sufficiently public that when David Ossman (future member of The Firesign Theatre) conducted a series of interviews with poets—published as *The Sullen Art* in 1963—Kelly, Rothenberg, and Creeley were pointedly asked to comment on it. 1963 was also the year in which Bly's influential essay "A Wrong Turning in American Poetry" was published in John Logan's poetry journal *Choice*; and while Bly did not then (or later) use the term "deep image," he invariably extolled the archetypal virtue of *depth* and poetic necessity of the *image*, thereby associating him with the term, particularly among readers who probably never saw *Trobar* or *Poems from the Floating World*.

Despite close contact between Rothenberg and Bly in the late fifties, deep image was largely restricted to the lower east side scene in New York. The conflation of this original initiative with Bly's circle, and the source of much subsequent disinformation, can be traced to Stephen Stepanchev's 1965 book *American Poetry Since 1945*. By that point, Kelly and Rothenberg had adopted a retrospective posture toward deep image, and the term began its quasi-academic afterlife where it has persisted to the present, almost invariably used with reference to Bly and James Wright. To his credit, Stepanchev quoted extensively from Kelly's "Notes on the Poetry of the Deep Image" (hyperbolically declaring it the theoretical equivalent of Olson's "Projective Verse"), thereby making more widely available a central statement that had had very limited circulation. Misleadingly, he claimed that Kelly and Rothenberg had *collaborated* with Bly, Wright, and William Duffy (co-editor of *The Fifties*) in "launching a movement toward subjectivism in American poetry"—a movement, no less, that "denied any influence from the Charles Olson-inspired groups" (*American Poetry* 175). Far from denying such influence, Kelly was actively soliciting it directly from Olson (whose response—"not imageS but Image" was repeatedly cited by Kelly

["Letter to the Editor" 26]), as was Rothenberg in his exchange with Cree-
ley. Stepanchev's focus on deep image, such as it was, served as prelude to
a discussion of the work of Bly and Wright, thereby effectively restricting
Kelly and Rothenberg to the role of theoreticians, since their poetry passed
without notice. This bias is understandable, given that *Silence in the Snowy
Fields* by Bly and *The Branch Will Not Break* by Wright were among the most
widely reviewed poetry titles of the early 1960s, establishing the public
face with which deep image has been associated ever since.

Why review this remote and apparently minor episode in literary his-
tory? After all, it's an episode in which the theoretical charter of deep
image served largely as accompaniment to two first books published by
Rothenberg's Hawk's Well Press, his own *White Sun Black Sun* and *Armed
Descent* by Kelly (neither of which has been reprinted, nor were they
widely available in the first place)—an episode made even more tenuous
in its significance because the original participants abandoned the term
not long after they took it up, and the one figure most associated with
deep image has always scorned the term. Given Bly's impatience when
asked about it, there is little to be gained by persisting in the common
application, even if "deep image" doggedly persists (as synonymous with
"subjective" image) in criticism on Bly and Wright. Forced by distaste for
"deep image," Bly came up with an alternative, "leaping poetry." If, as
Daniel Kane usefully suggests, "the 'deep image' was as much a politics
of dissent from mainstream poetics and what it suggested as it was an
effort to find new uses for the poetic image" (*All Poets Welcome* 91), is there
any reason other than the foregoing clarification of its history to revisit it
now? Before the question can even be addressed, of course, it's imperative
to attempt some conceptual coordinates.

The coordinates are most accessible by way of Gaston Bachelard rather
than the poets themselves. It's not clear that any of them knew his work,
although his cycle of books on the imagination of matter appeared in the
1940s. In *L'Air et les songes* (1943) Bachelard wonders, "Can the study of
fleeting images be a subject?" (*Air and Dreams* 13). Differently applied, the
question is: Can a deep image poem be composed? "We always think
of the imagination as the faculty that *forms* images," he writes. "On the
contrary, it *deforms* what we perceive; it is, above all, the faculty that frees
us from immediate images and *changes* them" and, in this capacity, the
imagination is "the human psyche's experience of *openness* and *novelty*" (*Air
and Dreams* 1). To imagine, then, means nothing less than "to launch out
toward a new life" (3). The theorists of deep image certainly felt the tug

of this liberating potential, but they failed to extricate the created image sufficiently from perceptual material, as is evident from the reactions of David Antin, Robert Creeley, and others at the time. Nevertheless, I suspect Kelly or Rothenberg would have been pleased to offer so clarifying a definition as this: "Both at the time of its birth and when it is in full flight, the image within us is the subject of the verb to imagine. It is not its direct object" (*Air and Dreams* 14)—to which might be added Aby Warburg's preoccupation with movement or rhythm in the image ("for Warburg the question of movement became associated with the subject's entrance into the image, with rites of passage, and with the dramatizations affecting his or her appearance" (Michaud 32).

With hindsight, Rothenberg admitted that, as far as deep image was concerned, the images "were probably in a Poundian way viewed as energy clusters" (Alpert 142). If Pound's vortex was the tacit model, it was the image of Imagism that all too easily prevailed, despite repeated protests and disavowals. "The poetry we have now is a poetry without the image," Bly complained (*American Poetry* 20). In 1959 he declared the Imagists "misnamed: they did not write in images from the unconscious, as Lorca or Neruda, but in simple pictures" ("Some Thoughts on Lorca" 8). Of course it might seem ludicrous to malign the Imagists for something they never attempted, but Bly's charge duplicates Pound's own shift in allegiance from *image* to *vortex*—which in turn has an intriguing historical parallel with Aby Warburg's critique of iconology, advocating that images in art might be better approached as "dynamograms" (Gombrich 244, 248). Robert Creeley shared Bly's concern that deep image could subside into mere pictorialism. He took that to be the trouble with Imagism, caught up in "the psychology of reference" and quickly becoming "a machine of manner" ("An Exchange" 28). Creeley was naturally aware of a deviant inflection of the image in Surrealism, but thought that this tendency, implicit in deep image, could "make sensational reference over-valued" (28)—as, in a fashion, it soon would in the work of the Confessional poets.

In fact, in the history of poetry it's hard *not* to find abundant examples of the image as anecdotal illustration. In "Frost at Midnight," Coleridge offers such an image precisely so as to question its grip on the mind as "a toy of Thought":

> . . . Sea, and hill, and wood,
> With all the numberless goings-on of life,

> Inaudible as dreams! the thin blue flame
> Lies on my low-burnt fire, and quivers not;
> Only that film, which fluttered on the grate,
> Still flutters there, the sole unquiet thing.
> Methinks, its motion in this hush of nature
> Gives it dim sympathies with me who live,
> Making it a companionable form,
> Whose puny flaps and freaks the idling Spirit
> By its own moods interprets, every where
> Echo or mirror seeking of itself,
> And makes a toy of Thought.
> ("Frost at Midnight" lines 10-23)

To what degree, then, are images putatively "deep" nothing more than "puny flaps and freaks"—suppositions of an "idling Spirit"? Creeley himself implied as much when, queried by David Ossman about deep image, he skirted the issue until, exasperated, he dismissively declared: "'deep image' is 'deep'—ok" (Ossman 61). His prickliness may reflect some memory of Bly's recommendation that "Mr. Creeley should try to deepen his own imagination . . . by searching for more richness of language and image" ("The Work of Robert Creeley" 21).

Deep image theory was haunted by the tautology its name insinuated. Like the emperor's new clothes, an image could be hailed as "deep" just because it was a "deep image." The liability was compounded by the terms most often used to evoke deep image: *visionary* apprehension, and the *unconscious*. Rothenberg aspired to a poetry in which "the unconscious is speaking to the unconscious" (Ossman 31). He suggested that a Zen koan was a more sensible analogy for the deep image poem "driv[ing] the mind into a *cul-de-sac*, in which it can only cry, 'Ah, this!'"—confronting "the perilous point where meaning is held in a tension on the sheer verge of meaninglessness" (*Nomad* 52). Oscillating between blankness and revelation, deep image was consistently thought to appear in a flash—sharing perhaps the messianic impulse, but not the historical dialectic, of Walter Benjamin's famous dictum, "The past can be seized only as an image which flashes up at the instant when it can be recognized and is never seen again" (*Illuminations* 255). An aesthetic of suddenness tends to dissolve continuity (provoking Karl Heinz Bohrer to ask, "Is the utopia of the moment a negative utopia?" [*Suddenness* 226]), but Kelly recognized that deep image registered a search for something determinate, like sonar scanning from a submarine. Deep image was not simply the 1912 Imagist image with depth as added value. So Kelly spoke of "a kind of poetry not necessarily dominated by the images, but in which it is the rhythm of images which form the dominant movement of the poem" (Ossman 34; cf. "Notes" 15); and this dominant movement is disclosed as a kind of hologram. Andrey Bely, the Russian Symbolist poet, evokes the elusive domain sought by deep image theory: "In poetry the words are grouped in such a fashion that their totality gives the image" (*Selected Essays* 97).

The original provocation behind Kelly's "Notes on the Poetry of the Deep Image" was the film, and film theory, of Sergei Eisenstein. Eisenstein was keen on the cinematic possibility of a "montage of attractions"—that is, the mobilization of "emotional shocks" deployed in "*a free montage with arbitrarily chosen independent . . . effects*" (*Selected Works I*, 35). The important thing, from a poetic as well as a cinematic viewpoint, is the rhythmic dynamic correlating emotional intensity with images. "Image is the rhythm of poetry," Kelly declared, attributing the insight to Nicolas Calas (Ossman 37). Calas was a Greek poet who had been initiated into the Surrealist circle in Paris in the 1930s, came to New York during the war, and eventually established himself as an art critic. In his first American book, *Confound the Wise* (1942), Calas discusses the "crisis of automatism" facing the Surrealist use of images drawn from the unconscious—a crisis typified by Rothenberg's early work, making it difficult in 1961-1962 for readers to distinguish deep image from Surrealism. Does Rothenberg's "rain that falls through my needle" qualify as one or the other, or both? Multiplied through the poem—with "an egg full of hours," "the rain of wet dollars," conveyed by burning eyes and hair taking root "like red trees" (*White Sun Black Sun* 30)—the potential of deep image clearly collapses back into Surrealist dirge. As Calas observed, "The application in poetry of the great Freudian discovery of the role of the unconscious has helped Surrealism to understand all the poetic import of the image but it did not help us to grasp immediately the rhythm of the free association of words" (*Confound the Wise* 27). In the case of automatic writing, there is no structural distinction between beginning, middle, and end, so the reader is given no principle for absorbing the cadence of images. However charged with the dynamism of the unconscious, the images are static. "What was audacious in 1925 gave the effect of unbearable repetition"—resulting in what Calas calls "the crisis of rhythm" (28).

In the second issue of *Poems from the Floating World*, in which Rothenberg first ventured the term "deep image"—not as a theoretical platform, but as an evocation of the magazine's name (reproduced below)—two epigraphs evoke the field, one of them by Calas and the other by Buber.

> "What can be learned does not matter; what matters is the self-abandonment to that which is not known."
>
> Martin Buber

> "The laws of the combination of images constitute the form of poetry; the movement of images is rhythm."
>
> Nicolas Calas

*   *   *

POEMS FROM THE FLOATING WORLD

> From deep within us it comes: the wind that
> moves through the lost branches, hurts us
> with a wet cry, as if an ocean were caged in
> each skull:

> There is a sea of connections that floats
> between men: a place where speech is touch
> and the welcoming hand restores its silence:
> an ocean warmed by dark suns.

> The deep image rises from the shoreless gulf:
> here the poet reaches down among the lost
> branches, till a moment of seeing: the poem.
> Only then does the floating world sink again
> into its darkness, leaving a white shadow,
> and the joy of our having been here,
> together.

(*Poems from the Floating World* 2, 1960: table of contents, rear inside cover.)

Supplementing the technical implications of Calas's proposition, Buber's exhortation to submit to the unknown established the mystical side of deep image. It's germane to the tradition of visionary poetry that "vision" is independent of eyesight. Likewise, pursuit of the unknown may mean pursuit of the unknowable. Ironically (or mystifyingly), then, the deep image may not be an image at all, but a "sound" provoked by, or in attunement with, a rhythm. So Kelly imagines deep image not in retinal but in auditory terms: "the image, after its first appearance as dark sound, still lingers as resonance" ("Notes" 15). "Sound is image. Touch is image" (*In Time* 8). It was "dark sounds" that, for García Lorca, defined *duende*, the otherwise unnamable force he associated with flamenco, bullfighting, and poetry at their perilous extreme. Duende is the dark side of creative endeavor. "Every image has its field of force, its shadow moving darkly through the poem, with which the poet must contend" ("Notes" 16). As with duende, deep image is a way of recognizing that ineffable point at which the work of creation intersects with—is pierced by—the work of destruction; and Kelly's concluding hope in his first proclamation is that deep image "restores the poetry of desperation" ("Notes" 16).

In a 1973 interview, Robert Kelly discussed his earlier attraction to deep image in terms that suggest why it could not last: "I was concerned to find the image in the imageless," he recalled. "Deep image to me was the image that was not perceptible to the senses, and that could be arrived at finally only syntactically" (Alpert 20, 21). The *syntactic* contribution to the apprehension of images as such was crucial to Creeley's resistance to puta-tive depth where image was concerned: "there is an 'image' in a mode, in a *way* of statement as much 'image' as any reference to pictorial element" ("An Exchange" 26). Syntax means putting together; syntax is the ar-rangement of the parts, or rhythm in the sense Kelly drew from Calas. In his exchange with Creeley, Rothenberg singled out the older poet's "The Door" as a consummate example of deep image. At three pages, "The Door" is one of Creeley's longer poems; and I recall Kelly telling me, in an appreciative reverie in 1973, that if you don't consult the clock "The Door" is an epic. Creeley's poem deftly intertwines a rudimentary image with alternating passages of self-scrutiny and emerging dream vision, until "The Door" rivals the work of the medieval Pearl poet. If by deep image we mean "The Door," then deep image is a rarity. Despite the lucid image of "the door / cut so small in the wall" (*For Love* 101), there's nothing uncanny or deep about it except through its cumulative effect in the poem, in which it operates more like a musical refrain than an enhanced or augmented image. To pursue *deep* image, in light of "The Door," meant paradoxically superseding the image in what Rothenberg called a "pattern of the movement from perception to vision" as in *visionary*—a tradition of venerable apprehensions of imageless images. The sense of transfiguration implied is handsomely accessible through a cognate term, *imago*: an insect in its sexually mature adult stage after metamorphosis. A butterfly.

In addition to being a solicitous posture toward poetic vision and a petition to the unconscious, deep image harbored a potentially social aspect. Significantly, this went unmentioned by Kelly or Rothenberg, but it contributed much to their friend David Antin's decision to steer clear of any commitment to deep image (refusing to be included in the deep image group in *Nomad*). As he recalled it in 1975:

> The idea was that the image was a kind of primitive psychological semantic construct. A kind of instant response that wasn't contaminated by a conventional syntax that tended, because of its orthodox structure, to assimilate all experience to what we used to call a "legislated reality," that was built up out of a handful of conventional cultural metaphors. At least that's the way I used to describe what we meant by an "image," and I think there was some agreement among us that that's what it meant. (Alpert 5)

As it happened, the issue of *Nomad* featuring deep image also included poems by Jackson Mac Low along with his essay "Poetry, Chance, Silence, &c." Mac Low was involved in the lower east side scene, and his performance work along with his chance generated compositions had a liberating effect on Antin, particularly in the linguistic turn signaled by "definitions for mendy." Antin recalls reading the poem on an occasion in which David Ignatow and James Wright were in the audience: "it must have sounded very aggressively remote from anything like 'deep image' poetry . . . I know from others that it sounded kind of fierce and antipoetic" (Alpert 16). The poem was an elegy, so its tactical submission to a technical definition of loss (from an insurance manual) cut loose any trace of deep image.

> loss is an unintentional decline in or disappearance of a value arising
>   from a contingency
> a value is an efficacy a power a brightness
> it is also a duration
> (*Selected Poems* 59)

Nonetheless, traces of deep image remain in the third page of the poem, which is blank except for two lines: "is there enough silence here for a glass of water" in the middle of the page, and at the bottom: "is it dark enough for bread" (61). These are not the only images in "definitions," but the *silence* and *darkness* recall aspirations of deep image to reach into, and engage, the unimaginable in the image. Of Mendy, Antin said, "It was his death and there was something about it I didn't understand and I knew I didn't, and the one thing I believe a poet ought to do is respect what he doesn't understand, respect its unintelligibility" (Alpert 17). But where deep image was the pursuit of unintelligibility by means of images, Antin was exploring instead the uncanny resources of linguistic banality drawn from professional jargons as well as common speech.

In 1965 Rothenberg and Antin co-edited the journal *Some/thing*. In the inaugural issue, Antin provided a text that might be construed as a charter, called "Silence/Noise" (printed largely in full caps). The modernist aspiration to purify the language of the tribe is reaffirmed, but with a shift of emphasis symptomatic of the cold war/Vietnam era. Antin resists talk of a new aesthetics, saying: "WHAT WE NEED IS A SURVIVAL TOOL . . . I AM TALKING ABOUT LANGUAGE HERE A HUMAN COMMUNITY CANNOT SURVIVE WITHOUT ITS LANGUAGE" (60). Rather than see poetry as a refinement of language, Antin affirms a reinvigorating embrace of the full potential of language, including its supposedly antipoetic aspects: "THERE IS NO NEED TO ASSUME THAT POETRY NEEDS TO RECOGNIZE ANY CONSTRAINTS BEYOND THE FUNDAMENTAL CONSTRAINTS OF LANGUAGE" ("Silence/Noise" 60). Rothenberg's agreement with this position is reflected not only in the procedural compositions he embarked on at this time, but in his later assessment of the danger for deep image "that one might move into a limited poetic vocabulary (a new set of image conventions as culturally controlled as the old) without ever exploring the full range of language that might also lead to the deep image" (Power 141). Still, deep image was not altogether jettisoned in the context of *Some/thing*. Antin's concluding remarks link the magazine's title to utopian aspirations for *something* beyond reach, or deep: "THE FEELING THAT SOME/THING LIES OUT THERE THAT WE CANNOT LAY HOLD OF IS THE FEELING OF THE INADEQUACY OF THE EXISTING ORDER IT IS THE DEMAND FOR A DIFFERENT ORDER THE CONDITION OF POETRY" (63).

A coincidence of chronology invites attention to the fact that *Some/thing* began in 1965, the year Jack Spicer died. If it is plausible to speak of a "linguistic turn" in American poetry, Spicer and Antin are among the poets most responsible. While Antin was clearly uncomfortable with the deep image theorizing of his friends, he concurred with them that poetic practice needed to somehow go down, to submerge itself in *prima materia* in the alchemical sense, to achieve a new distillation of its resources—resources Antin thought of as language itself in its broadest (fullest, deepest) capacity. Perhaps not coincidentally, Chomsky's theories of deep grammar were taking shape at this time, although Wittgenstein had had an impact on Antin much earlier. Wittgenstein also evoked unfathomable depth:

> The problems arising through a misinterpretation of our forms of language have the character of *depth*. They are deep disquietudes; their roots are as deep in us as the forms of our language and their significance is as great as the importance of our language. —Let us ask ourselves: why do we feel a grammatical joke to be *deep*? (And that is what the depth of philosophy is.) (*Philosophical Investigations* #111, 41e)

Jack Spicer's work is a veritable carnival of grammatical jokes, stress marks of a surface irreverence that are also "deep disquietudes"—a poet for whom "pathology leads to new paths and pathfinding. All the way down past the future" (*Collected Books* 179). Going down is an Orphic obligation; and Spicer's fixation on Cocteau's Orpheus provided him with the functional mythology of his work, the generative grammar of a poetics of fracture and what he called "disturbance." In the project initiating his cycle of composed books, *After Lorca* (1958), Spicer's gnarled receptivity to the Spanish poet is playful but also anguished, as if he had glimpsed the prospect of deep image *avant la lettre* in its larval struggle with duende. "I would like the moon in my poems to be a real moon, one which could be suddenly covered with a cloud that has nothing to do with the poem—a moon utterly independent of images" (*Collected Books* 33). But of course the moon and the cloud are images, and "I would like" remains a wish— unless, that is, it's elevated to theory as it was for Goethe, for whom "The highest thing would be to grasp that everything factual is already theory. The blue of the sky reveals to us the fundamental law of chromatics. One would never search for anything behind the phenomena; they themselves are the theory" (Buck-Morss 72). Such pan-semiosis risks the suddenness of reversal from plenitude to poverty: all things signify something, or they signify nothing. The zero/sum game is implicit in Mallarmé's wager. Spicer rolled those dice and lost—a gamble addressed by Robin Blaser in "The Practice of the Outside," included in his edition of Spicer's *Collected*

Books. "It is within language that the world speaks to us with a voice that is not our own" ("Practice" 279), Blaser writes in an insight germane to the developing poetics of his own "Image-Nations" sequence, in which the "strange unfamiliarity / of the familiar" (*Holy Forest* 138) resonates dexterously between the lure of the hermetic and the imperative of public discourse.

Deep image theory, in light of linguistic considerations germane to American poetry prior to $L=A=N=G=U=A=G=E$ magazine—exemplified by Antin, Mac Low, Spicer, and Blaser—suggests aspirations alien to the practice and legacy of Robert Bly, unless Jungian archetypes are taken to be a kind of tribal deep grammar of the imagination. "On one level," suggests Kevin Power, "the deep image is a process that leads to the discovery of a universal language" ("An Image" 154). Robert Bly was very receptive to the universal cipher of nature in the doctrine of Jacob Boehme. Certainly for Rothenberg, as for Bly, the potential of the image had archetypal resonances. Rothenberg told Power that deep image "carried the hope, like poetry in general, of 'finding the center,' which is an activity the ancestors in the old myths of founding engaged in at the outset & that we have to learn to do again with all means at our disposal" (Power, "Conversation" 143). After *Some/thing*, Rothenberg went on to edit the anthologies *Technicians of the Sacred* and *Shaking the Pumpkin*, and the ethnopoetics journal *Alcheringa*—all manifestly concerned with mythopoesis; and he would also be instrumental in facilitating contacts between key participants in what emerged as "language writing." And while language writing inherited the procedural orientation of Mac Low and Antin, and expansively took in the challenge of Wittgenstein and Gertrude Stein, the issues surrounding deep image were left far behind. Or so it seems.

Should deep image be restricted to period connotations, and understood as the selective integration of surrealist-tinged duende into American poetry? This is how Edward Hirsch construes it in his study of the duende, *The Demon and the Angel* (2002). Assimilating Lorca, Neruda, and Vallejo into the politically charged American milieu, deep image—"an image saturated with psyche that was both archaic and new" (210)—came to fruition, according to Hirsch, in the work of Bly and Wright, as well as in *The Lice* by W. S. Merwin, *The Book of Nightmares* by Galway Kinnell, *They Feed They Lion* by Philip Levine, and *The Sorrow Dance* by Denise Levertov. Certainly there's a familiar obsession with darkness: Merwin's "There are still bits of night like closed eyes in the walls" (*The Lice* 79); Kinnell's "I, too, have eaten / the meals of the dark shore" (*The Book of*

Nightmares 29); and Levine's young wife with "a gift / for the night that is always rising" (*They Feed They Lion* 8)—not to mention the tone set, definitively, by Bly in "Snowfall in the Afternoon," the final poem in *Silence in the Snowy Fields:* "If I reached my hands down, near the earth, / I could take handfuls of darkness! / A darkness was always there, which we never noticed" (*Silence* 60).

Bly's subsequent turn to political poetry in *The Light Around the Body* and *The Teeth Mother Naked at Last* mobilized deep image strategies for paradoxically public ends, the paradox being the wish that the unconscious might somehow be shared with an entire population in congregational rapport. In the form of Jungian archetypes it is in fact shared as a sacramental commemoration of images; and Bly went from being celebrated as the author of "newly discovered archetype[s]" (Libby, in Peseroff 38) to being accused of practicing a "Jungian evangelism" (Kramer 214). Whether it's been consistently Jungian or not, the evangelism has escalated with each passing decade. In retrospect, it is Bly's vigor as an advocate that has had a more enduring impact than his poetry, particularly his advocacy of the poets he translated. The steady flood of Neruda in English, the ubiquity of Lorca, the availability of Vallejo, Trakl, Char and Ponge in a variety of translations: these may seem like symptoms of a healthy interest in foreign poetry in America, but it was Bly who first called for (and often undertook) translations of their work in *The Fifties* and *The Sixties*. Only Rilke, among the many poets Bly has promoted, had significant presence in English before he took up the cause. In the case of Tomas Tranströmer, his generational peer, Bly in effect discovered the poet most genuinely in touch with deep image; the poet whose life work fulfills the mandate of deep image theory, even if he never had any contact with it except remotely, through Bly. In any case, Bly's wish came true, the wish for an American poetry milieu infused with the "depth" that only images conveyed from abroad could bring it.

And what of Kelly and Rothenberg? How did deep image shape their careers? Kelly was more peremptory in dismissing deep image than Rothenberg, for whom it implicitly remained part of an expanding arsenal of approaches to poetry and translation. In his innovative anthology *America a Prophecy* co-edited with George Quasha (1973), Rothenberg pointedly extracted from Kelly's "Notes on the Poetry of Deep Image" with an informative headnote. But he was also given to retrospective adjustments, wondering in 1965 if "it might not have been better to speak of, say, an *open* image rather than a *deep* one" ("Letter to the Editor" 27).

Kelly, too, attempted a terminological correction: "Where we were wrong was to speak of deep *image* when the word we wanted was *depth*" (*Statement* 9). Kelly dismissively recalled the formative period in which deep image theory emerged: "O how we talked too much, primitive & deep image & duende, blithering slogans & all the gimcrack foolishness of the articulate young"—pointedly acknowledging Rothenberg's warning, "we'll be sorry if we give 'em a slogan! & so we were" (*Statement* [6]).

Despite the taint of a slogan, for Kelly—who declared "The gateway is the visible; but we must go in" (*Statement* 58)—deep image was a serviceable charter of his poetics for at least a decade. *Armed Descent* inaugurated a quest guided by alchemical lore and other aspects of the Hermetic tradition, persisting through the sixties (most successfully in *Songs I-XXX*, *Finding the Measure*, and *Flesh Dream Book*) and culminating in the four hundred page poem *The Loom* (1975), a neglected masterwork that amply demonstrates the unexpected potential of deep image for narrative. As *The Loom* also reveals, Kelly was an adept practitioner in the *ut pictura poesis* tradition (culminating in "Arnolfini's Wedding" in *The Mill of Particulars*) raising the question of whether deep image can have a manifest iconographic content. Does the poetic meditation on a painting qualify as "deep" if, rather than simply pondering the image, it renders it slightly creepy? Certainly this possibility arises in much post-1960s poetry, of which James Tate might be taken as the consummate practitioner; but the case of Tate suggests another after-effect of deep image—the seemingly motorized production of poems emitted from a kind of deep image popgun. Such a prospect seems to have been on Kelly's mind in 1965 when he denounced "phony primitivism and the decades-old search for discordant images," while conceding of deep image: "It is deeply painful to me to see its name applied to incompetent bourgeois romanticism" ("Letter to the Editor" 26).

During the epidemic spread of creative writing programs in the 1970s, deep image poems (as understood by way of Bly and Wright) became the privileged idiom of a "bourgeois romanticism" more competent than Kelly would admit. But there was an aura of carnival tents nearby—a happy carnival, not the monster midway of William Lindsay Gresham's novel *Nightmare Alley*—a carnival where the ball always hits the bulls-eye and the girlfriend takes the teddy bear home, stopping for a soda on the way. My pastiche is intended to evoke kitsch moments plentiful in the work of the most dominant figure in post-sixties American poetry, John Ashbery. *The Double Dream of Spring* is resonant throughout with an almost olfactory hint of deep image; and *Self-Portrait in a Convex Mirror* met the challenge of iconographic meditation; but the campy pop cultural foundations of Ashbery's swelling body of work gives a very different inflection to suppositions about what one encounters in the "sieved dark" (*Double Dream* 66)—an inflection possibly more attuned to the American psyche than the archetypal panorama of Bly or the episodic homespun Polaroid surrealism of the creative writing programs in their first flush. What Ashbery makes available, at least as supplement to deep image, is a complex apparition of "the loose / Meaning, untidy and simple like a threshing floor" (*Double Dream* 18). Insofar as Ashbery's readers are disoriented, the patently simple is haunted by some peripheral worry, deep image as shark's fin—or is it just a trick of light on the waves? Surface or depth? The sense that surface and depth may be snug against one another like two sides of a sheet of paper is even more insistently pursued by Michael Palmer, a beneficiary and agent of the linguistic turn in American poetry. Palmer, like Creeley, bears allegiance to the syntactic rather than the pictorial promise of poetry; and such images as do emerge ("A headless man walks, lives / for four hours" [*Sun* 59]) are enhanced (or rendered "deep") by syntactic perturbations rather than by rhetorical enframing.

Syntax—that labor of joining or putting together—has turned out to be a more fertile incitement to poetic possibility than the reassuring parade of images. As early as 1965 Rothenberg admitted as much, locating the incentive behind the deep image debate in a "freedom for the mind to move among words and things, to *invent* . . . relationships without finality" ("Letter to the Editor" 27). To invent relations without finality is a worthy prospect for poetry. Rothenberg's explorations of procedural composition (like Gematria) and performance strategies (linking Dada with ritual chant) released him from the trap of deep image as invitation to somnambulistic automatism. It's by way of his fusion of a performative transfiguration of "found" material that deep image came to fruition in Rothenberg's long poem "Khurbn," arising from his visit to a concentration camp in Poland (the term *khurbn*—the "dark word" (*Khurbn* 5)—is a Yiddish alternative to "holocaust": "too much smacking of a 'sacrifice'" [*Khurbn* 3]). This forty page poem (anticipated in "The Presence of the Dead is in Every Corner," the poem immediately following "Deep Image: Footnote" in *Nomad* in 1962) consists almost entirely of litanies and lists, but the historical context renders them not only accessible but even suspenseful, unencumbered by any sense of automatism. In contrast to Bly's tendency to replenish the dayworld with dark archetypes, "Khurbn" is a cry of pure loss, following the hypnagogic instruction "practice your scream" (11): "Let a picture begin to form with every scream / Let the screams tell you that the world was formed in darkness that it ends in darkness" (34). It is only by its exuberantly declamatory means that "Khurbn" emerges as an affirmative encounter with the blackest of black suns; and, in the process, suggests that deep image continued to beckon Rothenberg for decades after he abandoned the theory.

In conclusion, what can be said about the life and afterlife of deep image? As a concept abandoned by its creators, even as they held on in practice to the hopes it awakened, it remains unsettled, a trail of clues leading to a deserted worksite. The short career of deep image was plagued by a sense of overbearing advocacy, not because Rothenberg and Kelly were prone to issuing edicts, but because the term was quickly associated with Bly, who was. Nonetheless, an injunction remains in the form of a lesson learned: there can be no program of deep image, no programmatic relation to the composition of deep image, any more than one might choose *duende* from a flamenco menu. One can only be aware of deep image in peripheral vision, as it were; thwarting direct scrutiny, it cannot be assimilated to a program.

Because deep image was a misleadingly concrete specification of the unspecifiable, Walter Kalaidjian claims that in Bly's case it was an "essentially conservative aesthetic" draining his poetry of its "discursive power" (Kalaidjian 197). Bly's commitment to the redemptive power of the unconscious is an act of faith, where Kalaidjian wants self-awareness. The two have rarely been united, let alone reconciled, in poetry. In contrast to the novel, that eminently modern genre, poetry is archaic. Bly and Rothenberg both went tribal in their own ways, notwithstanding the irony that the original provocation of deep image was the poetry of cosmopolitan Europeans. Deep image aspired to renew the archaic resources of poetry, and such a quest could not help becoming ontological rather than aesthetic. "The basic enigma of 'deep image' poetry," wrote one critic in 1973, "is that it is not so much a technique as it is a state of being" (Piccione 53); and compounding the ontological enigma, suggested Charles Altieri a few years later, is that deep image is "man's way of experiencing the nonsubjective depths of his own being alive" (Altieri 134).

The existential imperative that drove deep image—this feeling around in the dark for something without predetermined shape or dimension, but which by that very indeterminacy (openness, "without finality") belongs to the darkness—was an act of faith that it (whatever it was) would be recognizable when it appeared. But recognizable to whom? After all, "the unconscious speaking to the unconscious" bypasses consciousness altogether: so one might be engaged with deep image and know nothing whatever about it, like a sleepwalker's oblivion to a nocturnal ramble. The valedictory aspect of the poet's commemoration of the stream of images lost to the dark is memorably put by Robert Kelly:

> I once had a deep intuition of . . . a place in us in which the images die, in which they mount up and falter to the back, almost literally going over the pons, over the bridge in the brain, back into the back and die, die there, the images die. And our obsessions die there too, the hundreds of thousands of perceptions that we have every minute go there and become washed clean, and some few of them become redeemed along the way. (Erwin 135)

In the end, deep image is the reader's share, not the author's prerogative; the deep image is that one that sucks you under the ongoing flow.

In its search for a tropological trap-door, deep image was clearly a belated inflection of Surrealism: not only the surrealism of associative discontinuity and cultivated perceptual mutation—not only a *style*—but Surrealism as understood by Octavio Paz, whose lucidity on the subject derives from a unique combination of participation and distance. "The surrealist adventure is an attack on the modern world because it tries to suppress the quarrel between subject and object," he wrote, in a passage that might equally apply to deep image. "The same acid that dissolves the object disintegrates the subject. There is no self, there is no creator, but rather a kind of poetic force that blows where it will and produces gratuitous and inexplicable images" (*The Bow and the Lyre* 153). The mystical assent is ominously at hand in the presence of this gratuitous force, as Paz well knows. "Inspiration is manifested or actualized in images. By means of inspiration, we imagine. And as we imagine, we dissolve subject and object, we dissolve our selves and suppress contradiction" (154); and as Paz infers from Reverdy's definition, "every image approximates or unites realities that are opposite, indifferent, or far apart. That is, it subjects the plurality of the real to unity" (85). There is much to savor in unity, even when it's achieved by suppressing contradiction, but there is always the morning after, the new day when contradiction and variety are reborn. That is a world that can, and must, be discussed, not hailed in the narcosis of deep image. We don't live in our dreams, but (and this is the unchanging allure of deep image, this reminder) our dreams do live in us, after all, loaded with all the darkness we pack into them.

WORKS CITED

Alpert, Barry. "David Antin—An Interview." *Vort* 7 (1975): 3-33.

—. "Jerome Rothenberg—An Interview," *Vort* 7 (1975), 93-117.

—. "Robert Kelly—An Interview," *Vort* 5 (1974), 5-43.

Altieri, Charles. *Enlarging the Temple: New Directions in American Poetry during the 1960s.* Lewisburg: Bucknell University Press, 1979.

Antin, David, *Selected Poems: 1963-1973.* Los Angeles: Sun & Moon, 1991.

—. "Silence/Noise." *Some/Thing* 1 (1965): 60-63.

Ashbery, John, *The Double Dream of Spring.* New York: Dutton, 1970.

Bachelard, Gaston. *Air and Dreams: An Essay On the Imagination of Movement.* Trans. Edith R. Farrell and C. Frederick Farrell. Dallas: The Dallas Institute of Humanities and Culture, 1988.

Barnes, Djuna, *Nightwood.* New York: New Directions, 1961.

Bely, Andrey. *Selected Essays.* Ed. and trans. Steven Cassedy. Berkeley: University of California Press, 1985.

Benjamin, Walter. *Illuminations.* Ed. Hannah Arendt. Trans. Harry Zohn. New York: Shocken, 1969.

Blaser, Robin. *The Holy Forest.* Toronto: Coach House Press, 1993.

—. "The Practice of Outside." *The Collected Books of Jack Spicer.* By Jack Spicer. Los Angeles: Black Sparrow Press, 1975. 271-329.

Bly, Robert, *American Poetry: Wildness and Domesticity.* New York: Harper & Row, 1990.

—. "On English and American Poetry," *The Fifties* 2 (1959), 45-47

—. *Silence in the Snowy Fields.* Middletown, Ct.: Wesleyan U.P., 1962.

—. "Some Thoughts on Lorca and René Char," *The Fifties* 3 (1959): 7-9.

—[as "Crunk"]. "The Work of Robert Creeley," *The Fifties* 2 (1959): 10-21.

—. "A Wrong Turning in American Poetry," *Choice* 3 (1963): 33-47.

Bohrer, Karl Heinz, *Suddenness: On the Moment of Aesthetic Appearance.* Trans. Ruth Crowley. New York: Columbia University Press, 1994.

Breton, André, *Conversations: The Autobiography of Surrealism.* Trans. Mark Polizzotti. New York: Marlowe & Co., 1993.

—. *Manifestoes of Surrealism.* Trans. Richard Seaver and Helen R. Lane. Ann Arbor: University of Michigan Press, 1969.

Buck-Morss, Susan, *The Dialectics of Seeing: Walter Benjamin and the Arcades Project.* Cambridge: The MIT Press, 1989.

Calas, Nicolas, *Confound the Wise.* New York: Arrow Editions, 1942.

Creeley, Robert, *For Love: Poems 1950-1960.* New York: Scribner's, 1962.

—, and Jerome Rothenberg, "An Exchange: Deep Image and Mode," *Kulchur* 2.6 (1962): 25-42

Eisenstein, S. M. *Selected Works, Volume I: Writings, 1922-34.* Ed. and trans. Richard Taylor. Bloomington: Indiana University Press, 1988.

Erwin, Mike, and Jed Rasula. "Excerpts from an Interview with Robert Kelly," *Vort* 5 (1974): 135-144

Gombrich, E. H. *Aby Warburg, An Intellectual Biography.* 2nd ed. Oxford: Phaidon, 1986.

Hirsch, Edward, *The Demon and the Angel: Searching for the Source of Artistic Inspiration.* New York: Harcourt, 2002.

Kaladjian, Walter. "From Silence to Subversion: Robert Bly's Political Surrealism." *Critical Essays on Robert Bly.* Ed. William V. Davis. New York: G.K Hall, 1992. 194-211.

Kane, Daniel, *All Poets Welcome: The Lower East Side Poetry Scene in the 1960s.* Berkeley: University of California Press, 2003.

Kelly, Robert, *In Time.* West Newbury, MA.: Frontier Press, 1971.

—. Letter to Kenneth Irby, *Sum* 1 (December 1963): 24-25

—. Letter to the Editor, *Eleventh Finger* 2 (Autumn 1965): 25-26.

—. "Notes on the Poetry of the Deep Image," *Trobar* 2 (1961): 14-16

—. *Sentence.* Barrytown, N.Y.: Station Hill Press, 1980.

—. "Statement," *Nomad* 10/11 (Autumn 1962): 58.

—. *Statement.* Los Angeles: Black Sparrow Press, 1968.

Kinnell, Galway. *The Book of Nightmares.* Boston: Houghton Mifflin, 1972.

Kramer, Lawrence, "A Sensible Emptiness: Robert Bly and the Poetics of Immanence." *Critical Essays on Robert Bly.* Ed. William V. Davis. New York: G.K Hall, 1992. 212-223

Levine, Philip, *They Feed They Lion.* New York: Atheneum, 1972.

Libby, Anthony. "Robert Bly: Alive in Darkness." *Robert Bly: When Sleepers Awake.* Ed. Joyce Peseroff. Ann Arbor: University of Michigan Press. 37-53.

Merwin, W. S., *The Lice.* New York: Atheneum, 1967.

Michaud, Philippe-Alain. *Aby Warburg and the Image in Motion.* Trans. Sophie Hawkes. New York: Zone Books, 2004.

Ossman, David. *The Sullen Art: Interviews with Modern American Poets.* New York: Corinth Books, 1963.

Palmer, Michael, *Sun.* San Francisco: North Point, 1988.

Paz, Octavio, *The Bow and the Lyre*. Trans. Ruth L. C. Simms. Austin: University of Texas Press, 1973.

Piccione, Anthony. "Bly: Man, Voice, and Poem." *Critical Essays on Robert Bly*. Ed. William V. Davis. New York: G. K. Hall, 1992. 53-56.

Power, Kevin. "Conversation with Jerome Rothenberg," *Vort* 7 (1975): 140-153.

—. "An Image is an Image is an Image," *Vort* 7 (1975): 153-163.

Reverdy, Pierre, "L'Image," *Nord-Sud* 13 (March 1918): 3-5.

Rothenberg, "Deep Image: Footnote," *Nomad* 10/11 (Autumn 1962): 52-53

—. "The Deep Image is the Threatened Image," *Poems from the Floating World* 4 (1961): 42-44.

—. *Khurbn & Other Poems*. New York: New Directions, 1989.

—. Letter to the Editor. *Eleventh Finger* 2 (Autumn 1965): 27-28.

—. *White Sun Black Sun*. New York: Hawk's Well Press, 1960.

—. "Why *Deep* Image." *Trobar* 3 (1961): 31-32.

—. and Robert Creeley, "An Exchange: Deep Image and Mode," *Kulchur* 2: 6 (1962): 25-42

Spicer, Jack, *The Collected Books of Jack Spicer*. Ed. Robin Blaser. Los Angeles: Black Sparrow Press, 1975.

Stepanchev, Stephen. *American Poetry Since 1945, A Critical Survey*. New York: Harper & Row, 1965.

Wittgenstein, Lugwig. *Philisophical Investigations*. Trans. G. E. M. Anscombe. Oxford: Blackwell, 2001.

"As Radical As Society Demands the Truth to Be": Umbra's Racial Politics and Poetics

Jon Panish

In the still too few histories of the Lower East Side's early-1960s-era Umbra poets, a consensus has formed that this group is most accurately seen as a precursor or link to the subsequent Black Arts movement. [1] The authors of these sociocultural and literary histories argue persuasively that there are numerous connections between the Black Arts movement and the Umbra poets, their poems, the workshop they participated in, and the magazine they produced. To generate these historical narratives, scholars construct a triumphal, linear progression that emphasizes, for example, the movement of key individuals in Umbra from the Lower East Side to Black Arts projects in Harlem, Newark, New Orleans, Oakland, and Atlanta; the change in supporting organization from Umbra to BART/S or the Free Southern Theater; the transformation of the critical apparatus from experimental, outsider poetics to the black aesthetic; and the conversion of individual and group politics from oppositional to revolutionary. Like most linear narratives, there is a certain degree of truth and usefulness to this history. The historical connections described are mostly factual: some members departed Umbra in 1965 and the few years following specifically to join or found organizations with a cultural nationalist orientation. Also, like many of their counterparts in the civil rights movement, members of Umbra developed politics and, in their case, poetics that were "blacker," separatist, and more politically revolutionary as a response to such national political events as the assassinations of Medgar Evers and Malcolm X. Using these facts, members of the group and interested scholars have since been able to emphasize the connections between Umbra and the Black Arts movement while also establishing and maintaining a useful distinction between these poets, as a black avant-garde, and the more numerous white poets on the Lower East Side who have always dominated the discussion of the era's various avant-garde groups.

Perhaps it is time, however, to alter slightly our understanding of Umbra's significance as a postwar poetic avant-garde while still maintaining its particularity as a *black* avant-garde group. There are several reasons I'm suggesting this change in perspective. First, the emphasis on Umbra as a precursor or link to the Black Arts movement diminishes the work of the Umbra poets and the significance of the magazine they produced. Second, this emphasis also unfairly and unnecessarily tames the unruly diversity of the poetry produced by members of the original Umbra Workshop and the even wider range of poems published by non-Umbra members in the magazine. Finally, and perhaps most controversially, focusing on the Umbra-Black Arts movement nexus rather than on Umbra itself misrepresents the link between race and culture embodied in both the actual community of Umbra poets and the imagined community represented by the magazine. Though race is obviously as central to Umbra's mission (the first issue of the magazine states that "the experience of being Negro" is its primary "orientation") as it is to the Black Arts movement, Umbra's approach to race is plural and flexible in ways that the development of mid-1960s nationalism did not allow. Following David Lionel Smith's general model, I am making a distinction between the Black Arts movement's "black aesthetic" and Umbra's "black aesthetics"; as Smith argues, "the former suggests a single principle, while the latter leaves open multiple possibilities. The former is closed and prescriptive, the latter, open and descriptive" (96).[2] Because of their approach to race, it is more accurate (and useful) to view the Umbra poets as having anticipated the complex and pluralist notion of blackness that is a hallmark of contemporary cosmopolitan conceptions of art than as immediate precursors to the cultural nationalism of the Black Arts movement. Let me reiterate, however, that this is not to say that Umbra as a group or *Umbra*, the magazine, are examples of a cosmopolitanism that rejects racial identity outright; clearly, neither was. Instead, the members and the magazine they produced are examples of the black cosmopolitan literary lineage traced by Ross Posnock, especially the tradition that he says recognizes plural black identities, rejects both particularism and assimilation, and accepts "the voluntary aspect of modern identity" (7-8). Most important for my purposes, Posnock says that this tradition also tacitly accepts the notion that, as Alain Locke wrote, cultural resources "belong to all who can use them; and belong most to those who can use them best" (11). In both the composition of the group (black and white members) and the selection of poets and poems (not only black and white poets but poets constructing different black identities) presented in the magazine, the example of Umbra demonstrates an understanding of the complexity of racial identity and, more important, racial expression in art that clearly sets it apart from the subsequent period of Black Arts, the black aesthetic, and black cultural nationalism in general. As such, Umbra may represent a more useful and usable example for contemporary black avant-gardists than the subsequent Black Arts groups.

Certainly, the social and cultural environment of the Lower East Side during the early 1960s was instrumental in contributing to the kind of community established by Umbra. As scholars and most participants have recognized, the Lower East Side was unusual during this time in its social and cultural diversity. As Christopher Mele discusses in his study of the area, young people of diverse backgrounds, experiences, and interests were attracted to the Lower East Side by its "long history of pluralism" as well as by its relatively cheap rents (140-42). Though there was some tension between the younger, more recent arrivals and the older, mostly white, residents, most of the black members of Umbra remember the area as being exceptionally harmonious. Lorenzo Thomas, for example, has described the atmosphere as "low-rent cosmopolitanism" ("Alea's Children" 573) while Calvin Hernton has written that "the neighborhood became truly a rainbow neighborhood" ("Umbra" 582). In addition to its social and cultural diversity, the Lower East Side during the early 1960s was alive with vibrant, diverse political and social activism. This activism ranged from recently formed community groups, with names like the Lower East Side Committee on Civil Rights and the Lower East Side Neighborhoods Association, who were fighting against local racism, slumlords and poor living conditions (Mele 149-50) to a variety of older leftist organizations (Smethurst 272). According to James Smethurst, these organizations included "national organizational headquarters, bookstores, newspapers, journals, and Left-influenced ethnic institutions, such as the Ukrainian Labor Hall, and a Left-wing artistic subculture that included some of the younger artists of the Lower East Side" (272). Most significant for our purposes, Smethurst describes this conglomeration of activist forces on the Lower East Side as "a politically radical interracial bohemia at the beginning of the 1960s" (272). Thus it was in the ferment of the Lower East Side's social, cultural, and political diversity that Umbra's particular brand of black cosmopolitanism took shape. Founded by, composed of, and providing support for primarily black writers and intellectuals, Umbra maintained an openness to individual aesthetic choices, to different political solutions to existing social problems, and to interracial linkages and alliances that displays its members' debt to the environment of the Lower East Side but also signals its singularity among the area's various cultural and political groups.

Highlighting Umbra's uniqueness need not mean erasing the Black Arts movement or its significant accomplishments. As Brian Ward has stated (following Claybourne Carson), the broader black power movement, in both its political and cultural forms during the 1960s and 1970s, succeeded in firmly establishing and popularizing self-defined notions of African American culture and identity even if it ultimately failed to increase black people's political or economic power (408). Of course, as with the civil rights movement itself (and the rest of the 1950s and 1960s social movements), black power and Black Arts had a long history prior to its efflorescence during this time. Too often historians of these movements neglect precursors, such as Marcus Garvey, James Weldon Johnson, and Langston Hughes, and thus fail both to give credit and to contextualize developments in the 1960s, as David Lionel Smith has argued (107). In any case, to try to disengage Umbra from Black Arts as I am doing is not to denigrate the achievements of that movement but simply to shed more light on the movement's origins, as Smith has suggested, and to foreground Umbra's identity instead of allowing it to disappear, ironically, beneath the Black Arts shadow.

Without recapitulating the entire history of Umbra, I will first discuss more fully the link between Umbra and the Black Arts movement. This discussion requires that I make distinctions (distinctions that I will maintain throughout the essay) between Umbra, the group, and *Umbra*, the magazine. As a group of writers who met regularly in a single geographic place—the Lower East Side—Umbra existed for a very brief time. According to Michel Oren, as a "core group," Umbra was together from the summer of 1962 to 1964 or 1965, depending on whether one marks the end at the point of the first major rupture between factions within the group or of the failure of attempts to mend relations between the factions and the subsequent departure of some members to Harlem with Amiri Baraka (180-2). Even this statement is problematic because the group's membership wasn't stable during this short period; between the publication of the first and second issues of the magazine, influential members such as Ishmael Reed, Norman Pritchard, and Lorenzo Thomas officially joined the group. Nevertheless, there are several important aspects to the brief existence of the core group. First, the core group that Oren refers to included people (black men mostly) whose ages ranged from eighteen to thirty, who grew up in the North and the South, who were active in politics, community work, and literature, who were from middle- and working-class backgrounds, and who had different levels of formal education. They were, in other words, quite a diverse group of people who, like any diverse group, came together with already established ideological, artistic, and personality differences. Focusing on Umbra or any other group as "black" makes it easy to elide these differences to emphasize similarities instead. Though they were a group united by their racial identity, their dedication to poetry and the arts, their progressive political views, and their feelings of alienation from the mainstreams of bourgeois white and black society, they were by no means a homogenous group.

Next, the period of time during which the core group was together was a critical and volatile one in the history of American race relations. Although today this period is most often remembered as including the emblematized high point of the modern civil rights movement—the August, 1963, March on Washington for Jobs and Freedom—the period is actually more accurately represented as one of great violence and intense disillusionment for many black people. For many in Umbra, at least, the significant events of these years are better represented by the response of the Birmingham, Alabama, police to the freedom riders—the use of dogs and fire hoses, that is—the church-bombing murders of four young girls attending Sunday school in Birmingham, and the murders of Medgar Evers and Malcolm X than the March on Washington.[3] In any case, during these years, events connected to civil rights and race relations were occurring so rapidly and alternating so violently between the promise of hope and the disillusionment of despair that the work of writers whose sensitive antennae were tuned to this frequency is predictably filled with both optimism and pessimism, celebration and condemnation, joy and rage. As Rashidah Ismalli-Abu-Bakr puts it, "But in the '60s there was war and chaos and, simultaneously, hope" (585). Thus, the links to both the past—represented by poems that express a blues-based attitude of forbearance and suffering with a suggestion of hopefulness—and the future—represented by poems that are more raw in their expression of anger at the slow pace of change and a confrontational assertion of a grittier, street culture—are evident in the first two issues of *Umbra*. The former is represented in poems by a writer such as Julian Bond about Ray Charles, Miles Davis, and Martin Luther King as well as contributions by Lerone Bennett, in a poem "for Billie Holiday," and Robert Gore, in a poem titled "We Shall Overcome."[4] Interestingly, non-Umbra members wrote all these poems while such Umbra members as Tom

Dent, David Henderson, and Calvin Hernton wrote the poems that seem most like those to be written under the influence of cultural nationalism. Nevertheless, as Lorenzo Thomas says, the writers in Umbra's core group (and it seems this could be extended to the writers published in *Umbra*) shared "a common orientation" in that they "approached their world with a sense of outrage and with a missionary zeal borrowed from the southern civil rights struggle and heightened by an urgency bred by their surroundings" (*Extraordinary Measures* 119). Like the black population in general during this time, these writers saw the same problems but differed about how to solve them or even whether a solution was possible.

It is also because of the group's specific history that scholars have been so focused on Umbra as a link between periods rather than as a group that is significant unto itself. In fact, Umbra *appears* to mirror the very period it is set in: the group joined together a diverse collection of people interested in progressive political and poetic ideas but broke apart rather violently over, in part, differences related to racial ideology and practice. This reading of the group's history is underlined because the more or less official demise of the group in early 1965 is marked by Amiri Baraka's migration to Harlem to be joined by several members of Umbra's core group. Though Baraka was never a member of Umbra, he had been a visible and galvanizing influence among black writers on the Lower East Side for many years before his departure.[5] Again, however, to focus on what only in retrospect seems a significant historical pattern is to privilege continuity over particularity, the diachronic over the synchronic. It leads to inaccurate binary formulations such as the one in which one scholar has characterized Umbra as a "dynamic blend of integrationists and nationalists" (Gabbin 328). Clearly, when one looks at the poems included in Umbra's magazines (as I will do shortly), there is nothing in them that one could meaningfully label "integrationist," especially if one interprets this to entail assimilation as I think one must. By this distinction I mean to emphasize the difference between "integrated" and "interracial"; though *Umbra* was to some extent an interracial magazine (and by extension projected an interracial imaginative community), it was not integrated in the common usage of the time, which, as David Hollinger notes, "had little incentive to embrace the pluralist emphasis on the autonomy and durability of ethno-racial groups" (98). *Umbra*, on the other hand, was clearly a "pluralist" magazine in this sense; it staked out a literary and cultural tradition that is distinctively black. However, because of the *intraracial* pluralism of the magazine, it is also inaccurate to use the "nationalist" label. The poetry included in the magazine is "nationalist" only in the sense that it has a strong affective element related to the experience of racism, strongly evokes in some of its writing a sense of the everyday experience of being black in the U.S., and displays a strong sense of connection to an African past and an identification with contemporary African people throughout the world. However, as Tom Dent has remarked, trying to distinguish his group's writing from later nationalist work, "Umbra did not represent the style of black writing and black thought that became encrusted and almost formularized" (Oren 188). Lorenzo Thomas has also written that there are significant differences between the writing of Umbra members and those who followed them chronologically; he says that unlike "some militant blacks did in later years," Umbra writers did not idealize the "lifestyles and folkways" of black people in the U.S. (*Extraordinary Measures* 121). Dent's and Thomas's quotes suggest that Umbra members were not trying to construct a single, pure, and unified narrative of black authenticity the way that later nationalists were even as they were working within a framework that rejected conformity to white standards of writing and identity.

Moreover, this notion of Umbra as a group of "integrationists and nationalists" refers, I think, more revealingly to the struggle over the inclusion of white members in the group, a struggle that really only seemed to come to a head toward the end of the core group's existence.[6] By all accounts, this was a contentious issue in Umbra, as it was in all groups with a racially mixed membership during the time. The issue became more contentious as the decade progressed. However, it also seems clear that the motivation behind the inclusion of white writers in the group and in the magazine was not a matter of integration as such but a dedication to "art," and perhaps more significantly avant-garde art, as a social and cultural practice that enabled, and perhaps encouraged, race to be bracketed. Lorenzo Thomas puts it this way, "While race remained a powerful engine of social upheaval, the artists seemed able to work together almost in spite of it" ("Alea's Children" 575). While there are parallels one can develop between Umbra and a contemporary socio-political group such as SNCC—both included black and white members, members in both followed a similar trajectory of radicalization, both were involved in community action directed at eliminating racism and the socio-economic effects of it on black people—it's a mistake to evaluate them using the same terms. Unlike SNCC, for example, there is no indication that Umbra members ever saw themselves as creating a kind of "idealized integrated community" (Morgan 66). Instead, as Thomas's quote indicates, the inclusion of white people in Umbra *as members* (and this included only Art Berger and the wives of some black members) was more incidental than ideological. In part, the environment of the Lower East Side was, as stated earlier, more racially and ethnically diverse than the typical American community of the time. As a result, as Umbra drew members and participants for their activities and magazine, they inevitably included a few white people with whom they had already-established relationships. David Henderson affirmed this when he told Daniel Kane in 1998, "Of course we were nationalists and into the civil rights movement, but we also had a lot of white friends and people of other races. We were just not doctrinaire nationalists" (80).

This isn't to romanticize the relationships among the black and white members of Umbra either. It's clear from Oren's history and from various members' memoirs that many of the tensions accompanying race that existed within society as a whole accompanied members into the group. Some black male members, for example, were married to white women, and as Amiri Baraka has described, these relationships were increasingly becoming points of contention during this time. Moreover, as Harold Cruse has discussed, frustrations over the direction and goals of the civil rights movement caused tensions between white liberals and black intellectuals to simmer throughout this period before they boiled over in the mid-1960s (193). Thus, when one reads in Oren's history that Umbra member Art Berger believed himself to be a "token" white member who many black members had a "love/hate relationship" with or that Calvin Hernton felt the need retrospectively to describe Berger's role as that of a "servant," one should understand that these interpersonal conflicts were less about the clash between different ideologies of race relations than they were the result of the accumulation of a series of frustrations over the slow progress of change that increasingly made it difficult for black and white people to communicate with each other.

More important, though, is the fact that Umbra, if one judges more by the magazine they produced than the social history of the group's members, seems to have been designed to explode the integration/nationalism binary that was beginning to calcify in the early sixties. Even though the stated idea behind the formation of Umbra was to provide a place for black writers and artists who had already "integrated" the

Lower East Side avant-garde to combat their "isolation and anonymity" by meeting regularly apart from white artists and writers (Hernton 580), the magazine as practiced became a black-directed, black-defined vehicle of expression for a diversity of perspectives on blackness. What started out, in other words, as a kind of separatist support group became an enterprise that programmatically refused to limit itself to following a single principle of blackness (to follow David Lionel Smith's characterization of the Black Aesthetic [96]) or to capitulate to the Lower East Side's non-racial, universalizing notion of experimental poetics. Instead, they were, as Daniel Kane suggests, carving out their own artistic territory by using their own experiences and their own cultural knowledge in combination with their own study of Olson, Pound, and other innovative poetic stylists of the time (81-6). Their artistic territory, as represented by the magazine, became a space defined and directed by a politically radical black consciousness but inclusive of those white people whose poetic vision coincided with theirs. As such, their project resonated with the ideas of the more militant leaders of SNCC, such as John Lewis, who at the 1963 March on Washington had planned to say, "We will take matters into our own hands and create a source of power, outside any national structure, that could and would assure us a victory" (quoted in Morgan 61). That "march leaders" felt the need and were able to persuade Lewis "to tone down his remarks" indicates that Umbra's similar but even more militant posture was indeed path breaking for its time.

The foreword to the first issue of *Umbra* is where we can find the group's statement of its purpose and goals. In it, the editors stake out *Umbra*'s "orientation" in a commitment to two positions: "1) the experience of being Negro, especially in America; and 2) that quality of human awareness often termed 'social consciousness'" (3). Interestingly, neither of these positions limits *Umbra* in terms of its contributors' race nor their specific approach to black experience aside from a commitment to "social consciousness." The latter position is clarified in the third paragraph: "UMBRA exists to provide a vehicle for those outspoken and youthful writers who present aspects of social and racial reality which may be called 'uncommercial,' 'unpalatable,' 'unpopular,' 'unwanted'—but cannot with any honesty be considered nonessential to a whole and healthy society." Again, this orientation leaves room for quite a range of "aspects" to be presented, especially those that didn't toe the non-violent line. Even in 1963, racial discourse had become so entrenched in the *non-violent* battle over civil rights that any perspective that questioned, even symbolically, the value of this strategy or presented dissatisfaction with it could be considered neglected. Precisely what the editors mean by "uncommercial, unpalatable, unpopular, and unwanted" isn't made clear except in terms of a contrast with the previous paragraph's delineation of work authored by "those seemingly selected perennial 'best sellers' and literary 'spokesmen of the race situation' who are currently popular in the commercial press and slick in-group journals." This clearly sounds like a critique of James Baldwin, who, according to Henry Louis Gates, "was exalted as *the* voice of black America [with the publication of *The Fire Next Time* in 1963]. The success of *Fire* led directly to a cover story in *Time* in May of 1963; soon he was spoken of as a contender for the Nobel Prize" (8). Perhaps all the editors were implying here was that they wanted to combat what had been the typical black writer's experience of being chosen, one at a time, by the white literary establishment as spokesperson for the race (as had Richard Wright before Baldwin). After all, this interest in fighting the white establishment's anointing of a succession of single black voices had in part led to a tradition among the Lower East Side's black writers of reading "eight or ten at a time" (Kane 80). However, one cannot read through *Umbra* without also noticing that Baldwin's oft-heard call for black people to try to change white people with "love" (as he advises his nephew in the opening section of *Fire*)—a tactic Hernton calls "the compassionate type of attitude on the race question"—is absent in the magazine (Hernton *White Papers* 123). Still, it is also notable that the editors, while forsaking a "compassionate attitude" on race, are able to envision "a whole and healthy society" that might result from an uncompromising engagement with "social and racial reality." Strangely enough, this doesn't put them in territory too terribly far from Baldwin, who at the end of *Fire* writes, "Everything now, we must assume, is in our hands; we have no right to assume otherwise. If we—and now I mean the relatively conscious whites and the relatively conscious blacks, who must, like lovers, insist on, or create, the consciousness of the others—do not falter in our duty now, we may be able, handful that we are, to end the racial nightmare, and achieve our country" (105). Though, at the time, the *Umbra* editors may not have seen themselves, or wanted to present themselves, as being allied with Baldwin, the passing years reveal otherwise.

One final section of the foreword further enhances our understanding of the unorthodox "nationalist" position staked out by *Umbra*. In it, the editors state, "We maintain no iron-fisted, bigoted policy of preference

or exclusion of material. UMBRA will not be a propagandistic, psycho-
pathic or ideological axe-grinder. We will not print trash, no matter how
relevantly it deals with race, social issues, or anything else" (3-4). While
superficially this may seem to be a straightforward statement emphasiz-
ing the literary over the political (as Daniel Kane reads it), the choice
of words here—"bigoted," "preference," "exclusion," "propagandistic,"
"psychopathic," and "ideological"—clearly reveals that the authors are
also signaling their unwillingness to subordinate all other considerations
to the expression of particular racial ideas or emotions.[7] For example, the
clustering of those last three adjectives—propagandistic, psychopathic,
ideological—suggests that they were not interested in being dominated by
material that would advocate or imply the use of violence in the struggle
for black civil rights. This statement also, of course, suggests that the
magazine will not be limiting itself to black authors' perspective on the
black experience. While this combination of principles might suggest to
some that *Umbra* was retreating in its promise to publish writers who are
thought to be "too hard on society," I think they were more likely trying
to avoid what Lorenzo Thomas has since described as the "functionalism
of poetry"; that is, the idea that a poem can be an instrument used to
motivate people to action (Rowell 25). This implication is reinforced with
the paragraph's conclusion, "We are not a self-deemed radical publica-
tion: we are as radical as society demands the truth to be. We declare an
unequivocal commitment to material of literary integrity and artistic ex-
cellence." There are two interesting aspects to this, once again, broad and
somewhat conflicting statement. First, despite their reluctance to privilege
the political over the literary, this concluding statement suggests that the
editors would like to make a fine distinction between poetry that is purely
instrumental, that completely subordinates form to content perhaps, and
poetry that is, to quote Nathaniel Mackey, "an agent of change" (25),
that can, in Lorenzo Thomas's words, "creat[e] consciousness, which will
then inspire people to act" (25). As we will see, this is an ambition that
Umbra will not achieve with every poem; some clearly seem to have been
included more for their political ideology than their artistic merit. The
second aspect concerning the concluding statement that is worth noting
is the editors' apparent need to both affirm and deny the political content
of their journal: as a predominantly "black" magazine, they are forced to
declare their intention to pursue *both* truth and beauty.

While it is, I think, the second issue of *Umbra* that more successfully
fulfills the promise of the principles stated in the foreword, the first issue

is also noteworthy for its diversity of poets, themes, and styles. As Eugene Redmond first recognized (followed by Aldon Nielsen), *Umbra* was not the only black-directed magazine of its time to pursue a policy of interracial diversity. Redmond notes that *Dasein*, published by the Dasein Literary Society and featuring an advisory board that included Sterling Brown and Arthur P. Davis, was "original and experimental in content design and layout," included a wide range of material, and didn't limit itself to contributions from black writers and artists (553-4). While the first issue of *Umbra* is dominated by members and future members of the group, the issue is rich with striking differences.[8] To begin, among the poets represented here are experienced professionals, very young, aspiring writers, and others for whom writing poetry seems not to be their primary interest or endeavor. Among the latter group are three who are better-known for their civil rights activism—Julian Bond, Robert Gore, and Robert F. Williams—and one whose primary focus in writing was historical and journalistic, Lerone Bennett. Interestingly and perhaps fittingly, the poems by Bond, Gore, and Bennett show the clear stylistic influence of Langston Hughes (and not just because Bond writes a poem about him) and the blues. Their poems are straightforward and accessible, with uncomplicated structures, first-person narration, and colloquial language, and are infused with an intense sense of race pride and feeling. Three of Bond's four poems, for example, pay tribute to African-American icons: Hughes, Ray Charles, and Miles Davis. His poem on Langston Hughes is representative:

> He writes about Jesse Simple and home folks
> in Harlem,
> Biggety people read his stuff and frown,
> depressed,
> They just don't like to see themselves
> with their souls undressed. (9-10)

Thematically, this poem is typical of *Umbra* as a whole in its association with the "home folks" rather than the "biggety people." Bond's poems are also notable (though perhaps exceptional in the magazine) for their humor and light touch: "Look at that gal shake that thing / We can't all be Martin Luther King."

Bennett's and Gore's poems show the closest relationship to the civil rights movement. Their mostly somber poems effectively and evocatively develop themes related to struggle, suffering, and endurance. Bennett's two poems both present musical themes, but unlike Bond's celebration of triumphant performers like Davis and Charles, Bennett focuses in one on Billie Holiday's relation through her suffering to the brutal history of the African diaspora—"She was with Bigger / before Wright wrote, / was with Nekeela / in a slave coffle, / was stripped, branded / and eaten by the sharks / and rose again / on the third day in Georgia" (17)—and in the other to the black performer's need to satisfy white expectations: "Yesterdays, man, was yesterdays. / Play somethin' sweet / for them rich ofays" (19). Similarly, Gore's "Black Reincarnation" is a deceptively simple and effective blues statement that uses understatement and repetition to make a profound political point,

> If this is all there is to
> It
> Who in the hell would want to go through
> It
> Again, and again and
> Again? (37)

The inclusion of a poem by Robert F. Williams demonstrates both *Umbra*'s attention to the more militant wing of the civil rights movement and also the challenge of reconciling political ideology and artistic sophistication. With a very different resume than Julian Bond or Robert Gore, Williams is best known as the head of the Union County, North Carolina, chapter of the NAACP, which under his direction had a history of direct and forceful confrontation with racists. Williams attempted to integrate the Monroe, North Carolina, public pool, advocated the arming of black citizens and formed a self-defense club (he was an inspiration to and model for Huey Newton), led a group that confronted the KKK, and perhaps most famously ran into trouble with the national NAACP by remarking that in the future, "we would meet violence with violence." Williams wrote an account of his tenure as the Union County NAACP branch head titled *Negroes with Guns* (which is advertised in the back of this issue of *Umbra*) and was eventually forced into exile in Cuba and China on kidnapping charges (which were dropped more than fifteen years later). Williams's contribution to the first issue is a poem titled "An Ocean's Roar of Peace," which is perhaps artistically uninspired but is interesting in part because its theme conflicts with Williams's image as a

"Negro with a gun." The poem begins with what appears to be a call for interracial cooperation against white racists,

> tell me friend, what is your name?
> for we share a common blame
> tell me, what is your will for life?
> in this ominous age of ceaseless strife
> reason does not give us cause to hate
> as friends we must rise to forge our fate
> and proclaim liberty from the puppetmaster's
> string! (11)

Though this might have contradicted his public image, like many so-called militants, Williams was more, at this point at least, an antiracist hardliner than black separatist; though he wouldn't renounce violence (believing that is would be surrendering too much), he was willing to work with the Freedom Riders and urged people to support them when they came to Monroe. Still, given his image, it's a little jarring to reach the end of his poem and read,

> let us walk hand in hand;
> our numbers will increase til we are one,
> one great voice,
> an ocean's roar of peace. (12)

Williams's poem is surprising not just because it conflicts with his public image as a militant, confrontational public figure, but also because with its regular meter and rhythm, pedestrian end-stopped rhymes, and clichéd images, it is a thoroughly mediocre poem. Given that the issue's foreword states that the magazine will "not print trash, no matter how relevantly it deals with race, social issues, or anything else," how could the editors possibly justify including Williams's poem? On one hand, the inclusion of less-than-stellar poetry in a poetry magazine, even (especially?) a so-called avant-garde one, is not surprising; they are and always have been filled with such poems. On the other hand, the first two issues of *Umbra* seem to have more than their share of poetry that is artistically undistinguished, and most of these seem, like Williams's poem, to have been included because of their "relevance" to race and social issues. Though including these poems, then, contradicts the foreword's emphatically stated policy, it's apparent that in the end the magazine's political orientation trumped its artistic vision: either the editors were blinded to these poems' artistic faults or they chose to ignore them.

Beyond the inclusion of these movement-related writers, the first issue of *Umbra* includes poems by members and non-members that are diverse in both form and content. I won't discuss any of these poems in detail because others, notably Aldon Nielsen and Daniel Kane, have looked closely at the work of contributors such as LeRoy McLucas, Lorenzo Thomas, and David Henderson. As Nielsen and Kane have recognized about these three writers in particular there is a tremendous amount of formally innovative and thematically powerful work in the first issue. Also, among these three writers, and also Tom Dent and Calvin Hernton, there is a tremendous range of thematic emphasis; though all of their work engages "blackness," per the foreword's instructions, these more skillful, experimental writers engage race in complex and surprising ways. Dent's opening poem, "Nightdreams (Black)" exemplifies this with its blend of poetic styles and its combination of themes involving race, violence, and sexuality. Scholars of Umbra have neglected Hernton's strong work in this issue. Two of his poems, "The Long Blues" and "125th Street (Harlem, New York)" offer dynamic first-person narratives of urban life that stand out among the poems here in their emotional power, verbal creativity, and vivid imagery.

Finally, perhaps because of the core group's composition, the first issue offers poems by only one woman and one non-black male writer. As I'll discuss shortly, the second issue's makeup (presumably because of the foreword and call for submissions in the first issue) is more diverse in terms of gender and race. Still, these two poems in the first issue are interesting in their own right. Jay Socin, who is listed in the contributors' notes as being the publisher of Interim Books and who was also associated with Gregory Corso, contributed a poem titled "Hello, Goodbye," written about the deaths of twenty telephone operators in New York City in October, 1962. The poem, exemplified in this excerpt, displays more of a proletarian consciousness than a strictly racial one:

> twenty girls dead
> seventy more hurt
> too poor to survive
> the price of a meal out
> would have saved them (11)

Patricia Brooks's "Poem" uses the arresting imagery of slavery, the Underground Railroad, and lynching to describe her first-person (white?) narrator's growing awareness of and symbolic association with the plight of black men in the U.S. The poem begins with Brooks's narrator acknowledging her past lack of awareness,

> Black man, you are no part
> Of my past—
> No part of those soft-hanging summer evenings
> Insulating the eaves of my home
> From all catastrophe.
> You held no place
> At my hearth,
> Warmed by a love that burned
> Without your bitter fire;
> The four walls of my childhood
> Never knew the throbbing
> Of your song (39-40).

The poem ends, however, with her narrator as Eve symbolically marrying the "black man" as Adam:

> There is no shade from your shadow
> For us two
> Who bear the features of those actors
> Enacting that original ritual of damnation
> That has brought our birth.

Umbra's second issue, published later in the year (1963), features nearly twice as many poets as the first issue but approximately the same number of poems. Moreover, only nine of the thirty poets represented are Umbra members, and several of the most notable members contributing poems to the first issue—Tom Dent, David Henderson, and Calvin Hernton—do not have poems in the second issue. Nevertheless, the range in this second issue is enormous. Not only does the issue feature the appearance of Ishmael Reed (who had joined the group between the publication of the two issues), but it also includes poems by renowned member Norman Pritchard and by Clarence Major. More important, though there is still a clear emphasis on poems with thematic links to the civil rights movement (the first section, for example, is titled "The Coming Storm") and thus a return to the themes of suffering, endurance, and victimization, there is an even greater inclusion of poems that develop the theme of blackness in complex, suggestive (rather than obvious), and often conflicting ways (especially in the long middle section of the magazine titled, "Richard Wright Mnemonicon"). Finally, because the second issue reaches beyond the core group itself, there is an even greater diversity of contributors—in terms of age, region of the country, gender, occupation, and race—than in the first issue.

With its presentation of multiple perspectives on blackness and its inclusion of diverse national voices, the second issue of *Umbra* not only comes close to fulfilling the mission stated in its inaugural issue, but it also more clearly distinguishes itself from the other magazines being published on the Lower East Side during the early sixties. Unlike, for example, Ed Sanders's *Fuck You/a magazine of the arts* or Ted Berrigan's *C*, *Umbra*'s ambition transcended the Lower East Side and the goals of smashing social taboos or transforming the writing and reading of poetry. While clearly the Umbra poets themselves were influenced by some of the same social, cultural, and literary values as the white poets on the Lower East Side, racial identity and politics dominated *Umbra*'s mission. This focus on race didn't mean, certainly, that social taboos weren't smashed nor that poetry wasn't transformed in *Umbra*; however, these goals were subordinated to one that the black editors believed to be more serious and neglected by both the dominant culture and the oppositional one on the Lower East Side: the expression of black beauty and truth. Though Sanders, Berrigan, and other avant-garde white poets could be, and to some extent were, allies in the fight against the cultural and political establishment's hypocrisy and conservatism, they couldn't, wouldn't, foreground race.

"The Coming Storm" section, which is placed at the beginning of *Umbra*'s second issue, explicitly comments on the progress of the civil rights movement with a poem by a young woman who participated in the freedom rides and other poems that pick up themes presented throughout the first issue. However, unlike certain poems in the earlier issue, there is almost no optimism in these poems. Ishmael Reed's poem "Time and the Eagle," which leads off the initial section, works with Yeats's ideas/images from "The Second Coming" to forecast an approaching apocalypse. The poem is full of frightening imagery, from the first line, "The shackled Black, being torn in innocence," through stanzas featuring an "age of madness," "scaly sea creatures," "the blood tide," an "evil flapping demon bird," "victims . . . dangling from dark trees," and an "unknowing egg" that "wobbles in the terror / Of recognition and is devoured" (5-6). The other poems in this section reiterate many of Reed's pessimistic images (especially "blood") and lead to Charles Anderson's poem "Complaint on Passive Resistance," which develops a slightly mocking portrait of white freedom riders as liberal tourists. Interestingly, Anderson's poem is followed by a short story, "A Far Off Sound," written by Ann Allen Shockley that narrates a few scenes from an ill-fated relationship between two college students, a black, Southern basketball player and a white, Northern, sheltered, middle-class woman. Although the story is, as a whole, no less pessimistic than the poems that precede it (the relationship between the couple ends because of their ineluctable inability to understand each other's racial experience), its details create characters that are by no means one-dimensional. The basketball player's aggressive and antagonistic behavior toward the girl he is dating is explained by his memory of false accusations of rape (of a white woman) against his father. The young white girl, on the other hand, is presented as being typically naïve and attracted to the basketball player in part for his exoticism. Though these characters represent fairly typical types for the time, Shockley's humane, unsensationalized portrayal gives them an emotional depth that takes readers further into the interracial dynamic of the time than poems about movement politics can get them. Moreover, the inclusion of a secondary character, "a pretty tan girl" who sides with the white woman during one of her fights with the basketball player, slightly unsettles the story's racial order. Shockley's theme and depth is picked up later in the issue in a poem by Lorenzo Thomas called "South St Blues," in which he also describes the difficulty of communicating in an interracial relationship.

The bulk of the material in the second issue is found in two following sections, titled "Richard Wright Mnemonicon" and "Thursday's Collection" respectively. As in the earlier section, there are poems here that are filled with strong emotional content reflecting frustrations with the lack of racial progress. Rolland Snellings's (Askia Muhammed Toure) poem "The Song of Fire," which opens the "Richard Wright Mnemonicon" section, offers more apocalyptic images, including the fire of the title, which "will cauterize the Racist Plague!" and help enact a William Carlos Williams-like rebirth: "But to start anew—the old must fade away, / or burn . . . or . . . crumble in the savage wind" (20-21). Snellings's poem is especially interesting given that the first issue of *Umbra* contained a poem

of his, "Floodtide," that was dedicated to "the black tenant farmers of
the South" and celebrated their ability to "carry on." Though the earlier
poem also contained ominous images (including black rain clouds on the
horizon threatening to burst), they are nothing compared to the naked
anger and violence in "The Song of Fire." It's also interesting that Snel-
lings puts himself into the poem: "An angry, fiery man—awaiting nature's
call / to act out / my deadly hour upon the western stage." For him, one
who is even at this time on his way to a more nationalist position, there
is no hiding behind a poetic persona.

Though many of the poems following Snellings's poem also develop
themes of outrage or protest, they are much more nuanced and suggestive
than "The Song of Fire." In "Biography of a Guy I Know," for example,
George Hayes offers a sympathetic portrait of a heroin addict ("Bo")
who is "the first born son of a new breed; / A new breed of kiss my ass
Negroes" (26). Hayes distinguishes his friend from those who put their
"trust in Martin Luther King," and from "'Black church women' / [who]
Took numbers while praising God." Hayes says, further, that "Bo is the
author of goodness, but yet / He is akin to horror. / I love Bo, And I know
why . . ." Only vaguely reminiscent of the black prototype for Mailer's
"white negro," Hayes's portrait of Bo looks forward to the urban anti-
hero celebrated in late-60s/early-70s blaxploitation films. This issue also
offers poems by Ray Durem, a previously published poet (Rosey Pool's
Beyond the Blues) who received some blame for inadvertently provoking the
group's demise by submitting a poem, "A Decoration for the President,"
which contained disparaging images related to President Kennedy's for-
eign policy. When the editors deemed the poem in bad taste and refused
to print it after the president's assassination, Umbra split into irrevocable
factions, those supporting and opposing the editorial decision (Oren 181).
Still, Durem's poems that survived the controversy and were published
in *Umbra* are witty and angry simultaneously. One, "Night Prowl," uses a
biting humor to critique white hypocrisy:

> In Fillmore, late at night,
> the paddies gather, like a flight
> of pale bees,
> looking for brown sugar.
>
> What makes that sugar
> so sweet at night?

Don't it taste good
in the broad daylight? (29)

On the other hand, another Durem poem, "Sweet and Sour," is a relationship poem that only vaguely hints at any of the social issues typical of other poems in the magazine. It is followed closely by a poem by Susan Johnn, identified in the contributor notes only as a University of Wisconsin student, that complements Durem's "Sweet and Sour" by narrating a woman's conversion from a kind of suffering passivity to activism. The poem begins "Were I a man I would scream and tear out my guts for shame of it, / Because I am a woman, I sit and cry tortured: / Stop it, damn you, stop it!" (33). However, after recounting offense after offense—children "cinderized," "pregnant women insulted," and parents "herded / like cattle into vans"—Johnn's poem closes,

> I am only a woman—a dishwashing, supper cooking,
>> baby bearing, sex satisfying machine.
> The hell with that—move over brother—
> I'm coming too.

Finally, the issue includes poems by white authors that both directly and indirectly engage race. For example, Gil Jackofsky's poem "Bad" tells the story of his identification with a great grandfather whom he knew only from a painting that his family owned. The great grandfather, who "had fled from East Prussia— / A paradox, a Jew," fought on the Union side in the Civil War under General Sheridan but soon after the surrender killed himself (35-36). Though the painting of his great grandfather and the vague outline of his story remained in the family, Jackofsky says that "No one knows for sure if this face masked / hero / or coward." The last stanza recounts how when he was four, he stepped on the painting breaking the glass and eliciting a reprimand from his mother. The painting, he says, was then put away, never to be seen again, "But now, / Those eyes, fierce and troubled . . . / With . . . / Broken glass . . . / Are with me and they are mine." The poem thus develops its links with the magazine's mission only obliquely, through, that is, the Civil War association and the narrator's link to the soldier who served on the side of the Union as well as a possible link between the Jewish experience of violence in the Old World—signified by the broken glass—and the black experience of violence in the South. Also, the narrator's emotional identification with his great grandfather's "fierce and troubled" eyes links him to the general sense of frustration and alienation expressed by poets in the magazine. Most important, the narrator's averred link with a Union soldier who may have been either hero or coward implicitly acknowledges an "awful affinity" with an ambivalence that beset many white people involved in the civil rights struggle: how to participate in a movement that you believe is just but in which you are the oppressor. This ambivalence is enhanced by the poem's added element of a Jewish narrator. Will Inman's "The South is a Dark Woman" is a more straightforward statement of a white man's understanding and expression of solidarity with black people's struggle while also being a more artful poem than Jackofsy's. As the title suggests, Inman, a native of Wilmington, North Carolina, who lived in New York City at the time, personifies the South as a black woman who has given birth to his sensibility but from whom he is now alienated. Inman uses earthy imagery to describe the South's generative effect on him: her swampy nature nurtures him as he is growing. The power of this imagery is heightened by the clear suggestion of an intimate interracial mother-son relationship: "At her brown breast, I drank, / to her black mouth I pressed my white ear, / I leaned to her heartbeat, / I yearned to the stroke of her wounded hands" (41-43). Moreover, his connection to the South also links him to her other children, his brothers: black men in the North: "In the street everywhere / I see her face: and in the faces of dark men, / I recognize my own." Despite this identification, however, with the black South, there is also a sense in the poem that the narrator's alienation from the South is due not just to his physical separation from the region but to his unwillingness to associate with a place that is oppressing his mother, brothers, and him (at least the black part of him). And though he has been physically and spiritually separated from the South—"she was forbidden me"—he has faith that she will be liberated in the future—"she shall be released"—and when she is, and not until then, he will be liberated as well: "In my soul, she shall walk free, / and my blood shall not tremble / at her unrelenting gait."

These first two issues of *Umbra*, issued within a year of each other, are the group's major published documents. There were, however, subsequent issues published after the core group's dissolution with David Henderson at the helm in 1967 and the early 1970s. The 1967 issue, titled *Umbra Anthology 1967-1968*, is an especially worthy successor to the earlier issues. It offers another headspinning array of poetry and art by some of the regulars—Henderson, Hernton, Thomas, and Pritchard—as well as contributions by Alice Walker, Julia Fields, Henry Dumas, Sun Ra, Oscar Brown, Jr., and Bob Kaufman. Though published in the early days of Black Arts, this issue still seems to be adhering closely to the principles outlined in the first issues, especially with formally adventurous contributions by Kaufman and Pritchard, an Allen Ginsberg journal entry, a memorial tribute to Langston Hughes, and its first seven pages devoted to Sun Ra's unconventional poetry. As John Szwed has argued, though Sun Ra was embraced by black nationalists, his perspective, always an idiosyncratic one, wasn't so easily contained (311-12). An even later issue, 1970's *Umbra's Blackworks* is also a compelling magazine but shows the clear influence of Black Arts in the title, the selection of authors, and the content of the works included.[9] Whether one sees them as a precursor to the Black Arts movement or not, the four issues of *Umbra* are impressive but neglected publications that demonstrate that members of the black avant-garde of the early 1960s were perhaps more dedicated to higher principles of both art and politics than their more celebrated white counterparts.

WORKS CITED

Baldwin, James. *The Fire Next Time.* New York: Vintage, 1963.

Baraka, Amiri. *The Autobiography of LeRoi Jones/Amiri Baraka.* New York: Freundlich Books, 1984.

Cruse, Harold. *The Crisis of the Negro Intellectual: A Historical Analysis of the Failure of Black Leadership.* 1967. New York: Quill, 1984.

Gabbin, Joanne V. "Askia Muhammed Toure (Rolland Snellings)." *Afro-American Poets Since 1955.* Eds. Trudier Harris and Thadious M. Davis. Dictionary of Literary Biography, vol. 41. Detroit. Mich.: Gale Research Co., 1985: 327-33.

Gates, Henry Louis, Jr. *Thirteen Ways of Looking at a Black Man.* New York: Random House, 1997.

Hernton, Calvin. "Umbra: A Personal Recounting." *African American Review* (Winter 1993): 579-83.

—. *White Papers for White Americans.* Garden City, New York: Doubleday & Company, Inc., 1966.

Hollinger, David A. *Postethnic America: Beyond Multiculturalism.* New York: BasicBooks, 1995.

Ismaili-Abu-Bakr, Rashidah. "Slightly Autobiographical: The 1960s on the

Lower East Side." *African American Review* (Winter 1993): 585-89.

Kane, Daniel. *All Poets Welcome: The Lower East Side Poetry Scene in the 1960s.* Berkeley: University of California Press, 2003.

Mackey, Nathaniel. *Discrepant Engagement: Dissonance, Cross-Culturality, and Experimental Writing.* 1993. Tuscaloosa: University of Alabama Press, 2000.

Mele, Christopher. *Selling the Lower East Side: Culture, Real Estate, and Resistance in New York City.* Minneapolis: University of Minnesota Press, 2000.

Morgan, Edward P. *The '60s Experience: Hard Lessons about Modern America.* Philadelphia: Temple University Press, 1991.

Nielsen, Aldon. *Black Chant: Languages of African-American Postmodernism.* Cambridge, U.K.: Cambridge University Press, 1997.

Oren, Michel. "The Umbra Poets' Workshop, 1962-1965: Some Socio-Literary Puzzles." In *Belief vs. Theory in Black American Literary Criticism.* Eds. Joe Weixlmann and Chester J. Fontenot. Greenwood, Fla.: Penkeville Publishing, 1986: 177-223.

Posnock, Ross. *Color and Culture: Black Writers and the Making of the Modern Intellectual.* Cambridge, Mass.: Harvard University Press, 1998.

Redmond, Eugene. "Stridency and the Sword: Literary and Cultural Emphaasis in Afro-American Magazines." In *The Little Magazine in America: A Modern Documentary History.* Eds. Elliott Anderson and Mary Kinzie. Yonkers, N.Y.: Pushcart, 1978: 538-573.

Rowell, Charles H. "Between the Comedy of Matters and the Ritual Workings of Man." *Callaloo* 4.1-3 (1981): 19-35.

Smethurst, James. "Poetry and Sympathy: New York, the Left, and the Rise of Black Arts." In *Left of the Color Line: Race, Radicalism, and Twentieth-Century Literature of the United States.* Eds. Bill V. Mullen and James Smethurst. Chapel Hill and London: The University of North Carolina Press, 2003.

Smith, David Lionel. "The Black Arts Movement and Its Critics." *American Literary History* 3 (Spring 1991): 93-110.

Szwed, John F. *Space is the Place: The Lives and Times of Sun Ra.* New York: Pantheon Books, 1997.

Thomas. Lorenzo. "Alea's Children: The Avant-Garde on the Lower East Side, 1960-1970." *African American Review* (Winter 1993): 573-78.

—. *Extraordinary Measures: Afrocentric Modernism and Twentieth-Century American Poetry.* Tuscaloosa: University of Alabama Press, 2000.

—. "Umbra Writers Workshop." In *Encyclopedia of African-American Culture and History.* Volume 5. Eds. Jack Salzman, David Lionel Smith, and Cornel West. New York: Macmillan Library Reference, 1996.

—. *Umbra* 1.1 (Winter 1963). Society of Umbra.

—. *Umbra* 2 (December 1963). Society of Umbra.

Umbra Anthology 1967-1968 (1967). Society of Umbra.

Umbra's Blackworks 19701971 (1970). Society of Umbra.

Ward, Brian. *Just My Soul Responding: Rhythm and Blues, Black Consciousness, and Race Relations.* Berkeley: University of California Press, 1998.

"The New York School is a Joke": The Disruptive Poetics of *C: A Journal of Poetry*

HARRY THORNE

It takes an intrepid reader to track down every issue of Ted Berrigan's *"C" A Journal of Poetry*. The mimeo magazine is now only available in a select number of University archives, and even many of these archives have incomplete collections. Yet, despite its obscurity, *C* is a vital cultural document. Within the thirteen issues published between 1963 and 1966, we find that *C* harnessed the energy of the Lower East Side poetry scene but refused to provide a theoretical framework for the work that it showcased. Instead, Berrigan created a magazine that reveled in contrast and provocation, one that provides a challenge to critics who wish to define the magazine's place in the genealogy of the avant-garde.[1]

Beyond the New York School

In an interview that took place after *C* had folded, Berrigan stated, "The group is not important . . . it's not something to play up: there was by no means a group of *C* poet*s*" (*Talking in Tranquility* 56). These comments may be considered somewhat surprising as Berrigan is thought of as the primary spokesperson for the grouping known as the second-generation New York School.[2] In addition, the core members of the second generation, Berrigan, Ron Padgett, and Dick Gallup appear in almost every issue of *C*, while the work of the original so-called New York School of John Ashbery, Kenneth Koch, Frank O'Hara, James Schuyler and Barbara Guest is also heavily represented. Since "little magazines" are often designed to promote the ideas and aesthetics of particular poetic groups, it may seem strange that Berrigan actively denied the existence of his own group in his own magazine.[3] Yet, Berrigan's comments do make sense. Despite the preponderance of New York School poets in *C*, the magazine also contains work by a diverse array of poets active in the downtown scene including among many others, LeRoi Jones (Amiri Baraka), John Wieners, Harry Fainlight, Lorenzo Thomas, and Gregory Corso. Moreover, Berrigan did not present any kind of theoretical framework or manifesto in his magazine that would separate New York School poets (who were themselves hardly a homogenous group) from non-New York School poets. The resulting mix of poets and poetic styles and approaches in *C* means that it is almost impossible to discuss the magazine in terms of a unified poetic grouping. Berrigan's deliberately disorganized editorial stance means that *C* can be contrasted not only to obvious examples of coterie buildings such as Cid Corman's *Origin*, which self-consciously tried to build a community around Charles Olson's poetics, but also to seemingly likeminded publications such as Ed Sanders's *Fuck You/a magazine of the arts*. While *Fuck You* featured a similar mix of downtown poets as *C*, its material was more obviously slanted towards Sanders's ethic of "Gandhian pacifism, great sharing, social change, the expansion of personal freedom (including the legalization of marijuana, and the then-stirring message of sexual liberation.)"(*A Secret Location on the Lower East Side*, 167). *C* also contains a number of political poems, but unlike *Fuck You*, the magazine as a whole was not presented as a brazen political statement; instead, its anti-establishment ethos was channeled into an editorial strategy that eschewed the codification of a poetics in favor of contrast and idiosyncrasy.

As may be expected, *C*'s eclectic aesthetic poses a problem to critics who wish to view the magazine through the familiar framework of a group poetics. In her book *Career Moves*, Libbie Rifkin attempts to overcome this problem by suggesting that *C*'s eventual diversity was inimical to Berrigan's original vision for the magazine. She proposes that *C* was conceived as a "periodical workshop for the development of a group poetics" and as such it would be able to construct and validate the second-generation New York School: "(Berrigan) and his peers were to be the heirs of Ashbery, O'Hara, Schuyler, and Koch, and the execution of the estate would take place in the pages of a little magazine"(130). *C* was thus meant to be a unified publication; its eventual expansiveness was not something that Berrigan completely welcomed:

> the relatively fixed position on which the little magazine was founded began to generate itself; the collaborative circle widens, guest editors take over, the budget increases, and an institution was born. Berrigan was characteristically ambivalent about ripple effects of *C*'s success—thrilled by the society it enabled him to enter, but wary of the challenges to his creative control (132).

Rifkin's assertion that Berrigan was nostalgic for the group dynamic evident in the first few issues of his magazine receives some validation in Berrigan's notes to *C*. He describes the first three issues as "special" because they featured close friends and were "put together in almost the same way" as a poem, a statement that reflects the excitement of building a magazine around aesthetic and social alliances. However, while Berrigan may have looked back fondly on the first few issues of his magazine, it does not necessarily follow that he gave up creative control of subsequent, more diverse, issues. Berrigan's notes also refer to his "haste to get away from publishing only our group" and so it can be assumed that *C*'s eventual eclecticism was not an unwanted byproduct of success but a desired outcome. It may have been easier for Berrigan to maintain a smaller collaborative circle, but Berrigan's generous approach to editing led *C* away from simple notions of a group aesthetic and towards a more complex engagement with the idea of the New York School.

Rifkin's suggestion that Berrigan wanted to "execute the estate of the first generation" assumes that there was a concrete poetic tradition that could be passed down between the two generations of the New York School. Yet, the obvious contrast between the poetic styles of the first-generation poets, particularly between the styles of Ashbery and O'Hara, makes it difficult to define the New York School in positive aesthetic terms. Also, beyond the disparity in style among the members of the so-called New York School, the label was only initially conceived as a spoof on the New York School of painters; a fact that Berrigan showed himself to be aware of when he responded to a question about being associated with the group by saying, "it should be understood that the New York School is a joke"(*Talking in Tranquility* 90). Despite this understanding, it is hard to overstate both Berrigan's love of the poetry of Ashbery and O'Hara, and his attraction to the idea of the New York School. It could even be said that Berrigan was attracted to the New York School precisely because it was a joke, and as such it prevented critics from getting a handle on what it represented. Because Berrigan's understanding of the New York School revolved around contrast rather than coherence, he could effectively name anyone as a New York School poet. As he declared in an interview, "I had an idea that the New York School consisted of whomever I thought. And I could have that idea, see, because there was no New York School. I didn't have to consult John Ashbery to see if it was alright to think Philip Whalen was in it too"(*Talking in Tranquility* 91).

Berrigan applied this same flexible stance to his magazine. Even though poets conventionally associated with The New York School appear more frequently than others, they are not handed a monopoly. Rather, Berrigan sought to use the magazine to create moments of poetic disruption and volatility. It is these moments that this essay will concentrate on, since they best live up to the potential of Berrigan's editorial statement: "*C* will print anything the editor likes." This philosophy suggests a resistance to a group based New York School publication, as the idiosyncratic taste of the independent, unaffiliated editor is valued over the programmatic construction of a poetics.

The Early Issues

C's attraction to conflict and contrast goes back to its inception. In May 1963, Ron Padgett attempted to publish some of Berrigan's poems in *The Columbia Review,* a student magazine published by Columbia University. However, after a proof copy of the magazine was sent to the dean's office, the editors were ordered to remove Berrigan's poems due the presence of obscenities. As Daniel Kane writes about the saga, "cold war Puritanism was still pervasive enough in the early 1960s that word was easily linked to deed" (103). Columbia's censorship of Padgett's magazine created a considerable furor, one which went beyond the confines of the university's walls. As Berrigan writes, "There were TV appearances by editors, statements to newspapers like the Post, daily diatribes in the newspaper etc etc." ("Some Notes" 2). The principled opposition of students to the censorship of the magazine led to the formation of a committee of students called ACTION, and they eventually printed a few thousand copies of the suppressed issue with the appropriate title of *The Censored Review.*

It was the ability of the Columbia students to side-step the need for institutional backing that led Berrigan to believe he could run his own magazine. He writes, "the apparent cheapness of putting *The Censored Review* together inspired Lorenz Gude, a friend of mine and student at Columbia, with the idea of starting a little magazine, with me as editor and he and I publishing it" ("Some Notes" 2). The mimeo machine allowed Berrigan to create a magazine that was answerable only to his own literary tastes. It is easy to imagine *C*'s anarchic editorial policy as partly being a response to the anxious editorial wrangling that took place at institutional publications such as *The Columbia Review.* Freed from the restraints of academic publishing, Berrigan could produce a genuinely "alternative" magazine, one that did not need to have an easily definable identity and direction. When recently asked if Berrigan had a set plan for *C* from the beginning, Padgett replied in the negative, stating "Each issue reflected what Ted's life was like at the time."[4] This same openness towards spontaneity and change is discernible in the reasons that Berrigan gave for the magazine's title. He writes, "I wanted a name without connotations and so, while thinking about Marcel Duchamp, one day said to myself, "A" "B" "C" "Voila!" and there it was. "C" "See""Sea" "C# # (ad infinitum)" ("Some Notes" 4). Berrigan's desire for *C* to be free from connotations again suggests that Berrigan wanted a magazine that did not carry with it the baggage of a pre-assigned aesthetic. The ultimate trajectory of the magazine was to be left unknown.

The first issue of *C* was published soon after Padgett's *Censored Review* in May 1963. By the standard of its later, more flamboyant covers, *C* (1)'s cover art was exceptionally plain. A simple stenciled C and a list of the four contributors Dick Gallup, Ron Padgett, Joe Brainard and Ted Berrigan was the way that the journal was first announced to the alternative poetry scene. Berrigan made the decision to print *C* on legal sized paper, a move that he claimed would "infuriate collectors and dealers, but please Wallace Stevens who said he liked to see a lot of space on pages" ("Some Notes" 14).[5] As in later issues, *C*'s print was often unclear and uneven—a mark of the magazine's Do-It-Yourself aesthetic, and a reminder to the reader of *C*'s outsider status. While Berrigan certainly sought this status for his magazine, *C*'s somewhat unprofessional look was not just the result of stylistic decisions but also of a very real poverty: later issues would even include a request for new typewriter to be donated to the editor.

C (1) was to be the only issue that was devoted solely to poets from the second-generation New York School, and specifically to the editor's friends from Tulsa. Berrigan was excited by the dynamic that existed within the group—he described it as a "Picasso/Braque type of thing"— and was keen to stress the "newness" of the "point of view" which they had ("Some Notes" 3). To this end, in *C* (1), Berrigan published six of his sonnets alongside experiments in the same form by Padgett and Gallup. Rifkin's description of a "magazine in conversation with itself" is an apt one for this issue; the closeness of their poetry reflected the closeness of their friendship. As Padgett writes, "There was a tremendous camaraderie among us; it went without saying that we were all buddies working to make some interesting and new art, together and separately"(*Ted* 49). However, Berrigan's anarchic editorial policy of "printing anything he liked" meant that this initial emphasis of a group poetics could not be sustained. C (1) served to announce the previously unknown Berrigan and his friends to the alternative poetry communities of the Lower East Side, but once this announcement had occurred Berrigan was free to open up his magazine to those same communities. After C (1) was released, Berrigan immediately began to write to other poets and ask for contributions.

These contributions did not arrive in time for C (2), although it is clear from Berrigan's notes that he was eager for the magazine to make a "leap" into different poetic territories. C (3) did feature three new poets, Ruth Krauss, Jim Brodey, and Gerard Malanga, but it was with C (4) that Berrigan made his real breakthrough. He centered the issue on the work of Edwin Denby, a move which reflected Berrigan's concern for poets he felt were under-published. Although his writings on dance had garnered him considerable praise, Denby's poetry was not widely available, and Berrigan states that he conceived the issue because his "books had so little circulation" ("Some Notes" 9). Despite the relative obscurity of Denby's poetry, his work was revered by the New York School poets, especially O'Hara. Denby was from a different generation than O'Hara et al so it is difficult to consider him as being *in* the New York School, but even so he can be thought of as being a precursor to the New York School poets. Certainly, Berrigan's decision to dedicate the issue to Denby was partly due to his own desire to be associated with O'Hara. However, Berrigan did not make C (4) a simple homage to Denby and, by extension, did not seek to further establish a monolithic model for the New York School. Instead, he surrounded Denby's poetry with a series of complex framing devices that underlined his desire for C to have more than a single aesthetic perspective.

The most immediate of these framing devices is the artwork, which was created by Andy Warhol. The silkscreen print on the front cover shows the 65 year old Denby sitting down with the much younger Gerard Malanga standing behind him and holding Denby's hand. The back cover shows Malanga leaning over Denby and kissing him. Although the image is both staged and restrained, Berrigan received derogatory comments from poets who felt that Warhol was taking advantage of Denby (Wolf 24). Yet, in his diary Berrigan notes how pleased he was with Warhol's contribution; the cover which the artist designed was exactly the type of gesture that could not be made by institutional publications such as *The Columbia Review*. As Reva Wolf has shown, both the front and back covers of the issue act as socially subversive narratives. The formal portrait on the front cover is a "witty homosexual parody of conventional portraits of husbands and wives," while on the back cover Warhol "exposes" the two men kissing, an image which according to the "social codes of the time" should be secretive (Wolf 22-3). Warhol's images in *C* resonate with Douglas Crimp's description of Warhol's overall artistic strategy: "an ethical project of making visible queer differences and singularities." Certainly, Warhol's depiction of the relationship between the older Denby and the younger Malanga "made visible" a type of socially unconventional relationship.

However, the cover of *C* (4) was boundary breaking in more than one way as the image of the two poets symbolized the intermingling of two distinct spheres of New York's avant-garde. Malanga was Warhol's silk screening assistant and thus an intimate part of one of the city's most talked about new artistic movements, while Denby was associated with both the New York School poets and abstract expressionists such as Willem de Kooning. Although Berrigan expressed satisfaction with the cover, its challenge to the boundaries of artistic groups leads Rifkin to suggest that the cover cost the poet his ability to "control" *C*. She writes, "Malanga's compromising position on the cover of Berrigan's position-taking publication allowed Berrigan to make headway in the gay world of his poetry heroes, but it also compromised whatever sense of self-sufficiency he still maintained." According to Rifkin, Berrigan's self-sufficiency was compromised not only because his heterosexuality prevented him from enacting the intimate scene on the back cover himself, but also because Malanga was not an established member of Berrigan's own group. She writes, "Malanga moved freely in and out of Berrigan's cohort, transcending generic and sexual boundaries and thereby rendering them open in a way that would have been both enviable and discomfiting" (133). Yet, Rifkin's argument is diminished by the fact that Berrigan actively chose Warhol to design the covers for *C* (4). He also knew that Malanga would probably be involved in the production of the cover because it was through Malanga that Berrigan contacted Warhol. In choosing Warhol to design the cover, Berrigan knew that he would be given a challenging image, one that would enable *C* to transcend both "generic and sexual boundaries" as well the boundaries of New York's coteries.

As Wolf's detailed account of the making of the cover shows, Warhol was exceptionally aware of the literary politics surrounding the New York School. Warhol knew, for example, that O'Hara disliked him, and that the poet had written negative reviews of his work in *Kulchur*. The artist also knew that Denby was a hugely respected figure amongst the New York School poets and that Berrigan was a passionate supporter of O'Hara's work. According to Wolf, Warhol used the opportunity that Berrigan gave him to design the cover for *C* (4) as a way of insinuating "himself into O'Hara's circle of poets when O'Hara himself would not allow the artist in"(25). Yet, while Warhol may well have wanted to connect himself to poets associated with O'Hara, Berrigan's decision to feature work by Warhol demonstrates a counter-desire to question group allegiances and open the magazine to wider avant-garde influences. While Berrigan would certainly not have wanted to alienate O'Hara by using Warhol to design the cover for the Denby issue—the same issue features "Edwin's Hand," the first of many O'Hara's poems to be included in *C*—it does show that despite his fervent admiration of O'Hara's work, Berrigan did not want his magazine merely to reproduce the artistic tastes of his literary hero.[6] Because of O'Hara's complex personal and aesthetic response to Warhol, the cover to *C* (4) cannot be read simply as representing a meeting between older and newer generations of the New York School. Instead, Warhol's contribution highlights Berrigan's desire to undercut stable group definitions in favor of a volatile and provocative intermingling.

Berrigan's vision of *C* as a site of complexity and contrast is further underlined by his own contribution to the Denby Issue. He dedicated his poem not to O'Hara or Denby, but to John Wieners, who also had a poem included in the Denby issue. Berrigan had only just met Wieners, and would have initially encountered the work of the poet in Donald Allen's *The New American Poetry*. Allen placed Wieners in the final section of his anthology, dedicated to poets whose work had "no geographical definition" and who had "evolved their own original styles." Certainly, Wieners is a difficult poet to categorize, and although at various times he has been associated with the San Francisco Renaissance, the Beats, and the Black Mountain poets, none of these labels have really stuck due to his peripatetic existence. In "Grace After a Meal" Berrigan self-consciously identifies with Wieners's outsider status by describing a visit which the two poets made to Denby's loft:

> Out we go to get away from today's
> delicate pinpricks: awake and scheme
> to pay the rent; the room is littered
> with laundry, my desk turns
> my stomach; in my stomach a white pill

turns to warmth; I stretch and begin
to flow, and we join hands
for a journey to courage in a loft.
    A man signs a shovel, and
so he digs. I fear to become a crank,
alone in a dreary room, grinding out
poem after poem, confused, con-
cerned, annoyed
        But Edwin offers us
cookies, and coffee and beer and grace.
By his presence he offers us leads, and
his graciousness adds to our courage.

John,
We must not be afraid
to be civilized, meaning
Love.
    It is 5:23 A.M., and the sun
is coming. (*C* 3)

Although on one level "Grace after a meal" affirms the importance
of solidarity between poets, "I fear to become a crank / alone," it also
affirms the temporary nature of the meeting between Wieners, Denby,
and Berrigan. Denby's loft acts as a temporary creative oasis, and both
Wieners and Berrigan are given a spiritual refueling where the impor-
tance of the poetic career is reaffirmed. The equation of a "civilized" way
of being with "love" momentarily undercuts the primacy of the economic
concerns that cloud the beginning of the poem, and the two poets are
given renewed "courage" to pursue their artistic calling. Yet, while the
arrival of the sun in the penultimate line may be partly symbolic of the
reenergizing effect of Denby's loft, on a more practical level the dawn of
the new day also means the two poets must return back to lives marked
by poverty and insecurity. According to Rifkin, Denby's role in *C* (4) is
that of an "O'Hara substitute," yet even if that is the case "Grace after
a Meal" hardly solidifies the idea of the poetic group; other poets may
provide support, but the actual writing of poetry is done by outsiders
"alone in a dreary room." While the title of Berrigan's poem may pay
homage to O'Hara's famous line "Grace to be born and live as variously
as possible," "Grace after a Meal" does not monumentalize poetic kinship;

instead it travels between the temporary consolation of meeting other poets and the everyday reality of trying to write poetry while living on the margins of society.

Berrigan's attraction to the idea of the "outsider" is evident in his notes to the magazine where he proudly proclaims "no issue of *C* has less than half dedicated to unknown writers" ("Some Notes" 10). In *C* (5), for example, he included the first of several contributions from Harry Fainlight, another poet who "lived on the edge" and who was befriended by Berrigan. As Padgett writes:

> Harry was a British poet who wrote on LSD, a visionary poem about spiders. He was skinny, with big round eyes and wiry hair that stood up . . . he was barely scraping by in New York. He was a gloomy guy with a bitter, gurgling laugh, and he was intelligent and well educated. I heard he eventually went back to England and died, alone in a flat, of pneumonia. Ted was one of his best friends in New York. (*Ted* 68).

Fainlight's contribution to *C* is printed in the wrong order—the second stanza is placed before the first—an indication, perhaps, that Berrigan had to transcribe the poem from a disorganized original. The poem itself is a set in unnamed "Arab suburb"[7] and evokes a disorientating scene where the identity of the poem's narrator is dissolved by the surrounding scene: "Muezzins, buzzards, newspapers- like / Circling like / 'Till I am heavy with their whirling" (*C* 5, n.p). The disintegration of the self which occurs in Fainlight's poem mirrors the poet's position on the social margins; a position that Berrigan picked up on in his own contribution to *C* (5), "New Junket," which he dedicated to Fainlight. In this poem, Berrigan empathizes with Fainlight's outsider status: "Everywhere we went we paid the price / endurement of indifference." Even more so than his previous dedication of a poem to Wieners, Berrigan's poem for Fainlight is evidence of his attraction to the idea of the outsider, an attraction that resulted in the continued support of both unknown and socially marginal poets in subsequent issues of *C*.

Alongside Fainlight, Berrigan published three of the original New York School poets in *C* (5): John Ashbery, Barbara Guest, and James Schuyler. Of these three poets, Berrigan was particularly excited about the inclusion of Ashbery whose *The Tennis Court Oath* was a major influence on Berrigan's work. Ashbery's contributions to *C* (5) are reminiscent of his poems from that volume; their use of disjunction and self-referential language creates a consistently enigmatic wordscape. For example, the last lines of Ashbery's final contribution read:

> If you were a fast producer of say melancholy
> To scramble up the sand
> Fending off the waves
>
> A description of time, implanted
>
> As traffic grows. (*C* 5, n.p.)

Like the "you" of the poem, the reader is left scrambling and unable to find definite connections between the lines of the poem and an overall narrative. As Bruce Andrews wrote in L=A=N=G=U=A=G=E magazine regarding *The Tennis Court Oath*, "It is not just the accuracy of pointing which this work calls into question. . . . Rather we are led to question the efficacy of desire, *of getting through*" (n.p.). Ashbery's disjunctive strategies highlight the tacitly political undertones of his work by leading to a consideration of the way that linguistic norms are developed and used as socially disciplining tools. (We should note, of course, that the political effect of Ashbery's poetry takes place generally at the level of form, as the *content* of his poetry is mostly not overtly political).

The split between Ashbery's politicized use of form and his apolitical content is made explicit by Berrigan through his editorial decision to include Lorenzo Thomas's poem "Political Science" directly underneath Ashbery's contribution. Thomas employs Ashbery's disjunctive techniques, but includes more overtly political content:

> This is set of affairs
>   like warm adventures in darkest africa "Afric-ay
>   Ah forty years ago.
> entire geography history a jumbled a yellow in firesides
>   pages my yellow, O something tender about
>   the ending
>   lines the feminine poem
> "There will always be a place for you
> you can be the epee
>   when I paint the heart on my chest (*C* 5, n.p.)

Thomas takes the topic of imperial power and then subjects it to an Ashbery-like cut up. This allows the poem both to reflect the cultural disorientation that colonialism brings and to scramble the "rationality" that colonialism relies on to justify itself. Thomas poem shows that radical avant-garde practice does not need to exclude focused political content, and its placement after Ashbery's work shows how the New York School poet's method could be used in a different ways to produce more *overtly* political results. While Thomas was a huge admirer of the New York School poets, his association with the primarily African American Umbra group of poets also meant that he was interested in poetry as a form of political persuasion. As Kane writes about "Political Science," "Thomas's Olsonian use of the page combined with a content directly related to race marks it—and by association *C* itself—as a complication of New York School-style poetry rather than a mere mimicry of that style" (119).

The last poet to appear in *C* (5) was LeRoi Jones (aka Amiri Baraka), a poet who was to become a leading spokesperson of the Black Arts movement. Jones's "The New World" is more straightforwardly descriptive and philosophical than either Thomas's or Ashbery's contributions. The poem acts as a warning to would-be bohemians who are seduced by the romantic image of the poet:

> Being broke or broken, dribbling
> At the eyes. Wasted Lyricists, and men
> Who have seen their dreams come true, only seconds
> After they knew those dreams to be horrible conceits
> And plastic fantasies of gesture and extension
> Shoulders, hair and tongues distributing misinformation
> About the nature of understanding

While both Thomas's and Ashbery's poems aim to call into question the relationship between everyday language and reality, Jones's poem acts as a critique of poets who lose touch with social reality due to their "horrible conceits." These "conceits" and "plastic fantasies" lack what Jones later in the poem calls the "discipline" that is needed to control the "method of knowledge." Without this "discipline" poets become entangled in a self-destructive cycle: "And Beatniks, like bohemians go calmly out of style. And boys / are dying in Mexico, who did not get the word. The lateness of their fabrication: mark their holes / with filthy needles."

Unlike the disjunctive work found earlier in *C,* Jones's poem calls for a poetry that is able to frame the "nature of understanding." By placing Jones's poem at the end of *C* (5), Berrigan added to the multiple contrasts of the issue and once again scrambled the message that his magazine sent out.

The Later Issues

While the early issues of *C* certainly established the magazine's central place in the underground scene of the Lower East Side, they did not establish a predictable pattern of publication. In the later issues, unknown poets were placed next to established poets, O'Hara's poetry was published in an issue with a Warhol cover, and disjunctive poetic practice took its place alongside bohemian realism and philosophical reflection. *C*'s attraction to contrast only increased in the later issues, especially with the introduction of a number of so-called Beat poets.

As Kane notes in *All Poets Welcome*, Berrigan made frequent references to the influences of the Beats on his poetic sensibility (108). He described his "line of descent" as being "Beatnik cum Frank O'Hara" and this statement is backed up by the amount of space he gave to Beat poets in the pages of *C*. Yet, Berrigan's description of his "line of descent" is far from a straightforward one. While he certainly had friends in both "groups," Berrigan's "line of descent" covers an exceptionally broad aesthetic field. Like the New York School label, the designation of Beat has been applied to an extremely divergent range of writers and material. As may now be expected, Berrigan took advantage of this in his magazine, and instead of seeking a mythical hybridity between the New York School and the Beats, he chose material that emphasized the differences both within and between the respective "movements." *C* (9), for example, contains prose by William Burroughs as well as O'Hara's "For the Chinese New Year & for Bill Berkson" and Ginsberg's "The Change: Kyoto-Tokyo Express." Placed side by side these writings lend themselves not to a coherent "line of descent" but to dissimilarity and divergence.

> Now pay attention you young runners. Just here is the New York Times, July 7th, 1964. Barry Goldman waving his hat in Prescott Arizona . . . so lets turn to the financial page . . . financial Frankie is here to tell you the columns stand for something just look at the names: KY util plus one (Burroughs)[8]

Oh Crying man crying woman
Crying guerilla shopkeeper
Crying dysentery boneface on
The urinal street of the self (Ginsberg) (*C* 9, n.p.)

I'm looking for a million dollar heart in
A carton of frozen strawberries like the Swedes where
    is sunny England
And those fields where they still-birth the wars (O'Hara) (*C* 9, n.p.)

All three extracts are politically charged, yet their respective techniques and tones are radically different. Burroughs's newspaper cutup, Ginsberg's impassioned protest poem, and O'Hara's neo-surrealism were all brought together by Berrigan in order to create a literary environment characterized more by difference and dissimilarity than with neat aesthetic synthesis.

While the difference between the work of Ginsberg, O'Hara and Burroughs (among others) supplied C (9) with a typically provocative mix, the next issue of Berrigan's magazine went even further in cultivating an eclectic literary terrain. The issue was *C*'s largest, and it included over forty different writers from across the spectrum of the alternative American poetry scene. Some of the highlights of the issue include poems by the emerging second-generation New York School poets Joe Ceravolo and Tony Towle, a short poem by Charles Olson, a Jerome Rothenberg translation of a poem by the German Dada poet Richard Huelsenbeck, one of Michael McClure's "Ghost Tantras," a long poem by Philip Whalen about his relationship with music, a selection of Kenward Elmsie poems, a recipe for "hashish fudge" adapted from the Alice B. Toklas cookbook by Brion Gysin, and a number of "found poems" by John Giorno. This anarchic collection of material provides readers with a tangled knot of ideas, styles, and provocations. When confronted by this hodge-podge of styles, it is tempting to think that Berrigan's editorial approach was influenced by the writings of John Cage; Alice Notley writes that Cage's *Silence* was among the most heavily annotated books in his collection and it is easy to see how Berrigan may have identified with Cage's views on composition and order.[9] Cage writes that the "tendency in my composition means away from ideas of order to no ideas of order" (20), a tendency that Berrigan himself pursued through his arrangement of radically different material within *C* (10).

The End of C

C (10) was one of the many highpoints of the magazine's run, and it was also among the last issues that Berrigan produced. The magazine folded three issues later, after the publication of C (13), an issue that was guest edited by Ron Padgett and mostly dedicated to the work of French modernist writers and poets. In a personal interview, Padgett states that he had no idea that the issue was to be the magazine's last and that C ended its run without any kind of warning. This abrupt ending was an appropriate one because it was perfectly in tune with Berrigan's unpredictable approach to editing. There was no structured plan for the magazine at the beginning, and so fittingly there was no pre-arranged "final issue" either.

While Berrigan may have celebrated the temporary nature of mimeo publishing, the downside to such impermanence is, for us at least, the disappearance from public view of the magazines themselves. With the absence of these vital and eclectic documents, it is all too easy to pursue simplistic classifications that deny the fluidity of the underground poetry scene of the 1960s. Berrigan may have been one of the most enthusiastic supporters of the New York School, but his attraction to the anti-programmatic ethos of that same "school" prevented him from creating a coterie based publication. He was determined to reject a magazine that showcased a "certain type of poem" and instead created a publication that valued openness and experimentation.[10] As Anne Waldman writes in the introduction to the recently published *Angel Hair Anthology*, a magazine strongly influenced by *C*, "We weren't in the business of creating a literary mafia or codifying a poetics. There were no interesting models for that kind of life" (svii). *C* certainly avoided the codification of a poetics, as Berrigan's generous approach to editing created a magazine whose vitality cannot be captured by reductive labels.

Works Cited

Allen, Donald, ed. *The New American Poetry*. Berkeley: The University of California Press, 1960.

Andrews, Bruce. "Misrepresentation" in *L=A=N=G=U=A=G=E* ed. Charles Bernstein and Bruce Andrews. Vol. 12, June 1980.

Berrigan, Ted. "Some Notes on *C*." *C: A Journal of Poetry* collection. The University of Syracuse Library *C: A Journal of Poetry*. Rare books and manuscripts. New York Public Library.

Cage, John. *Silence*. Middletown: Wesleyan University Press, 1979.

Steven and Phillips, Rodney, *A Secret Location on the Lower East Side: Adventures in Writing, 1960—1980*. New York: Granary Books, 1998.

Crimp, Douglas. "Mario Montez, For Shame," in *Regarding Sedgwick: Essays on Queer Culture and Critical Theory*, ed. Stephen M. Barber and David L. Clark. New York: Routledge, 2002.

Kane, Daniel. *All Poets Welcome: The Lower East Side Poetry Scene in the 1960s*. Berkeley: The University of California Press, 2003.

Lehman, David. *The Last Avant-Garde*. New York: Doubleday, 1998.

Padgett, Ron. *Ted*. Great Barrington: The Figures Press, 1993.

Padgett, Ron. Unpublished interview with the author.

Ratcliffe, Stephen and Scalapinio, Leslie. *Talking in Tranquility*. New York: Avenue B/O Books, 1991.

Rifkin, Libbie. *Career Moves*. Madison: University of Wisconsin Press, 2000.

Waldman, Anne and Warsh, Lewis ed. *The Angel Hair Anthology*. New York: Granary Books, 2001.

Wolf, Reva. *Andy Warhol, Poetry, and Gossip in the 1960s*. Chicago: The University of Chicago Press, 1997.

Angel Hair Magazine, The Second-Generation New York School, And The Poetics of Sociability

DANIEL KANE

The Granary Books publication of *Angel Hair Sleeps With a Boy in My Head: The Angel Hair Anthology* is both cause for celebration as it is an invitation to assess the significance of the poetry and overall scene associated with those writers representing the so-called second-generation New York School.[1] This is a necessary step for literary and cultural history, as the *Angel Hair Anthology* quite literally recovers a decades-old avant-garde movement whose influence continues to be felt in New York and national avant-garde circles. Poets associated with the language writing phenomenon, spoken-word culture, and younger contemporary American innovative writers have all pointed to the poets and poetry scene of the second generation as especially significant.

The contributor's notes to the Poetry Project anthology *Out of This World* are telling in terms of the debts owed to the second-generation scene. Regarding the Poetry Project at St. Mark's Church reading series when *Angel Hair* editor Anne Waldman was serving as its Director, Charles Bernstein writes that it "provided an important alternative to the low energy, formally inert poetry of official verse culture" (621). Bernstein and Bruce Andrews went on to publish Bernadette Mayer's celebrated "Experiments" list along with essays on or by Mayer, Clark Coolidge, Lorenzo Thomas and other second-generation affiliated writers in their collaboratively edited *The L=A=N=G=U=A=G=E Book*. Andrei Codrescu remembers, "Ted Berrigan, who enjoyed my rudimentary English, taught me the poetry of the New World. It was a whole new kind of poetry: alive, anti-academic, bohemian, streetwise, political, open" (630). Amy Gerstler recalls, "Dennis Cooper [. . .] also introduced me to 'New York School' writers, and St. Mark's *Newsletter,* and numerous East Coast small-press magazines and anthologies. Those introductions provided me with what I felt at the time like a direction"(642). Michael Palmer gave his first reading at St. Mark's and recollects "Berrigan's barking laugh, half challenge, half support, in the background" and a "reading with Charles North and a Sunday 'conversation' with Clark Coolidge and audience about desire, silence, narrative, subversion, loss, subject, Sade, Bataille,

Blanchot, Olson, hymns, and fragments"(657). Punk legend Richard Hell credits Anne Waldman with inspiring him to start *CUZ* magazine, which would go on to publish work by Ron Padgett, René Ricard, and Eileen Myles (646).

Showing the influence not just of John Ashbery, Frank O'Hara, James Schuyler and Kenneth Koch but also of Padgett and Berrigan, David Lehman in his book *The Last Avant-Garde* demonstrates how second-generation poets inspired younger writers including Paul Violi, Alice Notley (who was married to Berrigan during this period), Tim Dlugos, and Eileen Myles (359-79). Bob Holman, one of the main impresarios of the "spoken word" performance poetry community, has stated, "I remember when Jim Brodey did *Howl* in five languages at the Poetry Project. They were read simultaneously—unrehearsed, just to do it. The performance dynamic at the church has been nurtured and important and was what allowed me to go down to the Nuyorican Poets Café and start my thing there"(qtd. in Kane 206). In *Statutes of Liberty* Geoffrey Ward draws a link between contemporary avant-garde publications and their predecessors: "Imprints such as Burning Deck, Roof, The Figures or Potes & Poets Press are the intrepid contemporary heirs of Corinth Books, Tibor De Nagy Editions, The Poet's Press, *C,* Angel Hair Books and other small-scale outfits that published the new American poetry of the 1960s" (179). It is clear in light of these references that we must take a critical look at the writing affiliated with the second-generation New York School in order to understand and historicize the contemporary innovative poetry scene more fully and properly.

Many writers associated with the second generation—including Ted Berrigan, Ron Padgett, Bernadette Mayer, Clark Coolidge, and Dick Gallup—certainly deserve to be considered as significant *individual* poets. The *Angel Hair Anthology* nevertheless reminds us that second-generation poetry was in many ways produced as and out of sociability, and invites us to consider how a conception of the poem as communal gesture affected literary reception, challenged established notions of what constitutes authorship, helped shape the arguably unstable tag "second-generation New York School," and most importantly led to the creation of some memorable, truly innovative texts that have been unfairly consigned to the "curio" section of literary history. In acknowledging this negligence, we should consider that even as earlier alternative writers including Allen Ginsberg, Jack Kerouac, Robert Creeley, Denise Levertov and other poets affiliated with Donald Allen's *The New American Poetry* were able to garner a relatively large amount of critical and public attention during the early and middle stages of their careers, poets including Warsh, Waldman, and Mayer are in many ways in the beginning stages of being read outside of small socially-determined circles.

While some critics may object to my use of words such as "communal" in reference to an admittedly diverse group of writers, I will argue we can infer what I call a "poetics of sociability" in second-generation work, and indeed, that failing to recognize the initial communal impulses behind these texts is to miss much of what is important about the writing. By analyzing the nature of second-generation sociability in contrast to earlier formations and by reading selections from *The Angel Hair Anthology*, I will take a look back into the construction of the so-called School as it manifested itself through the primary mode of dissemination—the small-circulation, community-based little magazine typical of what we now refer to as "the '60s" avant-garde scene.

Characteristic practices of the collective second-generation poetry scene include commitments to (1) the collaboratively-produced poem (of which there are dozens in *Angel Hair* magazines and books and related publications including the Poetry Project's still extant "house magazine" *The World*); (2) the collaborative book (which threatens privileged authorship and the fetishization of the book as organically connected to a single person in favor of a more collective vision); (3) the intersocial text (poems drenched with the proper names of those writers in the "scene" and/or serving as initiative rites welcoming new poets into the community); (4) the foregrounding of the public poetry reading as primary mode of literary reception.[2]

Such a communal approach to the production and distribution of texts positioned writers in *Angel Hair* more as a collective whose members worked in conscious *interrelation* to each other than as a group of perhaps likeminded, socially-related individual authors.[3] This stance coincided with the '60s counterculture's increasing vision of the collective—the commune, the tribal rock concert, the mass antiwar demonstration, the alternative drugs culture/community. As Lewis Warsh clarifies in his introduction to *The Angel Hair Anthology*, the scene the magazine aimed to in part create was "a community based on a feeling of connectedness that transcended small aesthetic differences" (xxvii).

There are several elements typical of the second-generation scene that mark its embodiment of community as appreciably different from other twentieth century literary coteries. Previous literary formations that influenced New York based writers—including Imagists, Dadaists, the Black Mountain School, and the Beats—represent a contemporary lineage of community-based poetry. However, writers within these previous "schools" did not perform such sociability *in their poetry* as relentlessly as second-generation poets did in their literary work. That is, earlier poetry communities and associated critics acknowledged the importance of writing within a scene primarily via reviews, manifestoes, essays on poetics and through organizing their own public reception in journals and magazines. (We can think of Pound in 1913 sending some of H.D's verse to Harriet Monroe's *Poetry Magazine,* appending the signature "H.D., *Imagiste*," Louis Zukofsky's "Objectivist" issue of *Poetry* in February 1931 and *An Objectivist Anthology* in 1932, the polemics associated with the Dadaists, or even Frank O'Hara's tongue-in-cheek "Personism" manifesto as primary ways for readers to gain an understanding of the social dynamics and shared aesthetics of those poetry scenes.) On the other hand, second-generation poets exhibited sociability and group affiliation not through developing an independent and carefully theorized poetics, but within the body of the poems themselves—affiliations and poetic stances were all performed within the stanzas.

Angel Hair 6, for example, makes references primarily to the authors featured within the issue. Frank O'Hara's "A Short History of Bill Berkson" will inevitably reecho eight pages later when one reaches Bill Berkson's poem "Sheer Strips." Berkson's "Sheer Strips" written in a wide-ranging open-field form where words scatter and burst all over the page, is engaged in lively textual colloquy with Anne Waldman's similarly-built poem "Sexy Things." Kenward Elmslie's "Easter For Joe" is addressed to Joe Brainard, while Ted Berrigan's "For You (to James Schuyler)" not only is dedicated to Schuyler, who himself appears as an author in Schuyler's and Padgett's collaboration "Within The Dome," but refers to Joe Brainard in the lines "[. . .] hand-in-glove and / head-to-head with Joe, I go reeling." The Schuyler/Padgett collaboration also refers to Brainard in the lines, "yes, as the great Joe Brainard once said, / "You can't beat meat, potatoes and a green vegetable." The title of Jim Carroll's poem "The Burning of Bustins Island" refers to a Maine island where many of the poets associated with the so-called second-generation New York School spent time together. O'Hara's poem "To John Ashbery" brings in the name of the only major male first-generation New York School poet *not* represented in this particular issue, so it still feels like Ashbery's invited. Meanwhile, the presence of Schuyler, Koch and O'Hara in *Angel Hair* 6 lends the authoritative note to the overall party of the issue, as if one's "cool" parents were there, legitimizing the goings-on. The proper names couched in these individual lines serve to create specific meaning suggestive of participation in the second-generation scene and a resulting poetics. These acts of naming also concretize the relationship between first- and second-generation writers (thus providing the reader with a real if casually evoked and willfully non-theorized interpretive framework), and invite us to consider if and how second-generation writers are building on their aesthetic inheritance.[4]

Again, groups that influenced the second generation in various ways can be differentiated by a sociability that is in marked contrast to what I have been describing so far. Black Mountain writers Creeley and Olson certainly designed work that was informed by their collaborative poetics, and many of us link these two within a group whose members include Paul Blackburn and Ed Dorn. Yet, at least through most of the 1950s and 1960s, we rarely find Black Mountain poets dropping each other's names into their poems or writing collaboratively (though multimedia collaborations among dancers, architects, musicians, painters and poets were part of the social norm at Black Mountain College). Writers affiliated with the Beats including Jack Kerouac and Allen Ginsberg, while certainly referring to each other in their work, did so obliquely or in such a way as to practically deify each other. Thus we have Kerouac's Japhy Ryder as a stand-in for Gary Snyder, or Ginsberg's cries of "Holy Peter holy Allen holy Solomon holy Lucien holy Kerouac" in his "Footnote to Howl" (134). Such naming tended more towards icon and myth building in opposition to the refreshing and radically quotidian impulses typical of second-generation writers.

Additionally, all of the aforementioned groups' "members" consistently threatened or rejected group affiliation or overtly emphasized and challenged positions of "leadership." We can refer back to Richard Huelsenbeck's claim to inventing the word "Dada" in opposition to Tristan Tzara's claim.[5] Other group-affiliated poets are notable as much for their infighting and resistance to collectivity as they are for their unified positions. To take the invention of Imagism as an instance, a glance back at the infighting between various competing groups of imagists (Amy Lowell versus Pound, for example), suggests that group ethos in Modernism is always complicated by the sense one has that the "group" in question is in many ways being used by a dominant figure to enhance that figure's own status and independence. While one could argue that Lowell and

Pound on some level did serve as team captains for these groups, their autonomy and separateness as individuals were always important—if not defining—aspects of their polemics.

One might be tempted to point to first-generation writers and Frank O'Hara in particular as models for the kind of sociability that results when poets name their friends with a kind of casual intensity. Admittedly, it would be hard to imagine such naming in second-generation work without such predecessor poems like O'Hara's "Adieu to Norman, Bonjour to Joan and Jean-Paul" which names figures including Norman Bluhm, Joan Mitchell, and Kenneth Koch in a willfully breezy fashion. Yet I would argue against charging second generation's figures with being wholly derivative. Where O'Hara's naming tended to fix personages like Bill Berkson, Vincent Warren, LeRoi Jones and fellow poets Koch and Ashbery firmly in the reader's imagination, the very excess of naming in second-generation work (as we see when looking at the references in *Angel Hair* 6) undermines the effort to establish clear individual presence typical of first-generation work generally and O'Hara's comparatively restrained practice specifically. We can think of this in terms of analogy. O'Hara's poems are akin to a dinner party where each individual is distinct, recognizable and charming. In the second-generation world, the party has turned much, much wilder, to the point where it is at times difficult to figure out who's who in all the commotion.

Our inability to get a clear sense of those independent "members" who constitute the second-generation world may go some way in explaining why its poets have not received their due as significant influences. The way in which the Beat, New York School, and Black Mountain group tags have been used by critics tends to reify individuals within the group, which is perhaps one of the reasons academic journals and presses continue to devote far more space and time to figures like Ashbery and Creeley than to writers including Waldman, Warsh and Mayer. Such journals generally tend to promote (and in a sense to *create*) individual achievement by rewarding it with critical and editorial attention. A willful group effort is thereby marginalized as secondary to the privileged single author. Taking this scenario into account might answer the question as to why Warsh, Waldman, and other second-generation writers continue to be frozen out of the academy. As editors of *Angel Hair,* Warsh and Waldman tended to foreground process and collaboration within the context of a decentralized community even as they published and promoted individual authors' oeuvres.[6] Second-generation work manifested more clearly than previous groupings had done before that the place of the solitary and muse-inspired author could productively give way to a poetics of sociability that, at least temporarily and by virtue of the collective, help create a truly alternative site of resistance against the literary and political establishment of the era.

"What More Can You Say About It?" Resistance to the Academy and Beyond

I use the phrase "site of resistance" to introduce a crucial characteristic shared by many second-generation New York School poets that will at once help us see how they positioned themselves as dissident to a conceived mainstream and to suggest a reason as to why much second-generation work continues to exist within a critically marginal space. Second-generation poets resisted classification in part by self-consciously rejecting academic discourse and (perhaps inadvertently) subsequent canonization. In his introduction to *The Angel Hair Anthology*, Warsh insists:

> I wrote a few reviews for *Poetry Magazine*, but to what purpose? I could only reiterate the ongoing decades long argument between academic and experimental writing and try to draw attention to the work of my friends (though I didn't have much say about what book I could review). Writing poetry criticism during the late sixties was to associate oneself with an academic world, and a tone of voice, which was considered inimical to the life of poetry itself. (xxiv-v)

Extending his anti-analytical position, Warsh (in an interview with Peter Bushyeager) responded to a characterization of his recent work as "impenetrable" with the following conversation-stopper: "I like impenetrability. Past a certain point, this book simply exists. What more can you say about it?" (13). Referring to his and other's early work collected in *The Angel Hair Anthology*—most of which would, in comparison to mainstream poetics, be considered fairly outré—Warsh characterizes the book as "a testament to all the inter-related friendships from that time when most of the contributors were fairly young [. . .] that's what the anthology is about" (15). The message here seems to be one that reinforces an arguably naïve binary that values direct, unmediated experience over extended analysis. Such a stance is only strengthened when the gathered work under consideration is defined more as an evocation of a system of actual, historical friendships than it is as a grouping of successful individual works.

While Warsh's general position is certainly arguable—after all, impenetrability can be seen to *invite* scholarly analysis and canonization due to its "difficult" status—Warsh appears to be encouraging us to *not* talk *ad nauseam* about second-generation literary work, to somehow consider it part of our daily life. There is a kind of resistance being enacted here, one that determines excessive analysis as detrimental to the spontaneous appreciation of the work.[7] Like Joe Brainard's "Flower Painting IV," his "Blossom" paintings and "Gardens" collages (images that are almost obstinate in their foregrounding of gorgeous flowers as simply *gorgeous flowers*), Warsh suggests his poems are there to be experienced, not analyzed. As Brainard once said "You know, there is not much you can do with a painting but look at it," (qtd. in Llewellyn 85) so one should apparently just read Warsh's poems as experiential phenomena that strive for beauty, humor, sorrow and surprise as opposed to texts ripe for scholarly analyses.

In her introduction to *The Angel Hair Anthology*, Anne Waldman also positions second-generation-affiliated work as necessarily independent of the range of the academic: "We weren't thinking about career moves or artistic agendas. We weren't in the business of creating a literary mafia or codifying a poetics. There were no interesting models for that kind of life" (xxvii). According to the way Waldman appears to want to position herself within a plural "we," these poets were living and writing in the here-and-now (or, more accurately, the then-and-there of the 1960s), and were certainly *not* scheming towards a future life in the archives and syllabi of the academy. *How dare you accuse us of such plotting/plodding foresight?* Waldman seems to say. In what might be read as indicative of a kind of refreshing if potentially adolescent spontaneity, Waldman seems to insist that poetry, like her life at the time, was being lived, not organized.

Indeed, I wonder if Waldman's scornful use of the phrase "career moves" is a reprimand to Libbie Rifkin for her book *Career Moves*, in which Rifkin argues that Ted Berrigan presciently and self-consciously organized and developed his writings and related archival materials in the hopes that they would one day be securely anthologized and canonized within academe. Anne Waldman's language can serve as a warning to Rifkin specifically and as a sentence on other "academics" who might attempt to "[codify] a poetics" out of an organic body of work. The very tension that Waldman and Warsh exhibit as regards poetic reception and their overt and still active anti-academicism might be consciously or unconsciously invoked to ensure their relative marginality and thereby to maintain the kind of innocence and spontaneity they value so highly in their work. Such a stance on Waldman and Warsh's parts may very well help fulfill one of the avant-garde's imperatives, that of resisting or undermining future recuperation. Possibly *this very essay* is breaking a basic rule related to the writers under consideration here—that which tacitly demands we romanticize collaborative literary production and refrain from defining the work via critical analyses. Academic criticism, with its tendency to draw lines and codify in one canon or another, is potential contamination of the very social world that generates the literary work.[8]

Second-generation New York School poets not only created an environment that froze out academic discourse, they also consciously kept their work apart from the gentleman's commercialism inherent in academic life—English department funding was not solicited and institutional affiliation was rejected. Somewhat ironically, *Angel Hair* did in fact rely partly on federal funding. *Angel Hair* received several grants from the Coordinating Council of Literary Magazines (based at the National Institute of Public Affairs in Washington DC) in February, 1968—one grant, a so-called "matching grant," was in part made possible by the contribution of $250 from "Mrs. Heinz" of the H.J Heinz ketchup company ("Letter to Lewis Warsh"). The National Endowment for the Arts also awarded the magazine several special one-time prizes of $250 for magazine development, and individual authors published in *Angel Hair* including Tom Clark and John Wieners received $500 grants. This particular grant program was deemed by the New York Times as "substantial" (Books 42). However, before we point cynically to *Angel Hair* as having a federally-funded bohemian vibe, we should recognize that federal funding of artistic programs in the 1960s served a far more insurrectionary function than it would in the post-Jesse Helms 1990s. After all, the still-extant Poetry Project at St. Mark's Church—perhaps the crucial avant-garde poetry reading scene of the 1960s, where Anne Waldman served as Director for 10 years—was itself financed from a federal program designed to pacify juvenile delinquents, yet the money was used in a way that was often in self-conscious opposition to the desires of the funders.[9] Additionally, the fact that the poet Carolyn Kizer (as opposed to an administrator unconnected to the poetry world) was overseeing the program in her role as Director of Literary Programs for the National Endowment for the Arts in many ways served to "cleanse" the funds emanating from the much-loathed federal government.[10] While partly funded from federal grants, magazines including *Angel Hair* were initially produced and published on tiny budgets and sent to "a range of family, friends, poets, other folk" as opposed to reviewers, distributors, and established bookstores (Waldman, *Angel Hair Anthology* xxi). Waldman's reference to "family, friends" points to *Angel Hair*'s place in creating an alternative economy designed to generate a self-sustaining interpretative community independent of traditional critical academic circles. Publication was as much planned to distribute new work as it was an instrument of community-building.

We should distinguish the kind of community and overall poetics of sociability described here from what Barrett Watten describes as language writers' "aesthetic of collective practice" (617). This is an important distinction to make, especially when we consider that language writers were influenced by a number of second-generation-affiliated writers including Bernadette Mayer and Clark Coolidge; that their collaboratively-written poems may have been inspired by earlier models found in magazines like Mayer's and Vito Acconci's *0-9*;[11] and that second-generation writers have generally failed to receive the kinds of attention accorded to Bernstein, Andrews, and other poets affiliated with language writing. I would argue that it is the second generation's refusal to engage in academic discourse and its approach to performing subjectivity that marks its enactment of sociability as fundamentally different from that of the language community.

We can differentiate the kind of collaborative practice associated with the second generation—and by extension a conceived sociability—from the kind of multi-author practice typical of those writers associated with $L=A=N=G=U=A=G=E$ magazine. Regarding *Legend*, a text written collectively by Bruce Andrews, Charles Bernstein, Ray DiPalma, Steve McCaffery, and Ron Silliman and published by $L=A=N=G=U=A=G=E$/Segue in 1980, Watten writes;

> [*Legend*] is located precisely in the place of the utopian elsewhere/nowhere invoked by $L=A=N=G=U=A=G=E$'s articulation of authorial subject positions. While $L=A=N=G=U=A=G=E$ was immediately recognized as an avant-garde tendency in its distance from literature, *Legend* demonstrates new formal possibilities of writing in the dialogic, collective practice of its five authors. The utopian counter-hegemony asserted in $L=A=N=G=U=A=G=E$ by virtue of the

missing referent of the work is enacted in *Legend* as in various forms of textual practice—generating a wealth of technical innovations, formal possibilities, and new meanings within a space of reflexive dialogue. (596)

He adds later, "The work explodes the presumption of authorship, dismantling and reconfiguring it in a series of multiauthored sections, each determined by the capacity of different techniques to generate new meaning." (597) Yet the decentered authority and multivalent meaning that Watten argues result from the collaborative gesture do not lead to the same kinds of sociability we find in much second-generation work. Collaborative poems published in *Angel Hair* magazine and certainly the dozens of collaborative poems published in *The World* generally acknowledged the identity of the authors only at the bottom of the page, and sometimes not at all. In Issue 10 of his *Adventures in Poetry*, editor Larry Fagin took this one step further by publishing an entirely anonymous issue; "no authors were credited; not even the name of the magazine appeared; the covers were pornographic comic strips" (Clay and Phillips 195). Poems in Bernadette Mayer's magazine *Unnatural Acts* were anonymous and collaborative—as participating author Ed Friedman recalls, "Everyone anonymously contributed a piece of writing, which someone else in the group used as the basis for composing a new work. The 'originals' were then discarded and the afternoon proceeded with everyone continuing to write works inspired by the reworkings of reworkings of reworkings" (Friedman). The sociability in *Legend*, on the other hand, is rather different. As Watten himself writes, "In *Legend*, authors *begin* from a position of self-assertion identified with one-sentence propositions; even if there is little of 'representation' or expressive subjectivity here, each author organizes a matrix of statements that bear his own idiosyncratic stamp" (597, my italics).

The five sections referred to by Watten that were written by individual participants are clearly marked and paginated in a table of contents. While individual names do not appear within the pages of the sections themselves, the potential sociability in the collaboratively written sections in *Legend* is nevertheless compromised by the initial impressions we have of individual writers independent from the collective, performing with their relatively stable voices or what Watten terms their "idiosyncratic stamp." We could even argue that these impressions happen earlier—that they occur the moment the reader picks up a copy of *Legend*. The cover consists entirely of the title LEGEND with the five participating authors' names printed boldly beneath it. (The cover is then duplicated on the seventh page). The urge towards what Watten insists is an attempt to "dismantle the limits and coherence of the authorial subject toward a wider politics" (603) is visually undermined by the five men whose names/presences are literally inscribed and centered on the front page of their *a priori* legendary work.

Such a positioning is in real contrast to the much less visible presence of the collaborating writers published in *Angel Hair* and related magazines and book series. The impulse towards community, far from being predicated on the understanding of a highly-specialized discourse typical of language writers, is instead based on far more casual effects. The lines "Don't be a horrible sourpuss / Moon! Have a drink! / Have an entire issue!" (109) in Ted Berrigan's and Ron Padgett's collaboratively produced poem "Waterloo Sunset" points to the way in which the agency for the creation of meaning and pleasure in the text is offered metaphorically to the potentially cranky and overly-serious Moon/reader, as opposed to being strongly determined by the specific theoretical positions of the authors. Second-generation writers deflate seriousness in an effort to enact an especially diffuse and amenable mood. Compare this to much of the work in *Legend*—Ron Silliman's lines including

9. It seeks the post-referential.
10. It dissolves the individual (qtd. in Watten 598)

indicate how language writers tended to determine reception by practically ordering the reader to situate the text within a clearly defined theoretical space defined by a commitment to poststructuralism.

Legend and related language writing may very well play a part in what Watten calls the "construction of community" (611), but we should ask ourselves what kind of community it is in comparison to the second-generation world. This world, defined in part by extreme whimsy and a refusal to engage overtly with its own poetics, invites readers to extend themselves quite easily into implicit sociability, especially in comparison to the world of language writers. I do not mean to suggest, however, that second-generation work is anti-intellectual or simply "fun" (nor, by the way, that all language writing is dull and doctrinaire). It would be a mistake to help establish a binary between "serious" language writing and frivolous second-generation work. As we shall see, the actual poetry of the second generation was as challenging and ambitious as it was whimsical.

"Come in Here"

The friendliness of the poetry community and the radical nature of the East Village itself as a major countercultural site found a metaphorical parallel in the production of *Angel Hair* magazine. Emphasizing the "sacred" nature of underground magazines and affiliating *Angel Hair* to predecessor mimeographed small magazines including Ed Sanders's notorious *Fuck You/a magazine of the arts*, Waldman writes, "We were already drawn to underground 'autonomous zones,' tender beauties of small press production," and then continues to describe the "modest" production values of the magazine (*Angel Hair Anthology* xxi). Autonomy, low cost, marginalization in the "underground," independence from the constraints of the traditional publishing and bookstore industries—these are all markers of a self-consciously avant-garde project, suggesting a quasi-Marxist utopia where the cultural workers are in control of the forms of production. For a historical moment, Waldman and Warsh owned the machines, temporarily achieving a high degree of autonomy.[12]

As the East Village from 1966 to the early 1970s found itself home to the Poetry Project at St. Mark's Church, the Kerista free love movement, the predominantly Latino Young Lords self-help organization/gang, Fluxus, the Motherfuckers anarchist group, the Bowery Poets Coop, the Fillmore East performance space, the East Village Other newspaper, and dozens of other countercultural "institutions," poems in *Angel Hair* served as lyrical counterparts to communitarian radical organizations.[13] The poems we encounter as we read through the six issues of *Angel Hair* are at times directly political. In Jack Anderson's poem "American Flag," Anderson uses a deadpan style to underscore his descriptions of the burning of an American flag: "A match is approaching the American flag. The American flag / is being set on fire. The match touches, first one stripe, / then the rest." In case the reader was wondering why the flag was being set on fire, Anderson informs us humorously in a later line, "The reason why the American flag has been set on fire is to / protest American policies regarding the Vietnamese war." While some may be surprised at the inclusion of such relatively straightforward and somewhat "obvious" politically-motivated poetry in *Angel Hair,* we should note that its tone frees it from the kind of earnestness Warsh and Waldman were wary of and that it mimics the kinds of cues to participatory action typical of a Fluxus performance. Additionally, such a poem benefited from the company it kept within the metaphorical community space of the magazine. As conventional leftist political action groups found a base in the Lower East Side in company with the more absurdist and irreverent elements listed above, so Anderson's poem coexisted with non-representational, absurdist poems. Bernadette Mayer's poem "Inventing Stasis" comes before Anderson's poem, and certain elements in the text seem especially designed to serve as a kind of playful echo or countermeasure to "American Flag."[14] The first stanza of Mayer's poem contains the word "saluting," as if it is in direct relation to the flag at the center of Anderson's poem:

> We were bored with them
> Why not, we said
> "Why not?"
> Come in here
> It is saluting
> To be there or here. (22)

Here we have all the various elements of a dissident poetics of sociability nicely contained within a single stanza. The pronoun "We" immediately ushers in representations of community, and the underlying exclusivity typical of community is further established by Mayer's mention of a "them" who are boring. The casual repetition of the phrase "Why not?" adds a kind of druggy noncommittal sheen to the poem, as the potential seriousness associated with the word "saluting" is deflated by the playful failure of the poem to fix stable subject, place or time. "Come in here" suggests a contrast with a tacit "out there," strengthening the overall "us vs. them" position. Sense is wholly subsumed by lyric by the time we get to the final line of the stanza—"To be there or here," read against the words preceding it, suggests the stanza is a kind of musical variation on the phrase "neither here nor there." As a reader, I was reminded of Charlie Parker's variations on "I Got Rhythm" more than I was of any stable point or moral. Sense—and order—are being threatened here.

We should consider that the Mayer and Anderson poems were in all probability chosen by Waldman and Warsh to sit closely to each other not just because they might be considered "good" poems, but also by virtue of their shared critique of American patriotism (the way "saluting" is elliptically critiqued in Mayer's case, and the manner in which the flag is burned in Anderson's). This editorial choice reflected in its own microsocial way the convergence of a variety of dissident political groups in the East Village, a mix that helped Waldman and Warsh to produce their own localized poetics of sociability and to mark a newly politicized turn, in contrast to the disengaged tenor of first-generation New York School magazines like *Locus Solus* and even more contemporary publications including *C* magazine.

Again, it is this notion of a collective sociability—one that in fact invites us to read and forgive Anderson's poem for its relative obviousness in light of its place within the "We" of Mayer's poem—that marks second-generation New York School work as compelling and problematic. While what might loosely be termed "conventional wisdom" imagines literature in a literary magazine to be published primarily because of the purported aesthetic value of the individual texts, Waldman and Warsh took common sense away from traditional notions of literary value by insisting (albeit indirectly) that value was partly defined by an attendant and clearly demarcated sociability. The few contemporary responses to second-generation work that we have available back up such an assertion in that they suggest readers respond to the poetry not as disengaged outsiders but as potential partygoers. For example, in his review of Lewis Warsh's *Moving Through Air*, Rich Mangelsdorff writes:

> Reminds me of court poetry; you can sense the power of references which would really explode given involvement with the intended people and scenes. One way to make the language rock, given a tight enough milieu; that's always been one of the reasons for going to New York anyway. (12)

Regarding *Angel Hair* 5, Mangelsdorff adds,

> This mag definitely projects the feeling of a time, place and scene. Too characteristic and too accomplished to be absent from the attention span of anyone digging the poetry of the present. (13)

Such a response justifies the potentially exclusive nature of listing names in poetry by identifying it as an act of group making. Such poetry is at once important "accomplished" work and a light-hearted incentive to move to New York. In opposition to the kind of interpretive community that is formed partly around the detection and appreciation of canonical

Western references or, as we see with the language grouping, a highly specialized theoretical discourse, we find that the more we recognize the names and know about (or imagine we know about and have access to) the poet's favored friends, writers, and texts, the more pleasure we are able to experience as a result of being so "with it." Again, poetry here is both aesthetic event and social game, in that the reader is invited to envision all the participants half-hiding behind the collaged and cut-up texts. The poems are not simply lyrical expressions of individuals but parts of a social system marking reflection, participation in, and extension of a poetics embodying group values.

The Generation Gap

The second generation is "second" because it owed many debts to earlier New York School figures, especially Frank O'Hara, John Ashbery, and Kenneth Koch.[15] However, the *Angel Hair Anthology* offers new readers of the work a chance to recognize that, while second-generation New York School poets were certainly imitative of the first generation in general and of Frank O'Hara in particular, they were extending, enriching and complicating a tradition as opposed to merely aping one. Such an achievement was realized via radical and politicized acts of collaboration, a more working-class inflected rhetoric in contrast to the stylized urbanity (and an attendant queer camp) of their predecessors, and a welcome infusion of women's writing and editing in a formerly male-dominated scene.

While first-generation figures O'Hara, Koch, Ashbery and Schuyler are legendary for their collaborations with each other and with visual artists, it is important to point out that the collaborative *poem* rarely makes an appearance in the books of the period.[16] Yes, Ashbery and Koch developed byzantine, Oulipo-inspired rules for their sestinas et al, but we don't read those poems in their books—instead, we read *about* them in David Lehman's literary-biographical account of the New York School, or we hear stories about them during conversations with other poetry fans. Poetry collaborations (to be distinguished from voluminous and accessible poetry-art collaborations or Ashbery's and Schuyler's collaborative novel *A Nest of Ninnies*) are important in the first-generation grouping more as an idea and a legend than as an accessible literary commodity. Compare this to second-generation work of the '60s and early '70s, which produced literally hundreds of collaborative poems and dozens of collaborative books. Again, while the difference here is in terms of scale, the scale is so extreme that one recognizes a shift in aesthetics.

For example, early issues of the Poetry Project-based magazine *The World* (variously edited by Anne Waldman, Lewis Warsh, and Joel Sloman) often contained collaborative poems written by five, six or more poets. Again, we can distinguish this from first-generation collaborative practice in that collaboration for O'Hara, Ashbery, Schuyler and Koch tended to mythologize individual practitioners as opposed to demythologizing and depersonalizing the participating subjects. There is no real doubt who O'Hara is and who the painter Norman Bluhm is when we look at their various collaborations, or who John Ashbery is in relationship to visual artist Joe Brainard when we read their collaborative *Vermont Notebook*. Even Ashbery's and Schuyler's collaborative novel *A Nest of Ninnies*, while certainly blurring the boundaries of authorship in the sense that no one line is identifiable as specifically belonging to either Ashbery and or Schuyler, maintained a consistency of tone that worked to concretize a reading of first-generation work as haute-urbane.

Compare such stabilizing moves with the collaborative poems in Tom Clark's and Lewis Warsh's little book *Chicago* (a collection of collaborative poems included in *The Angel Hair Anthology*). Issues of class and aesthetic tastes are foregrounded to the extent that the book appears designed to serve as an overt break from first-generation patrimony. Where first-generation poetry tended to reference the campy musical, jazz, and classical music, second-generation work rebels by extending the allusive field to include rock n' roll as poetry's new soundtrack. Thus in reading *Chicago* we find references to contemporary rock musicians including the Rolling Stones and Neil Young scattered throughout the poems.

Additionally, references to political figures such as Eldridge Cleaver add to the reader's sense that one is reading poetry that is far more tied into the historical moment, one which found rock n' roll positioned, quite literally, as utopian revolutionary gesture. (In John Sinclair's then-popular screed "Rock and Roll Is a Weapon of Cultural Revolution," we learn that ". . . MUSIC IS REVOLUTION. Rock and roll music is one of the most vital revolutionary forces in the West—it blows people all the way back to their senses and makes them feel good, like they're alive again in the middle of this monstrous funeral parlor of western civilization" [301]). The mood at the time tended towards a vision of rock n' roll as inextricably tied to notions of profound generational difference by virtue of its link to radical political consciousness. Simply naming the Rolling Stones or Neil Young, who produced overtly political music such as "Street Fightin' Man" and "Southern Man" respectively, helped Warsh and Clark establish their independence from first-generation predecessors via their alignment to the counterculture. Rock music was especially appropriate in terms of promoting a democratic poetics of sociability, distinguishing the second-generation scene from earlier Beat and New York School formations and publications, and linking the scene to developing values of spontaneity and tribe. As Daniel Belgrad writes, "Bebop musicians [favored by the Beats] had mostly avoided lyrics in order to communicate with the immediacy of pure prosody. Rock combined lyrics with prosodic soloing, sacrificing much of bebop's conversational dynamic but gaining the opportunity to deliver a verbal message. Second, rock was a music intended for dancing as well as for listening. In bebop, improvisational gestures of the body-mind were available almost exclusively to the musicians; but danceable rock music offered audiences the opportunity to get in on the act" (256-57).

Ashbery and Koch tended to maintain a kind of aestheticized distance from the revolutionary era in which they were writing—even O'Hara, who perhaps more than any other New York School figure included political gestures in his poetry—was not by any means interested in inserting counterculture rhetoric into his poetry with anything approaching sincerity. Thus we see that second-generation work quite literally introduces a far more youthful, class-inflected and populist tenor into a comparatively staid "uptown" New York School high art scene. Clark's and Warsh's poem "To John Ashbery" seems especially designed to mark such a break with the first generation—it actually reads like the kids are, in some sense, saying goodbye to their still cool if somewhat overbearing parent. For example, the lines

John

    it's
cold out. You are going
    uptown (278)

parodically emphasize the uptown, upper middle class comfort that Ashbery was headed towards. The coldwater tenement apartments of New York's Lower East Side, where the speakers of the poem are remaining, are positioned here as having a kind of dissident allure and charm. While

Ashbery may be on his way to comfort, Clark and Warsh maintain their bohemian status by staying downtown in both word and deed.

The next lines of "To John Ashbery" continue to differentiate first and second generations by pointing out the basic class distinctions inherent in the "downtown" versus "uptown" binary. The poets address Ashbery by saying, "If you were an Eskimo / we'd invite you / over for a frozen dinner." The fact of the frozen dinner, while vaguely humorous, also serves to lay yet another gauntlet down. References to fancy foods in first-generation work are manifold—we have James Schuyler in his poem "Milk" describing "milk-skins" looking "the way dessert plates look after everyone has left the table in the Concord grape season," O'Hara in his poem "Beer For Breakfast" insisting he's "happy as a finger / of Vermouth being poured over a slice of veal" and so on. On the other hand, the cheap, accessible, ready-made frozen dinner underscores the overall economy of the downtown scene. I would add that not only does the mention of the frozen dinner point to Warsh's and Clark's relatively empty pockets in contrast to uptown Ashbery, it also suggests a shift in aesthetic taste. The frozen dinner aligns the speakers of "To John Ashbery" to a distinctly pop-art world that values cheap, reproducible artifacts (Warhol's silk-screens) over the willfully massive abstract expressionism of first-generation-favored artists.

The final three lines of the poem are particularly loaded examples of the complicated relationship second-generation figures had with their predecessors:

> You're doing a lot better than us.
> You think.
>   Not dying.

"You're doing a lot better than us" asserts Ashbery's relative success compared to the straggly downtown types who so admire him. However, these lines also suggest Ashbery's own anxiety in relationship to his acolytes, as the next line surprises by clarifying that it is Ashbery himself who is engaged in thinking he's better than Warsh, Clark, and (tacitly) second-generation writers as a whole. The "You think" invites ambiguity—we are encouraged to wonder whether it's really *true* that Ashbery is "better," especially in light of the new references and sounds allowed into the poems of the second generation. The final line "Not dying" is especially rich. It evokes a kind of Monty Pythonesque vision of Ashbery insisting "I'm not dead yet!,'" while also referring to second-generation poets who are post-adolescents in their twenties (i.e., "Not dying"). Who's winning here?

I have used phrases like "haute urbane" and "queer camp" to set up another important distinction between New York School generations. While Ashbery and O'Hara brought a welcome dose of not-quite-closeted urban queer consciousness into post-war American poetry, their influence on younger poets and their publishing practices tended to manifest themselves within a male-circumscribed culture. While first-generation figures published women poets including Daisy Aldan and Barbara Guest in magazines such as *Locus Solus*, we generally find the first generation pretty much a men's club. *Angel Hair* and other second-generation publications rewrote the gender line by engaging women poets not just as muses and public performers but as editors, published poets, and career makers. As Linda Russo has recognized:

> Even though, as Lewis Warsh remarks in his introduction, in magazines and books, *Angel Hair* published "embarrassingly" few women, with *Angel Hair* Waldman and Warsh created a space open to continued change in the field of poetic production; it was, Waldman notes, a "seed syllable that unlocked various energetic post-modern and post-New American Poetry possibilities, giving a younger generation cognizance that you can take your work, literally, into your own hands." *Angel Hair* came to life in a decade when American Poetry was taken into the hands of unprecedented numbers of women as poets and editors, constructing through their work a productive relation to innovative poetic discourses. Throughout the 1960s, Diane di Prima, Margaret Randall, Rosemarie Waldrop, and Bernadette Mayer also co-edited little magazines and small presses (with men, usually a husband or lover). (260-61)

It is not hyperbolic to point to *Angel Hair* (along with other second-generation-affiliated journals, including Bernadette Mayer's and Vito Acconci's *0-9*) as partly setting the groundwork for the explosion in New York City-based women's writing in the '70s and '80s. As Russo adds, "since 1970 women have started over 70 little magazines and small presses devoted to poetic experimentation, almost half of these since 1990 alone."[17] Whether such a phenomenon would happen as quickly as it did without a figure like Waldman at the helm of the Poetry Project and the masthead of *Angel Hair* is anyone's guess, though I would suggest that

Waldman, and later Bernadette Mayer as organizer of celebrated poetry workshops at the Poetry Project, must be given at least partial credit as innovators and trailblazers.

Much of the writing that Waldman and Mayer produced in the 1960s and '70s is astonishing for its commitment to innovative writing and a kind of feminist consciousness that anticipates magazines like Kathleen Fraser's *How(ever)* and nineties post-feminism.[18] We can distinguish second-generation work from the strictly gendered feminist poetry of the '70s published in anthologies of the '60s, '70s and '80s like *No More Masks! An Anthology of 20th-Century American Women Poets* or *This Bridge Called My Back: Writings by Radical Women of Color*. These anthologies privileged what Kathleen Fraser has identified and critiqued as the feminist "call for the immediately accessible language of personal experience as a binding voice of women's strength" (58). Writing deemed "feminist" tended to be resolutely narrative, accessible, and didactic. Clear moral and political positions were staked, and previously marginalized stories were told. While a certain sociability is inbuilt in these books by virtue of the poets' shared political stances, this sociability was aimed at concretizing and essentializing identity. What was lost in such a mainstream feminist poetics was both the tradition of women's innovative writing (Dickinson, Stein, H.D, Laura [Riding] Jackson, and so on) as well as the attendant threat to conventional notions of what constituted a "gendered" identity.

Second-generation women's writing tended to undermine and move away from normative discourse and served as a real alternative to mainstream women's writing. For example, Mayer's and Waldman's collaborative prose-piece "The Basketball Article" (published as an Angel Hair book) promotes a kind of festive and dedicated feminism whose aim it is to show the simultaneous ludicrousness and sexiness of stereotypically gendered behavior. "[W]ritten in April 1975 as an assignment for *OUI Magazine*" but rejected "by a group of editors a few of whom thought it 'was a minor masterpiece,'" by "The Village Voice for whom the work was not technical enough," and by an agent who said that "THE BASKETBALL ARTICLE was fragmented and could not be handled"(481), "The Basketball Article" promotes a collaborative, sexualized, and experimental aesthetic wholly at odds with the conventional narrative techniques typical of feminist poetry of that era.

When "The Basketball Article" was finally published as an Angel Hair book, the authors made sure to thank a variety of men for making the publication possible—those thanked include a "Mr. Warsh" and a

"Mr. Padgett." Such naming troubles (albeit humorously) the assumption of easy participation in an egalitarian scene. That is, referring to Lewis Warsh and Ron Padgett as "Mr." is a distancing move, an acknowledgment that tension between the sexes existed even in such a freewheeling environment. Again, such inclusion of unmistakably politically-engaged gestures shows that second-generation figures were at least addressing gender politics and thereby complicating the disengaged, aestheticized surface of much first-generation predecessor work.

Lines throughout "The Basketball Article" evoke, as much second-generation work did, O'Hara's "I do this, I do that" mode, but the new feminist and counter-cultural consciousness enriches the practice. The beginning of "The Basketball Article" at once alludes to O'Hara's famous lines in "The Day Lady Died" (where he asks "for a carton of Gauloises and a carton / of Picayunes, and a NEW YORK POST with her face on it"), as it positions itself firmly within a dissident politics:

> The orange ushers of the Coliseum begin to wonder if smoking Sherman's makes you sexy. Should they smoke them? What magazine? *Oui.* We begin to dress in red, white and blue, we do not stand up for the national anthem. We always sit next to the opposing team. We distract them. We enter their consciousness. We carry a copy of Shakespeare's sonnets with us. We wear lipstick. We cheer for both teams (481).

Refusing to stand up for the national anthem will, even today, get you noticed and probably disliked by those around you. However, even as they are rejecting meathead patriotism, we discover that Mayer and Waldman don't come across as effete snobs doing anthropology in a sports arena. There is a real sense of play and appreciation for the proceedings here. The speakers distract the players with their lipstick, their sonnets, and their non-ideological cheers, and describe the movements of the players lovingly—those who "seem desperate running up and down court and the ones who do it like deer" (487). The lipstick displays a feminism more in line with the riot-grrrrllll and so-called "lipstick lesbian" phenomenon of the '90s than with the radical feminism of the seventies. Mayer and Waldman recognize, as they write in a subsequent line, that "There is grace in the men and women who play. A hedonism that turns into a sort of mysticism" (486). Pleasure *is* politics and vision, though a serious critique of the way gender manifests itself certainly still occurs within such a stance.

Who's in, Who's out? How to Judge a Poetics of Sociability

By 1966, Waldman and Warsh were certainly in the right place at the right time—surrounded by poets including Berrigan and Padgett living in the Lower East Side, and participating in the new federally-funded arts project that initiated the still-extant Poetry Project at St. Mark's Church. Waldman was named Director of the Poetry Project in the summer of 1967, and ran it for the next ten years. The social makeup of second-generation poets and their audience (which was for awhile practically one and the same thing), was crucial in determining the social nature of the work itself with its pointed references to favored poets and poems and its use of literary texts to swear in and consecrate new members. Such literary practice was employed within the community to semi-comically induct poets and readers into the order. As Warsh writes in his introduction to *The Angel Hair Anthology*, "From the start, the contents of the magazine mirrored our social encounters as much as any fixed aesthetic" (xix).

As a result of this relentless sociability in writing, I have found that reading much of the work in *The Angel Hair Anthology* can be a bit overwhelming. I felt initially as if I was looking through a window of a building across the street and witnessing a fairly glamorous group of people joking around, laughing, and talking about each other. Being outside looking in, of course, is not a comfortable position, and I suspect that some readers might be tempted to reject second-generation work because of its in-house, clubby feel, even as they remain attracted to its surprising technical innovations and to individual poems that are relevant and important independently of their coterie affiliation. Those readers put off by the incessant sociability of second-generation texts might ask themselves if they can impinge on the poetics of sociability by isolating one of the poems, getting it away from the rest of the crowd, as if they were focusing on a single person at a party. Is it possible to read one poem related to this group of writers without thinking of the dozens of related texts circling it? Must a reader be aware of the microscopic social exchanges that took place between these affiliated writers in order to receive pleasure from and insight into the texts? I believe that reading a number of poems as they appeared in *Angel Hair*'s third issue will help us determine that a poetics of sociability, while perhaps daunting for the new reader, is a marker of important work and enriches our understanding of the communal impulses in the post-war American avant-garde.

In Ted Berrigan's "Bean Spasms," the intertextual references and use of proper names typical of Ashbery, O'Hara and Koch are included alongside a resolutely 1960s hippie celebration of intoxication and relaxed unemployment that does not, however, preclude an affective transcendence. The following excerpt exhibits some of these characteristics:

THE HOTEL BUCKINGHAM

(façade) is black, and taller than last time
is looming over lunch   naked   high time   poem & I, equal in
perfection & desire (41)

Engaging Olson's conception of "field composition," Berrigan scatters words and phrases across the page in order to evoke the fragmentary, jump-start nature of thought itself—a practice that does not, however, refuse an almost corny lyricism, evident in "poem & I, equal in / perfection & desire." Nevertheless, while Berrigan as lyric voice is certainly evident in this poem, overall the text engages the page in such a way as to foreground and impel a kind of polyvocality that, unlike Pound's practice, generates a sense of immediacy independent of a link to a privileged past. It is worth quoting from the third-to-last stanza in the final part of the poem in order to understand how much of the writing in second-generation New York School work at once allowed for the lyric "I" while maintaining the poem as a vehicle for establishing a specific community grounded in '60s counterculture:

The rock&roll songs of this earth
commingling absolute joy AND

incontrovertible joy of intelligence
                                        certainly can warm
                                        cant they?   YES!
                            and they do.
            Keeping eternal whisperings around.
                                        (Mr. MacAdams writes
                                        in the nude: no that's not
(we want to take the underground   me that: then zips in &
revolution to Harvard!   out of the boring taxis, re-
                                        fusing to join the army

and yet this girl has   asleep "on the springs"
    so much grace   of red GENEROSITY
        I wonder!
Were all their praises simply prophecies
of this
        the time!   NO GREATER THRILL
            my friends (43)

Situating us directly within 1960s contemporary tribal youth culture ("The rock&roll songs of this earth"), Berrigan here reminds us that the "first-generation" New York School world that Allen Ginsberg implied was partly "a narrow New York Manhattan Museum of Modern Art artworld cocktail ballet scene"(qtd. in Gooch 280) has progressed into a more anarchic community. Ballet here makes way for bass, guitar and drums, and images of a primarily *collective* experience (think Monterey Pop Festival, Woodstock, the San Francisco Be-In) work their way into the erudite pep of the New York School.

The stanza then disintegrates into a variety of different voices beginning with "(Mr. MacAdams." Referring to his friend and fellow-poet Lewis MacAdams, Berrigan here introduces someone clearly within his social sphere. Yet this poem is innovative in the context of earlier New York School work by the time we get to the next line, "in the nude: no that's not." We are suddenly confronted with a text that suggests 3 or more radios being turned on simultaneously to different channels rather than one lending itself to easy paraphrase. We might be confused—should we read "no that's not (we want to take the underground," or should it be "no that's not / me that: then zips in & out" etc.? The question becomes even more complicated by the time we get to "and yet this girl has / so much grace / I wonder!"—a private lyric space juxtaposed compellingly next to lines about draft resistance ("re/fusing to join the army"). Tensions between disengaged hippies and committed politicos (and, metaphorically, between disengaged lyric and socially-engaged poetry) are all performed in a kind of wild welter that mirrors the conflicts between the laid-back hippie and anarchist yippie typical of the Lower East Side scene of the 1960s. Such disjunctive writing practices continue to provide new readers with fresh opportunities for creative reading. If we are tempted to read these lines in a "sensible" way, we could organize this section into three distinct parts, each containing a potentially distinct mode. First:

> (Mr. MacAdams writes
> in the nude: no that's not
> me that: then zips in &
> out of the boring taxis, re-
> fusing to join the army
> asleep "on the springs"
> of red GENEROSITY

This part clearly assaults anything resembling thematic linearity. Yes, Mr. MacAdams writes, but we immediately leave the purported subject and are pointed towards a variety of other voices and objects. Here, fragment replaces narrative in an effort to more fairly represent contemporary experience. A series of cut-up, grafted impressions are mediated by a constantly shifting process of thought as it is affected by the rush of life (the taxis, the army). Importantly, an implicit critique of the Vietnam war is encoded into the stanza when we learn that the semantic chaos has as its impulse MacAdams's refusal of the draft. Without resorting to jeremiad, Berrigan captures the absurdities of an urbane poet whose life embodies the O'Haraesque ideal of poetry writing, taxi hopping and so on even as he is threatened with being drafted. Second:

> (we want to take the underground
>   revolution to Harvard!

Here, the reader is placed back into "the sixties" via a simple, declarative statement aligned with functional political poetry. The lines here are exuberant, immediate, youthful, naïve, and utopian, ushering in the world of the Yippie chant that is by now so ingrained in the North American imagination. Third:

> and yet this girl has
>   so much grace
>   I wonder!
>   Were all their praises simply prophecies
>   of this
>   the time!

Here, the poem saves itself from becoming a mere historical artifact of "the '60s" by virtue of Berrigan's employment of a vaguely archaic syntax ("Were all their praises simply prophecies") and a graceful alliteration emphasizing "s": "this," "grace," "praises," "prophecies," "this." Such diction complicates what might otherwise be dismissed as a monologic hippie utterance.

We could divide the stanza in the preceding manner, but the poem certainly encourages a different creative reading, towards simultaneity, where all three modes are apprehended concurrently and thus no one style is privileged over another. Typical overall of the post-modern transformation of fragment-in-the-service-of-elegy to fragment-in-the-service-of-deep-play, we are invited here to read these lines in as wide a variety of permutations as we please. Getting back to the metaphor of text as party, we might imagine this stanza as representing a variety of voices talking at the same time. Sound replaces sense as the reader allows the jolly din produced by various romantic, whimsical, and youthful voices to characterize the stanza. Berrigan certainly appears to validate such a reading when he ends the stanza with a statement that could serve as a slogan for a poetics of sociability: "NO GREATER THRILL / my friends." Note the plural—the greatest thrill is of a number of friends appearing in the poem, and thus the sense we have of the text as social document is further established. This kind of invitation to creative reading is what keeps much of the best work of second-generation figures from becoming dated. Even as the work situates itself rather overtly within a cultural and historical moment that we can loosely define as "the counterculture," elements including the eclectic variety of tones; the amusing and surprising breadth of reference; the refreshing approach to inserting political subtexts into a deceptively lighthearted mode; and the radical assault on a poetics of sense and closure maintain the writing discussed here as innovative and often remarkable.

While a group aesthetic is certainly evident in the poems I've discussed, that should not be taken to imply that poets associated with *Angel Hair* and related magazines were boringly uniform. Some poems in *Angel Hair* 3, for example, introduced a highly conceptual and welcome minimalism into the overall New York School hegemony. Work in this issue and beyond serve as gentle alternatives to Berrigan's impressive if sometimes exhaustingly all-encompassing cut-ups, lists and collages. These texts at once complicate any uniform attempt to codify what "second-generation New York School" means *and* defer what would by *Angel Hair* 6 be a perhaps too-familiar aesthetic uniformity that Warsh and Waldman themselves rejected by ceasing production of the magazine and focusing their energies on a series of individual books. Aram Saroyan's single-word untitled poems "Blod" and "lobstee" are a case in point.

Saroyan, at the time publisher of the well-received magazine *Lines*, which featured ambitious serial, disjunctive and resolutely experimental verse, befriended poets Waldman, Warsh, Berrigan and Padgett. Not surprisingly, this act of friendship led to inclusion in *Angel Hair*, despite the fact that his work was about as far away from O'Hara's "I do this, I do that" narrative poetry as it could be. Saroyan's poem "Blod" is just that—the word "Blod" placed squarely in the center of the page. In the context of a poetics of sociability, we are encouraged immediately to find humor in the word. Where many of the poets in *Angel Hair* tell the reader what they do, what they think, and who their friends are, Saroyan intervenes with a weird blast of a muted tuba, a Blod. The virtues of quick surprise are manifested here. "Common sense" demands we treat the word as if it were *blood* or *blot* or *blob*, yet the omission of the one letter necessary to make sense leads to playful slippage and a resulting rejection of transparent reference that threatens stable meaning. If "blod," why not "Lobstee" for "lobster," Saroyan seems to ask. The implications of such a deconstructive approach towards socially-constituted meaning is now obvious, though still useful, funny and interesting. Say, "spondge," or "dridge." Saroyan invests us with interpretive and creative power as we are faced with the misprision of common-sense meaning—a misprision, we should acknowledge, that is a delight, one that leads to laughter (as so much of the work emblematic of sixties conceptualism, minimalism and performance art aimed to produce) rather than anxiety.

Berrigan's "Bean Spasms," Saroyan's playful experimentalism, Warsh and Clark's collaborations, Mayer's and Waldman's "Basketball Article"—these are all impressive texts on one level or another, yet overall writers associated with *Angel Hair* have not achieved the same kind of positive critical and/or popular reception that, say, poets of similar age including Sharon Olds, Robert Pinsky, or Billy Collins have achieved. In many ways, the fault for this critical invisibility lies perhaps not so much in the typical if questionable binary of purported avant-garde inaccessibility versus mainstream narrative ease, but with the poets and editors associated with the second-generation New York School themselves.

Quite a few pages in second-generation-related magazines contain poems bursting with proof of their eligibility in the New York School scene but lacking in the convincing imaginative practice evident in the texts I've discussed. Particularly in the early issues of *The World*, we find poems complete with O'Hara-esque references to time, awkward incorporation of sixties soul lingo, and mandatory-seeming references to given names within the second-generation nexus. Such work might very well lead un-suspecting, non-New York School readers to feel less amenable overall to reading poems affiliated with *Angel Hair* and the second generation. The very in-crowd feel of such poems, their uninspiring and forced-seeming evocation of proper names, and their insistent if dull light-heartedness tend to unfairly taint other poems in *Angel Hair* that share similar aesthetic characteristics. Yet social practices in the New York poetic community demanded democratic inclusion of such poems in a given magazine, es-pecially if the authors generated a New York School vibe. Unfortunately, such social and editorial practices perhaps played a part in setting the stage for the subsequent critical dismissal of individual writers who deserve a much longer shelf-life than they have so far received.

What I would argue is that one might fruitfully overlook or even accept such work in favor not only of the excellent poems so far dis-cussed, but more importantly to evoke and participate in the collective reading experience that *Angel Hair* and related magazines invite us to. The second-generation New York School, if taken as a group, may very well seem daunting and off-putting at first due to the unaffiliated reader's sense that he or she is barging in on an elite and even precious in-group. Yet, thanks to recent publications like Granary Books's *The Angel Hair Anthol-ogy*, and the continuing publication of important work by Lewis Warsh, Anne Waldman, Alice Notley, Bernadette Mayer, Clark Coolidge, Ron Padgett, and others in various small-press and major imprints, second-generation-affiliated poetry is making a comeback that invites new criti-cal assessments and reading strategies. *Angel Hair* and related magazines allow us to focus on one or two poets—the poetics of sociability does not in any way work to deny the value of reading a given poet in isolation from his or her social milieu. What I would suggest, however, is that we can approach such a poetics as an invitation to go to the party and read the texts as a collective, a babble, a joyful and worthy event.

Works Cited

Anderson, Elliot and Mary Kinzie, eds. *Little Magazine in America*. Yonkers: Push-cart Press, 1978.

Anderson, Jack. "American Flag." *Angel Hair* 23.

Andrews, Bruce, Charles Bernstein, Ray Di Palma, Steve McCaffery, and Ron Silliman. *Legend*. New York: L=A=N=G=U=A=G=E/Segue Foundation, 1980.

Belgrad, Daniel. *The Culture of Spontaneity: Improvisation and the Arts in Postwar America*. Chicago: The University of Chicago Press, 1998.

Bernstein, Charles and Bruce Andrews. *The L=A=N=G=U=A=G=E Book*. Carbondale and Edwardsville: Southern Illinois University Press, 1984.

Berrigan, Ted. "Bean Spasms." *Angel Hair*. 38-43.

—. Letter to Anne Waldman and Lewis Warsh. The Angel Hair Archive; MSS 4; box 1; folder 15; Fales Library and Special Collections, New York University Libraries.

Berrigan, Ted and Ron Padgett, "Waterloo Sunset." *Angel Hair*. 109.

"Books of the Times: Angel Hair, Partisan Review Et Al," *New York Times*, June 26 1968, 42.

Clark, Tom and Lewis Warsh. "To John Ashbery." *Angel Hair*. 278.

Clay, Stephen, and Rodney Phillips, eds, *A Secret Location on the Lower East Side*. New York: Granary Books, 1998.

Fraser, Kathleen. "The Tradition of Marginality." *Where We Stand: Women Poets on Literary Tradition*. Ed. Sharon Bryan. New York: W.W. Norton, 1994. 52-65.

Friedman, Ed. Personal interview. 3 Feb. 1999.

Ginsberg, Allen. "Footnote to Howl." *Collected Poems 1947-1980*. New York: Harper & Row, 1984. 134.

Gooch, Brad. *City Poet: The Life and Times of Frank O'Hara*. New York: Knopf, 1993.

Huelsenbeck, Richard. "En Avant Dada: A History of Dadaism." Motherwell 21-48.

Kane, Daniel. *All Poets Welcome: The Lower East Side Poetry Scene in the 1960s*. Berkeley: University of California Press, 2003.

Lehman, David. *The Last Avant-Garde: The Making of the New York School of Poets*. New York: Doubleday, 1998.

Letter to Lewis Warsh from Assistant to the Chairman, H.J Heinz Company, October 21, 1969. The Angel Hair Archive; MSS 4; box 1; folder 6; Fales Library and Special Collections, New York University Libraries.

Llewellyn, Constance, ed. *Joe Brainard: A Retrospective*. New York: Granary Books, 2001.

Magee, Michael. "Tribes of New York: Frank O'Hara, Amiri Baraka, and the Poetics of the Five Spot," *Contemporary Literature* 42.4 (2001): 694-732.

Mangelsdorff, Rich. "State of the Art; Young American Poets." Rev. of second-generation publications. *Kaleidoscope* 27 Sep.- 10 Oct. 1968: 12-13.

Mayer, Bernadette. "Inventing Stasis." *Angel Hair* 22.

Mayer, Bernadette and Anne Waldman. "The Basketball Article." *Angel Hair* 481-87.

Motherwell, Robert, ed. *The Dada Painters and Poets: An Anthology.* 2nd ed. Cambridge, Massachusetts: The Belknap Press, 1981.

O'Hara, Frank. "Beer For Breakfast." *The Collected Poems of Frank O'Hara.* Ed. Donald Allen. Berkeley, CA: University of California Press, 1991: 358.

—. "The Day Lady Died." *Collected Poems* 325.

—. "Adieu To Norman, Bon Jour to Joan and Jean-Paul." *Collected Poems* 328.

Out of This World: An Anthology of the St. Mark's Poetry Project 1966-1991. Ed. Anne Waldman. New York: Crown Books, 1991.

Plimpton, George, and Peter Ardery, editors. *The American Literary Anthology,* volumes 1-3. New York: Random House, 1968, 1969, 1970.

Rifkin, Libbie. *Career Moves.* Madison: The University of Wisconsin Press, 2000.

—. " 'My Little World Goes On St. Mark's Place': Anne Waldman, Bernadette Mayer and the Gender of an Avant-Garde Institution," *Jacket* 7 (1999), 9 September 2003 <http://www.jacket.zip.com.au/jacket07/rifkin07.html>.

Russo, Linda. "The 'F' Word in the Age of Mechanical Reproduction: An Account of Women-edited Small Presses and Journals." *The World in Time and Space: Towards a History of Innovative American Poetry in our Time.* Eds. Edward Foster and Joseph Donahue. Jersey City, New Jersey: Talisman House, 2001-02: 243-284.

Ribemont-Dessaignes, Georges. "History of Dada." Motherwell 99-122.

Saroyan, Aram. "Blod." *Angel Hair* 48.

—. "Lobstee." *Angel Hair* 49.

Schuyler, James. "Milk." *Collected Poems.* New York: Farrar, Straus, Giroux, 1993: 31

Sinclair, John. "Rock and Roll Is a Weapon of Cultural Revolution." *Takin it to the Streets: A Sixties Reader.* Eds. Alexander Bloom and Wini Breines. New York: Oxford University Press, 1995. 301-04.

Spahr, Juliana. *Everybody's Autonomy: Connective Reading and Collective Identity.* Tuscaloosa: University of Alabama Press, 2001.

Waldman, Anne "Introduction." *Angel Hair* xix-xxvii.

—, ed. *Out of This World: An Anthology of the St. Mark's Poetry Project 1966-1991.* New York: Crown Books, 1991.

—. *Vow to Poetry: essays, interviews & manifestoes.* Minneapolis: Coffee House Press, 2001.

Waldman, Anne and Larry Fagin. "Discussion of Little Magazines and Related Topics." *The Little Magazine in America* 496-513.

Waldman, Anne, Joel Sloman, Lewis Warsh, et. al, eds. *The World.* The Poetry Project at St. Mark's Church. (January 1967—January 1972).

Waldman, Anne and Lewis Warsh, eds. *Angel Hair Sleeps With a Boy in My Head: The Angel Hair Anthology.* New York: Granary Books, 2001.

Ward, Geoffrey. *Statutes of Liberty: The New York School of Poets.* New York: St. Martin's Press, 1993.

Warsh, Lewis. "Introduction." *Angel Hair,* xix-xxvii.

—. "An interview with Peter Bushyeager." *The Poetry Project Newsletter* 187 (Dec/Jan 2001-02): 12-15.

Watten, Barrett, "The Secret History of the Equal Sign: $L=A=N=G=U=A=G=E$ between Discourse and Text," *Poetics Today,* 20.4 (Winter 1999): 581-627.

Poetics of Adjacency: *0-9* and the Conceptual Writing of Bernadette Mayer & Hannah Weiner

LINDA RUSSO

PETER

Peter's foot is attached to Peter.
It is attached at the ankle bone,
adjacent to the leg.
This is true of the left foot
and the left leg
and the right foot
and the right leg.
Peter's leg
is attached to Peter's hip bone -
and this goes on, in the usual way,
until we have
the complete
Peter.

HANNAH

Hannah's hand
is attached to
Hannah's wrist.
What if it missed?

Published in *The World 13* (November 1968), this pair of poems by Hannah Weiner contrasts a universal confidence in the construction of the "male" poem ("in the usual way") with the fear that the "female" poem may fail to connect. While the "Peter" poem proceeds to list and assemble, from the ground up, parts necessary to form "the complete / Peter" so that the last line of the poem is in perfect symmetry with its title, the "Hannah" poem (having no ground to stand on?) fails to assemble beyond Hannah's displaced hand and wrist. The poem demonstrates with Nursery rhyme-like brevity and discomfiting humorous doubt its own inability to represent the female body, but suggests too that to do so might be child's play. Whether due to an innate flaw, uncertainty, or the desire to diverge from the Peter-way of doing things, the process and form illustrated in the successful completion of "Peter" are disrupted by the poem "Hannah." But rather than worry over a female "version" of "Peter," "Hannah" gestures toward other alternatives to be toyed with. A missed connection might reveal new possibilities: "What if"?

On the other hand, the poem makes play of dismemberment that is also a reflection on *membership*—*what if* Hannah wasn't "put together" like Peter or didn't proceed in the same manner? Would it make a difference? It is an apt question in the context of poetic community centered around St. Mark's Church-in-the Bouwery in the late 1960s. Ted Berrigan's "Early Sonnet," appearing in *The World 3* (May 1967), included the lines: "Peter exists / so he's in as who isn't?"; another poem, a collaboration between Berrigan and Dick Gallup entitled "80th Congress," made note of "Peter Schjeldahl / Who is new and valid." This act of validating and community-making, the naming of who's in and inquiring "who isn't," is a powerful gesture coming from Berrigan and Gallup, who in the same poem "approved" Lewis Warsh's and Anne Waldman's apartment at 33 St. Mark's Place as the official new center of the second-generation New York School poetic community.[1] "Peter" and "Hannah" are so uncharacteristic of Weiner's style that, in light of the coincidence, it's necessary to question whether they weren't purposefully deployed as a response to Berrigan's "Early Sonnet" and the homosociality and boundary-making of such gestures more generally. Was Weiner expressing her "outsider" status while commenting candidly on how many (other) "Peters" successfully assembled socially and in the pages of *The World* and other magazines as the result of gendered mechanisms of inclusion and exclusion?[2] Was she offering a subtle critique of the solipsistic list poem—a popular means of signifying acceptance of (and in) the coterie poetics illustrated in *The World*—by suggesting that "Hannah" would rather run amiss?[3] Establishing a style of writing that was quite distinct, Weiner was in the late 1960s composing and performing Code Poems based on the fragmentary phrases from the *International Code of Signals for the Use of All Nations* (primarily flag codes for ship-to-ship and ship-to-shore communication), to create disjunctive and humorous dialogic "communications" in poems that often paired "senders" and "receivers." In this way she experimented with the possibilities for a poetics based on notions other than that of the individual speaking to his or her community, which was central to the poetics of the Lower East Side and the postwar New American poetry more generally.[4]

For Bernadette Mayer, too, "what if" guided an experimental writing practice that departed from the ethos of the recently-established Poetry Project at St. Mark's Church-in-the-Bouwery. One might say that Mayer is the only second-generation New York School poet who never wrote "New York School Poetry"; although she appeared in four of the twelve issues of *The World* published between June 1968 and Winter 1972, she contributed only non-narrative prose compositions that were extremely disjunctive and dense. Even as Mayer and Weiner announced (and maintained to differing degrees) an affinity to the Poetry Project, "what if" was a mode that would serve to distinguish their work such that their texts offered little in the way of extending and reflecting the poetic community associated with St. Mark's at that moment. At the close of the 1960s both were publishing in *0-9*, a short-lived mimeo magazine published as a joint venture between Mayer and Vito Acconci that exhibited a refreshed interest in performance-oriented avant garde works from Fluxus to conceptual and environmental art, and participating in the dense weave of the new experimental and performative arts—visual art, music, performance, and dance—that were actively defining the avant-gardism of Vietnam-era New York.

This fact tends to get overlooked in genealogies of avant-garde poetry that cut from second-generation New York School Poetry to Language Poetry; as yet it remains undocumented how the poetic innovations of Mayer and Weiner have contributed to the articulations of dissent the explorations of alternative writing practices that came to define the latter movement. And yet, as this essay will reveal, the experimentation of Mayer and Weiner is central to the aesthetic shift that occurred in the 1970s. In making what might be called their conceptual writing projects—Weiner's *Code Poems* and related performances and her *Clairvoyant Journal 1974: March-June Retreat* and Mayer's *Memory*—they set out to problematize or avoid altogether the concept of a coherent self or vatic "I" at the origin of text, an innovation that was of crucial importance to the developing ideology of poets located on both coasts, in particular Charles Bernstein, Ron Silliman, Barrett Watten and Bruce Andrews. By the mid-1970s, Mayer's work was frequently solicited by a number of poets who would become associated with Language Poetry, and among them Weiner, too, found an enthusiastic audience for her work.[5]

Publishing poetry and essays, formulating criticisms and claims, and publishing definitive anthologies throughout the latter part of the 1970s and into the 1980s, these poets came to include the work of Mayer and Weiner into the Language corpus. Mayer's and Weiner's writing has not been wholly misplaced in a milieu in which questions about ideologies of poetic form were central. The inclusion of their writing by a younger generation of poets has provided a meaningful context in which to read their work (even as their inclusion was accompanied by occasional conflicts[6]), but at the same time the means and methods of their conceptual writing—namely, to engage and construct experiential environments—get overshadowed in a focus on the materiality of language and a related attempt to highlight the ideological nature of transparent, "natural" writing. And, perhaps more importantly, the feminism at the heart of their experimentations gets eclipsed as well.[7]

Regarding Mayer's *Memory*, for instance, Bernstein commented on the "artifice" of the natural look of consciousness that determined its formal construction: because her text was "based on what is supposed to be the look of energy, the invisible, natural flow, etc." it exhibited (and this is apparent in the archived drafts of *Memory*) a refusal to "sanctify as natural something wch [*sic*] is essentially a procedural decision."[8] Such refusals on the part of both Mayer and Weiner *were* formulated and purposeful, but were not proposed within the theoretical matrix that Bernstein himself assumes. Rather their refusals arose out of a gendered awareness of a community poetic practice that asserted a certain look and idea of the poem and the poetic subject that composes it.

Their conceptual writing projects could be aligned with radical feminist performances that partook in the "consciousness raising" of the Women's Movement: works that examined gender, representation and social spaces, like Martha Rossler's "Semiotics of the Kitchen" (1975) and Carolee Schneemann's "Interior Scroll" (1975). However, up until this point, very little is known about Mayer's and Weiner's connections to avant-garde formations both poetic and feminist, and it is not yet apparent that their innovations have a foundation in an engagement with both conceptual art and performative and performance-oriented texts gathered in the pages of *0-9* and enacted in related events and activities.[9] In collaboration with other contributors, Mayer and Weiner created spaces contiguous to the Lower East Side poetic community that allowed for an exploration of writing's potential as an investigative and performative medium. This shift in venue suggests that they had to abandon the social and ideological context of the Poetry Project in order to experiment with "removing" the presumed "self" at the origin of writing and with this to dispense with the singular and coherent "I" at the center of perception. The modes of conceptual writing they established address issues of form and procedure that would be influential to Language Poetry's departure from poetic practices guided by unquestioned assumptions regarding language and representation.

0-9: *From Material to Conceptual*

In his 1967 article "Poets and Painters," *Village Voice* art columnist John Perreault takes the occasion of a gallery showing of Joe Brainard's paintings to lament the dissolution of collaborative activity in the "brotherhood of painters and poets" and to celebrate its revival in the work of Brainard in collaborations with second-generation New York School poets. Over the next two years, Perreault would follow in his columns the development of poet-artist collaborations. In his critique of and commentary on different forms of art attendant to the concept (events, happenings, multi-media performances and environmental art, and forms of poetry attendant to the visuality and materiality of language) Perreault charts the dissolution of the generic boundary between poetry and visual art. Such dissolution—not a new concept—could be traced back to the anti-formalist innovations of John Cage at Black Mountain College in 1952, where he produced his multi-media "Untitled Event," now considered a cornerstone of postwar experimentalism. People, it seemed to Cage, were becoming more aware of the spaces around them, and art could emphasize that experience through the "purposeless purposefulness" that his event gave rise to.[10] Cage's classes in experimental composition at the New School for Social Research influenced the New York avant-garde; among his students was Allan Kaprow, whose "18 Happenings in 6 Parts" (1958) became the namesake of the "Happening."[11] This event was for art audiences in New York what the reading at the Six Gallery on October 13, 1955 had been for poetry audiences in San Francisco in its abashed disregard of traditional forms. Ten years later, *0-9* set out to document further manifestations of conceptual art with a concerted focus on the "dematrixing" of the "information structures"[12] and institutions in the creation of new ways to explore relations between individual, culture and public space.

Individuals in the New York art and poetry scenes set out to radically fuse the verbal language of poetry with the visual language of art, effecting new sets of relations between subject and object, text and page. This is true on the one hand of the Concrete poetry of Emmett Williams, Aram Saroyan, and others.[13] On the other hand, poetry departed from the page altogether, developing a significant public dimension, as in the verbally-repercussive performance poetics of John Giorno, the (quasi) chance-generated, performance-oriented texts of Jackson Mac Low, the "total translations" of songs from oral cultures and the ritual poetry of Jerome Rothenberg,[14] and the transcribed oral performances of "talking poet" David Antin. While all these new poetic modes together participate in a trajectory of thought that became a point of focus for *0-9*, poetry was also incorporated as a component in multi-media, multi-sensory "environments" in poetry-event performances (such as Perreault's "Film Poem" and the "Fashion Show Poetry Event," a collaboration between Perreault, Weiner and Eduardo Costa).

It was work that explored new media and new perceptual relations that the proletarian-looking mimeo *0-9* would document in its six bi-annual issues and four supplements (including Mayer's first book, *Story*).[15] A single volume of the collected issues, read like a book, would not tell one story. Among its multiple texts and textures, however, a design does emerge. In its earliest, thinnest issues, pages demonstrate intersections of text and performance and together chart a shift from an interest in "end text"—i.e. prose work or poem—to an interest in "process" texts that score or document pieces, performances, or events. When *0-9* debuted in 1967 many venues in lower Manhattan were showcasing all manner of new performances. The few issues bespeak a period of rapid expansion in terms of the range and kind of work published and an incurring exploration of public space as a site of artistic production. *0-9* tapped into a cross-section of poetry and performance—from Fluxus to Concrete to Carolee Schneemann's *Meat Joy*—exhibited in the earlier on-site magazine *Some/thing* (ed. Rothenberg and Antin, 1965-68) and likewise took an interest, via Mayer's editorial influence, in Ethnopoetics. But unlike its predecessor, *0-9* lays less emphasis on incorporating ritual and other elements of oral cultures into poetics and more on the alignment of textual and non-textual practices in an exploration of language, performance and the material page. While Mayer's and Weiner's peers published chatty and urbane prose and poems in *The World* and other magazines, Mayer's and Weiner's work appeared in *0-9* amidst a range of performative and performance-oriented texts as well as works by choreographer/soon-to-be-filmmaker Yvonne Rainer, and artists Jasper Johns, Robert Smithson,

Sol LeWitt and Lawrence Weiner. This mix constituted *0-9* as a unique space entirely open to conceptual art and experimentation—indeed, as a textual counterpart to such activity.

The first three issues of *0-9* do little to suggest this alignment, describing mainly an interest in linguistic and textual experimentation, but the accumulated issues show these experiments to be a portal in to conceptual art for both Acconci and Mayer while they were both still poets-of-the-page. An inclusive site of heightened typographic activity, each issue explored a diverse historic and generic terrain that included transcribed songs and tales from oral cultures, Renaissance and Medieval lyrics and tales, translations from Modern European authors, drawings (many by Bernadette's sister Rosemary Mayer), and contemporary poems and other texts that addressed every aspect of the visually-encoded page from punctuation mark to margin. Writing as it was being practiced by the poets associated with the Poetry Project does not make much of a showing in *0-9*.

With Renaissance "echo" poems and Weiner's Code Poems, the fourth issue (June 1968) contains the highest proportion of performative and performance-oriented texts, including Emmett Williams's "m u s i c a," a text that reorganizes the contents of Dante's *Divine Comedy* (employing "computer-tabulated data" collected at the University of Genoa) in a 213-line litany that documents the disappearance of the epic's nine most-repeated words, and Mac Low's *biblical poems* and methods for performance. Amenable to less conventionally readable works, *0-9* published documentary texts that became a necessary component of site-specific conceptual art, thus becoming *an extension* of events and performances. In "The Fashion Show Poetry Event Essay" which appeared in no. 5, for example, the collaborators write that The Fashion Show Poetry Event (January 14, 1969), was not finite "but the initial cause of a series of events which are a set of translations that add up to a total work"; their documentation-essay, as yet another translation, interpolates *0-9* into the "total work."

This exploration of the relationship of text and/as phenomenal space culminates in *0-9* no. 6. Among the contributions is Mayer's first published documentary poem/text, "Definitions at the center of the Newspaper, June 13, 1969." "Definitions" is a verbal map of a constricted reading of the newspaper. Each line describes what is encountered at the center of each page and "defines" it if possible. At times note is made of "the empty space next to a word," recalling the material through which the news is disseminated. This exercise in limiting the reception of information is also a random investigation that reveals, through a composite image, what is current in terms of the "news stories" and their paratexts. A range of objects is invoked: a bridal veil, a man's beach jacket, an air-conditioner, a piano, the skirt of a dress, the back end of a convertible car, a dish, a map, a sash, an oil tank being used as a lunch box, soap bubbles, a graduation gown, a house door, grass, a plant, the left eyebrow of Joanne Woodward. By re-assembling the objects and icons of consumer culture, this investigation reports on the social body constructed and reflected in these pages.

"Definitions" partakes in what seems to be a larger objective of this issue: to investigate the magazine itself as a medium. This objective proceeds variously. Material limitations are sought out in two short and untitled contributions by Robert Barry, "The Space Between Pages 29 & 30" and "The Space Between Pages 74 & 75." Their inclusion clearly demarcates the "contents" of the magazine as *conceptual* as well as material. The "space between" pages 74 and 75—facing pages—is enacted by opening the magazine to either page. But the "space between" pages 29 and 30, recto and verso of the same sheet of paper, is not represented mimetically in the print medium. With this conundrum the magazine as a container of information is challenged. Similar pieces by Douglas Heubler and Adrian Piper contribute to this investigation of "mental" space. Heubler's effort includes a page reading only across the bottom "LOCATED ON THE ABOVE SURFACE IS AN INDETERMINATE QUANTITY OF THREE DIMENSIONAL SPACE," whereas Piper's refers to a "void space" of undefined dimension that a page represents. Together these conceptual text-events contribute to the *idea* of the magazine by enacting and extending what it is "about" more so than contributing to what it *contains*. As reader-centered events, these three pieces work together to contrast the magazine as a surface with an unlimited space "above" and beyond it activated by words which are at once the visual site that constitutes the material object and a hinge that opens out from the print and enacts its dematerialization. These small acts of conceptual writing call attention to the limits of representational norms through which the magazine itself operates. While they can be interpreted as individual departures from word, text, and page as loci of attention, these short texts (more like labels), it should also be noted, transform the page into a site of activity. In this sense, conceptual text-events continue to develop a performativity apparent in earlier issues in the transcriptions of oral texts that enforce action through verbal repetition (as in this line from an Andamanese song: "I am cutting a canoe, / I am cutting a canoe") and in the documentation of events on the part of a writer/performer. With performative utterances, conceptual text-events engage the reader in the production of textual effects that neither deny nor affirm "what is" but set out to ascribe a third possibility: "what if."

It is at this point that *0-9* ceases to be an artifact and becomes an activity—a fact that was literalized in a series of three collective and chaotic events held during the spring of 1969. Street Works I, II, and III (March 15, April 18, May 25), a set of occasions where art could be encountered in the "non-art" spaces people traversed daily, was the brain child of Perreault, Weiner, and Marjorie Strider. As Perreault wrote in "Outside Art," in 1968 artists were taking to the streets and "to the wide-open spaces and [were] less and less involved in turning out precious objects. What they [were] offering to their audiences [was] an art experience rather than material artifacts that create that experience." His admission that galleries "do seem a little old-fashioned" and "geared to an elitist, neo-capitalist clientele" reflects a growing sentiment among artists of his generation: art for people not for purchase, free, open, and participatory.

What began as a 12 hour event with 20 contributing poets and artists grew to be an open-ended nighttime event with several hundred participants. (It ended prematurely due to police intervention.) Each Street Works event turned several blocks of city street into an environment for a range of theatrics. Acconci, for example, performed "Recognition" by simply walking up and down the street (a preliminary exploration of the boundary between public and private that would become focal to his later body work); Perreault performed "Street Music," a complicated score involving every payphone in the designated area; Strider hung up empty picture frames; and Steve Kaltenbach worked from Polaroids to reconstruct litter sites using litter transported from its original location near his apartment outside the designated Street Works area. For poets, Street Works was a venue for the exploration of public poetic acts—poetry enacted off the page and outside of the poetic community. An anonymous, indeterminate "Trash Poem" lay scattered on the sidewalk to be read in the order its words were encountered; Anne Waldman wore a sandwich board-poem; on another occasion she and Lewis Warsh handed out poems on roller skates; and John Giorno elicited the aid of volunteers to leaflet passers-by with his Kama Sutra poems, provoking objections to the somewhat obscene material.

The contributions of Mayer and Weiner, in contrast, were highly conceptual; Weiner posted blank labels on objects, performing an *absence* of writing, and attempted to tie up a city block with a fabric tape depicting the flag code from which she'd derived her Code Poems. She also performed "Hannah Weiner Meets Hannah Weiner" by arranging to meet the only other Hannah Weiner in the phone book (a psychotherapist). Mayer's events included handing out index cards communicating one of "101 constructions"; this is documented in *0-9* with one painstakingly filled neatly handwritten page bearing instructions: "Place a building on rollers. control the sunset. give out cards covered with blue chalk. bump into something moveable. circle a red-haired girl. walk two miles at intersections only. throw away large white balls. connect two travel agencies," etc.[16] Her "Polaroid Street Works" involved taking a Polaroid photo of the street, walking until it developed, then attaching it to the nearest surface.[17]

0-9 reached its acme when it attempted to meet up to the challenge of documenting this public-oriented and performative work in its final supplement to no.6, STREET WORKS. It gathers materials unevenly, including a partial list of contributors, some plans, reproductions of materials used, scripts, drawings and reports—many of these cryptic in and of themselves. As an incomplete representation of individual contributions, it reflects the spontaneity and simultaneity that characterized the events even while it does little to "document" the unscheduled, overlapping activities. Its failure to give a comprehensive account suggests, in other words, that one really had to be there. A precedent set by writing, assembling, and publishing was replaced by the precedent to make art in the streets.

Mayer's return to the Poetry Project in 1971 to teach a workshop (in which Weiner was a student) was an occasion to put to practical and poetic use the experience she acquired in the editing, writing, and performing that constituted her engagement with *0-9*.[18] The "Experiments list" that developed over time in collaboration with her workshop students begins with a call to somewhat systematically eliminate or alter components of a form of writing, blurring the boundary between writing and thinking, writing and dreaming, writing and living, "art" and "life." A very early draft of this list bears witness to the prevalence of a mode of thought derived from avant-garde performance and conceptual art. In the spirit of her own *Memory* (published in 1975), Mayer suggests that one "construct an expanding/evolving history thru random accumulation of found photos. Incorporate known personal photos; begin an integration of the two." She also suggests writing "a private detective journal" by "observing a specific part of the street every day . . . and recording every detail," as might befit Acconci and "creat[ing] your own 'prepared' typewriter" after Cage and Tudor.[19] In her workshop, Mayer encouraged her students to expose themselves to a vast range of new materials and composition methods and to incorporate collaborative practices, a combination that helped to rattle a firmly-entrenched aesthetic of rapid production, wit, chattiness and coterie politics. It was also where she encountered the ideas of a younger generation; among her students was Charles Bernstein, who would in time exert a connecting influence.[20]

Between the Lines: 0-9 *and the Making of Mayer's* Story

If the Poetry Project represented the establishment of a poetic community, *0-9* represented an adjacent space of anti-establishment possibility. As Mayer recalls:

> I was thinking of all the great artists, and surrounding your work with an environment that had all the visual things that you like. Certain kinds of poetry, Robert Smithson's art, just doing that, trying to make an environment that you liked, instead of wanting to be published in a magazine that you had second thoughts about.[21]

The material and conceptual environment of *0-9*, because it was not modeled after a literary journal proper, freed Mayer's poetry from formal imperatives of poetry magazines that she "had second thoughts about." Though they were friends, Mayer recalls being wary of Berrigan's mimeo'd *"C"* and other magazines:

> What I objected to was the way poetry was published in *"C"* and other magazines; it was always a certain kind of poetry, surrounded by white space, seen as precious, pretentious, maybe. I wanted to remove poetry from that context and just let it be, surrounded by conceptual art, anything but that precious feeling that you get from many magazines. ("Interview")

Mayer felt *"C"* "wasn't revolutionary." Libbie Rifkin describes editing *"C"* as an act consistent with the "imitative reverence" (111) with which

Berrigan inserted himself into the ongoing lineage of the so-called New York School. In *"C,"* Berrigan put forth an aesthetic agenda; the magazine was uniform, in a sense, in the way poems occupied the space of the page and because "lines echoed across contributors" (Rifkin 131).[22] *0-9*, "a way of exhibiting that you didn't have to publish staid, boring poetry" ("Interview"), was Mayer's effort to create a context to develop her breakaway notions of poetic form.

In fact, much of the work Mayer printed in *0-9* displays a tension between the poetic line, the prose fragment, and the prosaic sentence. For example, in "Untitled," a prose piece of several pages in which blocks of text cover a different area of each page, Mayer plays out her desire to break away from specific visual features including the stanza and the conventional positioning of the poem on the page:

> I wanted poems to be able to wander around and not to be restricted to certain concepts. . . . I was kind of wary of any way of picturing the poem as being a rectangular box surrounded by white space. Why not have the white space up there, if you have to have white space? I was just annoyed by convention, being told what do to. . . . And that's why I started writing prose. . . . I realized I could do all these other things, I didn't have to be restricted, there was no reason I couldn't be a poet who wrote prose. ("Interview")

As if to emphasize her decision to be "a poet who wrote prose," Mayer published only prose in *The World* in the years she was editing *0-9* and placing her experimental writing beside visually diverse texts. Her work during this period avidly questioned the distinction between poem and prose as it critiqued the use of language geared toward transparent forms of representation.[23]

This is the case in her first mimeo'd book *Story* (0-9 Books, 1968), formed of interlocking source texts, highly fragmented, and rejecting any narrative structure the title might imply. In *Story* Mayer is free, as she seemed to recognize somewhere between manuscript drafts, to liberate the line from its role in establishing a comprehensible narrator or furthering a teleological narrative. She describes *Story* as an accumulation of text "in a structure that is like a diamond shape" in which the number of different interwoven texts reaches its acme at the middle of *Story* and then tapers off toward the end ("From" 95). The content of *Story* is pure information, an apparently random sampling from library materials both ephemeral and enduring: Native American Myths, a Louis Agassiz article on coral reefs, a list of contemporary furnishings, quotes from Edgar Allan Poe, and a recipe for sponge cake, among other things. Characteristic of Mayer's work, beginning and ending are not necessarily distinct as such; the apparent organicism of accumulated and shed diamond-"layers" suggests that *Story* is processing rather than "telling." The process itself is mechanical, cognitive, and whimsical, but not product-oriented or synthetic as one might expect. The absence of synthesis is announced by in-text section headings—perhaps taking a cue from Raymond Queneau's *Exercises in Style* excerpted in translation in *0-9*—reading "fairy tale," "memoir," "epic," "thriller," "lie," etc. These seem to offer unrelated structuring principles to which the text never adheres. The effect is of a series of recurring, interlocking themes laid over the story Mayer originally tried to write—in the end undetectable—about, of all things, falling.

Story, despite its name, engages a poetic tactic popular with the second-generation New York School: the list. Where in that oeuvre the list serves to organize items or entries of a particular theme,[24] in *Story* the list serves to instill disorder. Rather than arranging the phenomenal and social world around the poet, the list, lifted out of the poem and placed within a larger textual field, becomes a means of effecting a "conversation" between texts. *Story* takes up the dictionary definition as a site of such "conversation"— after all, in the dictionary words "speak" about themselves. Yet Mayer deploys its listed components to destabilize meaning. For example, general descriptions paired with specific actions make the content of dictionary entries available for different "definitive" possibilities:

> To begin a ceremony or an elaborate course of events: as, to commence something or other.
> Prices fall.

> To leave a point of departure in any kind of progression: as, to start something, something started something.
> He marries and has a son. (*Story*, n.p.)

In the spaces between these lines—whether they suggest a critique of economic practices or of gender, language, and power—the authority of the dictionary is challenged; the ostensible purpose of the dictionary is questioned; and, like the newspaper page in "Definitions at the center of the Newspaper, June 13, 1969," the dictionary as a site of cultural information is re-read via juxtapositions that reveal alternate connections. This goes a step beyond Modernist collage to effect a dialogue between text and text, a drama of meaning-making. Language Writing would more fully engage such fertile, associative paratactic schisms.

Performative re-reading gives rise to alternate meanings in another section of *Story*. The effect is exacerbated when the specificity of the source text is distorted under the pressure of generalizing vocabulary; "We all live under the pressure of the atmosphere," in the original draft becomes in the published version "We all live under some of this and that" (*Story*, n.p.). This playful ambiguity, while it doesn't effect the truth-value of the sentence, becomes an effective means of vocabulary cross-fertilization productive not only of alternate meanings, but of an altogether new discourse. In the original typescript, a string of small stories are interspersed with random textual elements; these more coherent stories are then split up into their component lines and dispersed into the final text of *Story*. Mingling listed sentence/components of one source with those of others while downplaying the specificity of each list (with the use of general words like *this*, *those*, *something*), blending and bending definitions, *Story* avoids using the list as a form of creating distinctions. And among these distinctions we must list the poet of the self-referential list poem, a poem that gestures toward surroundings and friends in a presumed act of inclusiveness which is in fact a reification of the border between self and other. *Story* dissolves this border by putting different categories of information into a dialogue that never reaches a conclusion (or produces coherent characters) but instead remains a site of change.

The semantic challenge reflected in Mayer's writing process expresses a more significant change—that of the work in relation to categories of writing. For example, in the original draft:

> On the side, poems fall.
> Others [i.e. fish that live in shallow water] would be killed at
> once by the same pressure.

becomes in the published version:

> On the side, poems fall into two categories: these and those.
> Others would be killed at once by the same thing. (*Story*, n.p.)

These lines recall a reductive logic that is applied to poetry for the sake of understanding—a logic fatal to "other" kinds of poetic texts that don't easily fit generic either/or distinctions. As a poet interested in working in prose, this is of particular concern to Mayer. *Story*, despite the fact that it is composed by and large of prose, is for all practical purposes poetry: it is not composed of paragraphs but of a series of lines: each line, whether it occupies one line of type or three, is one syntactic unit; line breaks occur only at the end of a phrase or a sentence. As such the text of *Story* transgresses generic boundaries, defying easy categorization into "these" or "those." In the final paragraph of *Story*, the parenthetical phrase "already something else had begun between the lines" describes this generative transgression. The process *Story* commences is accurately summarized in its closing lines:

> Or the forming of a new one.
> Interlocking something or other.
> this is one of those.
> At the end, final: as end one, end the other. (*Story*, n.p.)

At the nether "tip" of this diamond-text, the dual ending of "one" and the "other," *Story* is a poem. It is "a new one" that is "forming" despite the text's refusal or inability, throughout, to replicate or define any one of its announced narrative forms. Derivative, between genres, "interlocking something or other," *Story* creates new textual and cognitive ground.

Mayer's writings often deploy tactics to modify poetic practices she didn't desire to reproduce. This both distinguished her work from and connected it to that of her peers affiliated with the second-generation New York School and the Poetry Project more generally, securing her, from this retrospective, an aesthetically peripheral yet highly effective position. Editing *0-9* was a manifestation of an experimental "malpractice" that made such transgressions and cross-fertilizations possible. Acconci's and Mayer's editorial selections produced a magazine that bore just enough resemblance to maintain an aesthetic connection to the poetic community (the poems of Padgett and Berrigan appear in *0-9* infrequently[25]), while at the same time creating an environment in which Mayer could display her own poetic strategies.

Environmental Art: Weiner's Code Poems

In May of 1967, Perreault devoted a *Village Voice* column to the "rapidly developing new art form" of Environmental Art, commenting on the sensory experience of aural and/or visual environments that position a viewer "inside" a work of art in an "attempt to make the 'viewer' an equal partner in the art work/viewer (participant) relation." The best example, he writes, "should be a total enclosure that opens up the responses of the participants to new levels of sensory consciousness." Perreault might have been describing the complexly constructed Code Poem performances of his co-conspirator Hannah Weiner, whose works quite literally explored the possible "programming [of] sense impressions" by providing combinations of aural and visual signals. Weiner had created a series of individual and collaborative events for performances, gallery showings, and street festivals dating back to 1964, when, in her exploration of visual and aural communication, she'd taken up the *International Code of Signals for the Use of All Nations*, a system of visual signals in use in the 19th Century.

Weiner's Code Poems-related events illustrate a trajectory of thought in the development of her clairvoyant works. Experimenting with varying intensities of sensory experience—from artworks that effected simple, single channel "circuits" to complex multi-channeled performances—these early works focus on information processing, although, anticipating her book *The Fast* (1970), energy transfer is intricately involved in the exchanges she sets in motion. "Long Poem for Roy Lichtenstein," for example, was a contribution to "Visual Arts Concrete Poetry" (1968). The piece consisted of the title spelled letter for letter in signal flags stretched across one wall of the gallery.[26] The flags might be enough for the receiver/viewer to "get the message"—that reading is decoding information—yet Weiner adds another information channel by offering a "decoder" list poem in the NATO phonetic alphabet, beginning "Lima / Oscar / November." Substituting a word from every letter in the phrase "Long Poem for Roy Lichtenstein"—26 lines hardly comprise a "long poem." With *long* Weiner makes a play on the distance between sender and receiver that the flags serve to bridge visually. And the "message" is translated from visual to textual to aural media, becoming literally "longer" at every turn—both spatially and temporally. Caught in this play of ephemeral sound and permanent visual information, the viewer/receiver participates in an endless circuit of "decoding" that never points outside the visual and verbal poems. In other words, the viewer/receiver activates the sites of communication, and, bearing the necessary knowledge, is even *instigated* in communication.

Weiner designed several performances as well, incorporating non-literary materials and contexts as possible sources of communication. These employed a complex system of signaling including anything from hoists of one to four flags in sequence, flashing lights and horn blast Morse signals, and semaphore.[27] In June 1968, for example, an elaborate performance of her short play "Romeo and Juliet" engaged U.S. Coast Guard flagmen performing semaphore and blasting Morse code against a backdrop of code flag slide projections, black light, and other media.[28] A repeat performance with the addition of flag hoists and flares followed at the Central Park Poetry Events later that summer. Even as a "play" "Romeo and Juliet" is characteristic of the code poems, which work through the humor of near-misses derived out of juxtaposing message-phrases from the International Flag Code. "Poem Between Vessels Towing and Being Towed" offers this "conversation":

T Take in Sails	I will take in sails
U I am coming nearer I wish	Come nearer. I wish to
to speak to you	speak to you
V I cannot carry out your order	I cannot carry out your order

The fact that a signal—the flag code for the letter T, for instance—was dually coded and could signify both command and reply enabled Weiner to "cross wires" and disrupt the dialogics of "I" and "you" that structures lyric poetry—a disruption she brought to bear on gender ideologies constructed in language as well.[29] This poem and its pair of "I"s are a send-up of a lyric ideology that required an active "sender"/I and a passive "receiver"/you. Both are also *you* and it becomes impishly unclear who is giving orders and whi is failing to carry them—despite the mutual desire to "speak to you."

The International Code of Signals presented the possibility of translating "simultaneous equivalents," as Weiner phrased it in *0-9*. The same "message" could be transmitted simultaneously in different forms appealing to different "circuits," visual, verbal and aural, and each flag signal could be read in seven languages. She set out to understand "sending and receiving" in "four, five, (and six?) dimensional space" through an exploration of "what can be transmitted through this space."[30] In this case, the performance environment was a field designed to test transmission in an investigation of the limits of linear thinking in the age of cybernetics: given that the amount of available information has more than doubled since World War II, she asked, how does the brain respond? Neurological repatterning and more efficient brain function were the desired outcome. Because one kind of signal "may equally be substituted for another with the exact same meaning," Weiner related this system with non-linear or schizophrenic thinking "which has served the binary neurological function of the brain."[31] What took place between the hemispheres of the brain—this would come to figure prominently in her clairvoyant writing.

The technical nature of Weiner's solutions would seem to prescribe their application. Did she, like others of her generation, simply want to alter perception—or did she see her work as engaged in the project of effecting social and political change? The latter is suggested in her contribution to Charles Bernstein's *The Politics of Poetic Form* (1990), where the terms of her exploration are modulated somewhat to suit the collection's ideological project; she writes that changes in states of consciousness made possible by disjunctive and non-sequential (*i.e.* clairvoyant) writing "awaken the reader to reality . . . and the need for political change" (226). Yet Weiner's focus remains on cognition and consciousness: "at heightened states of consciousness, both sides of the brain are energized, thus making the mind in action more effective because it has more power and knows more" (227).[32] Indeed, her focus on transmission of energy and knowledge sharpened considerably in the clairvoyant writing she practiced throughout the 1970s and 1980s.[33]

Group Memory and Group Mind:
Mayer's Memory *and Weiner's* Clairvoyant Journal

> Your own space & plenty of motion. Now why should you
> bother to be me in this way as a mix which is final insult as ax
> on the head of the murderer & this is this a public act . . .
> —Mayer, *Memory*

> Clairvoyantly I am other to myself, usually addressing myself
> by name or nickname, the mind dictating to the person.
> —Weiner, "Other Person"[34]

Avant-garde performance of the 1960s incurred "real time" and "real space" into its practices. John Cage in particular attributes the multiple, simultaneous construction of spaces in the intermedia environment to the use of language: "space arises out of the fact that the words are superimposed and accumulate their own spaces. There is no single space, finally—there are several spaces and these spaces tend to multiply among themselves" (*Birds* 132). If reading is, as Michel de Certeau asserts, "the space produced by the practice of a particular place" (4)—"place" here referring to the text that is constituted by a system of signs that becomes through reading an inhabited "space"—then it is possible to "malpractice" that place, to disrupt its rules and procedures and undermine its authority. The interruptive syntax of Weiner's clairvoyantly written texts and the undifferentiated, streaming shifts in mode and register of Mayer's *Memory* enact, out of a refusal to adhere to a normative and stabilizing semiotics of text, a purposeful malpractice through which writing, like reading, produces not a "space" but instead a proliferation of spaces. As such, *Memory* and *Clairvoyant Journal* are works of conceptual writing that entail a displacement of the subjective "I" as a point of origin and coherence precisely because the "I" is perceived as delimiting consciousness and the perception of spatial complexity. Because Mayer and Weiner refuse to import the logic of a coherent, perceiving "I" into writing, meaning that arises is "alogical"—neither logical nor illogical, but devoid of intellectual relationships altogether: unintentional.[35] Their writing addresses textuality as a means of perception rather than its product, and it is through this shift from structural "place-making" to inhabited "space-making" that both journals, with several information "channels" open, enable autonomous reading practices. The act of writing "performs" perception and the text functions as a site of collective cognitive action: the reader/viewer is invited to engage in the process of meaning-making that perception initiates.[36]

Cage defined theatre as something which engages both eye and ear, the "two public senses," because he wanted to be able to view everyday life itself as theatre. Similarly, the conceptual writing of Mayer and Weiner engages these two public senses in an attempt to create texts that are also generative experiential environments. For Mayer this is summed up in the community ethos of *Memory*, particularly as it was originally experienced by gallery-goers in 1971, and for Weiner it is evident in the multiple, fragmented clairvoyant "I" in *Clairvoyant Journal* that partakes in what she referred to as "Group Mind."

An extensive documentation project that consumed Mayer in pho-
tographing and writing, *Memory* attempts to reveal behavioral changes
over an extended time and space while clarifying the limits of conscious
perception as a source for memory. Shooting a roll of 36-exposure film
every day for the entire month of July 1971, Mayer made "a sort of
film diary of still pictures but with the added idea of forcing my self
to do this, to do it for one month. The purpose of it is to see how the
idea of what you photograph would change & to amass a large no. of
pictures (about a thousand) with their own (unpredictable) continuity."[37]
These were taken naturally, *i.e.* as one sees rather than as one "takes a
photograph," to avoid framing visual data according to a selective "I"
behind the camera. The written component, composed during and after
the month-long photography project, would "relate to the idea of the
relationship of memory & recording of the past with points of focus,
visual & imaginary, & the attempt to recreate that past by intuition—a
sort of déjà vu."[38]

Mayer did not envision *Memory* as a sole textual artifact—a now out-
of-print book—but as a simultaneous inscription of visual and aural
space, a work of saturated experience, a conceptual environment. For
the month of February 1972 at 98 Greene Street (New York) it could be
experienced in this way, its 1116 photographs hanging in a horizontal
band 13 photographs wide on the four walls of the gallery with text laid
out beneath while a six hour tape of Mayer reading *Memory* filled out the
aural environment.[39] Mayer comments: "if you spent the whole day listen-
ing to the tape and looking at the photographs you could follow along"
("Interview"). But what is it that a reader "follows"? The overabundance
of text and image effaces any trace of the singular "she" that initiates
the spatio-temporal experience *Memory* offers for consideration. The focus
is never on the self, but on the materials, gestures and actions which
involve others. As a collaboration between Mayer-as-writer and Mayer-
as-photographer, *Memory* invokes "other" perception from the outset. Her
compositional method included projecting slides of exposures on a wall
and using them as "points of focus, one by one, and as taking-off points
for digression, filling in the spaces between."[40] Her decision to "deframe"
photographs, to write down everything, to gather and blend and blur
rather than sort, select, and arrange experience, amounts to a refusal to
re-enact a "form" of memory as a form of cultural authority, a making of
history accomplished by giving the past a recognizably meaningful—i.e.
value-laden—form. Early drafts that recall and narrate with simple, even

banal, diaristic clarity expand through the accumulation of materials
including taped conversations, other peoples' journals, her own letters,
handbooks and event programs—in effect all the information she'd come
across during the month—and accompanying formal changes: repetition,
the mutating of poetic lines into prose, and modifications to grammar
and syntax. The result is a streamlined text and a composed "realism"
that many readers identified as reflecting the workings of consciousness.
Memory is *not* a document that reifies the consciousness of the autonomous,
experiencing individual. Highlighting its "assembled" quality, it is suscep-
tible to successive interventions and encourages what Juliana Spahr calls
"connective" reading.[41]

Practicing writing as action or event, inseparable from life, Mayer
avoided reproducing habits of representation and perception. In place of
the intentionally disappeared frame and the singular narrative it would
have directed viewers to reproduce, individual accounts proliferate on
the part of its viewer-participants; it invites acts of communal remem-
bering in place of any artifice of "reality." By recreating cognition as
a communal experience (thus getting as near to the idea of pre-literate
memory as possible), *Memory* retrieves history-making *for* the collective
from the individual. The documents become a source of other memories,
not of "original" memory. Mayer saw *Memory* as contributing to an in-
vestigation in human behavior—not as a form of autobiography or an
investigation of the individual, but as an exploration of the social body
as a whole: "you're not saying what's happening to you. You're actually
saying what's happening to everybody."[42] It is a practice set up amidst
the processes of the mind and memory and not a record of mind and
memory, and like Weiner's writing, excites cognitive action on the part
of its viewer/participants.

In the clairvoyant journals Weiner began keeping in 1970, her inten-
tion was to attend to perception, consciousness and language: "to show
. . . the mind working in relation to events happening" ("Mostly" 63).
Her idea of "mind working" is quite similar to Julian Jaynes's concept
of the bicameral mind in which "mind" and "other mind" (in Weiner's
terms) unmediated by consciousness are in direct communication with
one another.[43] Jaynes's notion that "consciousness has no location except
as we imagine it has" (46) might be the motto of Weiner's clairvoy-
ant writing, premised as it is on the validity of locations "outside" the
individual mind as originators and receptors of information and on the
role of writing as materializing imagined locations. As Weiner writes:

"SOS I LISTEN."[44] That is, while *Clairvoyant Journal* is composed as a "spontaneous" typewritten document, it is quite distinct from the "spontaneous prose" of Jack Kerouac. Weiner did not consider herself a source of language or ideas; she did not consider it the purpose of writing to tap into the "undisturbed flow from the mind of personal secret idea-words" or to free-associate in the "infantile pileup of scatological buildup words" as did Kerouac in his rhythmic jazz *"blowing"* (57). Her "spontaneity" proposed a means of investigating the structure, and not so much the content, of consciousness. Indeed, the "content" of her clairvoyant journal appears somewhat random. Weiner "talked to" words "as if they were separate from [her], as indeed the part of [her] mind they come from is not known to [her]" ("Mostly" 60). Multi-channeled and marked by disjunction and interruption (as opposed to a single-minded flow), the journals are oriented "externally." The self is de-centered and in place of "voice" differently-functioning voices are distinguished typographically: the "seen words" of voices that manifested themselves visually and gave commands appear capitalized in the text; words that materialized on nearby surfaces and made comments while she was typing appear underlined in the text; and her daily descriptions, the more traditional "journalistic" aspect of her project, appear conventionally in upper- and lowercase.[45] The results are journal pages of visually-active typography that performs multiple disruptions to Weiner's train of thought (see Figure 1).

Weiner capitalized, underlined, and spaced text "in laborious mimesis" (Jaynes *375)* of the clairvoyantly seen and heard, transcribing acts of cognition to create a space of *potential* (but not absolute or definitive) intellectual connection. Weiner's work is anti-rational and interruptive due to a refusal to logically connect fragments according to the schema of what Jaynes calls an Analog I—the singular, rational, expressive "I" of Western philosophy—just as it meticulously disrupts conventions of usage (mechanisms such as grammar, syntax and even spelling) that formalize and unify perception in the medium of language and produce the effect of such an organizing consciousness. As P. Inman relates it: the disruption of "interpenetrating narrative lines" in *Clairvoyant Journal* "frustrates an homogenized reading of the text. A viable identification of its author" (223). Much like the Code Poems, clairvoyant writing "throws at the reader such a quick multitude of words" that the reader is denied a "consistent ego building response"; in the absence of the writer's "ego" (and an apparent loss of Weiner's control over language and the

2/28

GO FOR A SAMADHI
feel different

   1st CHAKRA   BEGIN
               BEGIN WITH ME

Hooray GET OUT is a JOE musical not an order COME SOON NO I PASS
NO pass the *paper* wine YOU HAVE ORDERS *fix the page* WRONG BAR
Too late u met Michael at the Tin Palace PARTY free pass OMIT to La Mama
good night Bernadette BEGIN Going backwards: QUARTER TO TEN:
see GO OUT WHERE YOU TRY SOBOSSEKS FIRST. *agent* ^{London}
ACTION. *dont hesitate* MISS TIN PALACE SEE MICHAEL GO WORDS
He knows an agent WOW*get linoleum* TALK TO MARJORIE see Joe, hello to
Bob *conscious person* at NO
NOW SINGLE DONUTS eat the glazing NO DOUBLEDAY POPULAR
SO ELSE WOW*ie* DRUNK *leave more space* *dont underline that's an
order* SO WHAT

     serious now *dont hesitate* tonight followed *all wrong go to bed
no periods orders go to bed* glad get out is *New York* *dont repeat* *3 months
dont sit down dont perspire dont do it leave get it* *get it* at door non*ey
mother's word be careful drunk also* HERE where? *bed alright dont per-
spire* hear shout NO *dont explain* GO TOMORROW *Explain the interference*
it stops you from *bed* doing what the other words tell you *omit* DONT GO
BE A FOOL It's 7 1ST CHAKRA see clock DONT EXPLAIN THE CHAK-
RAS NOW RHYS KNOWS FOUR GO TO BERNADETTE'S it's 7 WOW
BEGIN Going to Phil Glass concert POPULAR WIFE GO TOMORROW
Tomorrow is Joe's musical and a party DONT GO BOTH This is silly
2 MOS *dont comment yourself* SO HUMBLE ENOUGH Rosemary is
back in town Read THINK Einstein's definition of thinking *Bernadette* doing
No more periods.
pre thought thinking SO AM I says the refrigerator in the pink bulb GET OUT
Change the bulb Bernadette's MAYER EXPERIMENTS this book is mind con-
trolled the WALK *Bernadette* language *ex communicate her words so through* it
goes through The way I QUOTE to destroy a word is to change its *litters* *too*
heavy Systematically derange the SIS I MUST DO IT *cut it short* SLOW
I QUOTE Pick any word at random let mind play around until ideas pass try this
                           through
with so SO WITH RHYS it's CHARMING'S word He *behave*
yourself SAW ME YOUR NOVEL CUT IT SHORT PLEASE PASS THE PAGE

Figure 1: Page from *Clairvoyant Journal 1974:*
March-June Retreat by Hannah Weiner

text) readers have to "put together" and "finish" sentences or "pause and separate the words" ("Mostly" 66). This emphasizes the role of sources outside the self—*i.e.* the community—in this journalistic composing of a self. The subjective "I," she suggests, is not definitive of perception but an imposed limit upon it, and working within that limit our knowledge of self is hampered.[46]

Weiner related the sentence to a "natural desire for closure" and singled it out as the target of destruction; it was "defeated" by the "more important" desire for writing as a form of "mind" rather than individual expression ("Mostly" 55). By dealing only with phrases, accumulating disruptions rather than completing thoughts, Weiner proceeds to "discontinue the sentence" ("Mostly" 55), to revoke its authority as a unit of meaning; to become clairvoyant is to become "denaturalized," to learn to perceive outside of naturalized, enculturated desires and expectations. On the level of individual usage, in other words, *verbal* articulation is not employed as a means of conveying the effect of the naturalized subjective "I" as such—and, supposedly, the "natural" desires and expectations it would operate with and express. There is nothing natural, Weiner suggests, about writing that represents the individual as a coherent product; rather this concept of self is mediated through literacy and is an effect of entering into negotiation with the options that communication via print presents.

The page in clairvoyant writing is a site of pre-literate (or bicameral) consciousness and bears witness to a dialectic of Antiquity and Modernity through which a new form of mind—"group mind"—is realized. She explained in a letter to Charles Bernstein:

> at this point i cannot talk about there being one mind because [I don't] know it from my experience, but i can talk from my experience [about] there being group mind. . . . This group mind operates in any or all of us, or in the radio, the newspaper, local agents my underlines. We can all tune in on it and it will say something relevant. it has information for us . . . mostly we get the information that is useful and truthful. that could be knowledge.[47]

Active typography accounts for (and produces) heightened cognitive "group mind" activity. As with much of her work, Weiner's clairvoyant writing enacts a struggle between orality and a contingent social praxis dependent upon a "collective cognitive imperative" (Jaynes 324) and textuality and the permanence of singular authorities. Whereas the latter signals the decline of mental action that characterizes the former, "group mind" reopens the processes of writing and cognition to the collectivity by removing these acts from the realm of the individual, interiorized self. In an interesting contrast to a mode of writing derived from the same dialectic relation—the scoring of the page called for in Charles Olson's "Projective Verse" (1950)—the "I" has difficulty appearing in Weiner's text, where a Cartesian dialogics of thinking and being is no longer valid. For Olson, the page is material evidence of the cognitive action of a man on his feet talking (to a community of poets to whom Olson takes his centrality for granted) and the poem becomes the province of the mythic Maximus, the uber Analog I, assembling the materials of history. For Weiner, the page can't possibly convey the projective force of an individual's thoughts; it is impossible for the writer to claim such authority in clairvoyant writing because "the person writing is bossed around by the voices, and gives up her autonomy to other parts of the self"("Mostly" 66)[48]; she, as in her "Hannah" poem, cannot stand her ground. All she has is the dislocated (clairvoyant, typing) hand. She refuses to document an authoritative history as a product of the already-assembled self, because no sufficient female self is constructed *through* a history that has excluded the cultural work of women in the constitution of the subject as universal (*i.e.* male). Rather than arrange text to assemble a history around her as though it reflects her presence, Weiner's clairvoyant writing reveals the female subject to be a surface available for the projection of (often conflicting) aural and visual texts. This concept Weiner literalized in writing "I SEE WORDS" across her forehead (on the "inside" of this surface she often received messages) and choosing this as the cover image of *Clairvoyant Journal* (see figure 2). The clairvoyant page is a public space for documenting what is heard and seen rather than what is expressed as "hers" because there is no historic or mythic self constituted as such to make fragments cohere. Thus this same image signifies the "between-ness"—as opposed to the centrality—that is constitutive of Weiner's subjectivity.

Her writing practice is located between a conceptual "group mind" and the concrete planes it inscribes, whether these be the page, the doorjamb, a friend's sweater, or her own skin—all surfaces on which words appeared to her. As both documenting subject and object of documentation, this between-ness suspends teleological determinations and enacts a sustaining ecology of presence that overwrites extant histories in which Weiner's future as a female member of the male avant-garde is already inscribed.

Figure 2: Cover image of *Clairvoyant Journal 1974:*
March-June Retreat by Hannah Weiner

Working amidst the cultural productions of men—performances by John Cage, Philip Glass, Steve Reich, John Ashbery and William S. Burroughs are all mentioned in *Clairvoyant Journal*—her clairvoyant documentation style places their productions within a stream of events, disassembling gendered hierarchies of "who's in and who isn't," of who is visible and represented in and through cultural productions.

The conceptual writing of both Mayer and Weiner raises the very question of what writing *is* in relation to the self. It taps into the circuitry of "self" and "other," "mind" and "world"—group memory or mind serves to bridge the two—to present mind in connection with, rather than as apposite to, the material and social world. In this mode, the "group"—sender and receiver, writer and reader—is allowed to dwell in the inscribed environment, a continuous stream of sometimes overlapping visual and aural information that arises out of Mayer's and Weiner's refusals to subjectively select or assemble facts from among information and abstractions. To do so would be to organize, define, and ultimately claim a limit on the world, or reinforce a limit (such as a "self" and "other") that had so often been claimed for women in the service of defining male identity in a history of avant-garde poetry and poetics. The crucial innovations of Mayer and Weiner, in other words, were impelled by their rejection of culturally-inscribed notions of gender. Since the *male* self was clearly central to avant-garde poetics, they did not premise their writing on a notion that would reproduce the female self as counterpart—particularly where that self could only be seen to serve in the maintenance of exclusionary gender dynamics that put men at the forefront and center of poetic community. In making contiguous performative spaces and incorporating the new concepts of performance-oriented arts into their writing, Mayer and Weiner questioned the working models of gender, self, writing and form at the very foundation of the poetic community centered around the Poetry Project at St. Mark's. They catalyzed poetic discourse by importing ideas, so to speak, as conceptual artists. Their experiments shaped and inspired the developments of an upcoming generation of avant-garde poets.

WORKS CITED

Bernstein, Charles. *Content's Dream: Essays 1975-1984*. Evanston: Northwestern UP, 2001.

—. Papers. MSS 519. Mandeville Special Collections Library. University of California, San Diego.

Cage, John, and Daniel Charles. *For The Birds: John Cage in Conversation with Daniel Charles.* Boston and London: Marion Boyars, 1981.

Clay, Steven E. and Rodney Phillips, eds. *A Secret Location on the Lower East Side: Adventures in Writing (1960-1980).* New York: Granary, 1999.

Damon, Maria. "Hannah Weiner Beside Herself: Clairvoyance After Shock or The Nice Jewish Girl Who Knew Too Much." <www.fauxpress.com/t8/damon/a.htm>

de Certeau, Michel. *The Practice of Everyday Life.* Trans. Stephen Randall. Berkeley: U of California P, 1984.

Duberman, Martin. *Black Mountain: An Exploration in Community.* Garden City: Anchor/Doubleday, 1973.

Goldberg, Roselee. *Performance Art from Futurism to the Present.* London: Thames and Hudson, 1988.

Inman, P. "One to One," *The Politics of Poetic Form,* ed. Charles Bernstein. New York: Roof, 1990. 221-225.

Jaynes, Julian. *The Origin of Consciousness in the Breakdown of the Bicameral Mind.* Boston: Houghton, 1976.

Kane, Daniel. *All Poets Welcome: The Lower East Side Poetry Scene in the 1960s.* Berkeley: U of California P, 2003.

Kerouac, Jack. "Essentials of Spontaneous Prose." *The Portable Beat Reader.* ed. Ann Charters. NY: Penguin, 1992. 57-58.

Mayer, Bernadette. "From: A Lecture at Naropa." *Disembodied Poetics.* ed. Anne Waldman and Andrew Schelling. Albuquerque: U of New Mexico P, 1994.

—. *Memory.* Plainfield: North Atlantic, 1975.

—. *Story.* New York: 0-9 Books, 1968.

—. Papers. MSS 420. Mandeville Special Collections Library. University of California, San Diego.

Mayer, Rosemary. Papers. MSS 520. Mandeville Special Collections Library. University of California, San Diego.

Perreault, John. "Poets and Painters." *The Village Voice,* April 20, 1967: 12.

—. "Outside Art." *The Village Voice,* September 26, 1968: 18.

—. "Environmental Art." *The Village Voice,* May 4, 1967: 14.

Rifkin, Libbie. *Career Moves: Olson, Creeley, Zukofsky, Berrigan, and the American Avant-Garde.* Madison: U of Wisconsin P, 2000.

Sandford, Mariellen R., ed. *Happenings and Other Acts.* London and New York: Routledge, 1995.

Sayre, Henry M., *The Object of Performance: the American Avant-garde since 1970.*

Chicago: U of Chicago Pr, 1989.

Silliman, Ron, ed. *In The American Tree*. Orono: National Poetry Foundation, 1986.

Spahr, Juliana. *Everybody's Autonomy: Connective Reading and Collective Identity*. Tuscaloosa and London: U of Alabama P, 2001.

Vickery, Ann. *Leaving Lines of Gender: A Feminist Genealogy of Language Writing*. Hanover and London: Wesleyan UP, 2000.

Weiner, Hannah. "Mostly About the Sentence." *Jimmy & Lucy's House of K* #7 (1986).

—. *Clairvoyant Journal 1974: March-June Retreat*. New York: Angel Hair, 1978.

—. "Poem Between Vessels Towing and Being Towed." *0-9* 4 (June 1968): 39.

—. Papers. MSS 504. Mandeville Special Collections Library. University of California, San Diego.

Faulting Description: Clark Coolidge, Bernadette Mayer and the Site of Scientific Authority

LYTLE SHAW

> Write about a place you know: a streetcorner, a pond, a phone booth, a riverbed, whatever. Bring to it everything you know or can know about the place, from its most distant past to the most recent thing you can remember about it. If you haven't got the time or inclination to research all about the place's deep past, make it up yourself, but keep in mind the general sorts of changes that the earth has gone through in the last billion years or so.
>
> —Bernadette Mayer (*The Art of Science Writing* 48)[1]

> our book made full in faulting more than statement
>
> —Clark Coolidge (*The Cave* n.p)[2]

Seeming at first to advocate the familiar category of place, Bernadette Mayer's paragraph destabilizes the very ground it presents—fabricating the natural historical authority on which such a ground would rely. A similar displacement is at work in the above line from Clark Coolidge—a line that seems to summarize what he and Mayer have set about doing in their unpublished collaborative book, *The Cave* (written between 1972-1978), which moves from a description of an actual cave exploration to a multi-faceted account of the linguistic and philosophical "grounds" of this account.[3] Despite his training in geology, Coolidge tends not to present the authority of science as a basis or armature for his poetry.[4] Instead, his characteristic claim that *The Cave* has been "made full" by "faulting more than statement" works to intertwine the geological and the poetic, suggesting an inescapable linguistic dimension to the former and a disruptive materiality to the latter.[5] That Coolidge and Mayer produced works that fed off the interrelationships between scientific authority and language both distinguishes them from most of their peers in American poetry and connects them to the Postminimalist artists of their generation (Coolidge was born in 1939; Mayer in 1945).[6] In a passage that Coolidge himself will quote in *Smithsonian Depositions,* the artist Robert Smithson reciprocally destabilizes the relationship between language and geology: "Words and rocks contain a language that follows a syntax of splits and ruptures. Look at any *word* long enough and you will see it open into a series of faults, into a terrain of particles each containing its own void" (*Robert Smithson: Collected Writings* 107).[7] If geology, like natural history, had seemed to provide a bedrock authority for some versions of the poetics of place ("I stand on Main Street like the Diorite / stone" writes Charles Olson in his 1968 volume II of *The Maximus Poems*) (221), for other poets the vertiginous relationship between scientific authority and language seemed to open abysses rather than ground claims. And these abysses attracted both poets and artists.

Inventive, prolific, conceptually complex and often hilarious, Mayer and Coolidge have both been significant influences on avant-garde poetry since the early 1970s—from the later iterations of the New York School to Language writing to the broad range of younger experimentalists that might be called post-Language writers. Still, while the terms, operations and goals of the Language writing movement they helped to catalyze, for instance, have become part of a literary historical debate, discussions of Coolidge and Mayer, when they exist, remain much more rudimentary.[8] Certainly Coolidge and Mayer's oeuvres—beginning in 1966 with *Flag Flutter & U.S. Electric* and stretching now to some 42 books in Coolidge's case, and beginning in 1968 with *Story* and now including 19 books in Mayers's—are far too various to imagine as strict parallels, especially given that large portions of both writers' work are still unpublished.[9] But it is not only the reception history that suggests links; the two writers identified with each other early on, collaborated on *The Cave*, and encouraged a kind of extreme experimentalism in each other that far outstripped the primary modes of quotidian and occasional writing that were coming to be associated with the later generations of the New York School.[10] In a 1975 letter to Mayer, for instance, Coolidge councils: "Don't worry! MEMORY is totally READABLE! No doubts, it now has its own life & should go on out to it (published)."[11] Despite Coolidge's assurances, the extreme experimentalism of books like the 1975 *Memory* (and of his own early works such as *Space* [1970], *The Maintains* [1974] and *Polaroid* [1975]) led in part to a fractured reception in which the two poets were claimed at once by the New York School and by the Language writers,[12] and yet could be "read" persuasively by neither of the main interpretive paradigms that came into play in the receptions of the two schools.[13] Both are included in David Shapiro and Ron Padgett's 1970 *An Anthology of New*

York Poets (Mayer as the only woman of the 27 poets printed). And yet
their influences via first-generation New York School poets are arguably
no more important than their connections to many other writers—from
Kerouac, science fiction and geology in Coolidge's case, to Melville, Haw-
thorne, and Stein in Mayer's. Nor do Coolidge and Mayer thematize New
York City as a recognizable background, location or "place" like other
"second-generation" New York School writers—from Ted Berrigan and
Ron Padgett to Alice Notley and Anne Waldman (whatever these latter
writers' other, significant, differences).[14] If we agree, for instance, with
Bruce Campbell's suggestion (in his excellent entry on Coolidge in the
Dictionary of Literary Biography) that the poet begins his first book with
"the allure of urban space," certainly the succeeding words and linguis-
tic particles—like those that follow for the next decades—float free not
merely from the urban New York of Frank O'Hara, and the bohemian
New York of Ted Berrigan, but from any consistent notion of place more
generally (*Dictionary of Literary Biography* 55).[15] And even if Mayer's early
works like *Moving* and *Memory* maintain a stronger link to the quotidian
details of New York City, the conceptual structures of these books go a
great length toward displacing and complicating any immediate relation
between self and site.[16]

How, then, does one position Mayer and Coolidge in relation to New
York as a site or context for their work? Answering this question will
involve not only considering their relation to the idea of site more gener-
ally, beyond New York City, but also focusing on their relationship to
the auxiliary scientific discourses often appropriated by both poets and
conceptual or site-specific artists when they become docents of sites. *The
Cave* may well be Coolidge and Mayer's richest response to these dilem-
mas. But before we approach its mouth we must first map out its position
within Coolidge's and Mayer's work more generally. One major compo-
nent of this mapping will involve a consideration of how their versions
of conceptualism, and their understandings of site, relate to those of the
Postminimalist artists of their generation.

Often evoking the language of scientific documentation, the Earth-
works artists, Conceptualists and Performance artists associated with
Postminimalism brought the problem of art's "site" to the center of
art-critical debate in the 1960s and early 1970s, and worked to shift the
emphasis of art from discrete objects, either painterly or sculptural, to
objects understood primarily in relation to contexts or environments. As
Robert Smithson remarked (speaking of his relation to the primary terms

of Minimalism—Robert Morris's "gestalts" and Donald Judd's "specific objects"): "I began to question very seriously the whole notion of Gestalt, the thing in itself, specific objects. I began to see things in a more relational way, [questioning] where works were" (RS, 296). Though some art historians understand the relational aspect that Smithson emphasizes as latent already in Morris's (if not Judd's) version of Minimalism, it is unquestionably the case that late 1960s art attacked the would-be autonomy of objects by a variety of means, refocusing attention (as Smithson suggests) on a set of relations between any object and its context or site.[17]

If this art historical shift has parallel relevance for the same period in poetry, it would not simply be in a new emphasis on site (or place) as a category, or even in a relational dynamic between a writing subject and a literal environment. Instead, we might think about the "environments" in which readers encounter poems—books—and their possible relations to the range of institutional critiques that artists began to direct toward the environments of the gallery and the museum.[18] For much as Postminimal artists downplayed the object status of art and thereby redirected attention toward durational and process-based events that engaged their viewing contexts, so many 1960s poets sought to dissolve the discrete poem, conceived as a distillation of experience, into the more extensive serial work—conceived *as* an experience.[19] But if a wide variety of poets were involved in a shift toward the book as primary unit of composition, we might notice a more specific reading of the book, as context or site, in Mayer and Coolidge's cases, one that treats each book as a discrete conceptual project, with its own vocabularies and formal structures, with its own self-imposed research methods and goals.[20] With each book understood as a kind of self-imposed conceptual frame, we might then see Mayer and Coolidge as quasi-scientists moving through a range of experiments. At the same time, because they construct their books not so much as neutral frames *for* experiments but as material embodiments and enactments of them—where all of the visual prosodic elements are semantically coded—we might say that the move away from a recognizable ground or context in the material world, the renunciation of "place" or "site," coincided with the increasing materialization of the linguistic and formal components of the book as a whole.

That both Coolidge and Mayer had significant ties to the Postminimalists suggests one historical basis for the homology of poems to books and objects to environments.[21] In fact, two of their closest ties—Mayer's to Vito Acconci, and Coolidge's to Robert Smithson—were to artists whose works and writings mobilize concepts of site or environment in ways that are absolutely central, in different ways, to the movement from Minimalism through Earthworks to nascent institutional critique—central, that is, to the dominant developments in North American art between about 1965 and 1975. Each, moreover, mobilized a new model of the artists as scientist: Smithson as the parasitic scientific theorist who would, anticipating the linguistic turn in the humanities, treat scientific discourse as material and posit disruptive entropy as the central principle of matter; Acconci as the subject of his own faithfully, even bureaucratically recorded experiments on his body in itself and in relation to public space.

Speaking of Smithson as a "generative" artist, Coolidge himself links the "fascination with word-fragmentation, building from syllabic plucks, particularly the *ends* of words" in his 1967 chapbook *ING* "to an interest in . . . Smithson," (*Angel Hair Anthology* 581) which emerged both because of their "geological connection," and because of Coolidge's admiration for Smithson's writing,"[22] which he engages most directly in his 1980 book *Smithsonian Depositions.*

While it is clear that Vito Acconci and Mayer were in close dialog in the late 1960s, neither cites the other as a significant influence. Indeed Mayer now distances herself from what she sees as the aggressiveness of Acconci's larger project, as manifest in such pieces as *Broadjump* (where the winner of a jumping contest was offered the opportunity to sleep with Acconci's two lovers), *Seedbed*, 1972 (where Acconci masturbated under a ramp in Sonnabend gallery to the sounds of viewers passing above, and projected his fantasies out to those same viewers via microphone), and even his 1969 *Following Piece* (where for one month he randomly followed a different stranger in Manhattan each day until that person entered a private space).[23] Still, from 1967 to 1969 the two did co-edit the magazine *0-9*, which published not only important experimental poetry,[24] but also some of the most significant writings and projects of the Postminimalist artists, including Sol LeWitt's "Sentences on Conceptual Art," Robert Smithson's "Non-Site Map of Mono Lake, California" and his "Upside Down Tree," Yvonne Rainer's "Lecture for a Group of Expectant People," Dan Graham's "Discrete Scheme without Memory" and an essay called "Eisenhower and the Hippies," along with works by Lawrence Weiner, Adrian Piper, Douglas Heubler, Les Levine, Robert Barry, and Michael Heizer. The shift from objects to contexts or sites was a consistent concern for the artists and writers assembled in *0-9*.[25] In his article "The Disposable Transient Environment," for instance, Les Levine argues that

"All paintings are landscapes. Very few of them have succeeded in shaking the nostalgic presence of the past. They allow the viewer to leave the time of his environment intellectually and enter into the time of the painting. Looking at paintings may be like going to sleep." The solution Levine envisions is "environmental art," which "can possibly overcome" the unnecessary separation between aesthetic and quotidian experience, "this change between life there and art there."

Beyond *0-9*, the traces of Mayer's dialog with Acconci can be located not merely in their common embrace of the would-be neutral, non-aesthetic, "objective" language of photographic and textual documentation that so many conceptualists turned to in the late 1960s,[26] but more specifically in the engagement with what might be called self-imposed research projects, whose object of study is oneself: "incidentally how long is my assignment here" Mayer writes in *Memory* (14).[27] Like Mayer's early work, Acconci seems to be carefully recording the results of his experiments on himself: how much of his hand he's able to fit inside his mouth before gagging (*Adaptation Study* [*Hand and Mouth*], 1969); how many times he can step up and down on a chair (*Step Piece*, 1970); how far he can follow strangers before being separated by locked doors (*Following Piece*, 1969).[28] Though never organized around combative psychological encounters and often much more funny, Mayer's early work could also be understood as a series of carefully monitored experiments on oneself.[29]

Emphasizing seemingly non-aesthetic, often scientific strategies for representing performances, processes and events, and stressing the relational aspect of artworks (their interactions with viewers and sites), the projects of the Postminimalists associated with *0-9* often coincided with what Lucy Lippard calls "the dematerialization of art." For late 1960s artists the goal of dematerializing art often meant the dream of independence from the art world's commodity system,[30] its traffic in things.[31] Whether or not any final and meaningful dematerialization was ever achieved, its goal was an important factor in the history of the avant-garde, since the claim that previous artworks were either too material or not material enough can be seen to drive a series of critiques internal to the history of twentieth-century art—the move from paintings to murals, from free-standing to environmental sculptures; and from objects generally to processes.[32]

If one expands the historical perspective to compare poetry from the same period, one is struck by a similar movement—but one that announces itself inversely as *the materialization of language*. For the desire to *materialize*, too, was directed against an easy "consumption"—now of poems as unmediated tokens of interiority. "Listen:" Mayer writes in *Studying Hunger,* "the world becomes progressively less edible" (SH, 46). To "materialize language" was not merely to emphasize its physicality—its spatial and sonic qualities—but also to acknowledge the lack of fit between words and things, to acknowledge the mystification of a view of the world as digestible in words. To materialize language was therefore also to cast readers back to the "raw material" out of which poems were built, raw material which, in some accounts, was also the socially charged atomic substance of identity—so that to disorder and recombine it beyond the code of the subject was to engage critically in the process of subject formation. This, of course, was one of the central ambitions of Language writing, articulated in a variety of keys throughout much of the critical writing by the poets themselves.[33]

Read back through the more self-reflexive and even at times activist critical climate Language writing has helped to produce, Mayer (like Coolidge) appears famously non-programmatic about her work's relations both to institutions and to the social world more broadly.[34] So much so that many readers tend to miss the complex conceptual ambitions that organize her books—that she tends to structure her works, for instance, by "exhaustively" or encyclopedically treating a string of inexhaustible concepts—from storytelling (*Story,* 1968), description (*Moving,* 1971) and *Memory* (1975), to states of consciousness (*Studying Hunger,* 1976) education (*Eruditio ex Memoria*) and collectivities (*Utopia,* 1983 and *Mutual Aid,* 1985). Extending this orientation to the problem of film in *Memory,* Mayer writes: "a movie is only the result of two to three months exploration of something" (M, 24).[35]

Mayer's 1975 book *Memory* comes out of a much larger 1972 exhibition at Holly Soloman Gallery in New York City in which Mayer had shot one role of 36 exposure film each day during July of 1971, then used the photographs (hung in a grid in the gallery) as mnemonic tools for an improvisatory seven-hour taped talk about her experience during that month. The only images in the book, however, are a small collection of the photographs collaged together on the cover; the text in turn is 195 pages of densely associative prose (linked primarily by commas) with occasional breaks into lines. Since the verbal material is already often obliquely related to the photographs, the fact that these possibly grounding images are not included in the text makes *Memory* all the more difficult. But while this format may have been a compromise (Mayer had proposed a version with images), accepting the imageless format was also a way to play up the gap both between verbal and visual understandings, and between present experience and memory.[36] That is, if Mayer's subject is, ostensibly, her experience during this month, the decisions first to mediate all access to this experience through the photographic records and then to withhold this record work to explore the inevitable gaps that structure one's access to memory, especially or particularly memories based on images. Throughout, she stumbles on images she cannot make present: "concentrated ash was all there was mind nothing sink . . . with my white-paints in it. I don't remember this dont remember thinking one on one white & whiter the word pictures, sing on the wall in pictures did you get it right thought" (M, 7). And if forgetting and mis-remembering become almost thematic devices that, through repetition, paradoxically unite the disparate material, so too does the act of gesturing toward photographic objects that Mayer refuses even to describe: "that is till much later but not that / one" (M, 10).

This deictic gesturing purged of description works not merely to distance us from the photographs, but to emphasize the complex temporality that Mayer's project establishes. As Mayer writes: "& this idea of my having had those ideas is a very complicated idea, including the idea of myself of the present moment remembering & that of myself of the past moment conceiving & the whole series of the states of consciousness which intervened between myself remembering & myself conceiving clouds make a wall, stop" (M, 181). Shifting between a meta-poetic statement about the book as a whole and another movement in it, the last clause of Mayer's formulation seems to enact the very problem she has pointed to in the first part of the sentence. The phrase "clouds make a wall, stop," that is, operates at once as a description of a new photograph in the series—a photograph of clouds, perhaps—and also as an oblique conclusion to her statement about the endless gaps that separate "myself remembering & myself conceiving," gaps that are themselves like clouds or walls.[37] Many of the syntactical folds and complexities of the book as a whole might be thought of as enactments of these temporal blurs and overlaps—linguistic analogs, that is, for the book's unstable tense. This tense is fractured and pluralized because the project of using photographs to help one "recover" ideas or experiences from the past gets continually overcoded (and even derailed) by the subsequent lives these ideas both have taken on, and continue to take on, in the book's present tense. Mayer's very first line remarks this problem as a "temptation" to revise the terms: "& the main thing is we begin with a white sink a whole new language is a temptation" (M, 7).

This may explain why phrases and events recirculate: where she mails a letter; where they stop to eat; how and where they cash checks for drugs; when "nikita kruschev [*sic*] dies" (M, 10 and 11). And while whole sentences do reappear in new positions in the text, and thus recode their meanings contextually, Mayer does not turn this into a structuring device the way that Lyn Hejinian will, for instance, in her 1980 book *My Life*. *Memory*, instead, shifts quickly among its strategies, banishing some and re-welcoming others.

While in *Memory* the use of an interlocutor, for instance, is but one of many devices, a speaking subject's relation to a "you" in some ways determines the very structure of Mayer's next book, *Studying Hunger*, which proposes to move beyond both description (which she associates with *Moving*) and memory.

> We asked how to communicate states of consciousness directly through a mass of language without describing or remembering. And, we wind up with the question, who is the YOU in this work. Or why is it there constantly switching. Even though this question seems to lead somewhere else, all my attempts to answer it eventually gave me the clue I needed to escape the code & begin to do what I was trying to do. (SH, 24)

As the experiment progresses, Mayer will circle back on the concept of memory, as though each of her works were an inquiry into a discrete concept that could be *exhausted* by its close and continued study: "theres a word memory I'll never use again, to rubber-stamp it. But more, sideways a space is used up. / Theres too much of it & I'm done" (SH, 31). The repetitive references inside these books both to their self-consciously extreme conceptual frames, and to the movement among these frames, suggests a strangely literal sense of Mayer as an "experimental" poet—a researcher studying herself as an object of what Mayer calls an "emotional science project" (SH, 9). This formulation suggests not the common project of artists wishing to reduce the range of human emotions into a scientific system, but the stranger, less stable goal of engaging the currents of desire, the swerves in subjectivity, that underlie any scientific inquiry, rendering it "emotional."

Mayer touches directly on her widespread, though subversive, interest in scientific authority in a passage in her 1989 *The Art of Science Writing*, a book ostensibly written to encourage scientific thinking in secondary school students. Like the famous writing experiments that she developed in her course at The Poetry Project in New York between 1971-1975, Mayer here suggests structures for composition:

> make different sets of index cards for the categories: information, interpretation, new ideas, hypotheses, etc., about a particular subject to be written about, such as clouds. Each card should have a title (cloud shapes, cloud literature, etc.). Tape them to the wall before your desk or table, so you can perceive the whole at once. Then make a chart or diagram that gives a visual representation of how aspects of the subject relate to each other. Include oblique or tangential material. Next create a verbal structure or outline for the piece. Tape the diagram and the outline to the wall so that a brief glance at all the material can remind you of where you are or where you might want to be. (AS, 41)

As with many passages in this book, the advice seems designed to locate the students' results less in the existing field of scientific writing than in the critique of this field offered by the burgeoning arena of Conceptual Art.[38] Mayer continues:

> The writer might also enjoy putting different paragraphs or sections of one piece of writing on different sheets of paper, then spreading them out on the floor and rearranging them in the way that seems most—and then least—logical. Draw conclusions from each. Another possibility would be to make a random arrangement of paragraphs or sections to see what you come up with.
>
> Instead of writing in essay form, it is unexplainably illuminating to create a set or series of reflections on a subject and number them sequentially, chronologically, or randomly. (AS, 42)

Ostensibly intended for another context, such passages constitute a kind of phantom poetics for Mayer.[39] Still, as all who read her closely realize, these descriptions are far from recipes for any of her books, since at the micro level, sentence to sentence, she tends to layer and superimpose procedures. What one gets from *The Art of Science Writing*, then, is something slightly different: an exploration of writing's possible relations to uncovering and arranging knowledge—to science and scientific authority in their broadest senses. These concerns situate Mayer firmly within the larger project of Conceptual Art.

Epistemology comes from the Greek word *episteme,* meaning "knowledge" and *logos,* meaning "word or science." Though it seems formidable to experiment with the origins, nature, method, and limits of knowledge, this becomes the simplest of writing exercises, and works equally well for people of all ages.

Invite students to write a series of ten questions on any or all subjects, and then to write a second series of ten questions about the subject of the class. Then, in a third exercise, have them write about how to find the answers. For instance, what book or library would contain the information I need? If I don't know, whom could I ask? Where is the nearest bird sanctuary? What means of transportation do I use to get there? Can I call the public library or the natural history museum to find the answers to questions? Can I call a professor at a college or university? Can I call someone who works in a private business? (AS, 73-74)

Experimenting with the "origin, nature, method and limits of knowledge," Mayer intertwines the scientific with the social throughout *The Art of Science Writing,* asking, for instance, not just where one goes to study birds, but which means of public transportation are available to get there.[40]

While Coolidge's book-based projects also seem to move from concept to concept (or at least from the scale of one linguistic object to the next), in his early work he tends not to include discursive meta-poetic meditations on his procedures.[41] Instead, such reflexive elements are nested within poems. For instance, from the first lines of "Acid," the first poem in his first book, the 1966 *Flag Flutter & U.S. Electric,* Coolidge invites his readers into a kind of geological underworld in which language's more pragmatic operations will be oddly attenuated. We might take the title to evoke both the corrosive agent that has eaten away all of the words that were at some point on the page and made the poem legible as continuous discourse, and as the experience of the hallucinogenic agent that the resulting poem now seems to evoke—or even be.

> Blackie was met at the subway
> advertising
> wished for pumice sunny flags
> WE GO   DOWN WE   GO DOWN

"Giant Grouper" said, in cold spray net tank
          GREENS deep at me
fade corridors
tapped the wrong uncle & spoke intimately

in foetal lift of potty stalagmites, resting
hair pillows edges of dead batteries
the leak
          Growth Mustard

earth vanity error: drainage , settle
     cigarette balls on umber pools
     the corners left to never return . . .

"call soon, I was underground"(1)

Whatever urban space Coolidge has alluded to with the subway in the first line quickly proliferates its referential bases, so that by the end of the poem the "subway" might as easily be a cave or an unconscious. In fact, the trope of cave exploration frequently recurs in Coolidge's work—making this poem a fitting introduction to Coolidge's later acts of descending into the word pits to mine language, to consider samples at a number of scales. At times this mining focuses on the sub-lexical specimen, chipped or chemically removed from its context: "ber // esting // ciple // ture // ent // tive // a ture / the ing // tions" (S, 119). At other points we get full lexical units dislodged, or partially dislodged from full grammatical units:

grammar a granite
               which   toddler
          so ban
               cram ifs which more
          tie modes
               so one
     eye tea half average
                    whens
     gore smug   (S, 70)

Coolidge is of course not the first to have linked poetry and mining:

Williams's famous soil sample in *Paterson* provides a vertical framework for thinking about site and its history, one that Smithson references in his essay on "The Spiral Jetty" and elsewhere calls "proto-conceptual art" (RS, 285); Coolidge may be referring to this moment in *Paterson* when in his book *Research* he writes of "buried treasure and the variable foot" (n.p). Still, for Coolidge the tools of the geologic researcher approaching his specimens are not brought to bear on a particular place or site, but mis-applied to language as a whole, so that entering into the space of composition or arrangement is also descending into the caverns of language, with hard hat and pick, to dislodge and rearrange the materials. Coolidge often thematizes his own writing space, his basement in particular, as a scene of ritualized, repeated encounters with recalcitrant objects like the generative crystal of *The Crystal Text*:[42] "I order myself to present myself to it. / How arrange my hands, the print of my face, / the interlogging of my legs, the shaft of trunk / to what sunrise? (CT, 90). Or, a few lines later: "My off-white pen scratches here / that I may enter in to that array, / morning opened into a corner of the underground. / The worst thing being a too few of the too many" (ibid.). Occasionally Coolidge will depict the lot of a poetry miner as a bleak one. "It is easy to feel distraught," he writes in an August 21, 1980 letter to Mayer, "about spending the last ten years in a room half underground with a limited view of trees against sky."[43] More commonly, however, he embraces the subterranean aspects of his vocation, taking pleasure in finding the fault lines at which descriptive discourses (which might once have been marshaled in service of normative topographical or descriptive effects) can decompose into arrangements of charged linguistic specimens.[44]

The "space" of Coolidge's pages is thus neither late Williams's unfolded speech rhythms occurring through the variable foot stanza, nor Olson's space of bodily self-realization through breath units whose arrangement on the page then have analogical links to the space of a town and its layered and (personally) mythologized history. Rather, in the early work at least, Coolidge parallels Mayer's literalization of the figure of the experimental poet, since his page can often be imagined as a linguistic/geological site, where chemical and physical operations have eaten away substance to reveal fragmentary linguistic orders, or provided a series of specimens that have now been arranged.

Consider the status of experiment and science in Coolidge's 1980 book *Smithsonian Depositions*—a work written in explicit dialog with the writings both of Robert Smithson and of Donald Judd.

Words and rocks contain a language that follows a syntax of splits and ruptures. Look at any *word* long enough and you will see it open into a series of faults, into a terrain of particles each containing its own void. This discomforting language of fragmentation offers no easy gestalt solution; the certainties of didactic discourse are hurled into the erosion of the poetic principle. Poetry being forever lost must submit to its own vacuity; it is somehow a product of exhaustion rather than creation. Poetry is always a dying language but never a dead language.

As for Apatite, fraud is a matter of bones. Biotite peels from Biot's sheets. In a pinch, Feldspar may be used as a field chalk. Garnet eats a granular pome. Mica becomes a lamina of the crumb. Oligoclase takes a little breaking. Olivine shapes an olive suffix. Orpiment, a gold's pigment. Pectolite is solid. Prase holds mastery of the Greek leek. Prsilomelane reveals a bare back. Quartz, the German unknown. Take a cave powder and you've Realgar. A french red may be got from Rutile. Sphalerite's a slippery blend. Sphene, a Greek wedge. And then there's Spodumene or wood ashes as gems. Stilbite? Shine it. Tourmaline's, to the Sinhalese, both Carnelian and a suffix. Zeolites are boilers. And Zircon, a silicate of jargon (26-27)[45]

Coolidge's experiment here consists in moving from an unmarked quote of Smithson's earlier cited 1968 essay, "A Sedimentation of the Mind: Earth Projects" (RS, 107) to a paragraph that seems to *enact* what Smithson describes. If this enactment shares Smithson's sense of the geological aspects of writing, and of writing as non-ideational substance, as "printed matter," (RS, 61),[46] Coolidge nonetheless accords the sonic dimensions of language a greater and more disruptive role. More so than Smithson, Coolidge frequently halts and reroutes semantic or discursive momentum by introducing paradigmatic word substitutions and chewy, mouth-slowing lexical combinations into his self-consciously built sentences: "Mica becomes a lamina of the crumb . . . And Zircon, a silicate of jargon." Indeed, the potentially disruptive play of sonic matter seems to open abysses in discourse that operate, one might even claim, as non-sites—as semantic elsewheres that haunt and destabilize the datum of legible discourse. In *Smithsonian Depositions* this datum gets established through extensive "depositions," quotations from 30 listed sources, including W. C. Williams, Godard, Robbe-Grillet, Kerouac, several textbooks on geology, Claude Lévi-Strauss, Donald Judd and Bernadette Mayer.[47]

Let us examine the deposition of the artist/critic Donald Judd, whose stop-and-start syntax Smithson had called both geological and abyssal.[48] In caring in to Judd's unmistakable prose, Coolidge reveals and playfully rearranges a vast network of subterranean anxieties about order and authority. Introduced by a fairly "straight" sentence placing the "field geologist" following a strike, Coolidge then presents a more hallucinogenic section in which giants and beehives throw columns and stones in this landscape (which may also be a tube), their activities seeming to produce the "bulging of the surface . . . termed The Turban." It is here, then, that Judd's art-critical tone comes in to remark on this created landscape (or perhaps on Coolidge's poem!): "It's fine. The black is discrete, hard, and projects. There aren't any other colors and divisions. The surface bends to the mark. The bands are often adjacent. It's not a coherent environment" (ibid.). Nor is Judd's new linguistic environment. Judd's description of a gallery sculpture has thus been collaged into a geological field description—just as his prose, more generally, has itself been turned into a kind of mining site.

> Quite a few of my pieces have been worn out. That came back. They sent a letter that seemed to be missing. Just information. I saw a painting by Newman with fingerprints down-room. Somewhere else a woman leaned the same way against a Rothko. A man, in time, become slow and careful. The room showed people, a few of whom are idiots. Newman one time leant back against a Pollock. You can't even get enough light. A man bought the face of a box. I counted sixty-four mistakes in the Still. The fast and constant space. Damage. Time too. (39)

Drawn perhaps to the conspicuous gaps between Judd's sentences, Coolidge goes about spelunking in them—increasing their effects at the level of the paragraph by extracting elements and therefore unhinging sentences from their antecedents: Judd's original text, from an essay called "Complaints: part 11" (published in *Arts Magazine* in March 1973) details a long list of problems the artist and his work have suffered from curators, art handlers and art administrators, including terse and incomprehensible correspondence, broken welds on artworks and a catalog with 64 mistakes.[49] Breaking the logical chains that would guide Judd's sentences, omitting conditions and circumstances, and generally leaving fingerprints, Coolidge transforms Judd's prose into a textual enactment of Judd's very complaint.[50] And on a larger level, just as Newman has rubbed against a Pollock, now Coolidge has the textual deposits of Judd rub against the linguistic strata of Smithson and Kerouac and Bernadette Mayer.

But it is important to stress that the tropes and operations that Coolidge transforms from geology do not always function solely as tools for analyzing and revising other texts. Like Smithson, Coolidge was interested in fieldtrips to *actual* geological sites. And it was around such a fieldtrip that Coolidge collaborated with Mayer to produce *The Cave,* a serial text that explicitly elaborates the shift I have been arguing is fundamental to both poets' works: from book conceived as collection of discrete poems, to book as site of process-based experimental project. Rather than a collection of poems or a single long poem *about* a cave, Coolidge and Mayer use the problem of describing a cave to construct a dialogic text that progressively circles back on its own incomplete or inadequate descriptive episodes, treating these as a datum or ground for a series of improvisations and transformations that eventually turns the book itself, in its various layers, into a textual cave. In a section of *The Art of Science Writing* that explains the Greek roots of "peripatetic scientists," Mayer suggests:

> Have students take a walk together, discussing scientific matters, observing, and making notes about everything. The scope of discussion can be limited to the sizes of things, the colors of things, types of trees, questions concerning the construction of cities, kinds of material and stone observed, the weather, and so on. . . . The ambience of this experiment can be either intensely serious or lighthearted and hilarious. It seems to work either way. Stress the importance of detailed observation. (AS, 59-60)

The Cave begins, in fact, as such a peripatetic experiment, one whose "detailed observation" of the "material and stone" and "notes about everything" drifts gradually from straight description toward an ambiance of hilarity. Its first section, "The Trip to Eldon's Cave," is a fairly conventional four-page narrative (written by Coolidge) of an actual cave exploration undertaken in September 1972 by Coolidge, his wife Susan and daughter Celia, Bernadette, and her then boyfriend, Ed Bowes.[51] Continued sporadically until October 1978, the full 66-page manuscript is comprised of 11 sections (6 by Coolidge, 5 by Mayer) ranging from 1 to 19 pages.[52] We find out in the first section that the cave, in Western

Massachusetts, had been discovered in 1875 by a 14-year-old boy named Eldon French, that it had been owned, until recently, by someone named Julie Harris, but that its new owners had posted no trespassing signs. Much of Coolidge's narrative is taken up with trying to find out if nearby residents know the new owners: "Kids on roof fenced-in with chairs & loud Rock&Roll Stereo that B says later remind her of some Manson scene, 'the way that girl kept talking about shotguns'" (C, 1:1). Failing to find anything out, they seek an alternative, less public route to its mouth: "Somehow it appears that I go first (with light), Celia next (no light), Ed next with unweildy (sic) fluorescent tube light for movies (& additional flashlight), Susan next (no light), Bernadette decides to stay out" (C, 1:2).[53]

While the primary source, the bedrock, of the collaboration to follow is the text of Coolidge's narrative, as each successive addition recycles vocabulary (and sometimes adds new terms) the manuscript descends into a linguistic netherworld of meta-descriptive abstraction. Terms that once designated physical surfaces or collective experiences now shift fluidly and playfully among several referential contexts.[54] The circling back on Coolidge's initial account begins immediately in Mayer's first response, "Modular?," which seeks out the fault lines in Coolidge's description:

> only information is transportable, but not precious or, a work that cannot be moved, as, as, / precise information that say many fields / one two three environment defines what is sculptural: wds, (the cave) were all over the paper, it is not necessary to say what they were it is not a game to figure out which they were, they were composed of letters from a to z, they all apex they all appear in _____'s Dictionary, but not in the order in which they appear on my (the opposing) page, for ex., now i'm going to tell you exactly what happened (C, 2:1)

Taking on a kind of literalist skepticism, Mayer refuses to match Coolidge's iterable, redeployable words with the non-repeatable, non-transportable cave that is their ostensible ground. At the same time Mayer seems to notice a (similarly destabilizing) *parallel* between words and caves: if "environment defines what is sculptural," perhaps it is possible to treat words as singular, sculptural objects that would resist definition, allowing "wds" to proliferate like caves "all over the paper," insisting on their abyssal singularity and resistance to definition. Mayer also remarks that a lot of experience has simply been left out of Coolidge's narrative: "they're ready to describe them they leave some things out walking down the woods is what you notice some things get pointed out, eyes tuned to dream all over the dream space extends forever theres no end to it" (C, 2:2). Picking up, perhaps, on Coolidge's emphasis of the bodily aspect of spelunking, Mayer reverses the genders, and now recodes this activity in terms of women's bodies: "Blouses without shirts, tied / I mean blouses for breasts & breasts in blouses, some pulled tight so / you could see the shape of the bodies of thought of the women who own them, / who invest them & plan to wear them & wore them, see-through / & tied in back / Black / Yes breasts You dont write around the words you dont really write around / them, Period" (C, 2:1).

In his response, "Karstarts,"[55] Coolidge first returns to Mayer's questions about the body: "Clear it with your ass to describe them. Leave a few more turns things out. You can never see more than you're ready to describe" (C, 3:10). In spelunking, the ass becomes a sensory appendage, replacing the hand, and alternating with the head—so that we pass over something on our ass, we "clear it." In fact, the ass seems to usurp the head's function, since we seem to need the ass's approval for a description. At the same time, the passage implies that the ass itself actually creates a description of the caves' surface by passing over, or clearing it.

> Ass space turns to wood. Slide the cave down a corridor. Knox Gelatin forever there's no end to it. We'll call it the water worm. Woods accommodate movement. Water laps an endless depict. Some things get pointed out then turn ahead at any one point. 20 feet of shoes. Movement is endless direction. Then it turns a corner. The trouble with style is an endless surround. The trouble with style is you can feel it with your ass. Never more than at this point of a discussion. Come out wherever you are. Paris pacific in concert as concept a continuous right turn. Mine. (C, 3:10)

Elsewhere in "Karstarts" Coolidge also illustrates how, as Mayer had said, "Clark eats away at the pronoun I" (C, 2:2). This happens when Coolidge substitutes Julie Harris and Wittgenstein (mentioned in Mayer's last round) as protagonists that replace the two poets and the range of pronouns that might reference them, so that suddenly we are remarking Julie Harris's and later Wittgenstein's breasts, rather than those in the blouses Mayer had mentioned. But "Karstarts" (like Mayer's "Modular?") also turns the cave and its description into protagonists—so that one might find "Words trespassing on the page" (C, 3:1). These anthropomorphized words struggle against containment by definition: "A photograph's silent as a definition's closed" (C, 3:1).[56] "The opposing viewpoint," for instance, "remains in the Environment Dictionary" (C, 3:5). Similarly, the poem spatializes the dictionary: "A closed drive down through definitions. Turn right in the dictionary a little ways" (C, 3:1). Intentionally conflating the struggle to elude property owners in their roundabout trip to the cave mouth with their attempts to liberate words, Coolidge writes: "We say OK thanks, we can go around back of where words end" (C, 3:4). If words, then, are new protagonists, the page is their site or context: "A photograph's silent as a definition's closed. Last there last year there. What are you invited to do. Big new white page closed to public registers" (C, 3:1).

This progressive dialog between Mayer and Coolidge generates two opposite trajectories: first, it allows one to trace the kinds of linguistic "abstraction" for which both poets are well known back to a variety of references or grounds that they usually do not include;[57] second, the layers of increasingly transformed quotations move further and further from the literal cave toward a kind of pressurized consideration of the descriptive vocabulary with which they had first thought to represent it.[58] In a sentence strung together by a series of "nows" that indicate different temporalities inside (from the distant geologic to the immediate, second-to-second present), Mayer adds a final twist to this figure of descriptive language as the failed protagonist of *The Cave:*

> Now I am having oceans fill the frame, now 4 people moving dumbly
> is a complete account of the imagined world, now obvious multiplications disapprove of the expressions of ordinary language, now
> imponderables, chalks, completed roofs all perform their office, now
> cracks in our heads conflict with the picture of our ordinary way of
> speaking (C, 4:4).

It has been Mayer's and Coolidge's self-assigned task to produce these "multiplications," the conceptual folds that would "disapprove of the expressions of ordinary language," so that the lexicon of the field explorer encountering a rare geological phenomenon emerges as the *site* of the poem.[59] As Coolidge writes: "like caves words leave a hollow in our past" (C, 11:1). But the question here is not only temporality, but also what Coolidge calls "that cleavable arrangement in the mind" (ibid.), the odd and infinitely rearrangable substance that language seems to take on in the present.

And it is this that allows Coolidge to characterize *The Cave,* in his last section, as a "book made full in faulting more than statement" (ibid.). Building off geological description only to "fault" it geologically, *The Cave,* like Coolidge and Mayer's work more generally, problematizes the kinds of immediate identification between place and language that had come to be associated, by the late 1960s and early 1970s, with the "poetics of place," a poetics that, from the early example of Charles Olson, and then subsequently in the various ethnopoetic movements—from Gary Snyder to Jerome Rothenberg—had mobilized the authority of science—archaeology, geology, botany, zoology—to position poets as authorized explicators of literal places. Unhinged, then, from a consistent spatial "ground" (a New York, a Gloucester, or a Paterson that would seem to contexualize their inquiries), Coolidge and Mayer's entrance into, and transformation of, the discourse of place in poetry coincides not merely with the rise of site-based works by Postminimal artists, but also, more generally, with the so-called linguistic turn in the humanities, in which science and philosophy were rearticulated not as privileged modes of establishing truth, but as written discourses on par with others. Having lived in this climate for nearly 40 years, many critics are justifiably growing tired of art or literature's often easy claim to undermine the authority of parallel discourses. Though Coolidge and Mayer come to related concerns quite early, it would be inaccurate to understand their work simply as positioned against the authority of science. Rather, their own "linguistic turn" might better be characterized as a kind of literalist framework that allows them to treat found vocabularies, especially those of science, as strangely physical things, and thereby, through their sequences of book-based experiments, to invent a series of deformed hybrid languages that produce their destabilizing and often humorous effects not just at, but almost literally in, the margins of epistemological writing.

WORKS CITED

Alberro, Alexander and Blake Stimson, eds. *Conceptual Art: A Critical Anthology.* Cambridge, MIT UP, 1999.

Andrews, Bruce. *Paradise and Method: Poetics and Praxis.* Evanston: Northwestern UP, 1996.

Beardsley, John. *Probing the Earth: Contemporary Land Projects*. Washington: Smithsonian, 1977.

Bernstein, Charles. *Contents Dream*. Los Angeles: Sun and Moon, 1986.

Campbell, Bruce. "Clark Coolidge." *Dictionary of Literary Biography*, ed. Joseph Conte, Vol. 193. Detroit: Gayle Research, 1996.

Creeley, Robert. *A Quick Graph: Collected Notes and Essays*. San Francisco: Four Seasons, 1970.

Coolidge, Clark. "Arrangement." In *Talking Poetics from Naropa Institute,* vol. 1. eds. Anne Waldman and Marilyn Webb. Boulder: Shambhala, 1979.

—. "Clark Coolidge." In "Memoirs" section of *The Angel Hair Anthology*, eds. Anne Waldman and Lewis Warsh. New York: Granary, 2001.

—. "From Notebooks (1976-1982)." *Code of Signals: Recent Writing in Poetics,* ed. Michael Palmer. Berkeley: North Atlantic Books, 1983.

—. *Flag Flutter & U.S. Electric*. New York: Lines, 1966.

—. *Space*. New York: Harper & Row, 1970.

—. *Smithsonian Depositions and Subject to a Film*. New York: Vehicle, 1980.

—. *Research*. Berkeley: Tuumba, 1982.

—. *The Crystal Text*. Great Barrington, MA: The Figures, 1986.

Doherty, Tyler. "Clark Coolidge in Conversation with Tyler Doherty." *Jacket* 22 (on line) May 2003.

Dworkin, Craig. "Fugitive Signs." *October* 95 (Winter 2001).

Foster, Hal. "The Crux of Minimalism." In *Individuals: a Selected History of Contemporary Art, 1945-1986*. New York: Abbeville, 1986.

Golston, Michael. "At Clark Coolidge: Allegory and the Early Works." *American Literary History*, 2001 (13): 295-316.

Gordon, Nada. *Form's Life: An Exploration of the Works of Bernadette Mayer*. MA Thesis: San Francisco State University, 1986.

Judd, Donald. *Complete Writings, 1959-1975*. Halifax: Nova Scotia College of Art and Design, 1975.

Krauss, Rosalind. *Passages in Modern Sculpture*. Cambridge: MIT UP, 1977.

Kwon. Miwon. *One Place After Another: Site-Specific Art and Locational Identity*. Cambridge: MIT UP, 2002.

Levine, Les. "The Disposable Transient Environment." *0-9* 5 (1969): 41.

Linker, Kate. *Vito Acconci*. New York: Rizzoli, 1994.

Lippard, Lucy. *Six Years: The Dematerialization of the Art Object from 1966 to 1972: a Cross-Reference Book of Information on Some Esthetic Boundaries*. New York: Praeger, 1973.

Mayer, Bernadette. *Memory*. Plainfield, VT: North Atlantic Books, 1975.

—. *Studying Hunger*. Berkeley/New York: Big Sky/Adventures in Poetry, 1975.

—. "From: A Lecture at Naropa." In *Disembodied Poetics: Annals of the Jack Kerouac School,* eds. Anne Waldman and Andrew Schelling. Albuquerque: University of New Mexico Press, 1994.

Mayer, Bernadette and Clark Coolidge. *The Cave,* unpublished collaboration, 1972-1978.

Mayer, Bernadette and Dale Worsley. *The Art of Science Writing.* New York: Teachers & Writers Collaborative, 1989.

Moure, Gloria, ed. *Vito Acconci.* Barcelona: Ediciones Polígraga, 2001.

Olson, Charles. *The Maximus Poems,* ed. George F. Butterick. Berkeley: University of California Press, 1983.

Shaw, Lytle. "The Labor of Repetition: Silliman's 'Quips' and Politics of Intertextuality." In *Ron Silliman and the Alphabet (Quarry West* 34), 1998.

Silliman, Ron. *The New Sentence.* New York: Roof, 1987.

Smithson, Robert. *Robert Smithson: The Collected Writings*, ed. Jack Flam. Berkeley: University of California Press, 1996.

Vickery, Ann. Leaving Lines of Gender: A Feminist Genealogy of Language Writing. Hanover: Wesleyan University Press, 2000.

Anne Waldman:
Standing Corporeally in One's Time

Ab Ioue principium Musae; Iouis omnia plena;
ille colit terras, illi mea carmina curae.
— Virgil, *Eclogue* 3

Muses, my song begins in praise of Jove.
He makes all flourish; my song is in his care.
— David Ferry, translation, Virgil's *Eclogues*

All is full of Jove.
— Waldman, from Virgil, *Eclogue* 3.

Ernst Bloch wrote about modernity, "one has one's time according to where one stands corporeally" (qtd. in Parkins 79).[1] This is a materialist position about standing in the now. Waldman extends this "now," as a global citizen in the name of possibility. She generates hope for a "new time" in glimmers, in her artwork, her manifesto-like performances: "an antithesis to bald commercialism, selfishness, spiritual vacuity, political advantage, double-dealing, lying, dishonesty" and so on—as she says in her mini-essay about the Beats in *Iovis* II (143). In this she has consciously assumed the "King of the May" mantle from Allen Ginsberg. Waldman generates event, conscience and a sense of possibility by her presence.

Anne Waldman's work in poetry exists at the intersection of activist passion, gender critique and wariness, and long poem ambitions. She is at root inspired by an Olsonic ambition to speak the whole social fabric as an incantatory, analytic cantor in shamanic voice. She is someone who can inhabit her own culture and play among a multiple of global sites with Blakean transformative lust. She calls us to account whenever she takes the witness stand: "Will some future generation look upon the ravages of the planet and the perpetuation of suffering by the powerful over the weak as a Second Holocaust? And see that no one attempted to stop the madness?" ("Notes for a Public Forum" 133).[2] Thus she stands corporeally in her time, in Ernst Bloch's phrase. Many of her poetic works present illuminating political outrage about the continuing crisis of failed social justice across the world. She flays power with words, ignoring or disdaining voices that say such gestures are impossible. To Waldman one could apply the comment Charles Olson made about Pound: "[Pound] would be the first to stake his work as social in consequence. He is no poet to separate his poetry from society."[3] Waldman tells us repeatedly and vividly that although we live in a modernity inflected by global oppressions, we nonetheless have the potential for global transformation.

Part of Waldman's political citizenship involves a specific kind of gender outcry and analysis. We can discuss this once we acknowledge that writing is not ever a gender-neutral site. Waldman tries to place herself corporeally into gender materials and relationships and, in her long poem (among other works), she investigates the damage and attraction of the gender sites we know. To the avant-garde, many feminisms have been inadequately mobile, uninterested in merriness, multiplicity of means, and chiaroscuro, too wedded to a monochromatic representation of the world of gender, too clear about univocal critiques and desires for healing or wholeness, too willing to buy a piece of power, or to engage in mono-dimensional naming rather than creating fissure and palimpsests.[4] On the other hand, since there are socio-political griefs in the world that must be addressed, to some feminists, the texture-oriented and performative avant-gardes have been inadequately materialist in their understandings of these griefs and urgencies. Could a feminist poetics of innovation make some dynamic syntheses of the politics *and* aesthetics surrounding gender questions? Some women contemporaries have confronted this seam between politics and the aesthetic with their long poems.[5] *Iovis* is Anne Waldman's intervention into this debate, a poetic analysis concerning patriarchy, subservience, psychic and spiritual struggle.[6] The form this takes in *Iovis* I is an investigation of maleness as an idea and set of subjectivities in culture, politics, psychology and religion.

To make this investigation means experimenting with the means of investigating. Who speaks? how will "data" be accumulated? What does judgment portend? What happens when love and criticism collide? What subjectivity and what text can a speaker create? What questions are there that necessitate this work? There have been several theoretical discussions of a female subjectivity adequate to rewrite culture; these in themselves offer enough claims and cross-claims to attract and trouble any female writer, and one could well find evidence of each and all ("both-both") in Waldman's *Iovis* (*Iovis* I, 2) One may call upon the new female feminist subject (in Rosi Braidotti's terms) or try to negotiate the wilds of a new heterogeneity (as does Luce Irigaray)—in the name of really achieving two sexes in dialogue, not just one. A person might find the idea of "writing the body" put forth by Hélène Cixous particularly liberating for women whose "bodies" have been so trashed or iconized in ideology as to be unrecognizable, and whose corporeal/intellectual bearing needs to be reseen as Waldman might, as "a construct of multiple meanings, like a multifaceted jewel. . . ."(*Fast Speaking Woman* 134). One may even continue to find that Jungian ahistorical frameworks have explanatory power, for those terms may function as compelling metaphors and as mythically-connected names for one's various subject positions, such as hag or puer. Waldman is frank about her allegiance to Jungian archetypes, noting certain benchmarks, for instance, her "'Puer' dreams. This possible, too, as she ages, having shed seductive submissive ingenue" (*Iovis* I, 177).

We have all lived in an era of the newly elaborated notion of the "feminine." In post-structuralist and post-modern thought, the feminine is defined as free-floating resistance, as excess, the outside, the beyond, the a-historical, non-symbolic otherness. This concept of the feminine is, in theory, unattached to gendered bodies—the male feminine is particularly powerful, as in Roland Barthes or Algernon Swinburne. There is also queered subjectivity that takes binarist gender (and its ideas) as moot, finished, untenable and untrue, and tries to imagine it is living in a world that has transcended these elements. To construct her speaking subjectivity, Waldman seems to have drawn, *ad lib* and variously, on a mix of those propositions from feminist theorizing, but she has also declared, with this poem, the space of the female masculine, a performative incorporative masculinity inside a female body. However, unlike the "female masculinity" studied by Judith Halberstam, with its emphasis on butch and drag king behaviors or performances, Waldman always insists on feminine panache. Halberstam indicates that her taxonomy is incomplete: "the more we identify the various forms of female masculinity, the more they multiply" (Halberstam 46); Waldman is certainly one of the exemplars of female masculinity. Indeed, Waldman might be closest in her ferocity, performativity, and aggressions to the picture Michael Davidson draws of Sylvia Plath in *Guys Like Us*, with those "self-conscious assaults on gender binarism" (Davidson 160) by someone who will "interrogate masculine aspirations from within a speaker who embodies many of those aspirations" (Davidson 170).

Waldman, like Alice Notley and other women loosely in the avant-garde and not in the women's poetry movement (as it centered its canon of interests in the mid-70s through mid-late-80s), was very resistant to any victimization theorizing and against any sense that women have little or no agency. For them, early feminist critiques had a hard time not sounding like self-pity. This as if in a belated replay of Woolf's Lily Briscoe's angry, poignant remarks, as if they were constantly saying "women can't write; women can't assert." Feminist thinking seemed, to these listeners, like an affirmation of disabilities, when it was, instead, trying to encounter and name the gender assumptions, the taboos buried in culture and in internalized/externalized values that blocked female striving. Indeed, as Ann Snitow and I argued in our introduction to *The Feminist Memoir Project*, any "victim status" thinking was viewed, in early second-wave feminism, as a naming of a thankfully temporary female condition, a condition soon to be rendered obsolete by the intensities and gains of feminist politics. Such terms were not meant to offer frozen and undialectical analysis (20). But despite having some common concerns, the two poetic worlds in which women were active did not meet or bond.

For at the same time, another aspect of early feminism was stirring affirmation of female power and transcendence. Waldman's *Fast Talking Woman* (1974) was a performance of assertive female power contemporaneous with semi-canonical works like Ntzoke Shange's performance piece *for colored girls who have considered suicide/ when the rainbow is enuf* (1975) and works taken as belonging to a lesbian-separatist world, such as Judy Grahn's *A Woman is Talking to Death* (1973). It is also true that in feminism's effort to bring women up to scrutiny, men and maleness were sometimes treated as a backboard, as hypostasized, and even distasteful, objects, not as mobile, in-process subjectivities, albeit ones with certain guarantees—or at least chits—of social power. Certainly *Iovis* responds transformatively to this issue. Thus Waldman may have been notably ambivalent to the women's poetry movement in certain of its manifestations, yet she also drew, *sub rosa*, on its feminist intellectual and cultural energies to confirm and extend her own evident energy.

Such writers as Waldman, active in Doing and Making (scenes, magazines, presses, work) felt they had disproved, by their own agency and bohemian élan, some of the claims made in other poetic circles of female powerlessness to be cured by allegiance to all-women communities. So these writers had a strong resistance to, and even some contempt for feminism as a movement, something visible in Notley's *Mysteries of Small*

Houses, for example, in which small-mindedness is displayed on both sides in the debate about "men." The Women of St. Marks thought their own life histories and productivity rendered irrelevant or moot the questions of access, representation, canonicity, and literary history that feminists raised. And this resistance continued despite the capacity of both sets of cultural workers to commit, or to construct, polemical "women's" poems. Waldman's recent poem "Abortion" (*Kill or Cure* 113), a simple poem of political outrage, uses the jeremiad genre to turn any accusation of a crime by women outward to speak of crimes (rape, patriarchal control) committed against women. In style, tone, and purpose, as an instrumental intervention, this poem could have appeared in *This Bridge Called My Back*. And this resistance continued despite the capacity of both sets of cultural workers to construct major critiques of gender and the social order, on the scale, for example, of Alice Notley's major mythopoetic intervention, *The Descent of Alette*, a magisterial feminist work, making a critique of patriarchy and tyranny and of the internalized consciousness and external society that supports these forms of social control.

Waldman's position can be framed with Denise Riley's insight—one wants to see gender, talk about gender, work through gender, transfigure gender, organize thinking to consider gender—and also wants sometimes to get beyond any such category. Denise Riley says about the female situation at the end of her book *"Am I That Name?"*: "while it's impossible to thoroughly be a woman, it's also impossible never to be one" (Riley 114). It is just a step to translate Riley's formulation in this way, a way I enjoy: "while it's impossible thoroughly to be a feminist, it's also impossible never to be one." For whatever the unevenness of approaches to feminism in this period (and there were plenty), from a historical point of view all the sectors of women writing were inflected with, touched by that particular "angel of history" (this, of course, Walter Benjamin), and touched with all due ambivalence and wariness, by its contradictory guises of positive assertion and negative skepticism and resistance. All female poets of the avant-garde (and always some male poets, too) had to—were compelled to—come to terms with feminist cultural and political challenges. All women writers, whether they did this consciously, or willingly, or not, were saturated with feminist questions, feminist demands, its cultural critique and its ferocity. The evidence is in their work and in the growing importance of feminist reception or gender analyses to the careers of women experimental writers—even if the writers themselves had ambivalent or resistant relationships to feminism, or to the women's poetry movement (which does not, and should not be the only container of feminist thought).[7]

In this, I would agree with the strategic formulation proposed by Steve Evans: it is vital to keep in play feminism and avant-gardism together in order to avoid the sharply articulated culs de sac he lucidly details: an avant-garde poetry without a sense of gender, a theoretical post structuralism without any sense of contemporary poetry and its practices, and a feminist institutionalizing of a single poetics. This essay, too, attempts to avoid "an avant-garde without women, a poetics without poetry, and a poetry for which entire registers of experience, innovation, and reflexivity are taboo" (Evans, ii).

For wherever one began in relation to writing, to call for, to notice, to comment upon the productive and compromised presence of women artists and writers, indeed, to be one of those writers, has entailed a negotiation (sooner or later) with the feminism of cultural critique, whether this critique features equality or difference (the great dialectic of feminist thinking) or tacks strategically between these. For it was feminist cultural criticism that articulated and foregrounded the roles that gender plays in culture—in the production, dissemination, reception and continuance of artists and texts. And feminist analysis really wanted—still wants—to change culture fundamentally. Thus while women's writing is not particularly self-similar at the point of production, there may be strategies and motifs related to the female position in culture that can be found in it. And women's writing becomes rather similar at the point of reception, so to speak—because (without intentional, subtle and concerted feminist reception) it is similarly treated by "the patriarchal government of poetry," to cite Clayton Eshleman's phrase (*Companion Spider*). It is for these reasons that the care and maintenance of feminist—socially located—reception has been my concern, and not the demand that people from certain groups write a certain way, nor that they attend only to certain materials or themes or modes of representation, nor the argument that certain themes and stances are *essentially* (rather than situationally) expressive of their social location.

But feminist critique is not simply about gender: it is also a challenge to the split between thought and feeling; a critique of values of profitability and wealth as social goods when in fact they create inequality, exploitation and immiseration; it is a rejection of all the forces that create the disenfranchised. The task of feminist critique is the pluri-decentering of binarism and hierarchy. It is a critique of power in the names of social justice and gender justice. The task involves standing corporeally within gender structures and other structures of oppression to break down these enormous pillars of patriarchal culture so that something new can be built as one is leveraging critique. So the feminism of critique is based on inquiry, resistance, disobedience, rage, and on placing yourself as if in utopian new time. It is in this enlarged sense that Waldman speaks in *Iovis*, a poem of feminist investigation and critique from "an oppositional poetics." (*Iovis* I, 298) *Iovis* is "a long piece which 'took on' male energy in all of its manifestations"—in the lives of the men around her, and in herself as bearer and critic of male energy (Christopher 1).

What is "a woman" but a person mainly gendered female whose subjectivities and masks may be far from female—may be boy, male lesbian, female masculine. A woman is a person human and parallel to man; a person some of whose experiences are different from a man's; a person socialized to the pleasures and temptations of dress-up femininity; a person intrigued by the mythic claim to otherness in the (so called) "feminine" space of language. Thus any woman in *Iovis* may be called polygynous— she has "married" many women, many meanings of woman and women, many meanings of man and men in a rapturous textual space. She is also investigative—like a detective—she wants to find out about power, and thus again she must examine men and maleness. She wants to tell her truth. Waldman's poetics of gender is put forth in "FEMINAFESTO" from *Kill or Cure*. She says: "I'd like here to declare an enlightened poetics, an androgynous poetics, a poetics defined by your primal energy . . . a transsexual literature, a hermaphrodite literature, a transvestite literature, and finally a poetics of transformation beyond gender. That just sings its wisdom" (145). It is clear that Waldman has some proto-queer ideas about how one's subjectivity is performative, how (to a certain degree), subjectivity does not necessarily go with body. The poem is like Blake's demonic printing presses coining new gender-money. Male—female—hermetic bisexual hermaphrodite or androgynous twins seems to be the plan for *Iovis* I, II and the projected III.

There are several versions of female subjectivity and social position in much feminist or proto-feminist thinking about women in this period, and the fact that these positions are in contradiction does not make them any less important, influential, powerful, or palpably generative. The positions are female equality, female difference, and [female] queerness. For instance, the second book of *Iovis* (*Iovis* II, 142-146) contains an important 1994 epistolary essay about the place of women among the Beats, an essay that opens the question of female difference in historical power and position. At one and the same time, the essay defends the Beats for their achievements and acknowledges what Waldman names their "sexism" and "racism" and their "fear of women's power." In the course of this letter, Waldman discusses the very narrow options for women in the 1950s if you were at all "strange," artistic or bohemian: madness and shock treatments, abortion and physical terror of illegality and, if you were really unlucky, infertility or even death, and/or suicide attempts from sheer nihilistic pain of non-conformity. (Sylvia Plath also discusses some of this in another register in her novel *The Bell Jar*.) This section acknowledges a specificity of female cultural history (that is, female difference at a certain time and place), and puts in evidence an interview with Joanne Kyger, that even somewhat undercuts her Beat-analysis, and indeed, puts in her headnote her own resistance to what she said: "sleepless, she rises once again to be an apologist for the macho Beat Literary Movement," (*Iovis* II, 134), suggesting a shift in her own upbeat attitudes between 1994 and 1996/7). In the important essay called "'I is Another': Dissipative Structures," Waldman speaks for "feminine energy." This seems to be a position for female equality as in "I am, as a woman, adequate, capable, inspired, in readiness, as good as anyone" (*Kill or Cure* 212).

This position is verified by Waldman's inclusion in this essay of her poem claiming her birth as a performative poet from the Zeusian head of Charles Olson during the 1965 Berkeley Poetry Conference (*Kill or Cure* 209). Waldman was present at the Conference in which the Olsonic genre of performance, crossing essay, poem, chant, and declaration was particularly rich and provocative/provoking. *Iovis* is a substitute Maximus, and Waldman deploys herself in ways like Olson and in ways like a critique of Olson as a figure. In part from Olson and others, the poem deploys tactics of heterogeneity of diction and allusion, and an enhanced textuality as the page of poetry holds more than usual—more space, marks, non-letters, pictures, gestures, diagrams. There is a heterogeneity of dissemination practices, too, that have one point of origin in Olson, with a strong emphasis on performance and poetic drama and a renovation of sound and the ear as means of poetic fabrication. The Olsonic impulse also enters with the "realism" of this poem in its documentary fervor.

However, "Feminafesto" also wants to claim female difference in ways that absolutely parallel claims from the center of the women's poetry movement. Mythic allusions, ancient wisdom's special functions for female are accepted as such, taken as compelling and applicable contemporary information—as the end of this essay in "Gaia worship" (*Kill or Cure* 212-13). And the essay also maintains a different female genealogy of poets, tracing her own poetic lineage to Sappho's singing school and its basis in ritual (*Kill or Cure* 194-198). Waldman's wobbling contradictions between female equality claims and female difference claims are very situational, not at all self-consistent. They are even opportunistic. One seizes the means that are to hand; "skillful means" (a Waldman phrase out of Buddhism) implies the analysis of situation and applying the right "nom de guerre" to triumph. So Waldman's position shifts in thesis-antithesis between equality and difference claims—this undecidability and situated analysis is in fact characteristic of much feminist thinking. It is this that enables the great power grab made by Waldman in *Iovis*: "Jove or Zeus or any procreative male deity is presumably filling up the phenomenal world with his sperm. He rules through possession, rape, and through the skillful means of the shape-shifter as well. From the psychological point of view (as a 'daughter'), I need to call him out, reveal him, challenge him, steal his secrets" (*Kill or Cure* 198).

Given that *Iovis* I opens—opens! with a citation from the famous so-called "Christological" passage from Second Isaiah: 52-53 about the man of sorrows, the claim Waldman immediately makes concerns female messianism (5), something one also sees in the great Victorian novel in verse by Barrett Browning, *Aurora Leigh*. The proposition is—when you want world-historical and ethical transformation, a woman shall lead them. This boldness does not stop, nor does the syncretic religious impulse falter; just a few pages later, the speaker imagines herself inseminated by Jove (*Iovis* I, 7). A world-cultural arc is evoked; Hindu and Buddhist tropes and mythologies will soon be engaged. This is a mythic-synthetic imagination at work, incorporative and "Golden Bough"-ish—but trying to re-torque mythology to discuss gender transformation. Thus one element of this work is its revisionary mythopoetic quality—an element significant to works of the women's poetry movement (like Rich's "Diving into the Wreck"), but also worked through in modernist mythic imaginations. In H.D.'s *Trilogy*, Christian mother Mary becomes a fertility goddess; in *Helen in Egypt*, H.D. examines the roots of bellicose violence as a repression of the passionate attraction to the mother, feelings of matri-sexual import.[8] Waldman particularizes these forces contributing to female power and sexuality with letters and interviews to her specific, local family—her father, her childhood (*Iovis* I, 10).

In the Allen Ginsberg ("Howl") and Allen Grossman (*Summa Lyrica*) narratives of poetic possibility, the Oedipal fantasy of being in the bed of the mother recurs for the male poet. This tenderness and hotness around incestuous fantasies is also visible in some work of Robert Creeley. One may have to confront a parallel? similar? or different? psycho-biography in Waldman. She claims the desire for the father, the freshness of the oedipal girl, the play with and through incests with a brother. Waldman makes the Jungian claim of archetypal repetition and offers a marital vow to these brothers and father "I honor & obey these first men in my life . . ." (*Iovis* I, 14), and she immediately writes a primary sex act that inseminates her with the ambition to accomplish this poem "It feels like the great sperm whale entered me" (*Iovis* I, 20).

However, insemination as one male act is not half of the "it" that will be this poem. The poem proposes allegorized interactions with men that attempts to diagnose them by revealing their potency—even through their weakness and fallibility, their losses, their self-deceptions, their assumptions. Waldman constructs the poem as a force field for gender, and what one quickly finds is that gender involves everything there is—school, children's games, war, Rocky Flats, random sex, old poems by Pound and Williams (or remakes of those hits), concepts like beauty, goodness, justice, the destruction of forests for "Happy Meal boxes" (*Iovis* I, 274). As Myra Jehlen notably argued, "gender has emerged as a problem [an issue] that is always implicit in any literary work," implicit in every cultural act (265). We pass to needy, whining men; we pass to male civilization giving benefits to men in great productive washes of power, and civilization hurting men, sacrificing them constantly. The speaker negotiates this influx and wash of contradictory material and findings constantly through the poem. This is her "both-both" poetics at work. Narratively, she, in her own oedipal desire for the father, and/or the power of the father and/or the phallus of the male, also, at the same time, negotiates the oedipal urgency of her son ("You are my wife Mommy you are the dream of me," *Iovis* I, 25). Simultaneity of conflicting transformations are both method, and technique. The poem seems to be the collection of materials put, in each section, into a rhetorical swirl calling for metamorphosis.

Section XIII of *Iovis I* offers the term Aetiological (etiology): a medical study of the causes, origins, reasons. Etymologically speaking, it is an allotting of responsibility. This is the key word for the diagnostic element of Waldman's epic. She will study causes and rationales of patriarchy especially in the cultural field, but also in the political, military, spiritual;

she will assign responsibility; she will analyze and implicate—and impre-
cate! There are multiple "plots"—but one plot is weaning herself from
Jove. She rehearses her own history, saying that she "stuck by her patri-
archal male companions" and was their "trusted confidante," but, alas,
the power she got was an illusion, and she must thus confront the Jovian
patriarchal center—no individual man can help you negotiate patriarchy
(*Iovis* I, 143). This is a pretty stark and bold position, one that makes a
feminist separation of blessed or helpful individuals from any patriarchal
system as a cultural artifact. The individuals are men (and sometimes
women) who never (or rarely) think they participate in the powers and
privileges of this system. There is a resemblance, in a different poetic
register, between this finding and Alice Notley's structuring of *The Descent
of Alette* around two key actions: the mid-book healing of the headless
Mother (by the affirmation of female intelligent compassion and by the
application of male blood given by a dead man) and, the climatic action in
Notley's book, the killing of the patriarchal Tyrant, who oppresses male
and female both.

In *Iovis*, there is an ongoing discussion of several contemporary men,
among them Robert Creeley and John Cage. Waldman asks what possibili-
ties they model, and whether (using John Waldman, her own father, here),
a woman in the "daughter" position finds it is plausible, easy, reasonable,
or forbidden to "inherit" from these men. The question of inheritance is
offered in its most condensed form in a play with French gender (*Iovis* I,
193): "(*père et son fille*) / sa *fille*." Waldman has an acute and observant sense
of genealogy, and filiations. This bearing is not innocent: she will write
herself into history as the daughtered son, or the sonned-daughter of a
great male figure. There are different Waldman attitudes in this work: she
is motivated to play the game of patriarchy accurately and with finesse,
but she also diagnosis its ills with resistance and suspicion. Her brilliant
performance piece in homage to John Cage, the penultimate canto in *Iovis*
I, memorializes an artist who is gentle, active, inventive, and productive,
allowing her to affirm androgyny because of his (*Iovis* I, 309). In general,
in this poem-long diagnosis, "She rides through the poem on / villains,
brothers, saints, deities / they speed her on" (*Iovis* I, 333). The astonishing
Kristen Prevallet letter in *Iovis* II (36-37) discusses Creeley, female writers,
and the beginning of female cultural consciousness, dramatically showing
the recurrence of issues and problems relating to female creativity in a
new generation. *Iovis* thus, in its own way, continually proposes the neces-
sity for feminist or gender-oriented analyses of culture.

In this letter Prevallet challenges and admires Waldman in equal measure, wondering precisely how she survived as a female writer:

> Interestingly enough, Creeley asked the class today [circa 1992] if anybody knew of anyone who was attempting to write an epic on the scale of Olson, and people mumbled this and that, and I said, but of course, A.W. and Creeley disagreed with me, and I still find it strange, not on the basis of writing/poetic skill etc., but EGO! What he meant is that your work is more personal in that you bring in letters, stories about your child, emotional instances, etc. (although admittedly, the boundaries get very shifty here—I mean Olson's persona was huge and was personal.) So I was thinking what was at stake here was not ego but gender, and I wonder how you felt about it. (*Iovis* II, 36)

She continues, noting that people do not complain about male EGO,

> Well, I am very confused about the whole thing because I am being confronted with the problem—to be forward, or to hang back—to perform or to whisper—to vanish or to shine forth. . . . And [speaking about another incident] I know this is only the beginning of similar kinds of interactions, where I speak my mind and get my hand slapped afterward, like I did something BAD, or even worse. . . . (*Iovis* II, 37)

Despite the examples of strong women writers in the generation before hers (Kathleen Fraser is also mentioned in this letter), here again a woman writer presents these recurrent questions: may a woman have EGO as an artist, who is it that allows her, what is the price of her engagements, and what are the internalized and exterior costs and even punishments that a woman writer risks. These are thoroughly feminist questions.

One way Waldman solves these cultural problems of access for women is by assuming that her subjectivity is not just female, but is also male. "Both-both," again. The subjectivity of the work *Iovis* speaks in response to Jove as shape-shifter; she makes herself Puer (boy or youth) as shape shifter or trickster figure ("Puer, picaresque adventurer," she says [*Kill or Cure* 144]). She conjures this figure, holding the mother at bay (*Iovis* I, 177). Being a puer figure leads her to the incisive command: "rise up paginal" (*Iovis* I, 187). *Rise up* meaning, appear, be prominent, increase in intensity, return to, or get erect. This "paginal," I read as a page or boy helper figure. As a pun on vaginal, as if the vagina could erect, and finally, the adjective pertaining to the pages of a book. Thus when things rise up paginal, they constitute a male vagina of the book. Which is what this book is—an active vaginal space in which sperm-words enter and inseminate. So there are (at least) two genders always on this page. Self-consciously and consistently making the claim of dual genders also at the same time confuses and transcends the issue of gender totally (which means a queered sensibility is also, sometimes, in play).

To appreciate the dual genders, we need to take seriously Waldman's playful and serious claim, made sometimes, that she disidentifies with her own gender, or certainly with its disabilities. This is both a dangerous and an entrancing, enchanting position. Her analysis is keen. Patriarchy says only itself and its men can be promiscuous, adventurous, far-ranging, seeking, piratical (that last, a Kathy Acker subject position) (*Iovis* I, 107-08). Patriarchy says females must be loyal and relatively meek. Waldman sweeps this demand for femininity and mildness away. But holding the mother at bay or "scorning the mother" is a rather problematic position, given that one is also a mother and a female (this in *Iovis* I, 177-187). "Scorn for women"—a position well-known from the first Futurist manifesto of Marinetti, is like playing with fire. Does this mean scorn for the parasitic, feminine, the enforcer of bourgeois social norms? If so, then scorn seems like an appropriate response, one often made by feminists. But if this means scorn for the whole female gender as an entity, such "scorn" is unalloyed misogyny. However, this trace of a Futurist position is not consistent in Waldman, for in the essay "Feminafesto," she speaks of the mother as model, suffering with unexpressed creativity that inspires her daughter's oeuvre.[9] Her determination to persist as a thinking, creative woman, her resistance to compromising her desires have their origin there.

As she gets older, Waldman also foregrounds the third phase of a Jungian triple goddess—the "hag" archetype. This raging witch and speaker of curse and imprecation is off the scale of binary gender, beyond the desire to please men and beyond the more timid women. Waldman finds these Jungian categories appeal to her; her revision of them lies in claiming both puer and hag. This is a typical Waldmanian "greed," as it sets her as the gatherer of multiple forces, and the sustainer of these forces in contradiction. It is clear that the struggles of gendered subjects are major struggles of loyalties and desires inside the speaking subject. Whole dramas and allegories of gender unroll inside Waldman as speaker no matter what subjectivity she assumes. That is why the genre "encyclopedic poem" is prime; it is a genre of inclusion and juxtaposition adequate to the matter at hand.

An encyclopedic poem is certainly heterogeneous in genre; and for Waldman one might easily identify ode, newspaper clipping, epistle, conversation, jeremiad, interview, documents, lyric, dream records, diatribes, arias, sestinas as among the genres included in *Iovis*. No matter how long the genre list, one can never account for all its genres.[10] Thus one point is the plethora or dynamism of her generic urges, which is a fact of many (although not all) long poems in this period. Both Smaro Kamboureli (speaking about the Canadian long poem) and Lynn Keller (for contemporary long poems by United States women) discuss the 20th century long poem in general as alluding to many genres—specific choices of materials from epic, lyric and serial poem, narrative—and thus a flexible and ambitious vehicle (Kamboureli, *On the Edge of Genre*; Keller in Parini, ed.). The encyclopedic long poem clearly functions as such a flexible genre compendium. As such a poem, *Iovis* is generically hybrid, polyphonic, intertextual, conceptual—a pooling of documents and acts of analysis and outcry.[11]

An encyclopedic poem is simply inclusive. Although encyclopedias are generally organized by the alphabet, giving a non-teleological order to things, the encyclopedic long poem insists that anything and everything could, in principle, be included in any order, so it gives the feeling that no cultural censorship has taken place—no exclusions for false norms, for standards of elegance or fitness. This aesthetic of inclusiveness is certainly Waldman's. When Waldman began *Iovis* in around 1985 or 1986, she remembers "feeling for a time I needed a long poem. . . . I often tend to get a bit too scattered, . . . so the idea of putting all of the writing into one place, under one rubric, was a relief! Anything that arose might go into that work. . . ." (*AWP Chronicle* 28, 3 [Dec 1995]: 1; "Interview with Anne Waldman," conducted by Lee Christopher). Waldman thus uses the poem to account for motion, meaning both change or flux and teleology of betterment. Unlike the analogous poems of Pound and Williams, this "poem is 4-dimensional in its performance" (Waldman, reference missing)—a way for Waldman to stand corporeally with the work, and to some degree a way for her to modify, to cut or to emphasize some of the materials in performance as a griot might. There is a sense that this poem is a multi-act opera without one singular or particular narrative, but a magical "Bollywood" production, incorporative, absorptive, dashing. This is her sense of channeling energy, but it makes of "writing" a

way-station or "go-between" to performance. This has some cost in word-
to-word attention or carefulness. A more static analogy for its form is a
"temple"—one with pluralities, polytheisms, and a sense that the sacred
is everywhere.

This inclusivity does not necessarily have a master-subjectivity orga-
nizing it, as one finds in *Paterson*, with the topos of the speaking subject
wandering among, but not totally participating in, his city. And *Paterson*,
like *Iovis*, offers a community of voices—wild, wary, hopeful, yearning,
needy, dynamic, critical, responsive voices that are not the poet's voice.
The use—part of her inclusivity—of letters and of some interview ex-
changes—are a feature of *Iovis* that tends to make subjectivity of the poet/
speaker a field site of cross-hatching vectors. It is not that the subjectivity
is decentered; it is that a zillion demands pull and tug at her, and she
attempts to satisfy all of them. While I don't want to romanticize female
difference here, this dilemma of overload takes on a particularly female
cast. Kathleen Fraser, "Tradition of Marginality" in her *Translating the
Unspeakable: Poetry and the Innovative Necessity* will sometimes note the female
relations to life-issues that lead to a sense of difference, and also refuse
to romanticize that position, resisting the separatist. The demotic form of
the encyclopedia poem is the scrapbook. And the scrapbook is a domestic,
artisinal, hobby-horse genre. It is this self-consciously "feminized" version
of the encyclopedic poem that Waldman has mastered.

Waldman uses the scrapbook-look of her page as a utopian space of
"both-both" attitudes—she can put things together in dynamic inclusiv-
ity because she will provide the syntax of connection within corporeal
passions of performance (*Iovis* I, 2). "Both-both" is a brilliant formulation,
rejecting as too binarist the notion of "both-and." The page as score for a
performance has a number of functions for Waldman. It is a place to locate
"other informations [that] weave in her" (*Iovis* I, 100)—that is, it is a hold-
ing place, a site in which you collect things because you do not want them
to get lost, forgotten, obscured. This tremendous sense of the rescue of the
lost marks particular periods in writing—here it marks women's writing,
whether the work is by Adrienne Rich or Susan Howe, and whether it
investigates lost women only, or lost aspects of history. *Iovis* is keen on this
necessity; for example, the poem collects her own principled political inter-
ventions, one of many letters of protest that enter this text, for example, "I
believe that Mr. wa Mulumba is a prisoner of conscience" (*Iovis* I, 31). The
materials tend to make faceted or nuanced our sense of "men" or "male-
hood." There are many letters included: a crackpot inventor offering his

ideas to women, not to men; and a winsome needy student waiting to be acolyte, epigone, and above all recognized (*Iovis* I, 32-33); and a poignant letter about a young boy discovering that he is gay (*Iovis* I, 54-56). Any few pages in this book run a wild tonal and informational gamut that one might simply note as Waldman's mode of "realism"—a precise use of realism in poetry (very similar to what Olson and Williams did), both trying to account for, to sound out what we are now by what has happened to a site (maleness) in historical time. The page is a dynamic instrument, a transformative forge in a Blakean sense.

Iovis is fundamentally a gigantic collage of materials located around issues for meditation. Every section cuts down through a time, takes place in a transfigured locale (sometimes a merging of geographical sites) that is essentially a meta-materialist space for meditation, and works through— or at least locates—a problem or issue: "How to change rhythms on a cellular level" (XI, p. 154, *Iovis* I) or "What did you see? he asks. What do I know?" (*Iovis* I, 241). The 'strands" of the poem "come together karmically" (*Iovis* I, 298). The advantage of collage modes—the collection dragnet—is also its weakness, an anything/everything goes mentality; the poem is an extension of "catchall notebooks" kept over many years (*AWP Chronicle* interview, 4). An encyclopedic poem always raises the possibility that there is just too much heterogeneity and fragmentation.

Some of that heterogeneity is galvanized by the sometime evocation of the manifesto genre; like "scrapbook," this is another key long-poem genre allusion. For the poem, like many specifically encyclopedic long poems (certainly like Pound's *Cantos*) has a manifesto impulse—the look of urgency on its page, the theatricality of now-time in its gestures, the sense of speed, immediacy and even crisis are admixed with rumination. A manifesto creates the sense that the "moment of social transition" is happening there on the spot; that the poem is not the representation, but the vehicle of this transformation, and that the poem as manifesto will "mark the artistic praxis that will create that new world."[12]

If the page is, as I've said, also a score, then any page stands in a position of conflict—it is a way-station on the way to something else (a performance), and it is a place where things accumulate and get pieced together in the here and now. The page in *Iovis* is a space of declarative urgency (the manifesto root), but it is never, or rarely, seen as a place of poise, of stability, of the iconic. Indeed, Alice Notley points to the documentary and autobiographical/accumulative impulse behind Waldman's work, with some skepticism—the poem, she says, is going to be "what happens next," but she nonetheless suggests that while "the form makes flaws possible" still "possibly poetry should make room for flaws, being a human form" (Notley, "Iovis" 121, 126). Waldman, inside her choices, justifies the looseness and assimilative flair of the work with a "Beat Buddhist" (and incidentally Olsonic) aesthetic enunciated (Notley "Iovis" 128-29) as an "energy pulse"—form is activity, form is energy. Form is choice on the run, is event, not stasis, or reflective choice. "Rather than have the poem be an extrapolation, a refined gist of a 'high' moment, I want it to be the experience—. . . a poem that would include everything and yet dwell in the interstices of imagination and action." (Interview with Lee Christopher, *AWP Chronicle* 28, 3 [Dec 1995], 6). The poem—a Western poem of potential, subjectivity and assertion—also tries to dramatize "the dynamic pratitya samutpada, the interconnectedness of the whole 'scene'" (*Iovis* II, 241) (This sometimes occurs in its adolescent deformation: "Mom, you are so random" as in *Iovis* II, 221.)

What interests me particularly in *Iovis* are its analogies to encyclopedic long poems by Pound and Williams.[13] In modern long poems like *Paterson* and the *Cantos*, there is a strong component of diagnosis. With their pileup of evidence, the encyclopedism gives the illusion (and it is an illusion really) that all elements of a given society and culture have been covered. This contributes to the sense of totalizing of these poems even when they have many loose ends. Further, such poems (and this is part of the pleasure) seem to adumbrate in their field and polyvalent accumulations a new society, and a new and total culture (as Pound once said). That is, the very form of the poem is a sociality and a hope for social transformation. This is quite true of Waldman's poem, although it is not clear that she allows this form to argue for final or rested; in contrast, Notley's *The Descent of Alette* is very conscious of its ending: a secular vision based on the resurrection in the flesh, of bodies emerging from the grave of the subway. In Notley's vision, too, everything is left to be done; there is no prescription for a new society. Such a society will be built by the values learned in the struggle with the Tyrant.

Waldman's speaking subject claims authority—but it is the authority of investigation—like a detective, a follower of clues, an explorer, a discoverer (and as I said above, there is often a sense that the subjectivity of the poem is on overload with the pressures and voices of all the others she allows to speak forcefully in her text). Especially Pound's subjectivity was the revealer of the hidden, occluded, structures—it is the voice of someone who has uncovered a gigantic conspiracy and does not doubt

his findings, their importance, nor his unchangeable subject position as
catalyst case-manager. This is the ambition to speak the whole social
fabric and articulate root issues or problems that can be analyzed by
means of the collage *coupure* and engaged juxtapositions the poem pro-
vides. For Pound, the issue was economic deception and degradation.
He called this usury instead of capitalism; he became fixated on Jews as
history's villains. Pound had a golden age vision with a sense of ultimate
restoration of that age with Mussolini. The *Cantos* were fundamentally
traumatized by WWI and then again by WWII. Pound offers political
and historical materials ("tales of the tribe"); an anthology boil-down—a
summa of what's really important; a declaration that the work is not
fiction (although presumably it is fictive), that there's real message, real
document in the work. This goal—that poetry should analyze, appreciate,
explore what is happening in the real world is vital to Waldman: "May it
be her ultimate sirventes, that old troubadour refrain of outrage toward
a botched civilization" (*Iovis* II, 287) sums up the Poundean motif, citing
Pound's "Hugh Selwyn Mauberley." The encyclopedic poem is evaluative
and judgmental.

In Waldman's *Iovis* scrapbook of array, as in Pound's *Cantos*, or Wil-
liams's *Paterson*, there are so many materials that the goal of judgment
may seem implausible. But it is a purpose central to the encyclopedic
long poem. Judgment may occur in a variety of ways. The paradox of
Pound's setting out the notes and glosses that constitute a lot of the poem
so that the reader can "draw his own conclusions" from the data—yet
the conclusions are predigested by Pound—is one of those "fake" So-
cratic projects that lead only to the conclusion the pedagogue proposes.
Williams's method of judgment was a tactic of field composition that he
called "rolling up," so that great chunks of material, as they crossed,
could have one key idea extrapolated from them—such as waste, or need
for "marriage"—explorations of sexuality, or a sense of wonder amid the
damage. Effective in one way, rolling up could also call for extractive and
reductive reading strategies.

Paterson is a somewhat more attractive poem because of Williams's will-
ingness to engage with criticism and doubts about the poem and the proj-
ect inside the very poem. Just like the fierce, lacerating letters from "Cress"
in *Paterson* that undermine the subjectivity of *Paterson* right where it really
hurts—in his own self-justificatory gender narrative—so in Waldman's
poem, severe self-doubt enter and inflect the project—a kind of "nekuia"
moment, as in the epic plot, of a descent to the underworld. The self-doubt

is striking: coming "to rest with her box of scraps, notes, journals, memorabilia, letters, unfinished versions, her major task continuing unsettled at her feet. She spreads the documents about her, and bows her head. She feels a burden to sustain the plan. The society is crumbling around her. She can barely withstand the daily news" (*Iovis* I, 279). One section later, she feels marginalized within her own community (*Iovis* I, 286). She incorporates the letter of a provocative, empathetic reader who calls attention to the "transport" of the writing, the sense of riding the words, the issue that language is often used instrumentally.[14] This letter is, unlike the Cress letter, a mainly appreciative note on her mediumship ("I see you as this kind of poet, who lets energy flow through her, while you do your best to manifest the patterned energies you sense" *Iovis* I, 297), but it pulls at her, as do all the letters—political, cracking up, sympathetic.

The ethnographic urge to take the measure of a specific culture is one of Williams's "contributions" to Waldman's poem. Indeed, Waldman's themes of the waste of possibility and the pollution of democracy by profiteering, the creation of waste from abundance, contemporary ecological destruction are close to *Paterson*; so too her use of inserted letters to offer a sense of a community sounding, and filiations to other people. The writer of *Paterson* emphatically proposes a male gendered and sexed subject position for the speaker of the poem. (Pound does too, but Williams is more overt because less universalizing.) But of course neither the *Cantos* nor *Paterson* revises maleness and its cultural authority. The male subjectivity of these poems and of Olson's is counterpoised—consciously and with lacerating fervor—by Waldman's parallel poem positing a female/androgynous subjectivity speaking the poem *Iovis*. Waldman has stood corporeally against (and for) these magisterial works of modernism—continuing them and criticizing them in one ambitious gesture.

WORKS CITED

Bloch, Ernst. "Nonsynchronism and the Obligation to Its Dialectics (1932)," *New German Critique* 11 (1977). 22-38.

Braidotti, Rosi. *Nomadic Subjects: Embodiment and Sexual Difference in Contemporary Feminist Theory*. New York: Columbia University Press, 1994.

Cixous, Hélène. "The Laugh of the Medusa," trans. Keith Cohen and Paula Cohen. *New French Feminisms*, in Elaine Marks and Isabelle de Courtivron, eds. Amherst: University of Massachusetts Press, 1980: 245-264.

Davidson, Michael. *Guys Like Us: Citing Masculinity in Cold War Poetics*. Chicago: University of Chicago Press, 2004.

Dienstfrey, Paricia and Brenda Hillman, eds., *The Grand Permission: New Writings on Poetics and Motherhood*. Middletown, CT: Wesleyan University Press, 2003.

DuPlessis, Rachel Blau. *H.D.: The Career of that Struggle*. Bloomington: University of Indiana Press, 1986.

—. *The Pink Guitar: Writing as Feminist Practice* (1990). Tuscaloosa: University of Alabama Press, 2006.

—. *Writing Beyond the Ending: Narrative Strategies of Twentieth-Century Women Writers*. Bloomington: Indiana University Press, 1985.

—. *Blue Studios: Poetry and Its Cultural Work*. Tuscaloosa: University of Alabama Press, 2006.

—, and Snitow, Ann. *The Feminist Memoir Project: Voices from Women's Liberation*. NY: Three Rivers Press (Random House), 1998.

Eshleman, Clayton. *Companion Spider: Essays*. Middletown, CT: Wesleyan University Press, 2001.

Halberstam, Judith. *Female Masculinity*. Durham: Duke University Press, 1998.

Evans, Steve. "Introductory Note: After Patriarchal Poetry: Feminism and the Contemporary Avant-Garde." *differences* 12. 2 (Summer 2001): i-v.

Fraser, Kathleen. *Translating the Unspeakable: Poetry and the Innovative Necessity*. Tuscaloosa: University of Alabama Press, 2000.

Friedman, Susan Stanford. "Craving Stories: Narrative and Lyric in Contemporary Theory and Women's Long Poems." In *Feminist Measures: Soundings in Poetry and Theory*, ed. Lynn Keller and Cristanne Miller. Ann Arbor: The University of Michigan Press, 1994: 15-42.

Friedman. "Gender and Genre Anxiety: Elizabeth Barrett Browning and H.D. as Epic Poets." *Tulsa Studies in Women's Literature* 5 (1986): 203-28.

Friedman. "When a 'Long' Poem Is a 'Big' Poem: Self Authorizing Strategies in Women's Twentieth-Century 'Long Poems.'" *LIT* 2 (1990): 9-25.

Frost, Elisabeth A. *The Feminist Avant-Garde in American Poetry*. Iowa City: University of Iowa Press, 2003.

Grossman, Allen. "Summa Lyrica: A Primer of the Commonplaces in Speculative Poetics." *The Sighted Singer: Two Works on Poetry for Readers and Writers*. Baltimore: The Johns Hopkins University Press, 1992.

Hejinian Lyn. *The Language of Inquiry*. Berkeley: University of California Press, 2000.

Hinton, Laura and Cynthia Hogue, eds., *We Who Love to Be Astonished: Experimental Women's Writing and Performance Poetics*. Tuscaloosa: University of Alabama Press, 2002.

Jehlen, Myra. "Gender," in Frank Lentricchia and Thomas McLaughlin, eds., *Critical Terms for Literary Study*. Chicago: University of Chicago Press: 263-273.

Kamboureli, Smaro. *On the Edge of Genre: The Contemporary Canadian Long Poem*. Toronto: University of Toronto Press, 1991.

Kinnahan, Linda A. *Lyric Interventions: Feminism, Experimental Poetry, and Contemporary Discourse*. Iowa City: University of Iowa Press, 2004.

Keller, Lynn. *Forms of Expansion: Recent Long Poems by Women*. Chicago: University of Chicago Press, 1997.

—. "The Twentieth-Century Long Poem," in Jay Parini, ed., *The Columbia History of American Poetry*. New York: Columbia University Press, 1993: 534-563.

—, and Cristanne Miller, eds. *Feminist Measures: Soundings in Poetry and Theory*. Ann Arbor: University of Michigan Press, 1994.

Lyon, Janet. *Manifestoes: Provocations of the Modern*, Ithaca: Cornell University Press, 1999.

Notley, Alice. *The Descent of Alette*. New York: Penguin Books, 1996.

—. *Homer's Art*, Canton, New York: Glover Publishing, 1990.

—. "Epic and Women Poets." In *Disembodied Poetics: Annals of the Jack Kerouac School*, ed. Anne Waldman and Andrew Schelling. Albuquerque: University of New Mexico Press, 1994: 103-109.

—. "Iovis Omnia Plena." *Chicago Review* 44 (1998): 117-129.

Olson, Charles. *Charles Olson and Ezra Pound: An Encounter at St. Elizabeths* (1975). Ed. Catherine Seelye. New York: Paragon House, 1991.

Parkins Wendy. "Moving Dangerously: Mobility and the Modern Woman," *Tulsa Studies* 20, 1 (Spring 2001): 77-92.

Perloff, Marjorie. *The Futurist Moment: Avant-Garde, Avant Guerre, and the Language of Rupture*. Chicago: The University of Chicago Press, 1986.

Pound. Ezra. *The Cantos*. New York: New Directions, 1971.

Retallack, Joan. *The Poethical Wager*. Berkeley: University of California Press, 2003.

Riley, Denise. *"Am I That Name?": Feminism and the Category of 'Women' in History*. Minneapolis: University of Minnesota Press, 1988.

Vickery, Ann. *Leaving Lines of Gender: A Feminist Genealogy of Language Writing*. Hanover: Wesleyan/New England Press, 2000.

Virgil, *The Eclogues of Virgil*, trans. David Ferry. New York: Farrar, Straus, and Giroux, 1999.

Waldman, Anne. "Notes for a Public Forum." *100 Days: An Anthology*. Ed. Andrea Brady. Cambridge: Barque Press, 2001.

—. *IOVIS I*. Minneapolis: Coffee House Press, 1993.

—. *IOVIS*, Book II. Minneapolis: Coffee House Press, 1997.

—, and Ed Foster. "An Interview with Anne Waldman," *Talisman* 13 (Fall 1994/ Winter 1995): 62-78.

—. "Feminafesto." From *Kill or Cure*. New York: Penguin Books, 1994, 142-146.

—. "Rocky Flats: Warring God Charnel Ground." *Disembodied Poetics: Annals of the Jack Kerouac School*. Ed. Anne Waldman and Andrew Schelling. Albuquerque: University of New Mexico Press, 1994: 482-490.

—. " 'I Is Another': Dissipative Structures." In *Fast Speaking Woman: Chants and Essays*. San Francisco: City Lights Books, 1996.

—. *Kill or Cure*. New York: Penguin Books, 1994.

—, and Lee Christopher, "Interview with Anne Waldman." *AWP Chronicle* 28, 3 (December 1995): 1-6.

Williams, William Carlos. *Paterson* (1946-1951; 1958). New York: New Directions, 1992.

Wolkestein, Diane and Samuel Noah Kramer. *Inanna: Queen of Heaven and Earth. Her Stories and Hymns from Sumer*. New York: Harper & Row, Publishers, 1983.

"fucking / me across the decades like we / poets like": Embodied Poetic Transmission

BOB PERELMAN

My title quotes lines from Alice Notley's *Songs for the Unborn Second Baby* (1979), and refers to *Doctor Williams' Heiresses*, a talk she gave the next year. I'm juxtaposing something that sounds normative—poetic inheritance—with something that sounds impossible—poetic fucking across history—to dramatize the notion of poetic generations. It's a term which is usually not dramatized, since the more it's taken out of its normal vaguely metaphorical usage the more preposterous it becomes to any but a mystical way of thinking. In normal usage, to speak of poetic generations marks chronological change while suggesting ontological permanence. The canonical Romantic poets are sometimes divided up into first and second generation to convey the overt information that Blake, Wordsworth and Coleridge began their careers decades before Shelley, Keats, and Byron. In a more tacit way the nomenclature assures us that each of the six is the same thing: a Romantic poet. But if we move beyond such a suggestion of family resemblance and take the word as claiming that the first-generation *engendered* the second generation, it seems a willfully naive use of language.

In the opening section of *Doctor Williams' Heiresses* Notley uses such willfully naive language. In what reads like a cross between fairytale and Biblical genealogy, she literalizes the logic of poetic generations to begin a canny intervention at a charged point in the poetic field where two poetic tendencies met. Intervention may well be too strong a word. Put it this way: whether or not Notley planned it at the time, in hindsight the talk now reads like a statement of poetic principles that didn't conform to those of a good number of the audience. The circumstances of its delivery highlight this. The talk was part of her residency at 80 Langton Street, and it was published by Lyn Hejinian later that year in her Tuumba pamphlet series. Thus both talk and text appeared in contexts closely associated with the coalescence of Language Writing. Although it was early in her career, Notley was already a major figure in the St. Marks scene.

I don't want to give the impression that the occasion was freighted with melodramatic opposition. This was not the Capulets and Montagues

circling in the plaza with the scent of shed blood already in the air. Nei-
ther literary tendency was as sharply defined then as now (or, if you
prefer as thoroughly reified). Hejinian often ranged beyond Language
Writing in her Tuumba series, and 80 Langton was a venue for all sorts
of innovative art work & music. Notley was friends with audience mem-
bers—she was staying with me and Francie Shaw during the residency;
and the atmosphere at 80 Langton was one of respect for, and interest and
pleasure in her work.[1]

Nevertheless, from my vantage 25 years later, *Doctor Williams' Heiresses*
can be read as an initial articulation of a basic difference in tendency
between the second-generation New York School and Language Writ-
ing, between—to use shorthand I will be amplifying a bit—writing that
foregrounds the fact of the poet writing in real time and writing that
foregrounds textuality. Such a distinction is far from iron-clad, and many
crossover poems could be cited from both sides. But let's let the binary
stand for now.

In reading *Heiresses* as articulating such a distinction, I'm not following
Notley's own disclaimer. Almost immediately after the opening fable, she
denied that there was any intentional logic behind it: "I can't remember
anything about what I was thinking about Williams & women writers 2
years ago. It was just a crackbrained theory so I could write some works
then." (But even this shrugging-off sentence now seems consonant with
New York School poetics—the pragmatic devotion to art, the everyday
speech, the pointed disinterest in thoroughgoing intellectualizing.)

Since the talk is not widely available, I'll be quoting at some length al-
though the quotations will not give a complete sense of the heterogeneity
of the talk. The opening fable is followed by some casual literary conver-
sation between unnamed characters who seem to be Notley and her then
husband Ted Berrigan; excerpts from Williams's *I Wanted to Write a Poem*;
a letter from Bernadette Mayer; bits from one of Notley's interviews;
and the talk concludes with a passage where Notley addresses Williams
directly. Throughout, poems and lines of Williams are interspersed. The
opening fable begins:

> Poe was the first one, he mated with a goddess. His children were
> Emily Dickinson & Walt Whitman—out of wedlock with a goddess.
> Then Dickinson & Whitman mated—since they were half divine
> they could do anything they wanted to—& they had 2 sons, William
> Carlos Williams & Ezra Pound, & a third son T. S. Eliot who went

> to a faraway country & never came back. From out of the West came
> Gertrude Stein. . . . [She] and William Carlos Williams got married:
> their 2 legitimate children, Frank O'Hara & Philip Whalen, often
> dressed & acted like their uncle Ezra Pound (*Heiresses*, n.p.)

Clearly, the tone here fends off professionalized literary historical serious-
ness, but it doesn't strike me as ironic. Its fairytale earnestness slants away
from its adult audience, addressing them as a special group of children
whose world is that of postwar innovative American poetry. In that world
poetic history is reduced to pure generation: nothing matters but lineage.
It's a hard pretense to keep up for long: Notley herself couldn't sustain the
tone; the other sections of the talk are nothing like this.

After mentioning Charles Olson, the illegitimate child of either Pound
or Williams and "the goddess Brooding," Notley strategically stops
naming poets who would be close to her own present: they are simply
"very many." But at the conclusion of the fable she does name herself and
Bernadette Mayer:

> Now O'Hara & Whalen were males that were male-female, as were
> many of the children of Williams by various goddesses & of Gertrude
> Stein & some gods. Olson was too big to be male-female as he would
> have liked. . . . Anyway it was striking how there were no females
> in this generation; & the first children of the male-females & of Olson
> & their other brothers were all males, and there were very many of
> them because of their fathers' incredible promiscuity. But the male-
> females also produced a second wave of children of which there were
> many females. These females could not understand how they came
> to be born—they saw no one among their parents & brothers who
> resembled them physically, for the goddesses their father mated with
> were evaporative non-parental types. As a matter of fact these females
> couldn't even believe that their fathers *were* their fathers. They came
> to indulge in a little ancestor worship—that is they each fell in love
> with a not too distant ancestor. One of them, Bernadette Mayer, fell
> in love with Gertrude Stein. And the one named Alice Notley fell in
> love with her grandfather, William Carlos Williams.

In the end, the fairytale tone of impersonal narration gives way to a slyly
polemic assertion of her presence in the same arena as their named ances-
tors. What started as a patriarchal genealogy, complete with evaporative

goddesses providing ineffable continuity, has become a map where living women poets look around, question affinities, and choose their ancestry.

Influence or Inheritance

The title of her talk, *Doctor Williams' Heiresses*, uses a conventional trope of transmission across generations, although the use of "Heiresses" is deliberately challenging: to say that Notley is Williams's poetic heir is unexceptional, but the change to heiress contains a tinge of a suggestion that she is calling herself, in a parodic redeployment, a poetess. But that's a subtle challenge in comparison to the lines I quoted from *Songs for the Unborn Second Baby*, where Notley, in the middle of a diatribe against Williams, describes him as establishing the most intimate (though ambiguous) contact with her: "fucking / me across the decades like we / poets like."

The idea of poetic DNA transmitted from one generation to another may be hard to credit, but something like this is said to happen in religious contexts, where a moment of contact with a crucial elder can be the site of doctrinal transmission: e.g., a Zen master passes the true teaching to the worthy disciple, who at that point becomes a master. Often enough in poems and anecdotes poets treat contact with the authenticating elder in similar ways. But there's a crucial difference. The Zen master acts to authenticate the new master, it's what Austin would call a performative speech act (as in "I hereby christen this ship the *USS Metonymy*"); whereas in poetic matters the fact of literary generation is a retrospective production. The first-generation New York School poets didn't act to create the second generation, the second generation authored themselves as the second generation by admiration, imitation and appropriation of, and some contact with, the older poets (who henceforward became the first generation).

Counter-evidence: Kenneth Koch actively promoted the work of his students, a number of whom are now considered second- (or third-/fourth-) generation New York School poets. John Ashbery was aware of Ted Berrigan, Ron Padgett, Joe Brainard and Dick Gallup as a group, which he named "the soi disant Tulsa school." So it was not as if the first generation was not aware of the second generation. Nevertheless, the initial impulses of appreciation and coalescence came from the younger poets.[2] The following two poems hardly nail down the point, but when "Memorial Day 1950" and "Cornkind" are juxtaposed, it seems that it is much easier for the younger generation to find ancestors than for the older generation to acknowledge heirs:

Picasso made me quick and tough, and the world

. . .

Fathers of Dada! You carried shining erector sets
in your rough bony pockets (O'Hara, 17)

and do I really want a son
to carry on my idiocy past the Horned Gates
poor   kid   a staggering load (387)

I realize that part of the attractiveness of any O'Hara poem is that it coruscates with irony and invites the reader to see at least two sides to the vividly presented arguments; and clearly these two poems are not exceptions. The "fertility motif" of "Cornkind" is handled with the campiest of rhetorical tissues: the "kid . . . becomes a strong strong man," etc. And "Memorial Day 1950" announces itself as the work of an apprentice poet while "Cornkind" is written by a confidently mature poet. Nevertheless, there is not a shred of irony in the early poem's praise of its ancestors; and the only place that "Cornkind" finds shelter from irony is in the erotic sincerity of its anti-generational conclusion: "you are of me, that's what / and that's the meaning of fertility / hard and moist and moaning." The creation/recognition of poetic generations is much easier when facing toward the past.

Identification and cathexis toward the past has long been a pattern (especially among male poets). It is the past where the magic spark is to be found, which is the point of Browning's "Memorabilia":

Ah, did you once see Shelley plain,
        And did he stop and speak to you,
And did you speak to him again?
        How strange it seems and new!

Any poet in subsequent generations can read Shelley's poems, study them, memorize them, collage them, but in the tacit logic of the poem the crucial fact that grants access to the authentically new is seeing and speaking with Shelley. "Shelley," i.e., his works, can have wide-spread, complexly mediated poetic influence; but immediate contact with Shelley, the embodied poet, is of a different order of value. The final stanza figures Shelley as a departed eagle, eclipsing the contextual world:

> For there I picked up on the heather
>> And there I put inside my breast
> A molted feather, an eagle feather!
> Well, I forget the rest. (Abrams, 1202)

Browning reports that the poem was instigated by meeting a stranger in a bookshop who had spoken with Shelley: "Suddenly the stranger paused, and burst into laughter as he observed me staring at him with blanched face. . . . I still vividly remember how strangely the presence of a man who had seen and spoken with Shelley affected me." It is not the presence of Shelley's books, which the shop presumably carried, that mattered, but the relay of immediate contact that the stranger represented.

Basil Bunting speaks of a similar species of contact (though in his case it was a probability of contact which did not quite occur):

> My father . . . knew some of the Swinburnes. . . . it's just chance that when I was a small boy Swinburne never met me. He'd do what . . . he did to all the children on Putney Heath: he'd pat me on the head and present me with half a crown. And that would have been very interesting to me because when *he* was a little boy . . . he was taken to Grasmere where he met an old gentleman who patted him on the head, but did not offer him half a crown—he was too frugal—and that was William Wordsworth! (qtd. in Terrell, 3).[3]

Such actual or imagined moments are quite distinct from examples of poetic influence. Bunting is not suggesting that he was influenced by Swinburne and Wordsworth; the underlying logic of his wistful almost-story is that the chain of Wordsworth touching Swinburne, then Swinburne touching Bunting, would grant Bunting the position of authenticated poet of Northumbria.

Poetic influence is a much safer concept than this, for poetic formalists and cultural critics alike. Poetic influence, since it has so many facets, is an incontestable fact. It's everywhere. The formalist would point to the heterogenous total of formal poetic acts—poems, prosody, subject matter, vocabulary, visual layout—as the substance out of which a new poem is configured; the cultural critic would emphasize the social totality of extra-poetic language uses and the topography of the poetic field as the important factors. In either case the emergence of any poetic feature of any poem could be traced back to a complex set of structuring configurations. Following out some of these relations could produce endlessly detailed, endlessly plural histories.

With poetic inheritance on the other hand, history becomes a singular and often polemic saga. Exoteric poetic influences are irreducibly democratic, their information available, at least theoretically, to anyone who can read. But poetic inheritance, on the other hand, is esoteric, a matter of luck or grace. It takes place in "a secret location on the lower East Side" to quote a recent history of the small press poetry scene. It only happens to specific poets, which makes the spark passed from older poet to younger poet utterly valuable.

Needless to say, problems arise with this notion. There are many other presumptive heirs. How do they know the will was read correctly or if there even was a will? At best, the claim of inheritance may provoke respect or envy in the non-inheritor, but it can also be read as a sign of presumption or narcissism.

From the outside, esoteric poetic inheritance is hard to credit. It's easy to see that Whitman was a central *influence* on Ginsberg: the form of both poets' line is similar, as is their democratic address and their bodily candor. But Ginsberg speaks of more direct, esoteric involvement.

> Neal Cassady slept with [Gavin Arthur] occasionally . . . and Gavin Arthur had slept with Edward Carpenter, and Edward Carpenter has slept with Walt Whitman. So this is in a sense in the line of transmission. . . . Kerouac's heterosexual hero [i.e., Cassady] who also slept with somebody who slept with somebody who slept with Whitman, and received the Whispered Transmission, capital W, capital T, of that love. (Ginsberg, 317)

(And Ginsberg slept with Cassady occasionally, it should be added.) The Whispered Transmission, which Ginsberg emphatically capitalizes for the ear of the interviewer, is not simply a verbal message, equivalent to a poem on a page. It involves physical contact which in its underlying logic is actually re-embodiment. A footnote mentions Gavin Arthur's description of "how Edward Carpenter made love to him in the manner in which Walt Whitman had made love to Edward Carpenter."

Ginsberg's connection to Williams, while considerably less fraught, follows a similar pattern. Rather than the poem on the page, which would be open to readerly interpretation and reaction, Ginsberg valorizes the fact of Williams's own enunciation. Ginsberg quotes the last line of "The Clouds," imitating Williams's pronunciation rather than the word "a" that is printed on the page:

> "Plunging upon a moth, a butterfly, a pismire, hupp. . . ." And then he waved his hands in the air—he just gave up. So I suddenly realized it was just like somebody talking in a bar, not finishing the sentence but just giving up with a gesture of impatience, and that it was a syntactical fact of speech that had never been written down before in poetry—and so I realized that his poetry was absolutely identical with speech. (268)

It's a common occurrence for a listener to receive a new, more sharply focused impression when hearing a poet read; but these examples go beyond the commonsense suggestion that the poet's body is an important nexus of circulation, they suggest that the author's body is needed to give the poem its most valid existence.

Notley's lines from *Songs for the Unborn Second Baby* toy with this notion, both stating and contradicting it. The rest of the diatribe against Williams is much less ambiguous: he's a swaggering male who fills Notley with scorn. In such a context, "fucking me across generations" has a more colloquial meaning:

> male principle of the poetry, you earnestly sexed
> character of your poetry fucking
> me across the decades like we
> poets like or centuries why aren't you
> my obstetrician, are you?
> for they forgot us a midwife
>
> but you're right, Bill Williams, I won't
> take it
>   your flattery, I hate
> Venus, you
>   can't flatten me, further
> you betray me with your fragrant
> infidelities to Floss and I toss off our
> whiskies to your impalement
>   on

our immense unflowery tooled up
universes, you unmitigable [*Songs*, n.p.]

There is ambivalence in the passage as a whole ("why aren't you / my obstetrician, are you?"; "infidelities" that are not flagrant but "fragrant"), but the gist is unambiguous. Take out "like we / poets like" and we would have Williams as the classic male victimizer, the "earnestly sexed / character of [his own] poetry fucking [Notley] across the decades," i.e., messing things up for her decades later. However, "like we / poets like" tugs against such easy resolution. "We poets" unites Notley with Williams: both are poets who like "fucking . . . across the decades." It's hard to pin down subject positions in lines as fluid as these, but Notley is writing from at least two situations at once: as objectified female subject she is getting fucked (impeded, condescended to, fucked over); as poet she is involved in some mutually pleasurable fucking (poetic intercourse).

Judging from *Songs for the Unborn Second Baby* and *Doctor Williams' Heiresses* poetic intercourse is a complex matter. While attacking Williams, the poem as a whole clearly owes quite a bit to his work in its casual but precise speech, its everydayness, its use of the stairstep line. So even while she (the person) continues to attack him (the person), turning his claim that he got his language "from the mouths of Polish mothers" against him [*Autobiography*, 311], their poetries remain entangled:

No Polish mother

                                        you weren't either

        Where is the female the polarity to you

                to my tongue?

                        Who would join the

    polarities is life's crank?

                        Who
    functions as formally normal, that is
                            a polarity—

to be an eye, an I-character, sturdy-lifed?

There's

no formalized dailiness for the androgynous?

When I

hate the diapers the dishes

just now those yellow

daffodils and you? [*Songs*, n.p.]

In *Doctor Williams' Heiresses* Notley shows that she is well aware of how thoroughly Williams's work informed the earlier poem. In many places, Notley speaks of what she learned from Williams; she claims that he was the greatest American poet and that it was his work that taught her to write as herself—her poet self. By the end of the talk she is speaking directly to him. She recounts her time in England, writing *Songs* amid bleak moods:

> I typed up all of your poem "Asphodel, That Greeny Flower," & Honey that took a long time. In that bad time there was always you. To love as a poet & to love & hate as a man. Immobile pregnant & isolate & unhappy, I didn't need to read about your attractions to women other than your wife. Your reasoning seemed specious & was enraging. . . . We poets take all words personally. But I wrote my poem & I used for its form your *Paterson* & an O'Hara ode & those Cantos . . . & it is held together by flowers, as "Asphodel" is—we had a bewilderingly luxuriant garden there—& by the presence of the opposite sex "you" & by the will to write poetry. I want to say this only for me I think, I think whoever hears this knows it & knows all about you— [*Heiresses*, n.p.]

The address here is intimate—Notley's I talking to Williams's you— but still literary: whoever is listening to this ultimately public statement can know what is being said. There is a further degree of privacy in the talk, however, and it is something that strikes me as a characteristic of second-generation New York School poetry. It occurs when private knowledge—or personal poetic inheritance that is intrinsic to the poet—is displayed very openly. If that description is opaque, then the following bit of dialogue from the talk should make it clearer. It does clearly seem to be a dialogue although the different speakers are not identified. I'll intersperse comments:

—I can't remember anything about what I was thinking about Williams & women writers 2 years ago. It was just a crackbrained theory so I could write some works then.

—Why are you working up to writing some incredibly baroque lecture? You should be worrying about whether or not your panties are gonna fall down while you're giving it.

There's no way to prove that the represented speakers here are meant to be taken as Alice Notley and Ted Berrigan. But I feel that I know who they are, and I predict that many other readers would share that impression. Where does my knowledge (or subjective certainty) come from? It seems a mixture of publicly available information (from reading their work), personal acquaintance, and the intermediate sphere of contact with many others who were involved in various degrees with their work and their lives.

Emblematic of this gradient between public and private knowledge are the two alternatives in "Ted's" remark: there's the baroque lecture (public knowledge) and the fallen panties (private, but in public view).

—Which pair should I wear in case they do?

—Your Philip Whalen black & white calligraphy panties with lower case letters stitched along the seams . . . Why don't you do something easy like play some records of Williams reading?

—Ah, they've all heard those records.

—Are you kidding? Young poets haven't heard shit—they all turn up their noses at the Caedmon records because they got famous on the Dylan Thomas records. Which is why we liked them.

It's a different comic register, a learned one, but the first half of "Ted's" answer provides the same display of private poetic inheritance. Philip Whalen stitches calligraphy only on Alice's panties.[4]

But in the second half of the remark "Ted" proposes a method of public pedagogy. The substance of what is to be learned about poetry is still embodied—it's Williams reading his poems—but that substance is more or less public: the records are available.

The reported conversation ends on a thoroughly pedagogic note. Even though the conclusion is that Williams's work showed Notley how to write as herself, this knowledge is offered as public, something that Williams could teach other readers and writers:

> —What Williams did for you—he consolidated a lot of what you knew already, but he allowed you to be fast, perky, sassy, talky, all these different ways that had to do with talking, in one poem. He helped you to be as fast as you are. And to consolidate these voices you were hearing in your head & in the house & on the street & put them in the same poem. Getting it off Williams was like getting it authentic & not a little thirties-movie-modern like in Frank O'Hara . . . What *I* got off of him was a sharp clear use of direct address. He had this way of using the imperative tone.

> —My theory had something to do with being for awhile the female to his male. You could use him without sounding like another imitation Williams poem. And how could you not use him since he was the greatest one? But you could use him to sound entirely new if you were a woman. It was all about this woman business. I thought we didn't need to read women—I mean find the hidden in the woodwork ones—so much as find the poems among whatever sex that made you feel free to say anything, including your own anything. [*Heiresses*, n.p.]

To reiterate, Notley is writing down (or possibly inventing) both these voices. Having "Ted" describe her own work involves a strategy that is quite like Stein's using Toklas's voice to describe her (Stein's) own work in *The Autobiography of Alice B. Toklas*. Here, Notley gets to characterize her own work as well as Berrigan's. An absolute connection with Williams is the source of this personal poetic autonomy. An emblem of this is the early Williams poem Notley quotes in between this conversation I've just cited and the opening fable. The fable ended with the statement that "Alice Notley fell in love with her grandfather, William Carlos Williams." Allowing for some poetic analogizing, the poem shows Williams reciprocating by falling in love with his [grand]daughter:

YOUTH AND BEAUTY

I bought a dishmop—
having no daughter—

for they had twisted
fine ribbons of shining copper
about white twine
and made a tousled head
of it, fastened it
upon a turned ash stick
slender at the neck
straight, tall—
when tied upright
on the brass wallbracket
to be a light for me
and naked
as a girl should seem
to her father. (Collected, 166)

Now, this poem can be read in any one of a number of ways. He's personifying and sexualizing the mop; he's sending up commercial personification; he's exploring a safe field of forbidden fantasy; he's working on his line breaks, etc. What I'm emphasizing here, though, is the embodied intimacy Notley is claiming by placing the poem where she did in the talk, framed to dramatize the impossible but compelling union of her poetic body and Williams's poetic body.

It strikes me that this fronting of private knowledge, contact, inheritance, membership in a select order of poetic authenticity was something distinct from the various practices of some writers in the audience at 80 Langton that were coalescing into what became known as Language Writing. Williams was as crucial a figure for Language Writers as for Notley, but the admiration was for a more textual poet. In another moment in the talk, Notley writes,

We still haven't caught up with what Williams meant by the variable foot. . . . Variable foot is maybe about the dominance of tone of voice over other considerations—I do my poems from here 'cause I talk from here—haven't you ever talked to anyone? I'm not an oracle or a musical instrument or a tradition or a bellows or even a typewriter: I am a tone of voice, warming, shifting, pausing, changing, including, asserting, exulting, including, including, turning & including. I break my lines where I do, as I'm being as various as my voice should be in our intimacy. (Heiresses, n.p.)

Notley's insistence on tone of voice does not preclude statements of her poetics, which she obliquely differentiates from the classical model ("an oracle"), the Romantic ("a musical instrument"—Shelley's and Coleridge's aeolian harp, say), the Eliotic ("tradition [and the individual talent]"), and the Olsonic ("bellows," "the breath," "typewriter," the poet using the typewriter to score the precise timing of the poem's enunciation). Possibly the typewriter—a machine that produces textuality—hints at Language Writing as well.

Notley's characterization of tone of voice certainly describes many moments in Williams's work. But only the "more textual" Williams could have written "Crustaceous / wedge / of sweaty kitchens / on rock / overtopping / thrusts of the sea," etc. It is not that "The Agonized Spires" (*Spring and All*, #13) is a major Williams poem; but the innovative panache of the poems and broken prose of *Spring and All*, the irascible darting attention in *Kora in Hell*, *The Great American Novel* and *The Descent of Winter* provided exciting tokens of how open things could get.

Perhaps a basic distinction of that moment can be found in the culminating focus of Notley's description of tone of voice: "including, including, turning & including." A single, vividly alert speaking subject is the source of a coruscating, changeable tone of voice—or, if you prefer, of coruscating, changeable tones of voice: either way, the variety of tone comprises a unified stretch of experience, which the poem is to register. It was such unities that many of the techniques that Language Writers were using at the time (the new sentence, collage, syntactic fragmentation) aimed to bypass.

A footnote from the 21st Century. It strikes me now that neither tone of voice nor textuality does justice to what keeps Williams so interesting. To pick a passage from *Paterson*—and there are scores of them—the following can't be reduced to either "Williams the poet" or to "words on the page" without having the life drain out of it. Perhaps Williams's own rather gnomic sense that poets think with their poems points in a more accurate direction.

> Invent (if you can) discover or
> nothing is clear—will surmount
> the drumming in your head. There will be
> nothing clear, nothing clear.
>
> He fled pursued by the roar.

Seventy-five of the world's leading scholars, poets and philosophers
gathered at Princeton last week . . .

Faitoute ground his heel

hard down on the stone:

Sunny today, with the highest temperatures near 80 degrees; mod-
erate southerly winds. Partly cloudy and continued warm tomorrow,
with moderate southerly winds.

Her belly   .   her belly is like
a cloud. a cloud
        at evening   .
His mind would reawaken:

He   Me with my pants, coat and vest still on!

She   And me still in my galoshes! (*Paterson*, 85)

Bodies Writing Poems

For all of the conversation, analysis, and polemic around the topics of
poetry and individual agency, no settled conclusions are in sight. 25 years
ago, Notley's insistence on a poetic embodiment that was powerful enough
to focus all poetic history in her body seemed very different from the
poetics of Language Writing, where the transpersonal social composition
of language was foregrounded to the point where any thorough emphasis
on the person writing seemed artificial. But choices that seemed stark 25
years ago have not proved to be mutually exclusive. As a nonconclusive
coda here, I want to bring two very different emblematic poets together
to give my sense of how contingent any division is between the territories
of text and body.

What has resonated most unescapably from Eliot's "Tradition and the
Individual Talent" is his championing of impersonality and his image of
the poet as a shred of platinum unaffected by the combustion it enables.
As we are told near the end, "To divert interest from the poet to the poetry
is a laudable aim" (Eliot, *Essays*, 11). But that essay has contributed greatly
to the continuing mystique surrounding the person of Eliot. This is not
simply due to Elioticians who need to get a life: throughout the essay

Eliot hints at a rather gothic narrative of a person in danger. There's the coy aside that "of course, only those who have personality and emotions know what it means to want to escape from these things" (10-1). "Escape" is a very charged word; but it turns out that escape is not possible. He has already been captured, as the familiar quotation indicates: "not only the best, but the most individual parts of his work are those in which the dead poets, his ancestors, assert their immortality most vigorously." Eliot closes the paragraph with stern (but odd) emphasis: "And I do not mean the impressionable period of adolescence, but the period of full maturity." The vigorous, assertive dead, who are more real than the live poet who merely inhabits the present, reappear at the conclusion of the essay: the poet "is not likely to know what is to be done unless he lives in what is not merely the present, but the present moment of the past, unless he is conscious, not of what is dead, but of what is already living" (4, 11). The normative message here is that "great poetry is timeless." But a different scenario can be deduced: that of a vampire taking over a victim's living body, making great poetry not so much timeless as undead. In a later essay Eliot gives us a bit more information about the victim (himself). The initial assault is during the "impressionable period of adolescence": "Consider the adolescent reading of any person with some literary sensibility. Everyone, I believe, who is at all sensible of the seductions of poetry, can remember some moment in youth when he or she was carried away by the work of one poet. Very likely he was carried away by several poets, one after the other" (Eliot, *Prose*, 101-2). In the same essay we learn the identity of one seducer: "I was intoxicated by Shelley's poetry at the age of fifteen" (86).

It's an improper association, but this reminds me O'Hara's "Ave Maria" where the adolescent artistic awakening takes place at the movies where "the soul / . . . grows in darkness, embossed by silvery images." There the young artist learns "where candy bars come from": knowledge which is "as gratuitous as leaving the movie before it's over / with a pleasant stranger whose apartment in is the Heaven on Earth Bldg / near the Williamsburg Bridge" (O'Hara, 372).

But isn't this a case of apples and oranges? The young Eliot is carried off by the poets he reads; the young O'Hara is—in the poem's scenario at least—willingly carried off by a person. And isn't that exactly the difference between their work? For Eliot genuine poetry needs full contact with the poetic "mind of Europe" in order to live; in "Personism: A Manifesto" O'Hara asserts that poetry needs "love's life-giving vulgarity" (499). The seduced Eliot reads Shelley; the seduced O'Hara has great sex at the Heaven on Earth Bldg—in the poem's scenario at least.

It's hard not to be curious about the Heaven on Earth Bldg. Did earthly activities go on there or was the whole thing just imaginary?[5] For readers who might want to salvage the great wit of "Ave Maria" from the troubling thought that it revolves around what we now consider child abuse, it is tempting to read the "pleasant stranger" as a deliberately out-rageous thought-experiment counter-balancing the equally exaggerated Norman Rockwell-esque family that is teased throughout by the poem's diction ("Mothers of America," "oh mothers you will have made the little tykes / so happy," etc.). In such a reading "the pleasant stranger" is merely a (complicatedly) naughty ogre, while the poetic payoff is the non-ironic phrase "darker joys," whose unspecified virtues are hard to deny, espe-cially in contrast to the brittle childish world evoked by the rest of the poem.

But then again, for most of O'Hara's poetry, the strategy that de-real-izes the "pleasant stranger" is exactly wrong. It is hard to imagine cel-ebrating his poetry with the enthusiasm it deserves while still considering "12:20 in New York," "a hamburger and a malted," and the "bottle of Strega" (325) as poetic symbols or as props for some reality effect. The charisma of "Personism" comes from O'Hara's verve in taking complex (and vague) matters of poetics and resolving them into concrete situations in daily life. "Measure and other technical apparatus"? Make sure your pants are "tight enough so everyone will want to go to bed with you" (O'Hara, 498). That's a lot clearer than Williams's attempts to explain "the variable foot" and a lot more memorable than Pound's "Use no su-perfluous word, no adjective that does not reveal something" (Pound, 4). Aesthetic questions are brought back to how the person feels—which is the original meaning of aesthetic in Greek—not that O'Hara cared about the classics. For him most contemporary poems taste as bad as mother's overcooked roast beef and feel as bad as the sad lectures she delivers while ladling out the gravy: "Too many poems act like a middle-aged mother trying to get her kids to eat too much cooked meat, and potatoes with drippings (tears)." By the way, this seems to be the same house that "the young tyke" escaped in "Ave Maria." How to judge poetry? By how much you like it. The canon of American poetry that O'Hara endorses is tiny: "only Whitman and Crane and Williams . . . are better than the movies." Would you rather see *Rebel without a Cause* or read *Lord Weary's Castle*? If you don't need poetry, "bully for [you]." At this point, it seems that when it comes to poetry, the person is all-determining. The manifesto is entitled "Personism," after all, and it was written immediately after O'Hara wrote "Personal Poem":

> Personism . . . was founded by me after lunch with LeRoi Jones on August 27, 1959, a day in which I was in love with someone (not Roi, by the way, a blond). I went back to work and wrote a poem for this person. . . . [Personism] puts the poem squarely between the poet and the person, Lucky Pierre style, and the poem is correspondingly gratified. (499)

In the midst of such celebration of the personal, where even the poem is granted personhood by being made into a person "gratified" to be the middle partner in a sexual daisy-chain (which is how I assume "Lucky Pierre style" functions), it is easy to ignore the surprising emphasis O'Hara puts on the impersonal. Personism, he insists, "does not have to do with personality or intimacy, far from it!" Even though the originary moment of Personism seems to involve a real telephone call to the loved one, the address in the Personist poem is only virtual. The phrasing is a bit tricky. O'Hara tells us that while writing a poem for the person he was in love with, "I was realizing that if I wanted to I could use the telephone instead of writing the poem, and so Personism was born." Now, I suppose this can be read as meaning that O'Hara's realization that he "*could* use the telephone" [my emphasis] was followed by his (unmentioned) actual use of the phone, and thus that Personism involves mixing real-time conversation with written direct address. But in the less strained reading he doesn't pick up the phone. The implication of this reading is that "Personism was born" as a shock of compensation at the poet's absenting himself from the everyday circuits of felicity. And while it's rather counter-intuitive to de-sexualize the Lucky Pierre configuration, if we read somewhat fussily, the initial description of the threesome—Personism "puts the poem squarely between the poet and the person"—differentiates the "poet" from the "person."

If we put this differentiation together with the claim that Personism has nothing to do with personality or intimacy, that "it's all art," then O'Hara can be seen to be saying something quite similar to Eliot's claim that "the emotion in [the poet's] poetry will be a very complex thing, but not with the complexity of the emotions of people who have very complex or unusual emotions in life" (10). Now I don't intend to prove that Frank O'Hara is T. S. Eliot's long-lost identical twin. And to be fair, one sentence after putting "the poem squarely between the poet and the person," O'Hara writes, "The poem is at last between two persons instead of two pages"—something that Eliot would never have countenanced.

While they're not twins, my purpose in bringing O'Hara and Eliot into such quasi-alignment is to suggest how thoroughly interlaced the notions of poet and poetry are. They seem so tightly bound up in fact that neither will serve well any longer as a useful binary term.

To return to Notley and the differences of her poetics from those of Language Writing. As I said at the beginning of this section, to contrast Notley's embodied poetics with the social textuality of Language Writing has become if not a perfectly false distinction then at least a tired one. There are plenty of examples of foregrounded language or foregrounded embodiment in the poetry on either side. In Ted Berrigan's *Sonnets*, a second-generation New York School work if anything is, textual manipulation—extensive recycling of lines and phrases—is central. And if Steve Benson's performance-generated pieces (e.g., many of the pieces in *Blue Book*) don't emphasize the moment by moment existence of the poet, nothing does. It would take careful editing, but selections could be made in which Bernadette Mayer was a Language Writer, Kit Robinson was a second-generation (third?) New York poet. And what about Clark Coolidge, who at the time Notley was presenting *Heiresses* was a beacon of textual activism for many Language Writers? His affinities through the '70s were with the second-generation New York scene. (I seem to be proving here that I do not have the temperament for the job of poetic passport control.) And, to repeat, William Carlos Williams was a formative influence behind both Language Writing and the second-generation New York School. The one abiding difference is the matter of lineage. While I would say that I, like Notley, love Williams's work and have (I hope) been deeply influenced by it, I also have to say that he's not my grandfather.

Works Cited

M. H. Abrams, et al., eds., *The Norton Anthology of English Literature*, sixth edition, Volume 2. New York: Norton, 1993.

Berrigan, Ted. *Nothing for You.* Lenox, MA & NY: Angel Hair Books, 1977

Clay, Steven, and Rodney Phillips. *A Secret Location on the Lower East Side: Adventures in Writing 1960-1980*. New York: Granary Books, 1998.

Eliot, T. S., *Selected Essays*. New York: Harcourt, Brace and Company, 1950.

—. *Selected Prose of T. S. Eliot*. Ed. Frank Kermode. London: Faber & Faber, 1975.

Ginsberg, Allen. *Spontaneous Mind: Selected Interviews, 1958-1996*. Ed. David Carter. New York: HarperCollins, 2001.

Notley, Alice. *Doctor Williams Heiresses*. Berkeley: Tuumba Press, 1980.

—. *Songs for the Unborn Second Baby*. New York: United Artists, 1979.

O'Hara, Frank. *The Collected Poems of Frank O'Hara*. Ed. by Donald Allen. New York: Knopf, 1971.

Perelman, Bob. *The Marginalization of Poetry: Language Writing and Literary History*. Princeton: Princeton University Press, 1996.

Pound, Ezra. *Literary Essays of Ezra Pound*. Ed. T. S. Eliot. New York: New Directions, 1968.

Terrell, Caroll F. "Basil Bunting: An Eccentric Profile." *Basil Bunting: Man and Poet*. Ed. Caroll F. Terrell. Orono, ME: National Poetry Foundation, 1981. 25-62.

Williams, Carlos William. *The Autobiography of William Carlos Williams*. New York, New Directions, 1967.

—. *The Collected Poems of William Carlos Williams*, Vol. 1, edited by A. Walton Litz and Christopher MacGowan. New York, New Directions, 1986.

—. *Paterson*, revised edition prepared by Christopher MacGowan. New York: New Directions, 1992.

"A generous time": Lee Harwood in New York

NICK SELBY[1]

> All distances in time and space are shrinking. Man now reaches overnight, by plane, places which formerly took weeks and months of travel.
>
> —Martin Heidegger, "The Thing" (165)

When British poet Lee Harwood first visited New York in the summer of 1966 he discovered an energetic and open poetic, artistic and social environment that had a profound effect upon his poetry. Harwood recalled in 1993 that he found himself in the United States "hungrily exploring a country that seemed to produce such great new art and meeting all the people I'd previously only known through letters" ("Lee Harwood" 144). Such a sense of hungry exploration is evident in the poetry Harwood wrote in, and as a result of, his time in America. Learning at first hand from New York poets, Harwood begins to see ways in which his poetry might operate through open forms that did not tend towards (as he felt his earlier work, and that of The Beats, had done) "an egotistical dead-end."[2] Indeed, America generally, and New York especially, seems crucial to Harwood's developing maturity as a poet (he was 27 in June 1966) primarily because it was in New York that he discovered a time and place where poetic experiment was part of a lively collaborative artistic environment. In New York, then, Harwood's poetics discovers a mode of being that is inclusive, exploratory and experimental. Writing in the "Memoirs" section of the *Angel Hair Anthology* (2001), Harwood notes,

> When I went to New York for the first time in summer 1966 I stepped into exactly the right place at the right time. New York seemed the centre of an immense energy and openness in the Arts. Everyone was exploring and pushing the boundaries of what might be possible. It felt especially rich for poets with them collaborating with painters, musicians, film makers, theatre people, and other poets. . . . A generous time. (*Angel Hair Anthology* 589)

215

This essay seeks to explore the impact of the "generous time" of the New York poetry scene of the late 1960s upon Harwood's work. Its overall suggestion is that Harwood's poetic development across his three collections *The Man With Blue Eyes* (1966), *The White Room* (1968) and *Landscapes* (1969) can be traced through his engagement with and involvement in that New York poetry scene. Although the poems collected together in *The Man With Blue Eyes* were written before Harwood had first visited New York, they display clear poetic affinities to first-generation New York poets such as John Ashbery and Frank O'Hara. As Harwood's "first real book," it is also important that this collection was also the first book to be published by Angel Hair, in New York. This essay will consider first, then, some of the poems in *The Man With Blue Eyes* in terms of Harwood's response to New York poetry and poetics before he had actually visited the city. It will then move on to examine how Harwood's next two books build on gestures learned from his time as part of the New York poetry scene. However, it will also argue that while Harwood's work at this time deploys a responsive generosity and restless energy that seem signals of the New York environment from which it arose, it is also marked by a poetics of diffidence, hesitation and uncertainty, a "reserve" that seems part of Harwood's British poetic accent. In short, New York will be read as "exactly the right place at the right time" for Harwood precisely because it allowed him to move towards a mature poetics in which his open forms make fully articulate the energies of both proximity *and* distance that his work seeks to thematise.

What is especially interesting about the passage quoted above from the *Angel Hair Anthology* is that it so clearly announces many of the concerns that Harwood's poetry was working through in the late 1960s. New York itself, with its inclusive energies, openness, exploratory ethos and sense of community, becomes a model for Harwood's poetry. As with his reading of New York, the impulse behind Harwood's poetry is generous. Its openness draws on the experience of an exciting, experimental and energised artistic community. Indeed, as the jacket-blurb of *Landscapes* (1969) makes clear, it is seen by Harwood as a collaborative venture, "The poem is always unfinished and open ended and only complete (and then only in one way) when read by someone else." That this is something Harwood learned from John Ashbery is, as this essay will argue later, crucial. But that it also stems from a more general sense of New York poetry at this time is one of the underlying assumptions of this essay. What the following discussion of Harwood's growth as a poet under the influence of the New York poets (both first and second generations) will show is that such poetic openness in his work is also deeply freighted by a sense of loss, fracture and anxiety. His sense, that is, of the artistic generosity of this time is delicately counterpoised by an exploratory poetics in which distance, separation, and paranoia play just beneath the glitteringly energetic poetic surface.

As this essay hopes to demonstrate, this sort of tension witnesses a changing sense for Harwood of the poem as an open form. And this *poetic* quality also reflects a developing *thematic* concern in Harwood's work. Living between America and Britain becomes a concern that is increasingly entangled in questions of geography, location and poetic mapping. The growing maturity of Harwood's poetry over this period, then, seems to rest in its ability to gesture to a politics of power that underpins and structures personal, poetic and transatlantic relations. Harwood learns, that is, a politics of commitment from New York. While such commitment might, initially, seem to go against the grain of the apparently off-hand tone of many New York poets at the time (O'Hara's "walking and talking" style, Ted Berrigan's expansive yet generous sexual energies, for example) what it does register are the entanglements of the personal within the political which they are seeking poetic means to explore. Indeed, Harwood's poetics of generosity signals just such entanglements. The gaps and hesitant articulacy of Harwood's poetic surfaces allow him to explore—and be open to—the ways in which lyric might come to generate political meanings.

By 1965 Harwood was already writing poems that bore the inflections of recent American poetry and poetics in the attention they threw upon making articulate the energies of their composition. He had been "enthused" by Donald Allen's groundbreaking anthology of 1960 *The New American Poetry*, as well as books published by New Directions and City Lights and the "little magazines" that had found their way across the Atlantic ("Memoirs" 588). The impact of open field poetics, with its associative leaps and sense of provisional, rather than closed, meanings is seen throughout *The Man With Blue Eyes*. In fact, in this collection the imaginative leaps that such an associative technique allows turn New York into a place (and image) of surreal longing. New York is the point towards which Harwood's poetic and personal attention turns. So, whilst the poem "New York will welcome me" might be seen to derive its surreal urban setting from the French poets Harwood was reading at the time, its tone is clearly indebted to the Beats ("Memoirs" 588).[3]

The poem opens:

> the blue cadillac
> sweeps round the sky
> into its tower sun setting
> people file out of the offices
> and crocodiles move into the subways
> a grey man standing on a column
> of sponge cake
> shook himself awake (n.p)

New York is important here as an icon of Americanness. Such a sweep-
ing panorama registers the mythic freedom of a car culture heading into
a west of sunsets played off against a crowd of undifferentiated, grey,
office workers. And although Harwood's imagined New York is a place
of generous welcome, it is also one defined for him by his difference and
separation from it. New York, therefore, becomes a marker of the physical
and emotional dislocation, and subsequent longing, that underpins the
whole of *The Man With Blue Eyes*.

Tellingly, the objects against which this poem measures such a sense
of cultural distance are distinctly American: cadillacs, subways, and later
in the poem, dollars and eastside tenements. Even the sinisterly surreal
image of "crocodiles" in the "subways" (with its nod towards a popular
New York "urban myth") derives from a semantic slippage—another type
of distance—between British and American usage. Only rarely to Ameri-
can ears does a "crocodile" denote a line of moving people. It is because of
such slippages that Harwood's poetic New York becomes unfixed from its
imagined scene of American "things." The poem's surreal jump-cuts pres-
ent, therefore, an apparently solid place that is neither solid (a "column"
is revealed to be "sponge cake") nor quite so easily accommodated into
the myths that seem to sustain it. Effectively this means that New York's
iconic status is felt by the poem to be subject to the energies of both
the poet's disjunctive imagination, and to wider cultural forces, however
hazily these are articulated.

While this conjunction points toward a key concern for Harwood,
namely how lyric voice is rendered politically articulate via a disjunctive
poetic surface, it is in this early poem only a partially successful strategy.
The poem's impact certainly rests on Harwood's ability to suggest a dis-
tance between the poet's desire and the (poetic) scene of that desire. And

it is indeed important that such a scene is New York. However, the poem's suggestion about the violence that underpins America and our desire for American things is fogged somewhat by a collapse into a rather hazy over-sentimentalizing of the forces of that desire, of the poet's want for New York. At its close, then, the poem suggests—but cannot fully articulate—the violence on which its American scene stands. Its final gesture is, therefore, to overwrite such violence through an evocation of sexual desire and a sense of lyric distance.

> "life gets tedious . . . . ." he said
> as the last indian arrow
> passed through the breast pocket
> of his last check-shirt
> one dollar is seven shillings and tuppence
> and at present there is a water-shortage
> in new york meaning water cannot be
> served at table unless requested
>
> so the love song and finger strokings
> and eyes meeting on the stairs
> of eastside tenements
> all at a meeting planned a year
> > a head

Ultimately for this poem, New York's welcome relies upon Harwood's sense of emotional separation. His surface disjunctions operate through a sort of transatlantic poetics of exchange that ends up by sentimentalising the distances of his longing. Any critique of consumer capitalism and commodity culture that might be implied in the poem's references to check-shirted cowboys and arrow-firing Indians (and also, incidentally, submerged in the name "Cadillac"), and in the attention given to the power of the dollar within a transatlantic exchange economy, collapses under the fleeting touch of lyric, the desire of "the love song."

Other poems in the collection are also fascinated by the tension and distance between the "things" of the world and the lyric poet's containment of them. Throughout the collection, America is very often the space of that distance. In "London—New York," for example, the solid fact of rain beating on the window of a transatlantic aeroplane images Harwood's distance from, and yearning for, his lover:

> but now
> an airplane over an ocean
> with rain beating its windows
> & you inside, riding back
> to another city & stranger nights

Despite an undoubted lyric poignancy, within which distance and desire are both technologised and Americanised (both Harwood's spelling of "airplane," and the fact that the lover is flying back to New York emphasise this), this poem collapses the terms of its attention. It struggles to make its transatlantic occasion part of the poem's critique and rests upon sentimentalising the distances of its desire.

In a more sinister, and surreal, mode that points forward to Harwood's more mature style, the poet's imaginative discovery of and travels through the new world in the poem "Summer" find Mexican railroads raised upon "aztec ruins." This is a poem in which the history of the Americas comes to be seen as subject to a kind of lyrical porosity. It traverses a troubled emotional terrain where the land and the body become, together, scenes of troubled possession, " 'it's all a question of possession, / jealousy and . . .' " Most obviously, the effect of this poem is somewhat different from the wittily camp description of columns like sponge cakes in "New York will welcome me."[4] This is namely because any surreal humour of the previous poem is replaced here by a darker undercurrent, a nervy "half-light," in which Harwood seeks to conflate colonial and sexual desires. In this poem we are party to the enactment of a set of tense crossings between its evocations of a lover's body and of America's body politic. America's institutions of power ("senate," "independence") are thus swept up into a Roussel-like imaginative and surreal fantasy of poetic touch. Disturbingly personal *and* political, the poem's imagery of broken and demolished communications across distances of time and space indicates one of the strategies by which Harwood's developing poetics seek to go beyond the "egotistical dead-end" of its earlier mode. In a sense its broken and disjunctive articulacy becomes a measure—and a refutation—of lyric's refusal of the political:

> at intervals messages got through
> the senate was deserted all that summer
> black unmarked airplanes would suddenly appear
> and then leave the sky surprised at its quiet
> "couldn't you bear my tongue in your mouth?"

skin so smooth in the golden half-light
I work though nervousness to a poor but
convincing appearance of bravery and independence

mexico crossed by railways. aztec ruins
finally demolished and used for spanning one more ravine
in a chain of mountain tunnels and viaducts
and not one tear to span her grief
to lick him in the final mad-house hysteria
of armour falling off, rivets flying in all directions like fire-crackers,

Such a sense of "flying in all directions" typifies the rather uneven emotional register of *The Man With Blue Eyes*. But if such startling juxtapositions and jump-cuts indicate a certain poetic immaturity, they also, however, allow Harwood to sound a note that is rather different from the fluid articulations of the poets associated with the Black Mountain and New York "schools" he was reading at this point. So, although Harwood has noted that *The Man With Blues Eyes* is full of "raggedyness and mistakes" that result from his "undigested" enthusiasm for the new American poetry, it is also this quality that marks it off as different from the poetry of the American avant-garde that he was reading so enthusiastically at the time ("Memoirs" 588-89).

On the one hand, then, the "undigested" quality of *The Man With Blue Eyes* shows Harwood attempting a poetry that explores new territory, a poetry that, to adapt Frank O'Hara's words, "goes on its nerves," or in which, as Charles Olson's "Projective Verse" essay hammers home, "ONE PERCEPTION MUST IMMEDIATELY AND DIRECTLY LEAD TO A FURTHER PERCEPTION." But, on the other hand, the nervy energies of this collection leave a sense of ragged displacement—emotionally, poetically, and spatially—that is very different from the rapid onwards surge of poetic movement encountered in projective verse, in O'Hara's New York streets, or in, say, the fluid daydream mapping of Guadalajara in Ashbery's "The Instruction Manual" (1955). In contrast to such fluency, which seems to be about the invention of a poetically inhabitable place through the force of an imaginative energy,[5] and from which Harwood has clearly learned, *The Man With Blue Eyes* dwells on (in) moments of hesitation, doubt, and nervousness. The perceptual leaps are rapid, but also jarring, disjunctive. At its most accomplished *The Man with Blue Eyes* explores spaces—both real and emotional—as they are rendered poetically uninhabitable, as they stammer at the edge of speech. In this sense it is a collection that marks the direction in which his poetry could mature, and the possibilities it was taking from its reading of American poetry. In effect, the "raggedyness" (whether emotional, thematic, or in terms of poetic form) inheres in Harwood's increasingly insistent, but at this stage rather unformulated, poetics of touch.

The strongest poem of the collection, "As your eyes are blue," demonstrates this tendency powerfully.[6] Clearly showing a debt to the poetics of the new American poetry in its objective clarity and sense of the immediacy of its poetic perceptions, the attentive details of its poetic touch are shot through with a delicate and hesitating intimacy with the things of the world. The poem's distances and separations and its crushing sense of loss build from its detailing of the things of the poet's immediate perceptual environment. But the grey roof slates, half-open doors and windows, clothes and coins, taxi cabs and half-lit rooms of this poem are not, strictly, "objective correlatives" that *stand in*, as it were, for the poem's emotional environment. The poem's hesitant enumeration of these things renders them in themselves emotionally permeable and the poem itself an object in, and of, the world to which it is open. In its opening lines the poem maps a series of dependencies and tailings-off, of grammatical suspensions (seen in the "As . . . yet . . . even you" structure of the first stanza) that intimate the poem's halting emotional narrative:

> As your eyes are blue
> you move me—& the thought of you—
> I imitate you.
> & cities apart. yet a roof grey with slates
> or lead. the difference is little
> & even you could say as much
> though a foxtail of pain   even you
>
> when the river beneath your window
> was as much as I dream of.   loose change &
> your shirt on the top of the chest-of-drawers
> a mirror facing the ceiling & the light in a cupboard
> left to burn all day   a dull yellow
> probing the shadowy room   "what was it?"

"cancel the tickets"—a sleep talk
whose horrors razor a truth that can
walk with equal calm through palace rooms
chandeliers tinkling in the silence as winds batter the gardens

outside   formal lakes shuddering at the sight
of two lone walkers

Any "grand" story of separation, loss and sexual betrayal—though ges-
tured towards—is carefully kept at bay. The poem is not about revelation
in this sense. This is largely because its lyrical insistence is less confes-
sional, or personal, than it is attentive to the processes by which we might
speak ourselves as lyric subjects. The poem's open form, that is, is one of
continual revelation, a moment-by-moment discovery of itself through its
use of apparently disjunctive poetic textures and surfaces.

As Robert Sheppard has noted, the effect of this poem is one that
"teases [its reader] with possible semantic resolution" such that it "de-
familiarizes the other [and] pluralizes subjectivity" (330-31). Curiously,
though, such effects are not ones of exclusion. If they make apparent a
sense of the multi-faceted possibilities of poetic subjectivity then in doing
so they perform a key gesture in a poetics of inclusion. We are invited,
that is, *into* the poem feelingly, to complete the gaps, hesitations and half-
articulated phrases for ourselves. Rather than experiencing the world and
the poem as different environments, then, the poem's delicacy allows it to
trace a single environment of interaction. What is strange, or defamiliar-
izing, about this is the way in which the poem's seeming equanimity and
calmness of surface belies its apparent narrative of restless and troubled
emotional depths. This is not to say, though, that the poem works by
opposing surface and depth, form and emotional content. What it care-
fully attends to, rather, is its own (lyric) deployment of tropes of surface
and depth in order to generate its specific poetic environment. "Equal,"
in Charles Olson's phrase, "to the real itself," Harwood's poem is also
intensely self-aware about the qualities of its equalness.[7]

Such awareness is played-out in the poem's imagery of various surfaces
and their gentle disturbance. From the start the poem deploys a language
of inscrutably calm surfaces. The lover's blues eyes, for example, are
merely the first of a number of impenetrable surfaces throughout the
poem that reflect only the self-reflection of the poem's speaker. The con-
ditional clause of the first line, then, sets in train a series of surfaces that

"imitate" each other: "your eyes" and "the thought of you"; you and me ("I imitate you"); one city and another; blue eyes and a "grey roof"; "slates / or lead." Despite an apparent tonal evenness (registered in the repeated phrase "even you") and a seeming placidity of movement from one surface to another, such imitative equations do not flatten the poem's emotional reach but mark its fine, discriminating distinctions. The difference is, indeed, little. What the poem begins to discover is that the "equal calm" with which it attends to the things of its world actually covers them over. The poem's lyric gesture, then, is one of discovery, one that sees through its reflective surfaces ("*through* a foxtail of pain") to open onto its hidden emotional landscape. Whether looking at "the river beneath your window" the interior of a room, or a palace and its gardens, the sweep of the poem feels for the ripple in its calm texture. In the shuddering surface of a formal lake, or a chandelier jangling in the wind, we see scenes of a placid exterior world disturbed by an apprehension of an inner poetic truth. Here, in an image of surprising violence, Harwood's poetic calmness and quietness opens onto the poetic "real" as it "razors a truth."

Such a textual rending substantiates, as it were, the sudden appearance of the poem's dream life through its calmly articulated but nevertheless disjunctive poetic surface. But this sudden irruption of an inner world through—into—one of sharply realised exteriors is not, as might be suspected, simply psychological. Part of the powerful impact of the poem's "sleep talk" is that we are unable to distinguish who is actually speaking the disturbing dream-words. Effectively this means that no psychologically expressive speaking subject is suddenly revealed at this point as the "real" that lies underneath the poem's lyric surface. Rather, what we do see here are the ways in which the poem's disjunctive utterance is an equal part of its strategy of (emotional) openness. Under the poet's exploratory touch, poem and reader come to map a series of imaginative journeys and memories of journeys that, in the following sections of the poem, suggest a deeper rift in the fabric of human relations than the mere fragmenting of a love affair. In a moment that could be read as one of sad resignation, or of recognition of a sort of evenness between the parts of its disjunctive surface (another moment of "equal calm"), the poem states "why bother one thing equal to another." But the poem itself is bothered precisely by the ways in which it can—poetically—feel that evenness between things.

It is this, indeed, that might be felt to be the poem's generative principle. The poem suggests, but never asserts, connections. It is left for the reader to make them, to feel that, somehow, with "meetings disintegrating," poet and reader, love affairs and "affairs of state," meet equally over this poetic ground. And such meetings open into other possible poetic dwellings:

> you know even in the stillness of my kiss
> that doors are opening in another apartment
> on the other side of town   a shepherd grazing
> his sheep through a village we know
> high in the mountains the ski slopes thick with summer flowers
> & the water-meadows below with narcissi
> the back of your hand &—
>
> a newly designed red bus drives quietly down Gower Street
> a brilliant red   "how could I tell you . . ."
> with such confusion
>   meetings disintegrating
> & a general lack of purpose only too obvious
> in the affairs of state

The shifting in these lines from one scene to another imitates a sort of poetic opening of different doors, successively. Things meet, briefly, at these points of opening, only to move on again and disintegrate even as they touch. And touch, itself, is the medium of such dissolving connections and curtailed intimacies. The lover's kiss cannot still an inevitable departure and is oddly echoed by the image of sheep grazing. In both cases lips brush surfaces. The carpets of flowers "high in the mountains" and in the "water-meadows" likewise image surfaces kissed, this time with colour. Their mirroring touch, however, seems hopelessly self-reflective, narcissistic even. And in the grammatically disconnected phrase "the back of your hand &—," touch and intimacy are seen to disintegrate. Playing with the notion of knowing something "like the back of one's hand," the lover's touch—"your hand"—both rhymes with, and withdraws into, the lost touch of the copula "&—" which withdraws, itself, into silence.

Quite properly, the poem resists any sweeping gesture of closure, preferring instead to keep open the suggestion that, properly articulated, the personal somehow touches upon "affairs of state." In its final moments the poem yearns for touch, for the intimate, only to find its narrative even more forcefully interrupted by a resounding single word line "but." Tonally this is very different from the variety of connectives ("As," "even you,' "&," "of course," "you know," "yes, it was . . . ," etc.) that, however fragmented, have characterised the poem's disjunctive surface up to this point. Here, a failure of touch becomes the poem's measure of the distance, separation and broken desire that its hesitant articulations make manifest:

> but
>
>   the afternoon sunlight which shone in
> your eyes as you lay beside me watching for . . . .—
> we can neither remember—still shines as you
> wait nervously by the window for the ordered taxi
> to arrive   if only I could touch your naked shoulder
> now "but then . . . ."

Such a sense of emotional rupture and departure leads to the powerfully suggestive doubleness of the poem's final two lines in which distance is asserted even as it is denied: "& the distance is nothing / 'even you—." The poem remains open as a result of this hesitant trailing-off. Touchingly, we are not even sure who speaks these last two words, they remain in unclosed quotation marks.

Some considerable time has been spent on this remarkable early poem precisely because its concern to make articulate the disintegrating meeting point between the personal and the political, and its employment of a poetics of touch, signals the way in which Harwood's poetry would respond to the conditions of New York, and its poetry, when he finally did visit it in 1966. Both the quiet deliberateness of this poem and its generosity can be seen to become signal characteristics of the poetry Harwood wrote during, and after, his brief time spent as part of the New York poetry scene. Although his work was already maturing in this direction (and largely through his reading of American poets, especially those involved with Ashbery in the magazine *Locus Solus*[8]), it was New York itself that provided the impetus and stimulus for him to test his very English poetic voice against those voices of the emerging "second-generation" New York poets with whom he found himself involved. As Sandy Berrigan has put it, "I don't think of [Lee] as a New York poet and I definitely see him as British in his feeling for nature, the non aggressive stance he usually takes, the softness . . . Lee is more historical and political (in narrative ways) than the NY poets."

Similarly, John Ashbery remarks upon the "softness" of Harwood's poetic as a defining characteristic of his Englishness. As he describes it, there is a very English note to the "pearly, soft-focus quality one rarely sees in American poetry" but which he finds in Harwood.[9] Because of its American influences, though, Ashbery feels that Harwood's poetry encapsulates a transatlantic tension. Interestingly, he suggests that this has something to do with Harwood's dealings with issues of landscape, and geography. He notes that Harwood's poetry is more like "recent American poetry than English poetry" because of its open landscapes—it "lies open to the reader like a meadow. It moves slowly toward an unknown goal like a river."[10] What this description makes possible is a consideration of how Harwood's developing fascination with issues of landscape, geography, mapping and journeys in the two collections subsequent to *The Man With Blue Eyes* indicates his growing maturity as a poet precisely because they provide the means for him to confront that fraught transatlantic relationship in which his poetry of this period is embedded. Because of the transatlantic context for Harwood's poetics, the imagery of distance, separation, and departure that pervades *The White Room* and *Landscapes*, then, bears both personal and geopolitical resonances. Despite Ashbery's claim that "Harwood's English is like American English in that it lacks a strong sense of possession," its examination of the transatlantic dynamic from which it arises seems most expressly to be about strong senses of possession. We may, in fact, recall the line "it's all a question of possession, . . ." from the earlier poem "Summer" as a key to understanding how Harwood's poetry comes to respond to his experiences of New York, and of transatlantic dislocation. As modes of poetic possession, proximity and distance, touch and departure become crucial issues in Harwood's maturing style precisely because they are the felt forms of his experiencing of New York in the Summer of 1966.

Although Harwood was only a briefly present figure in the New York artistic "scene" at this time he was, nevertheless, important and influential. In a letter to this author describing his experiences in New York in the summer of 1966 he has noted that "there was a whole network of poets who got to know each other through the world of little magazines and who became friends. It was . . . a lively poetry and art scene, very open and generous and wide ranging. It was a very exciting atmosphere when everyone was experimenting and discovering and sharing enthusiasms and collaborating and having a lot of fun." One simple marker of just the sort of artistic generosity that Harwood encountered in New York is his easy acceptance—as an important figure—into that scene. As part of this exciting artistic network he worked with Joe Brainard on comic strips for the *East Village Other* newspaper, thus drawing upon his experience of having edited various small press magazines in London in the early sixties (such as *Night Scene*, *Night Train*, *Soho*, *Horde* and *Tzarad*).[11] His involvement in the lively St Mark's Poetry Project led to his befriending such people as Ted and Sandy Berrigan, Ron Padgett and Peter Schjeldahl as well as Anne Waldman and Lewis Warsh whose apartment at 33 St. Mark's Place on the Lower East Side, as Daniel Kane has noted, "proved to be a center for the New York School and the relationship of that coterie to the Poetry Project" (161). It also gave him the chance to renew his friendship with Tom Clark and Larry Fagin who he had first met early in 1966 when they were living in England.

As a result of his getting to know Anne Waldman and Lewis Warsh in that summer of 1966, a number of Harwood's poems were published in their *Angel Hair* magazine and—as already noted—they published his collection *The Man with Blue Eyes* as the first Angel Hair book. This book, for which Joe Brainard provided the cover artwork and Peter Schjeldahl its Preface, received the Poets Foundation Award in 1967.[12] The award, decided by an anonymous committee in New York, was for "a new or first collection of poems by a young &/or promising poet," and that year was given in commemoration of Frank O'Hara, who had died in the July of the previous year (Letter to the author). Though it is culturally intriguing that the award was given to a British poet, it also seems especially fitting, given that *The Man With Blue Eyes* was so clearly indebted to the work of both O'Hara and Ashbery (Weatherhead 173).

Indeed, both these first-generation New York poets were powerfully important to Harwood. Harwood had first met Ashbery the previous summer in London and had subsequently travelled with him through France and Switzerland (Ford 47). He has described Ashbery's impact on him as crucial, "Meeting John, in a near inexplicable way, turned me round . . . I finally realised one could make poems that worked like Borges" fictions. Poems that created a world and invited the reader to enter, to wander round, to put in their own two cents, to use.'(*Angel Hair Anthology* 588).[13] Ashbery had returned to New York from Paris in 1966 and Harwood had gone there too to be part of the vibrant cultural scene that heralded Ashbery's return. However, despite Ashbery's central importance to Harwood, being exposed to second-generation New York poets, allowed him to see ways of using an Ashbery-esque poetics of journeys and worlds spun-out imaginatively for effects markedly different from those of *The Tennis Court Oath* and *Mountains and Rivers*. In terms of O'Hara's influence on Harwood, it is tempting to see his tragic death in the summer of 1966, only a few months after Harwood met him, as casting a dark light over both Harwood's experience of New York and over the poetry that he wrote out of that experience. It would seem that O'Hara did encapsulate for Harwood the spirit of generosity and artistic openness that he associated with the New York scene. He remembers "the openness and intelligence of a man like Frank O'Hara, and his wit. I wanted my poems to have that too. I still treasure the memory of his care and delight as he told me, a stranger, which paintings to see in Washington." ("Lee Harwood" 144). However, as we shall see, although Harwood's work does take on darker undercurrents of foreboding, loss and departure this seems not specifically due to O'Hara's death but to a growing awareness, for Harwood, of his poetic differences from the New York poets amongst whom he found himself.

At times, in fact, *Landscapes*, and especially *The White Room*, seem explicitly attempts by Harwood to write away from the influence of Ashbery and O'Hara, so as to learn from later New York poets and in doing so discover his own, distinctly British, voice. A case in point might be the poem "When the Geography was Fixed," to which we will return in further detail later. In dismissing the superficiality of its own ability to describe the past, saying it is "only a figure . . . clumsy as most symbols," this poem obliquely refers to Ashbery's long poem "The Skaters" (1964).[14] Harwood notes, "And what's in the past / I don't know anymore—it was all ice-skating." Thus the intricately spun-out surface of Ashbery's discursive poetics (his attending to how "the water surface ripples, the whole light changes" [34]) is here countered by Harwood's attempt to write a poetry that gets beneath the surface, one that acknowledges that "This formality is just a cover" (90).[15] An attempt by Harwood to move away from the model of O'Hara's poetry might also be detected in this poem. The poem's imagery of painting, and its description of a gallery-opening has clear, general, affinities with O'Hara's work. Most specifically, though, the poem seems anxious to acknowledge and differentiate itself from O'Hara's famous poem "Why I am Not A Painter." Like O'Hara, Harwood writes a poem about the similarities and differences between acts of making a painting and of making a poem, one—moreover—that makes semiotic indeterminacy its point of enquiry ("clumsy . . . symbols"). However, if for O'Hara the differences between painter (Mike Goldberg) and poet (O'Hara) are encapsulated in the poet's use of the word "ORANGES" (in contrast to Goldberg's use of "SARDINES"), Harwood's poem makes a very different use of this colour. For Harwood, the distinction between inner and outer landscapes, as well as between poetry and painting, is marked by his poem's struggle to clarify a series of distinctions between shades of red and orange:

> The hills and room are both in
> the white. The colours are here
> inside us, I suppose . . .
> In the water a thick red cloud
> unfurls upwards; at times it's almost orange.
>   . . .
> The clear droplets of water sparkle
> and the orange-red cloud hangs quite seductively.

If, on the one hand, O'Hara captures the atmosphere of a self-enclosed, self-referential New York art scene, one that manifests an apparently unstoppable expansiveness in its attention to surface ("One day I am thinking of / a color: orange. I write a line about orange. Pretty soon it is a / whole page of words" [112]),[16] on the other hand, Harwood's delicate investigation of orange and red allows for an entirely different set of associations to unfurl by the end of his poem. Through his poetic attention to distinctions of colour, Harwood is able to hint at an expansiveness—very different from O'Hara's—that haunts his poetic landscape. Geographies are fixed, Harwood suggests, in acts of nation-building. The colonial spread of whiteness across the American landscape leaves only a trace, scant record, of redness, though the scene is coloured, distantly, by it.

> During the whole gallery-opening a record of primitive red
> indian chants was played—and this music
> seemed to come from the very distant hills
> seen in every painting—their distance was
> no longer fixed and they came nearer.
> But recognitions only came when all
> the veneer was stripped off
> and the inexplicable accepted in the whiteness.

So fine and delicate are the manoeuvres of this poem in finding a way beyond the poetic examples of Ashbery and O'Hara in particular, and New York poetics more widely, that it would be insensitive to claim that it is a direct political critique of such poetics. What it does register, though, is Harwood's willingness to frame his own poetic questions about cultural distance, otherness, even colonial and sexual possession, as a response to New York and its poetries.

In many ways, then, what Harwood learns from his exposure to the vibrant New York poetry scene is a delicacy of poetic touch whereby he can balance his sense of cultural distance against that of his fascination with the things of the world around him. His poetics, that is, grows to exploit the tension (a transatlantic one) between the energies of generous commitment he encountered in New York and that of his soft, hesitant articulacy. Feeling away from home, both in and out of the "scene," being in New York allowed Harwood, therefore, to write poems in which questions of dwelling and space, and of landscape and geography are opened out as refractions of a wider political economy. As his poetry matures it does so by revealing an awareness of the historical and political conditions (of power, of colonialism) upon which a sense of the geographies we inhabit, the landscapes through which we travel, are raised. Throughout *The White Room* and *Landscapes* we encounter repeated scenes of departure and journeys as analogues to broken relationships. But the sense of fragmentation and "gappiness" that these lend to the poetry is very different in effect from the "raggedyness" of Harwood's earlier work. The poetic breaks and sense of distance and dissolving landscapes of this later work resonate with vague political menace, often, as in "The Argentine" by explicitly commenting on acts of colonising the land: "This was not the first migration / nor would this country be in anyway final— / the movement had been an agony dragged across / many lands   it was a well known process" (83). On other occasions in these collections figures are left stranded within an open landscape such that geographical and emotional distances come to reflect each other. Thus "The Seaside" begins with the lines, "You wrote such a love poem that I was / dumbfounded and left to scratch the sand / Alone in the surf" (60), and in a similar vein, another poem in this collection, "The Doomed Fleet," begins, "The entire palace was deserted, just as was / the city, and all the villages along the 50 mile / route from the seaport to the capital. / It was not caused by famine of war— / 'It was all my fault'" (92). "Plato was Right Though" strips bare its poetic landscape—"The empty house—the empty country—the empty sky. / Reverse it to A—B—C."—and declares "All the previous locations are impossible" in its contemplation of Plato's banning of poets from the Republic (101-04)

Generally, the idea of location itself (both poetic and geographic) is more fluid in the slightly later collection *Landscapes*. The quieter tones of this collection nevertheless still register a mistrust (like Plato's) of poetry's ability to reflect the conditions of the real. As we have seen, this indicates a drawing away from the kind of hard and fast street-wise poetry of poets such as Frank O'Hara, Ted Berrigan and Lewis Warsh who became friends of Harwood's in New York. As his poetry learns from the New York scene, and moves away from it, landscape itself becomes the increasingly anxious focus for his poetic articulations. So, while learning from the briskness and energetic surfaces of New York's first- and second-generation poets and their concern with the immediacies of their poetic environment (for instance, Berrigan's series of O'Hara-influenced poems each entitled "Personal Poem"), Harwood wants to attend to the landscape of layered histories that can be discovered beneath such poetic surfaces. This is evidenced in poems such as "When The Geography Was Fixed" and "The House" which, despite their seeming simplicity of statement, take place in uneasy locations, ones that are marginalized, at a distance from the centre. These settings reflect the delicate unease of Harwood's position as a poetic-insider and cultural-outsider to the New York scene. We are told (in "When The Geography Was Fixed") that "The distant hills are seen from the windows. / It is a quiet room, & the house is in a town / far from the capital" and (in "The House") that "The rain over the hills—the shades of blue & grey / in the clouds on the horizon with the evening coming— / The house is on the outskirts of the town." (12, 14).[17] Located at the edges geographically, many of the poems in *Landscapes* reveal a self-conscious edginess about their underlying artistic conditions. They interrogate, that is, the relationship between senses of geographic and of poetic place, an investigation, it would seem, that results from his having spent time in New York. In 'The House" the question of location underpins a consideration of the real. The landscape is English, though the process of its poetic investigation, how it unreels across that landscape, is indebted to American poetics:

> & this question of painting & vision
> & which seems the more real is fascinating—
> I can't explain this. But beyond the hills
> are the moors (14)

The poem, as it were, digs in and reveals the various strata and faultlines on which it is erected. Harwood's poetic eye is fascinated here by a twin vision, firstly, of that which lies just beyond and, secondly, of its own position of beyondness, or inexplicability. Poem, then, becomes both the vehicle and the object of a complex investigation of the space occupied by us as lyric subjects.

For "When The Geography Was Fixed," and "Question of Geography" the poem itself is both place and process of stripping away layers, it performs an attempt to get to the real geography that lies underneath the poetic, or painterly, façade. Both poems are disturbingly fascinated by what lies underneath, and they both see this fascination in painterly terms. "Question of Geography" self-consciously explores the position it can occupy as a poem, given that "all [is] inevitably reduced to the question of / geography or memory" (22). Such a poetic layering of present and past places ("geography or memory") provides the poem's conclusion with some kind of aesthetic compensation in the fact that although we are told the real place is painted over, "all the same it's still there / beneath the fresh plains of colour."[18] Questions of geography are therefore explicitly seen as aesthetic ones too. In "When The Geography Was Fixed" (along with many other poems in *Landscapes*) plainness of speech becomes a question of getting beneath the surface veneer. The poem tells us that "This formality is just a cover," but its interest is not so much in revealing what is covered over than in detailing the poetics of that process of uncovering (12).[19] As with "The House," this stripping away of poetic, geographic and paint layers leads to an acceptance of the inexplicable, "But recognitions only came when all / the veneer was stripped off / & the inexplicable accepted in whiteness" (13). We are left here with a fresh plain of white, the poem's acceptance that it can never be anything more than an incomplete landscape.

In fact, in many of the later poems in *Landscapes*, gaps in the text, literal white spaces, indicate the hesitant poetic margin between real and emotional landscapes that Harwood is seeking to explore. The ruptured (textual) landscape at the opening of "Question of Geography," for example, displays a rather troubled indeterminacy on the part of the poem's speaker wherein an unspecified "somewhere" lies "hidden" and forgotten:

Facing the house	the line of hills
across the valley	a river somewhere
hidden from view	the thickets there
I can't remember	the colours (22)

Such hesitant articulations are explicitly about testing the margins of poetic experience. In this sense they provide a poetics that is edgy, and which pushes against the limits of the space occupied by the poem. Such gaps demonstrate, therefore, how distance, separation and beyondness are more than simply thematic concerns for Harwood. A sense of landscape as the occasion of the poem's lyric utterance is powerfully conveyed in "You Become a Star." Once more its textual gaps suggest its theme of (transcontinental) distances reconciled

> Your face so near   your body
> at the sea's edge   many continents
> away in the distance   the whole shoreline
> vibrating   the blue grey sky at night (46)

Superficially these poems have affinities with American experimental poetics in general, and with those of the New York scene most especially. Specifically, though, they were inspired—as Harwood has pointed out—by the work of Joe Ceravolo.[20] They develop through an Olson-like poetics of the open-work, and—formally—seem closely related to a poem such as Lewis Warsh's "Inside Long Treks" that was published in *Angel Hair* # 3 in the Summer of 1967, at the time Harwood was writing the poems in *Landscapes*, and which he supposes was equally influenced by Ceravolo.

But in their attention to margins and limits, their sense of poetic articulation as continually ruptured, not seamless, and their work to expose the underlying conditions of their utterance, they show Harwood's departure from such models. Harwood's interrupted poetic voice is a counter to what he heard in New York poetry. Writing in 1975 he noted that "The danger of most New York poetry is that you get a tone of voice going, and it's very elegant and witty, and the rest of it, and then it comes out as yards of material which you just reel off." ("Surrealist Poetry Today" 13).[21] The implication—however reductive—about New York poetry is that it deals solely with surfaces, tones and striking attitudes. And Harwood certainly felt this as a danger in his own poetry. In writing *Landscapes*, Harwood sought to respond to F. T. Prince's charge about *The White Room* that, under the influence of New York poets, he was merely "pattering on." (Sheppard, "Lee Harwood and the Poetics of the Open Work," 219). So, Harwood's response to New York is to develop his own kind of poetic seriousness. Rather than simply skating over surfaces and reeling off material, Harwood attempts to "feel" for distance, separation and the gaps in human relations. Though undoubtedly such themes result from his New York experiences, they actually lend his poetry a quality that is very different from that of his New York friends. While New York poets disdained overt seriousness, and practised insouciant forms of poetic disengagement by focusing upon an environment of (urban) surfaces, Harwood's interest is increasingly to attend to what lies behind such surfaces.

It is in this sense that, however much it is connected with an American processual poetics, the slow unfolding of Harwood's poetry before us like a river, as John Ashbery has described it, is in fact part of a careful poetic examination of one's place within, and possession by, the environment in which one finds oneself. However much *The White Room* and *Landscapes* are indebted to Harwood's New York experience (and many of the poems they contain were either completely written, or at least started, in New York [Letter to the author]) these collections develop a quiet deliberateness, and a poetic generosity that is very different from the sorts of generosity Harwood described himself as encountering in New York. His poetic narratives, as we shall see (and picking-up on Sandy Berrigan's point), often turn or break or dissolve as they discover the political or the historical as it emerges through the surface of personal "patter." His stance is, indeed, non aggressive and thus—I want to argue—a subtle counter to the politics of an aggressive and (apparently) imperialist power that was being enacted at the time by The United States in South-East Asia, and which the New York poetry scene is often felt to have avoided tackling.[22] Though, as David Herd has clearly pointed out, it would be rather too simplistic to maintain that the conflict in Vietnam had no impact upon the radical, experimental art scene in mid-sixties New York, it is true to say that the pressure of it as a form of ideological conflict is registered rather differently in Harwood's work when measured against that of his New York contemporaries.[23] Perhaps it is simply that the energies Harwood is able to give to the New York "scene" are ones that derive from his greater political distance, and from a poetic desire to see a broader ideological picture. Quite clearly, though, the voice we hear in the poems Harwood wrote during, or shortly after, his time in New York, has the generosity of a different ideological commitment to that artistic scene from that of his American contemporaries. Despite this, much of the energy of his poetry in this period seems due to his actual contact with poets previously known to him only through correspondence. Indeed, while distance—as we have already seen—is a common theme in his work of this period, a feeling of transatlantic contact also pervades the poems written at this time and is clearly one of the most important aspects of those few months Harwood spent in New York in 1966.

Being importantly involved in the New York scene, then, crucially lent much of Harwood's poetry in *The White Room* a restless energy similar to that of his New York school peers. With a bravura to match Ted Berrigan, "His July Return" details a re-union of lovers before contemplating the scene of its own writing, "When I had finished writing this, I looked at / my watch. It was 2.30 in the morning. / I decided to go to bed" (58). The camp literariness of "The Late Poem" sounds a note familiar from Frank O'Hara, "Today I got very excited when I read some / poems by Mallarmé and Edwin Denby, and later / in the evening, by F. T. Prince. / . . . / Ted Berrigan has met Edwin Denby. / I don't know anyone who has met F. T. Prince. / I wish I could meet F. T. Prince; / maybe I will one day, but it will have to be soon / as he must be getting old" (59). And the fascinating and funny poem dedicated to Tom Clark, "I'm Stoned, Tom" takes—literally—a double perspective on Harwood's feeling of displacement in America. Excusing his earlier bad-temper at a café, the poem's speaker (whose words appear throughout the poem in quotation marks) notes "'Tonight I'm so stoned that / when I look at my favourite postcard of / Kit Carson's tomb I see two gravestones / and I know that's not right'" (64). The speaker's feeling of things not being right for him in America, of his own sense of cultural displacement (and those of the Indians of "Taos, New Mexico" mentioned in the penultimate stanza) within a mythical Western setting, leads to the poem's concluding note, "It's so difficult being 27 years old / and still not sure where one is." What is heard here is the undercurrent that marks the whole of *The White Room*, namely Harwood's sense of his distance and difference from the dynamic American scene in which he was participating. Here the transatlantic tension that drives this collection resonates through his sense of being an outsider. It becomes the driving force of his poetics.

This is seen expressly in the longer, more narrative, poems of *The White Room* through Harwood's detailing of scenes of parting and departure. In "The Argentine" and "The Book" such scenes owe much to Borges's stories of Argentinean ranches, though these are played off against a different vision of America, one that take place in New York. The city's grid system, with its crossings of avenues and streets, becomes an analogue for the crossing traffic of human relations. This is turn intersects with the larger political dimensions of these poems. In both cases a personal (that is, emotional and erotic) sense of loss and exclusion is thus mapped onto a political, or at least, geographic system of relations. "The Argentine" plays-off a mythic South America of gauchos "discontent with the ranch" riding off in search of new pastures against the leave-taking on the New York streets that takes place in its fourth section (82-5). The poem thus interweaves the taking—or missing—of personal and sexual chances with the bold moves of nation-building frontiersmen. It discovers that lurking equally beneath colonial and sexual desires is a sad discontent driven by the pressure of distance between Old and New worlds. New York is the location of that distance:

> On the sidewalk in Fifth Avenue just below 12th Street
> 3 men were parting outside a German restaurant.
> The older one had to go uptown—it was late—
> and the 2 young men were
> separately going to drift round the Village for a few hours
> Then, as the taxi arrived, Joe reached up
> and kissed John on the forehead.
> The 3 split up. It was a hot june night—of course.
>
> The second young man left outside this action
> evidently felt something
> It would seem that he was really more concerned
> with the older man and that he now regretted
> his passiveness in the street . . .
>
> . . . The frustration at a missed chance is universal
> and a slight jealousy of the successful equally common
> There were other days, and usually the older and the younger man
> succeeded in gaining some degree of harmony
>
> But . . .
> the pressure of a train and a plane schedule
> put a simple end to that development (84)

Part of the disturbing sense of rupturedness in this poem (and signalled, above, by the "But . . .") is the way its six sections cut between different scenes in, and narrative perspectives upon, the American landscape.

America itself becomes, therefore, a scene of displaced histories of op-
pression and violence, where the clear view "from the mountain pass"
is unnervingly too easy "and the whole geography somehow too simple"
because, it seems, the "violence" underpinning "past journeys" will too
easily be forgotten (85). But another sense of displacement is witnessed
here. Because of the oddly stilted third-person narration Harwood him-
self stands at some considerable distance from the action. Both the poet
and the "second young man" are effectively "left outside this action."
Given the poignant detail of the "train and plane schedule," it would
seem that once again Harwood's sense of distance from the New York
scene, his outsider position within it, is a subtle indicator of wider trans-
atlantic relations.

"The Book" would seem to confirm this. Again this is a poem of many
departures: we see motorcyclists who ride "fast along the highway" in
its first section; "The 5.25 Pullman train, painted chocolate and cream"
leaving Brighton station, as well as a car journey conducted "in silence,"
in section two; and another parting on New York streets in section four.
Such departures betray Anglo-American tensions. The "highway" down
which the motorcyclists ride contrasts sharply with the English coun-
tryside of an "early Norman village church" and "ploughed / fields,
with rooks in the elms" that is seen from the car and train windows in
sections two and three. And the "churchman" who is seen spilling tea
whilst "leafing through his sermon" on the train journey from Brighton
is clearly not part of the New York scene of the poem's final section. The
imagery of the poem's New York ending emphasises points of cultural
crossing and divergence, in the meeting of Avenue and Street and in the
contrasting "cream-coloured suit" and "dark glasses" of the departing
lover (that incidentally recalls the colours of the Brighton Pullman, and
perhaps hints at the simmering racial tensions of urban New York in the
mid-sixties).

> We parted at 1st Avenue and 51st Street—it was July.
> Wearing a cream-coloured suit and dark glasses
> he crossed the street and then turned to wave—twice—
> the lunch-time traffic was very heavy and I soon
> lost sight of him.

Such notes of distance, departure and the fleetingness of everyday mo-
ments in the face of the traffic of modern experience are part of Harwood's

response to New York. These tell us much, though, about Harwood's poetics of dwelling—of how his poetry attends to a sense of longing for, and belonging to, the landscape of experience. Being an outsider in New York allowed Harwood to feel more keenly the generous spirit of the New York artistic scene in that summer of 1966 and how his poetry might learn from that.

To conclude, I should like to return to the epigraph with which this essay opened. At the start of his essay, "The Thing," Heidegger considers how a concept of "things" and "thingliness" is related to a consideration of distance (and the contraction of distance) in modern space. The world, that is, is made manifest in our feeling of nearness to it. He goes on to examine how "thingliness" inheres in the notion of containment, that an object defines itself as a thing by its containment of, or definition of, the space it inhabits (165-82). Harwood's poetics represents an attempt to respond openly to the world it inhabits, or to the "things" it lays possession of. By traversing the distances between New York poetics and his own British voice, and in his willingness to leave a poetic space open for us, the reader, to explore, Harwood continually examines how poetry might be a generous dwelling place. His poems provide, then, a measure of the distances of transatlantic poetic relations by testing, feelingly, the spaces and surfaces upon which they dwell. While Harwood's attention to the poem's "thingliness" might be seen as something he has learned from New York poetry, his work is also inflected with—possessed by—a particularly English sense of the density and texture of its poetic landscapes. These themes are perhaps best expressed in another of Harwood's New York poems, "Central Park Zoo," in which centrality and marginality, possession and freedom, as well as New York's generosity as a poetic space, are all played out.[24] This poem ends:

> We walk among the animals
>   the cages upset you
> When I really think I know you're always right
> there's no worry   we're on the same planet
> & so very lucky
> that the poem should end like this
> is very good

Works Cited

Anon. "Harwood Bibliography," *Poetry Info*, 14 (Autumn-Winter, 1975):17-18.

Ashbery, John. *Some Trees*. New York: Ecco Press, 1978.

—. *Rivers and Mountains* New York: Ecco Press, 1977.

Berrigan, Sandy. Letter to author, 21st June, 2004.

Costello, Bonnie. "John Ashbery's Landscapes," in *The Tribe of John: Ashbery and Contemporary Poetry*, ed. Susan M. Schultz. Tuscaloosa: The University of Alabama Press, 1995. 60-80.

Ford, Mark. *John Ashbery in Conversation with Mark Ford* London: Between The Lines, 2003.

Friedlander, Benjamin. "Strange Fruit: O'Hara, Race and the Color of Time," in *The Scene of My Selves: New Work on the New York School Poets*, eds. Terence Diggory and Stephen Paul Miller. Orono, Maine: The National Poetry Foundation, 2001. 123-41.

Harwood, Lee. *The Man With Blues Eyes*. New York: Angel Hair, 1966.

—. *The White Room* London: Fulcrum, 1968.

—. *Landscapes* London: Fulcrum Press, 1969.

—. "Surrealist Poetry Today," *Alembic* 3 (1975): 13-14.

—. "Lee Harwood," in *Contemporary Authors: Autobiography Series*, vol. 19, ed. Joyce Nakamura. Detroit: Gale Research Inc., 1994. 135-53.

—. "Memoirs," *Angel hair sleeps with a boy in my head: The Angel Hair Anthology*, ed. Anne Waldman and Lewis Warsh. New York: Granary Book, 2001). 588-89.

—. Letter to author, 7th April 2004.

Heidegger, Martin. "The Thing," in *Poetry, Language, Thought*, trans. Albert Hofstadter. New York: Harper and Row, 1971. 165-86.

Herd, David. *John Ashbery and American Poetry*. Manchester: Manchester University Press, 2000.

Kane, Daniel. *All Poets Welcome: The Lower East Side Poetry Scene in the 1960s*. Berkeley: University of California Press, 2003.

Lehman, David. *The Last Avant-Garde: The Making of the New York School Poets* New York: Doubleday, 1998.

O'Hara, Frank. *Selected Poems*, ed. Donald Allen. Manchester: Carcanet, 1991.

Olson, Charles. *Selected Writings*, ed. Robert Creeley. New York: New Directions, 1966.

Sheppard, Robert. *Some Aspects of Contemporary British Poetry: With Particular Reference to the Works of Roy Fisher and Lee Harwood*, unpublished PhD thesis, University of East Anglia, 1987.

—. "Lee Harwood and the Poetics of the Open Work," *New British Poetries: The Scope of the* Possible, eds. Robert Hampson and Peter Barry. Manchester: Manchester University Press, 1992. 216-33.

Shoptaw, John. *On The Outside Looking Out: John Ashbery's Poetry.* Cambridge, Mass. and London: Harvard University Press, 1994.

Warsh, Lewis. Email to the author, 3rd April, 2004.

Weatherhead, A. Kingsley. *The British Dissonance: Essay on Ten Contemporary Poets.* Columbia and London: University of Missouri Press, 1983.

Spring in This World of Mad Angels: The Poetry of Joseph Ceravolo

PATRICK MASTERSON & PAUL STEPHENS

"Strangely enough, it's better to be unrecognized as an exceptional poet, at least for a while" ("Scattered Poems by Jack Kerouac" 77). So begins what appears to be the only review Joseph Ceravolo ever published in his lifetime. Ceravolo's own exceptional poetry has gone, for the most part, unrecognized—particularly when compared to the standard of Jack Kerouac that Ceravolo invokes. Ceravolo ends the opening paragraph of this review of Kerouac's *Scattered Poems* with the slightly off-color statement: "How great it is to be forgotten and then come back to life again, even though you are dead. (Jack!)" (78). And since he said it first, we repeat after him: "How great it is to be forgotten and then come back to life again, even though you are dead. (Joe!)"

Ceravolo remains one of the more enigmatic figures of what is now called the second-generation New York School. His life and works, in fact, call into question many of the term's typical associations. Ceravolo, during his most productive years, was not a Bohemian, not a Manhattanite, and not, for the most part, greatly involved in the kinds of self-promotion that characterized the small-press and small-journal publishing of younger writers in New York in the 1960s. Both David Shapiro and Ron Padgett tell the story of Ted Berrigan having to go in person to Ceravolo's home in Bloomfield, New Jersey to collect the manuscript that would become (via mimeograph) Ceravolo's first book *Fits of Dawn*. The story, like many others, illustrates that Ceravolo tended not to go out of his way to circulate his work—in marked contrast to many of his friends who compulsively published themselves and each other. Though a well-produced selected poems, *The Green Lake is Awake*, appeared posthumously in 1994, otherwise none of the six books he published during his lifetime remain in print. Indeed, a great deal of his work remains unpublished. The mini-epic poem *Hellgate* (a recording of which was played at the memorial reading for him at the Poetry Project in 1988, and the title of which refers to the Hellgate bridge in Astoria, Queens, where Ceravolo was raised) remains in manuscript, as do the poems that he was working on in the 1980s which he placed under the title *Mad Angels*.

The hope is that more of Ceravolo's poetry will become available to a wider readership over time. In the meantime, this essay is intended to serve as a critical thematic introduction to Ceravolo's diverse body of work. Though Ceravolo's work has appeared in numerous anthologies, and has been cited as an influence by other poets, there has never been, to the best of our knowledge, any kind of detailed scholarly analysis of his work.[1] Through the course of writing this essay, Joseph Ceravolo has come to seem to us to be something more of a mysterious angel than a mad one. His poems are often as lucid as they are visionary, and if his poems often seem personal they are never simply allegories of what we know of his life. We were impressed by the accounts given of him by his fellow poets David Shapiro, Ron Padgett, and Paul Violi—nonetheless our account remains at a certain distance from the poet himself.[2]

Ceravolo's first book publication seems to have occurred as an indirect result of his having been on a list of poets given to Ted Berrigan by Kenneth Koch.[3] Berrigan and Ceravolo were both born in 1934, which makes them less than ten years younger than the poets usually thought of as first-generation New York School. It could be said that Berrigan and Ceravolo, in terms of age, were something more like first-and-a-half-generation New York School—although we acknowledge that the two poets are generally considered alongside other important younger second-generation poets like Ron Padgett (b. 1942), Anne Waldman (b. 1944), Bernadette Mayer (b. 1945), David Shapiro (b. 1947) and Paul Violi (b. 1947).[4] Daniel Kane suggests that:

> One can argue that what characterized the difference between the "First-" and "Second-" Generation New York School poets was the Second Generation's occasional use of typically Beat writing practices, including a slightly more rough-edged approach and (particularly in Berrigan's case) a greater tendency to disclose personal information that emphasized the speaker's use of illegal drugs or other stereotypical dissolute activities. (109)

All of these considerations are generally true, but in the case of Ceravolo none of them are true. Ceravolo does belong under the second-generation rubric, but with certain qualifications. Another rough distinction might be made within New York School poetics, for instance, between "uptown" poets and "downtown" poets. This distinction would be less about literal geography and more about socio-economic origins (in the pre-gentrification senses of "uptown" and "downtown"). Poets like Ceravolo, Tony Towle, and Frank Lima were native New Yorkers who emerged from working-class backgrounds. Ceravolo was born in Astoria, the son of a tailor and a seamstress. He would go on to graduate from City College, and later to take poetry classes at the New School. By way of contrast, none of the poets that David Lehman considers first generation—Ashbery, Koch, Schuyler, O'Hara—actually grew up in New York City. With the exception of Schuyler, all attended Harvard and all had ties to "uptown" institutions like Columbia or the Museum of Modern Art. There were Ivy Leaguers among the second generation, of course, but many of those who had been taught and influenced by the first generation came from less privileged and more local backgrounds. This tended to make "downtown" second-generation poets less likely (particularly during the 1960s) to be employed in art world or academic positions. In Ceravolo's case, his occupation as a civil engineer does not fit well into either an "uptown" or a "downtown" model of New York writing in the 1960s.

In other respects too, Ceravolo's works are not typical of second-generation New York School writing. Though he was clearly influenced by his teachers Kenneth Koch and Frank O'Hara, Ceravolo, while he is often humorous, is rarely ironic. Unlike the poetry of Ted Berrigan or Frank Lima, Ceravolo's poetry has few direct affinities to Beat writing. Ceravolo's 1960s poems offer personal information only on the most oblique terms, and there is little to speak of in the way of "dissolute activities." The locations of Ceravolo's poems are seldom urban—more characteristically they are suburban. The Jersey Shore and Newark's Olmstead-designed Weequahic Park (the location of the green lake in "The Green Lake is Awake") frequently appear in the poems. Unlike Ted Berrigan or Frank O'Hara, Ceravolo offered few references to contemporary New York social life.

If Ceravolo was not himself directly involved in publishing the works of others, as were many other New York writers of the time, his poetry was nonetheless well-represented within the small-journal and small-press culture. Ceravolo's publication credits—in journals like *Locus Solus, Art and Literature, C Magazine, Angel Hair, Adventures in Poetry,* Aram Saroyan's *Lines,* and *The Paris Review*—demonstrate that an admiration for Ceravolo's poetry held broadly throughout the New York School. Ceravolo's earliest extensive foray into publication seems to occur, in fact, in a 22-page section of his poetry in the double issue of *Locus Solus III-IV* edited by John Ashbery in 1962. At least during the 1960s, Ceravolo was well-connected to both first- and second-generation publishing organs. Writers like Towle, Ceravolo, Charles North, Bill Berkson, and Frank Lima—all of whom attended workshops at the New School taught by Koch and O'Hara—had a unique and somewhat belated relation to their first-generation predecessors. Koch certainly did more than any other figure to champion Ceravolo's work, but their correspondence shows that they for the most part maintained a respectful student/professor relationship. Ceravolo sought Koch's approval of his poetry while it was still in manuscript; the reverse does not seem to be true of Koch. Though Ceravolo for a time was close to the inner circle of Koch, O'Hara, and Ashbery, he was not himself, so to speak, a full-fledged member of the inner circle.

The earliest poems we have by Ceravolo, which are not yet as experimental as those of *Fits of Dawn*, are included in the volume *Transmigration Solo*. Not published until 1979, *Transmigration Solo* included a mix of poems from a 1960 trip to Mexico, as well as a group of poems from 1965.[5] These early poems demonstrate an early Koch-esque metaphoric intensity, although they do not tend to share Koch's Francophilic humor. A couplet like "The light is mattress lipped, / and the pages born curtains" (*Transmigration Solo* 30) typifies Ceravolo's approach—surrealistic, yet detailed and serious. The poem "Invisible Autumn" is more Williams-esque in its language and compression:

> The blade days—
> like Summer rush
>
> Apollo leans.
> The way the sun comes up,
> the sun leans.
> The sun leans less than
> in the north, but one lean
> is as good as another.
> Now it's autumn, but
> you would never know.
>
> The blade days
> like Summer, rush. (*Transmigration Solo* 19)

The poem displays Ceravolo's lifelong fascination with the seasons, as well as with the short line, but it does not yet display the mid-60s difficulty that characterizes his best-known works.

Ceravolo's first book *Fits of Dawn* shows the influence of Ashbery, Koch, and O'Hara, but it also departs from their models in its stylistic ambitiousness. *Fits of Dawn* is arguably one of the most challenging and experimental works produced in New York during the mid-1960s. In its use of neologisms, non-sequitur themes, and fractured syntax, *Fits of Dawn* was every bit as unorthodox as Ashbery's *Tennis Court Oath* or O'Hara's "Second Avenue." By the time of *Fits of Dawn*, Ceravolo's writing had changed dramatically. The minimal had become maximal, though the internal assonance and sonic intensity of the earlier poems remained. Compare "blade days" with "Tierra . . . overture" or "apple . . . axles" in the passage below:

> Tierra! nothing less overture
> dirty summer of wear the
> apple   Pine causes axles
> sung stupor of nests
> Beg injun actual of beneath clarteaux
> dead   Slying!
> mountain!   oh mountain!   un-
> torn scat scat indestruct.
> wakens so cupped of ascending
>   farms ah the muslin
> Muslin! of stash compel
>   Voyez! terrace retournelle
> migrate sax   the rail drape so
> desire   Listen! Made up!
> Of! gist, crocus, the among (*Fits of Dawn* n.p. Book II)

Although the writing bears much in common with Koch and O'Hara in its use of exclamation marks and French interjections, *Fits of Dawn* is even more densely-packed and narrative-thwarting than Koch or O'Hara at their long poem extremes. Whereas long poems like Koch's *When the Sun Tries To Go On* and O'Hara's "Second Avenue" are filled with recognizable literary and pop-cultural allusions, *Fits of Dawn* rarely employs proper names. Given that it is only sporadically punctuated, perhaps the poem *Fits of Dawn* most closely resembles is Ashbery's "Europe." But even here, *Fits of Dawn* diverges. "Europe" is divided into small lyrical chunks, and it tends toward short lines (much like Ceravolo's later poetry). *Fits of*

Dawn employs long lines and projective spacing, and it seldom aims for comedy. It is this period of Ceravolo's writing that has drawn particular attention from Charles Bernstein and Ron Silliman (though Silliman offers his most extended consideration of Ceravolo in the context of the early poem "Migratory Noon" from *Transmigration Solo*). Charles Bernstein, for instance, isolates several instances of New York School texts that were especially amenable to Language writers' interest in multiple referentiality: "Koch's 'When the Sun tries to Go On' or Ceravolo's 'Fits of Dawn'—I was looking for a certain kind of work and these poems fit that bill" (qtd. in Kane 191). Given that the book is highly disjunctive, polylingual, and uncompromising in its methods, the line "rigor rubbing outset" (*Fits of Dawn* n.p.) might well stand as a description of the book as a whole. While an early Ceravolo poem like "Invisible Autumn" occupies the world of the precision lyric, the world of *Fits of Dawn* has become that of Dada, Stein, and perhaps *The Tennis Court Oath*. *Fits of Dawn* is not ironic or clever in the ways of Kenneth Koch or Ron Padgett or Ted Berrigan or even Bernadette Mayer; it does not offer emotional metaphors to ground experience as in much of Ashbery's work; it does not have the everyday world detail of Frank O'Hara's "I do this, I do that" mode. While its anti-metaphorical jazz-influenced verbal intensity—"terrace retournelle / migrate sax the rail drape so / desire"—may remind some readers of the early Clark Coolidge, we note that Coolidge did not publish his first book until a year after *Fits of Dawn*'s appearance.

Fits of Dawn is also somewhat unique among second-generation New York School works in the degree to which it combines a deep interest in non-western literature with an intense emphasis on the materiality of language. Ceravolo writes of Kerouac's *Scattered Poems*:

> it's a pure relief to read a poet so unburdened by western academic poetics . . . Kerouac makes me forget about the pretensions and immortalizations of western poetry and exudes a freshness of the combination of reality, fantasy, and spirit that the best of western poetry shows. This links it with all the poetry of the world . . . *Scattered Poems* takes the embarrassment out of being influenced by poetry from the east or anywhere else in the world.("Scattered Poems by Jack Kerouac" 118-19)

The embarrassment Ceravolo speaks of is presumably associated with a tendency to view non-western "primitive" literature as simple. One might recall here the important statement by Jerome Rothenberg in the 1967 preface to *Technicians of the Sacred* that "where poetry is concerned, 'primitive' means complex" (xxvi). *Fits of Dawn* operates along similar primitive-complex premises, incorporating Bushmen literature at various points, for instance. As such, *Fits of Dawn* is the clearest expression of Ceravolo's life-long fascination with the primordial and the pre-cultural—the entire book can be read as an attempt to approach language in such a pre-cultural, primordial state. Music becomes one avenue by which Ceravolo tries to find a proto-semantic language. With its allusions to jazz ("scat scat" and "migrate sax"), it is possible to discern the influence of free jazz. Like the mid-60s compositions of Archie Shepp, Albert Ayler, and Cecil Taylor, *Fits of Dawn* offers jarring sounds emanating from seemingly unidentifiable sources. Highlighting the procedural and multireferential nature of the text, the book opens with one of its few directly identifiable allusions, an epigraph from Jung: "He did not think, he perceived his mind functioning." The titular fits of dawn are themselves a kind of heightened pre-conscious perception. The book begins with the stanza:

> That should what I habitude
> warmer hatchet please killed
> too fast lilac mads wait
> fly life eat one anything
> say curiously caress ago (*Fits of Dawn* n.p. Book I)

In a way, everything that takes place in the book takes place "too fast," in some remote time "ago." The book does not slow down; it continues into a world that more closely resembles that of the later Joyce than anything else. Like *Finnegans Wake*, *Fits of Dawn* is insistently and ambiguously mythographical, probing the origins of speech with a "langwedge" (Joyce's term) of the future. *Fits of Dawn* engages in neologisms, deliberate misspellings, and puns, but in a seemingly nonsystematic way:

> Flow hot gust wall
> cry crazy shower unbeeleave mom late
> earlier   crush thrown kill
>   skycolory—
> ness matter not no colony
> de la cruise imagine wish form (*Fits of Dawn* n.p. Book I)

Without any kind of recognizable poetic persona driving the poem, *Fits of Dawn* flows freely through languages and eras. Spanish is the most frequently detectable foreign language, but there are also traces of French and Latin. In its radical compression of language, *Fits of Dawn* tends to tilt toward nouns and verbs and away from adverbs and articles, as in a passage like:

> Cage are sentence force
> Dive sumac pace mil herb thanks,
> man alogof loathe-bells
> excellentations scritted imitate, lie. (*Fits of Dawn* n.p. Book I)

Perhaps poetry itself is a series of "excellentations" which lie by their very imitative nature—and Ceravolo is opposing himself to "sentence force" (and perhaps alluding to John Cage). Ceravolo seems throughout the work to be divided between utopian and dystopian linguistic views. Language imposes artificial civilizing impulses on humans, but it is also the only means we have to convey "excellentations" of all kinds, from poetic epiphanies to domestic reassurances. When *Fits of Dawn* is allusive, its allusions rarely form a coherent pattern. The poem can be impenetrably conscious of its own "scritted" imitations:

> Etes-vous coast   Attend less
> tail on, tail on stall funny by look
> voiceless taming gel
> eros acre   A middle you grow
> I steep ah sunk coolie
> douce and kiss fu thought
> of currants yes stiffle (*Fits of Dawn* n.p. Book II)

It is unclear who is speaking or whom is being spoken to in this passage, and yet Ceravolo's wistful seriousness is still evident. Given the difficulty of the first two books of *Fits of Dawn*, it is perhaps not surprising that the first two books have never been reprinted.[6]

Book III of *Fits of Dawn* features typically shorter lines and shorter stanzas (or blocks of lines) than the preceding two books. The poetic contexts of Book III are more recognizable, and the syntax less fractured, as in lines like: "Partly in skies in weak muzzles, fertile / communal dodging America." A number of themes and images persist from the earlier books.

One recurrent pattern is Ceravolo's use of exclamatory commands, often in French, such as "Voyez!" and "ecoutez." These French exclamations would seem to point to the Francophilic moments common to much first-generation New York School Writing. But Ceravolo's intensely written exclamations again cannot be linked to authoritative sources. The exclamatory gestures look as if they had been transmitted, like the poems of Sappho, through damaged manuscripts:

> O
> hilly erg of
>   young
> being of otter being
> apollo
> O Voyez! O whelm
>   Succumb
> painty of dommage
> Bloom! O tox
> destroy N
>   oregon of motion (*Fits of Dawn* n.p. Book III)

The poem is performing its own kind of whelming. It exists in a world, perhaps, without subjects—in a world that is both pre-subjective and post-subjective. No one can be commanded when there is no *one*. The last two lines that come before the final "A story from the bushmen" offer the ambiguous:

> . . . . . .   O
>   breathe

Breath seems to be the only identifiable quality left in this apocalyptic or precolyptic world—breath representing a kind of pure life-force before and after the intrusion of civilization. In this gesture, there is an Olsonian emphasis on the centrality of breath. In Ceravolo, the breath becomes all-important, not just as a force which avoids the "interference of the lyric ego," but as a central unknowable energy that cannot be acculturated.

In "A story from the bushmen," which ends *Fits of Dawn*, the poem makes a momentary detour into an almost decipherable, albeit fantastic, narrative. A husband and wife have a child, an "eland," which grows up to be jealous and vicious. Meanwhile, the father has "created all the animals." When the mother cooks the eland, it turns into many elands which then attack the mother. The other sons of these parents are then ordered to hunt these new elands. If Ceravolo has for a moment turned to a more recognizable sequential language, such a gesture is only momentary. Soon the book returns to chaos. The creation myth turns out to be hopelessly circular and misleading—Oedipus times a thousand. "The song from the bushmen" ends again with the emphasis on breath:

> To need am the fly
> The breathe no pavilion to this
> pain. Nape, so
> the precipice is june But for the
> villainous level joyful
> as the town so play (*Fits of Dawn* n.p.)

At this point, the poem returns to play, away from pain and close reading. The ending has a tragicomic feel—the energy of its verbal collisions making up for the bleak pain-inflected uncertainty of *Fits of Dawn* as a whole.

Fits of Dawn was unique within Ceravolo's oeuvre, just as it was unique within 1960s New York poetry. *Wild Flowers Out of Gas*, a chapbook printed by Tibor de Nagy, appeared next in 1967. It was to be followed shortly thereafter by the full-length *Spring in This World of Poor Mutts*. Both books had much in common with each other, and little in common with *Fits of Dawn*. Of the twenty-four poems printed in *Wild Flowers Out of Gas*, eleven were reprinted in *Spring in this World*. The poems in *Wild Flowers* show Ceravolo moving back toward a more compressed episodic lyricism, and away from the maximalist longer lines of *Fits of Dawn*. Only two poems in *Wild Flowers* are longer than a page, and those two poems are serial poems made up of smaller lyrics. The poems from this period refer consistently to children and childhood. The last few lines of "Indian Suffering," for example, generate a sense of childish indignation:

> Bow wow wow I am
> going home.
> The children called
> him ugly boy. I am not
> afraid of anything. Boy-not-afraid.
> Ugly boy a magic. (*Wild Flowers out of Gas* 8)

Ceravolo often takes on the persona of a child in these poems, but his assumption of a child-like identity is never simple. One of Ceravolo's better-known short lyrics, "Drunken Winter," shares a similar structure to "Indian Suffering":

> Oak oak! like like
> it then
> cold some wild paddle
> so sky then;
> flea you say
> "geese geese" the boy
> June of winter
> of again
> Oak sky (*Wild Flowers out of Gas* 17)

If the paired repetitions are seemingly Steinian, the degree of poetic compression is uniquely Ceravolo's, as are the poem's themes. Again a season, this time winter, appears in a manner contrary to what would be expected. The world is unworthy of its wild flowers and its springs and its winters—especially when viewed from the vantage of its ugly boys and poor mutts. David Shapiro recalls Ceravolo telling him that he wanted "to create only one school, The School of Everyday Life, with courses in the seasons" (Hoover 291). Such a school would be open to students of all ages and would be run from the perspective of the student—a student of the universe, or more particularly of the student's immediate experience of the cosmos. Admission to such a school would be free, not costing even the five dollars that Berrigan asked for entry into the New York School (Ratcliffe and Scalapino 91).

If Ceravolo's poems of the late 1960s are fascinated by innocence and by immediate experience on a cosmic scale, they are also deeply interested in problems of intimacy and detail. As Charles North writes: "Ceravolo's poems strike one as intensely personal, despite their modernist strategies. Many are gentle, intimate, about love, sex, family . . ." (North 26). David Shapiro characterizes Ceravolo in an unpublished essay as "a poet of grammar and a poet of love." The poem "Ho Ho Ho Caribou" offers a good introduction to these mid- to late-1960s themes within Ceravolo's writing, and as such was well chosen for the *Norton Anthology of Postmodern Poetry, From the Other Side of the Century: A New American Poetry 1960-1990,* and *An Anthology of New York Poets.* In an ambiguous setting we might envision as a zoo, the poem opens:

> Leaped at the caribou.
> My son looked at the caribou.
> The kangaroo leaped on the
> fruit tree. I am a white
> man and my children
> are hungry
> which is like paradise. ("Ho Ho Ho Caribou" 25)

Again, Ceravolo's trademark strategies of repetition show themselves. In three lines, "leaped," "looked," "caribou," and "kangaroo," all quickly bounce off one another. The narrator is conscious of his whiteness and his anonymity, and he derives a certain kind of pleasure from the dependence of his children. There are no proper names or allusions to specific places or events in "Ho Ho Ho Caribou." The caribou becomes an unlikely source of meditation upon the exotic and the transcendent, as the poet addresses both the caribou and his children:

> Everyone one has seen us out
> with the caribou but
> no one has seen us out in
> the car. You passed
> beyond us. ("Ho Ho Ho Caribou" 26-27)

The poem here is unusually straightforward, and Ceravolo's typical verbal dexterity subdued. Passing back into the world of the highway, the poem retreats from the territory of the standard Ceravolo meditation on modern life—the park, the beach, the zoo—and back into a world of suburban anonymity.

It is tempting to try to read Ceravolo's career as an engineer into his poetry—and into poems of suburban alienation like "Ho Ho Ho Caribou" in particular—but to a surprising degree there is little direct evidence of his career in the poems themselves. Like Wallace Stevens, Ceravolo seems to have kept his career and his poems separate.[7] While there is a tension between the working life and the poetic life in Ceravolo's poetry, for the most part the working life tends only to appear in large, amorphous terms. The poem "Red Sun," for instance, begins:

> You can't take me with a look.
> These are the keys
> to an orgy
>
> after work
> but they will not work
> of beautiful sensuality.
>
> Yes, work is so remote, here beneath the tides.
>
>   (*Spring in This World of Poor Mutts* 20)

The dullness of work and the excess of the orgy exist at opposite poles—
somewhere between these is the domestic inspiration of the Jersey Shore
tides. Throughout his career, Ceravolo's poems are more often concerned
with love and marriage than they are with his employment. Ceravolo's
important long poem "Sea Level," originally published in *Art and Literature*
in 1965, is a long rambling meditation on married life that takes place,
like "Red Sun," presumably at the Jersey Shore. As in other Ceravolo
poems, the poet is consumed by problems of intimacy and the obstacles
to intimacy:

> I'm walking over here. I'm not
>   like a prisoner. Don't
>   bother him, flies toward the cells
>   Spread their cells. There's free
> misery in the cell
>   ***How does***
> this cheap kiss
> (walking over) find the real you
>   and your cells? ("Sea Level" 79)

The poet muses over the biological, the minute, the banal, and how they
condition everyday interaction. "Sea Level" also offers rare moments of
Ceravolo writing in prose, and in them Ceravolo is typically elliptical yet
emotional: ". . . I know my controls peeking at all the people evaluates
me and changes and dependent over a veiny sea, that I love to swim in.
But am afraid of the nutrition of this lust . . ." ("Sea Level" 81). In "Sea
Level" the New Jersey landscape takes on strangely female characteristics:
"where is / the river of cuntelating light, where is / the Passaic or Nile?"

These feminine characteristics seem to threaten a kind of early sixties paternalism, when the speaker of the poem asks:

> What do
> the moms do to us?
> Where is the tomb of my
> passion as a man ("Sea Level" 85)

The feminine seems to be associated with a certain mythical consistency. The Passaic and the Nile equally represent archetypes of femininity that presumably "cuntelate" the male poet.

All of this may seem rather crude, but it should not be taken as diminishing the poem's verbal ingenuity or its attempt to create tenderness. Like many of Ceravolo's poems, the emotions presented are complex and never sentimental. The poem concludes with a sort of self-indictment on the part of the poet for his inability to realize the beauty of his own situation:

> Coming essence adorns
> the poor pages of honesty inflamed
> as rice in your heart:
> love pitted and rising in your
> arm, thieves holding a season, placenta,
> and miracles of balms
> constructed of what you are o
> drill; under this drought
> beholding, the thief of living with you,
> of living with you. ("Sea Level" 90)

Ceravolo, his "honesty inflamed," questions his ability to create an essentialist poetic statement about his life and family. The poem ends with reconciliation and with a valentine-like invocation of the beloved. Within a pattern of fractured syntax, the poem offers a sincerity that betrays a deep love for family and for region—without ironic detachment and without operating within a rarified world of allusion. By the end of the poem, Ceravolo has largely undone his initial dissatisfaction with his surroundings.

William Carlos Williams is perhaps the central influence on this middle period of Ceravolo's poetry. But whereas Williams's New Jersey is often a tough, gritty, inhospitable landscape peopled by its "pure products,"

Ceravolo's New Jersey is less bleak and more domestic—featuring parks, zoos, and beaches, rather than vacant lots and industrial debris. Ceravolo may have shared a middle-class suburban lifestyle with Williams, but Williams railed against middle-class suburban life much more directly than did Ceravolo. Still, Ceravolo must have identified greatly with Williams personally: both led professional lives very much outside of an artistic milieu, both were husbands and fathers, and both maintained contacts with more Bohemian counterparts in New York (and elsewhere for Williams).[8] Williams's lack of artistic pretension, and his responsiveness to the everyday and the local, shapes much of Ceravolo's sensibility as a poet. Ceravolo was equally devoted to the transformative powers of the imagination, and he, like Williams, summons the imagination through the seasons, as is particularly evident in the poem "Spring in This World of Poor Mutts":

> I'm thirty years old.
> I want to think in summer now.
> Here it goes, here it's summer
>
> (A disintegrated robot)
> over us.
> We are mortal. We ride
> the merry-go-round. A drummer like
> this is together.
> Let's go feel the water.
>   Here it goes!
> Again and it's morning "boom" autumn
> "boom" autumn (*Spring in This World of Poor Mutts* 45)

Later in the poem one finds the apostrophe: "Oh imagination. That's how I need you" (*Spring in This World of Poor Mutts* 46). In one way of reading, Ceravolo's poetic "disintegrated robot" of summer could be thought of as a remarkable twist on Williams's statement: "A poem is a small (or large) machine made of words" (54) from the introduction to *The Wedge*. Individual imagination, in both cases, is resisting the "merry-go-round" mechanisms of contemporary industrial society. The poems in *Spring in This World of Poor Mutts* show Ceravolo at his most Williams-esque in other ways as well. A poem like "In The Grass" is Williams-like in its spare punctuation:

> Here in the grass
> where the flowers
> walk softer than birds
> to their nest
> in the clouds
> Where the rain
> falls from the sky,
> the small breath
> of the insect
> is like a breeze
> before rain (14)

If this is a kinder, gentler Ceravolo, it is also a Ceravolo who is fascinated by minutiae and by the stasis of the larger world in the context of its smaller parts. The poems of *Spring in This World* feature more children than the poems of any other period of his writing. This must have been, in large part, a reflection of his role as a father. The poem "The wind is blowing west" seems to belong to another universe when compared to *Fits of Dawn*. The poem opens:

> I am trying to decide to go swimming,
> But the sea looks so calm.
> All the other boys have gone in.
>
> I've been waiting in my tent
> Expecting to go in.
> Have you forgotten to come down?
> Can I escape going in?
> I was just coming
>
> I was just going in
> But lost my pail (7-8)

Soon the poem, which is divided into four sections, begins to repeat itself. The poem itself becomes a kind of suspension of decision. There is no epiphany; the personified renewal of the Shelleyan west wind takes place regardless of the activities of the boy-narrator. The simplicity of the poem is deceiving; like many of the poems from *Spring in This World*, the poem is deeply inconclusive and takes place within the space of an unending immanence of things.

Spring in This World of Poor Mutts, published in 1968, received the first ever Frank O'Hara Award, probably through the maneuvering of Kenneth Koch and John Ashbery. It was Ceravolo's most widely circulated book, and his only book to be published by a university press.[9] After *Spring in This World of Poor Mutts*, Ceravolo would not publish a book for over a decade. From what records there are, in the pages of the *Poetry Project Newsletter* and *The World* for instance, he seems to have given readings and published sporadically during this time. Larry Fagin's *Adventures in Poetry* seems to have been the one journal that published Ceravolo's work with any consistency during the 1970s. A statement by Rosemary Ceravolo (writing under her pen name Mona da Vinci), which appears in the Anne Waldman-edited *The World* in 1976 seems to illustrate a certain degree of disillusionment with the New York poetry community:

> Having been on the mailing lists of numerous mimeographed and off-set poetry magazines for a period of ten years or more because my spouse is a contemporary poet of substantial value, and a hydraulics engineer who formulates concrete systems of drainage for society's water diversions [. . .] I have inadvertently become aware of the question as to whether these magazines offer anything of poetic substance or [. . .] are they being produced as edifications edited by self-designated rulers, policy makers, supervisors, and directors of particular systems, schools, styles, i.e. forms of verse. (da Vinci 77)

The passage makes the New York small publishing scene out to be remarkably bureaucratic and systematized, and the passage betrays a surprising degree of resentment directed toward the so-called "self-designated rulers," a social network that the Ceravolos seem to have felt excluded from. Rosemary Ceravolo does not specify who precisely these "self-designated rulers" of mimeographed and off-set poetry are, but she must be thinking of Anne Waldman and others. It was not a very large fiefdom to be fighting over—and yet it is almost impossible to know to what degree the Ceravolos's exile was self-imposed.

Ceravolo's last two books, *INRI* (1979) and *Millennium Dust* (1982) are particularly difficult to categorize. The increasing religiosity of these two books seems to have distanced Ceravolo from his peers and from the New York scene in general. Here again, Ceravolo, in his open religiosity, defies second-generation New York School preconceptions. Judging by the near silence that greeted these poems, no one knew how to place them. To use just one rough measure, the selection in *The Green Lake is Awake* is comprised almost entirely of Ceravolo poems from the 1960s, and Kenneth Koch's introduction to the volume makes no reference at all to the religious content of Ceravolo's late poems. Ceravolo's later work is distinctly less interested in syntactical disruption than his earlier work, though his late poems often retain his characteristic lyric brevity. If the later poems are more direct, they have nonetheless not abandoned the visionary qualities that characterize Ceravolo poems from all periods. Many of the later poems are not overtly religious, but *INRI* and *Millennium Dust* are both pervaded by crucifixion imagery. *INRI,* with its reference to Pontius Pilate's inscription on the cross (John 19:19) and perhaps to the J.C. of Ceravolo's initials, is mostly made up of three to five line poems. The book features a dramatic cover drawn by Mona da Vinci. The drawing is of a face superimposed on an EKG diagram of a dying friend of the Ceravolos, Joseph Robinson, to whom the book is dedicated. The poems in *INRI* are often melancholic and brooding and employ a deliberately simple vocabulary. The poems can be straightforwardly mystical, like:

MACRO

My screams
can't annoy the stars.
Come, Holy Ghost
enlighten me!
Continue me on. (*Inri* 16)

The poems can often feel like gnomic translations in their unrelenting fatalism:

MANURE

Death is a seed
and Spring its manure
Love in the language
of science
becomes my name
(Insane) (*Inri* 41)

Ceravolo seems to find comfort in a kind of self-detachment from the world, in a kind of poetic asceticism. It is possible to infer some kind of Chinese influence, or perhaps the influence of Pound's *Classic Anthology*, in a poem like:

ANOTHER WORLD

Everything is part of me,
even the heart of inhumanness,
now that I'm exiled. (*Inri* 4)

And yet this is not a literal exile from a given place; it would seem to be an exile from the sensual world of "humanness" altogether. Or rather perhaps, this is an exile through the senses into a post-sensual world of devotional fervor.

Though many of Ceravolo's later poems were increasingly religious, it would be wrong, we think, to conclude that there were two halves to his career. While Ceravolo was a somewhat solitary figure within the New York poetry world in terms of social groupings, his closest associates seem to have been David Shapiro and Frank Lima—a group of three which might in itself constitute an intriguing New York School subset. Shapiro maintains that it was probably their religious upbringings (Jewish in the case of Shapiro and Catholic in the cases of Lima and Ceravolo) that united them. A poem like "Rocket," for instance, which was written in 1967, but not published in book form until 1982, shows that mystical and religious themes were present in Ceravolo's work even during the period in which he most deeply involved in the mainstream second-generation New York School scene. The poem "Note from St. Francis," written in 1965, is beautifully spare in its ambiguously religious asceticism. The poem opens:

In the world today
there is
no world so attached as I am
to worlds. (45)

The influence of Kerouac's Buddhist-Catholicism might be discerned here. Both Kerouac and Ceravolo attempt to renounce worldly things, and find themselves unable to escape the sensible world, unable to create

what Kerouac called a "no-poem non poem" (202). Kerouac and Cera-
volo struggle to reconcile Catholic renunciation with the celebration of
everyday experience—and their sacred and their profane epiphanies are
often not far separated. Given that Ceravolo himself spent time writing
in Mexico, he almost certainly would have been familiar with the scat-
influenced poems of Kerouac's *Mexico City Blues*, published by Grove in
1959. Even in Ceravolo's non-overtly religious poems there is a constant
tension between the worldly and the otherworldly. A more dramatic shift
than the religious turn in Ceravolo's poetry occurs stylistically in the
decreasing degree to which his writings are disjunctive syntactically. A
poem like "Millennium Dust," for instance, operates within a much more
conventional syntactic structure than a poem like "Ho Ho Ho Caribou":

> The spread of suffering
> rolls away like dust into the moon.
> Flesh of the arid bodies
> are more than what man reduced them to.
>
> (*Millennium Dust* 120)

As he was in *INRI*, Ceravolo in *Millennium Dust* is intensely concerned
with human suffering and with the possibility of resurrection as a release
from suffering. It is tempting to interpret "After Image," the final poem
in *Millennium Dust*, as a *Tempest*-style farewell to poetry. The poem begins:
"Nobody can get inside me / until the angels get there first." The poem
goes on:

> *Think what you want*
> about the uselessness
> of art for art's sake,
>
> or science as a social metaphor.
>
> Neither can change
>   this world
>
> or become a comrade to the enslaved
> embittered masses
> or a ruby in the elite crown
> of the greedy few.

> That's why nobody is allowed inside me
> until the angels
> bring their defiant message
> to reconstruct the resumption
>   of life everlasting
>   of love, of hope. (126)

This is perhaps Ceravolo's fullest *ars poetica*. One way to read these lines is as a sort of retraction, in the tradition of Chaucer and others. "After Image" disavows any attempt to renew the world through metaphor, as the earlier poems had implicitly attempted to do. If *Fits of Dawn* offers a kind of pre-symbolic, proto-metaphoric language, then perhaps these final poems offer a post-symbolic, post-metaphoric alternative. In the Gospel of John, Jesus says to his followers: "I have said these things to you in figures of speech. The hour is coming when I will no longer speak to you in figures, but will tell you plainly of the Father" (John 17:25). The Ceravolo of *Millennium Dust* is interested in plain speech, in the world beyond figures.

Ceravolo's late post-symbolic self-isolation, defined in terms of Christian redemption, is a "defiant message," and ultimately a deeply oppositional vision of redeeming the "enslaved" from the "greedy few." Except for the strongly felt presence of his family in the poems, it would be safe to say that Ceravolo was always on a kind of *Transmigration Solo*. As the title would imply, the transmigration of souls usually takes place between souls in the plural. Andrew Epstein has suggested that what particularly defines first-generation New York School poetry is the sense of friendship and community to be found among the poets.[10] David Lehman makes similar claims in *The Last Avant-Garde*, as does Daniel Kane in his reading of the communal spirit of the 1960s New York scene.[11] But Ceravolo does not fit this pattern. Though he knew and admired many of his contemporaries, he never refers to them directly within his poems. There are only two Ceravolo collaborations (beyond collaborations with Rosemary) that we know of: a poem co-written with John Perreault which appeared in *Locus Solus 2* in 1961, and a "collaborative writing experiment" with participants listed as "joe ceravolo, rosemary ceravolo, peggy decoursey, ed friedman, yancy gerber, john giorno, kevin kerr, bernadette mayer, ann powell, anne waldman & hannah weiner" which appeared in the journal *Unnatural Acts II* in November 1972. It is not clear if Ceravolo participated in other such events, but he seems not to have. The one recording available of Ceravolo reading was made not in a public setting, but in the Spring of 1968 at his home in Bloomfield.[12] From all that we can tell, Ceravolo was always somewhat indifferent to his welcome in New York.

In comparison to his peers, who often prided themselves on the collectivity of their writing, Ceravolo was defiantly on his own for most of his poetic career. Kenneth Koch suggests that his poems "make no gestures or appeals outside themselves" (*The Green Lake Is Awake* 13). This is in turn perhaps another cause of the lack of attention paid to Ceravolo in recent years: he wrote virtually no criticism, left no poetics statements or interviews, and was uninvolved in publishing his fellow poets. Ceravolo made few, if any, explicit political claims, and his work makes no appeal to any specific social group. Italian-American studies courses seem unlikely to begin clamoring for his work as historically representative. By default, Ceravolo is thrust into the role of "poet's poet." With the current difficulty in finding a copy of *Fits of Dawn*, Ceravolo becomes even more a lyric "poet's poet." It is hard to tell what this might mean for Ceravolo's reputation in the long run. We believe that based on their uniqueness and based on their relevance to 1960s poetic experimentalism as a whole, Ceravolo's writings collectively make a strong claim on posterity. In his late poem "Hills" Ceravolo portrays himself as particularly isolated: "People think I'm out of my mind, / but I'm only beaten up in memory" (*Millennium Dust* 55). If Kenneth Koch is right that "Modern poetry takes a large step in this poetry that has not yet really been followed by others" (*The Green Lake Is Awake* 9), then we can only assume that Ceravolo is "beaten up in memory" only temporarily.

WORKS CITED

Ceravolo, Joseph. *Fits of Dawn*. New York: "C" Press, 1965.

—. *The Green Lake Is Awake*. Minneapolis: Coffee House, 1994.

—. "Ho Ho Ho Caribou." *The Paris Review*. 44 (Fall 1968): 29-34.

—. *Inri*. Putnam Valley, NY: Swollen Magpie Press, 1979.

—. *Millennium Dust*. New York: Kulchur Foundation, 1982.

—. "Scattered Poems by Jack Kerouac." *The World #29* (April 1974): 118-19.

—. "Sea Level." *Art and Literature* 7. (Winter 1965): 79-90.

—. *Spring in This World of Poor Mutts*. New York: Columbia University Press, 1968.

—. *Transmigration Solo*. West Branch, IA: Toothpaste Press, 1979.

—. *Wild Flowers out of Gas*. New York: Tibor de Nagy Editions, 1967.

Clay, Steven, and Rodney Phillips. *A Secret Location on the Lower East Side: Adventures in Writing 1960-1980*. New York: Granary Books, 1998.

da Vinci, Mona. "Poetry and the Beast." *The World #30* (July 1976): 77-78.

Hoover, Paul, ed. *Postmodern American Poetry: An Anthology*. New York: W.W. Norton, 1994.

Hornick, Lita. "Joseph Ceravolo/Night Bird." *Nine Martinis*. New York: Kulchur Foundation, 1987. 91-98.

Kane, Daniel. *All Poets Welcome: The Lower East Side Poetry Scene in the 1960s*. Berkeley: University of California Press, 2003.

Kerouac, Jack. *Mexico City Blues*. New York: Grove Press, 1959.

Lehman, David. *The Last Avant-Garde: The Making of the New York School of Poets*. New York: Anchor Books, 1998.

Myers, John Bernard. Letter to the editor. The New York Times Book Review March 31, 1968, Section 7. 22

North, Charles. "Wild Provoke of the Endurance Sky." *No Other Way: Selected Prose*. Brooklyn: Hanging Loose Press, 1998. 25-29.

Ratcliffe, Stephen, and Leslie Scalapino, eds. *Talking in Tranquility: Interviews with Ted Berrigan*. Bolinas, CA: Avenue B/O Books, 1991.

Rifkin, Libbie. *Career Moves: Olson, Creeley, Zukofsky, Berrigan and the American Avant-Garde*. Madison: University of Wisconsin Press, 2000.

Rothenberg, Jerome, ed. *Technicians of the Sacred: A Range of Poetries from Africa, America, Asia, Europe & Oceania*. 2nd revised and expanded, 1985 ed. Berkeley: University of California Press, 1968.

Silliman, Ron. "Migratory Meaning." *The New Sentence*. New York: Roof Books, 1985. 109-26.

Williams, Carlos William. *Collected Poems, Vol. 2: 1939-1962*. Ed. A. Walton Litz and Christopher MacGowan. New York: New Directions, 1986.

"Everyone you've ever been with for a moment": The poetry of Lewis Warsh

GARY LENHART

In the summer of 2003, I traveled to Montreal to see an exhibition of art by the French painter Edouard Vuillard at the Musée des Beaux-Arts. The day before, I spoke with a friend who had seen the exhibition earlier. She volunteered that she had not found it particularly impressive because the artist was "all over the place." As I strolled through the many rooms of the museum filled with Vuillard's intimist domestic paintings, his landscapes of the Swiss and French countryside, Parisian cityscapes, portraits of close friends and demanding rich clients, dinner plates painted with graceful sketches of young women, large decorative "tapestries" intended for bourgeois dining rooms, Kodak snapshots, quotations from European masterpieces and Japanese prints, lithographs and etchings, stage designs and book illustrations, I realized that my friend had indeed been correct about Vuillard being "all over the place." But instead of finding that variety a sign of dilettantish indirection, I thought Vuillard's wide-open readiness to attempt any professional commission, try on passing artistic fashions, or pursue his personal whims and inspirations, to be a mark of adventurous confidence and artistic ambition. Nor did it matter what genre he attempted or how widely he ranged; everything he made bore the impress of his imagination.

Reading Lewis Warsh's writings from beginning to end, it's apparent that he too has been "all over the place." Like Vuillard, Warsh was also nurtured by a community of artists that gave him early approval and the subsequent confidence to experiment. Though he divides his writings into categories of poetry, fiction, or autobiography, his poems range from intensely lyrical passages to flat technological jargon, often serve to document his life, but may also seem remote from it; his short stories, if not his novels, often read like prose poems or memoirs; and his autobiographical writings alternate between fantastic conjecture and stark impersonal analysis. So many of the characters in his fiction slip easily and passively out of old identities and into new as they experience alterations in their surroundings and acquaintance that human character comes off as fragile and accidental, an interaction between wayward personality, social coercion, romantic imagination and sexual seduction.

The earliest painting in the Vuillard exhibition is dated 1889, the latest dated 1938. As you view paintings and drawings from the intervening years, it's remarkable how frequently the same faces and figures repeat, including not just members of the artist's family, but also a repertory troupe of friends and fellow artists. Anyone with a slight acquaintance with French painting from the same period will appreciate that the changes in Vuillard's techniques and subjects owe as much to his attention to the work of his contemporaries as they do to alterations in his personal circumstances and environs.

Though the practice of poetry, at least in Lewis Warsh's lifetime, has been insulated from the commercial demands of fashionable patrons or anxious dealers, the large autobiographical and diaristic elements in Warsh's writings likewise allow us to read them in light of the surroundings from which they sprung. Though Warsh has described himself as a poet in particular thrall to "inner voices," his career has also been, from a precocious age, public and social. He was early near the center of an active poetic community, and his "inner voices" often include echoes of those acquaintances. Though his writings are strongly individual, it's also possible to notice how those inner voices emerge in poetic forms modified by his reading and extensive shoptalk with other poets. The high school correspondence that Warsh collected and published as *The Maharajah's Son* makes clear that for Warsh a writing vocation was from his adolescent beginnings an inherently communal activity. Using the extensive autobiographical evidence he has supplied in his writings, I wish to consider the development of his poetry in light of the shifting communities to which he belonged, the poetry that surrounded him, and his imaginative response toward the events and ambiance of his experience.

Some will see this approach to poems as obscuring their particular distinction or masking the poet's individual genius. Those who write poems while hearing voices, some of which they can't identify, some of which they recognize as familiars, will think the approach needs no justification. Yet others will find this conception of poetic composition as a mediation of communal voices a fairly radical idea, de-emphasizing the vision of the author as a single, agonistic individual, and reading the poem instead as part of an ongoing imaginative discourse between artists. As the comparison to Vuillard implies, it's possible for anyone to appreciate individual poems by Lewis Warsh, but an appreciation of the full spectrum of his poetry is enhanced by attending to the context in which those poems were composed.

Lewis Warsh was born in New York City and has lived most of his life there, with the exception of significant stretches in northern California and rural New England. In 1965 he met Anne Waldman at Robert Duncan's reading during the Berkeley Poetry Conference. They soon married and together published *Angel Hair* magazine and books. When Waldman succeeded Joel Oppenheimer as director of the St. Mark's Poetry Project, she established the direction of its programming for years to come. The young couple's apartment at 33 St. Mark's Place became a hang-out and meeting place for their cohort of poets and artists. The poets published by *Angel Hair*, the poets who read regularly at the Poetry Project, and the poets who habitually dropped by 33 St. Mark's Place were largely those we have come to associate with Ron Padgett's and David Shapiro's *An Anthology of New York Poets*. Yet neither Waldman nor Warsh were included in Padgett and Shapiro's anthology. Though inclusion or exclusion in any one anthology is seldom defining, the exclusion in this case seems more insight than oversight. In his introduction to *The Angel Hair Anthology* Warsh states that his poetic allegiances were always complex:

> I must admit that in my first readings of the *New American Poetry* anthology the poets in the New York School section interested me the least. My tastes were with the Black Mountain poets, especially Robert Creeley, Denise Levertov, and Paul Blackburn, and with the San Francisco poets, Jack Spicer, Robert Duncan, and Robin Blaser. The way these poets internalized experience made sense to me; I'd always been involved with inner voices, and it was the tone in which these voices were speaking to me that became the 'voice' of my early poems. These poets also taught me that psychology, magic, history and dailiness could exist in equal measure. (*Angel Hair*, xx-xxi)

Of course, Donald Allen's anthology doesn't divide these poets quite this way. There Duncan is included among the Black Mountain poets, with Creeley, Levertov, and Blackburn. But it's understandable that Warsh would associate Duncan with his San Francisco associates. The young Warsh had traveled to San Francisco in the summer of 1963, where, on his first night in town, his friend Harris Schiff took him to Gino & Carlo's bar to meet Jack Spicer.

Spicer asked the eighteen-year-old Warsh what he did, and as soon as he replied, 'I'm a writer,' he saw their faces close down, knew he'd made a mistake. Went home kicking himself for not replying, 'I'm a poet.' He had failed a crucial test. But soon he felt comfortable enough to begin 'going to Aquatic Park on Sunday afternoons where Spicer held court.' (*Poet Be Like God*, 266)

Warsh became such a regular among the Spicer group that summer that Spicer nicknamed Schiff, Warsh, and a third young poet from New York City the "Blackheads" (*Poet Be Like God*, 266). At the end of that summer he returned to school in New York, but when he traveled again to Berkeley two years later he resumed spending Sundays with the Spicer group in Aquatic Park.

It was back in New York City in 1963, at 18 years old and attending Kenneth Koch's poetry workshop at the New School, that Warsh wrote what he calls his "first good poem." It was a 10-part serial poem titled "The Suicide Rates." Though written while studying with the New York School dynamo Koch, Warsh says it was "influenced mostly by Robin Blaser's long poems, 'Cups' and 'The Park'" (*Angel Hair*, xxi) and "ideas of distance and intimacy I'd picked up from reading" Blaser and Spicer (*Angel Hair*, 606).

2

How many ways to die for a window

It is dead night, far from home,
I sit back, dazed,
for a moment we affect the equality of places
of other nights, eyes, and a casual stare, a price.
. . .

6

Now I see photographs of the wild
and open vehicles of our time.
Too many means which transport the wavering eye.
. . .

9

Like small foreign villages whose gates have been
destroyed by bonfires

so the cities nearest my hands
are destroyed by the rust and the rustling of cool ashes.

Cool gray enters my throat.
. . .

To the young Warsh's surprise, though his teacher's "aesthetics at the time seemed antithetical to what I was interested in . . . he liked the poem nonetheless."

> It made me wonder about all the boundaries that had been drawn by the Don Allen anthology, and elsewhere . . . all the different schools that were enmeshed with one another but somehow at odds. I had the simple thought that if Kenneth could like this particular poem then those boundaries didn't really matter. It was the enmeshment that mattered. (*Poetry and Poetics in a New Millenium*, 151)

The poem was included in Warsh's first book, *Moving through Air* (1968). Though it would be many years before he returned to composing serial poems, his later books rely heavily on the form.

> I've never felt quite like a bona fide New York School Poet, whatever that means. The poetry world, especially during that time, felt more communal to me than a cluster of different schools, and I saw no contradiction publishing poets associated with the west coast—Ebbe Borregard, Philip Whalen, Robert Duncan, Joanne Kyger, John Thorpe, and Jim Koller—alongside the poets from the New York School. (xxvi)

In conversation just after Kenneth Koch's death in 2002, Warsh told me that the poetry of Whalen and Koch (both published in *Angel Hair* 4) had been particularly important to him, and added that he thought it odd that he had never become close friends with either—an indication of the interweave of personal and aesthetic, reader and companion, that runs through his work. The younger poets he lists were acquaintances from his trips to the West Coast in 1963, 1965, 1968, and after the dissolution of his marriage to Waldman in 1969.

In 1966 Warsh and Waldman moved to St. Mark's Place on the Lower East Side and became friendly with a group of young poets living in that neighborhood. In their biography of Jack Spicer, Lewis Ellingham (also a contributor to *Angel Hair*) and Kevin Killian describe the exchange between the Spicer circle and the lower East Side poets thus:

> The so-called 'second generation' poets of the New York School— Anne Waldman, Ted Berrigan, Bernadette Mayer, Ron Padgett, Bill Berkson, Clark Coolidge—caught on quickly, spurred by the presence among them of several who had known Spicer well—Lewis Warsh, Joanne Kyger, Harris Schiff, Larry Fagin, and others. (*Poet Be Like God*, xi)

From one viewpoint, Warsh seemed instrumental in bringing the news from San Francisco to New York. But *Moving through Air* also included "Halloween 1967," a diary entry which, in its rapid gossipy catalogue of friends (first names only) busily coming and going, is a quintessential "New York" piece.

> Sandy calls. She's coming over with David & Kate. Katie, Debbie & the kids leave. Sandy arrives. Shelly leaves to return to the Halloween party at the Village Theatre. Jim calls. Anne & Ted arrive, home from the reading. David falls asleep in my arms on the couch. Shelly returns. The party is obviously dragging. Jim arrives. He needs to use Anne's typewriter to type poems. Wren comes. Ted, Sandy & the kids leave. Anne cooks me a hamburger. Shelly leaves, Wren leaves. Jim is still typing. Ron & Pat arrive. Larry has disappeared somewhere. . . . (*Angel Hair*, 210-211)

The Ted mentioned in the poem is Ted Berrigan. In an interview with Ed Foster, Warsh stressed the importance of Berrigan in his life during this period, both personally and poetically.

> I came out, so to speak, around Ted, and my poetry began evolving in some new ways. . . . Around 1967 I began to realize I could use an *I* in my poems in a way I hadn't done before. . . . I realized I could mention the names of people in my poems, something everyone takes for granted now, but which was for me a big breakthrough. And I discovered that I could tell a little story out of my direct experience. No need to hide, or obfuscate, or pretend I was someone else. . . . Gradually I discovered I could write a kind of personal poetry that was different

than Ted's, or Frank O'Hara's. There's a vast difference between being an Irish guy from Providence or Baltimore and being a Jewish guy from the Bronx. (*Poetry and Poetics in a New Millenium*, 152-3)

Published while Warsh was in his early 20s, *Moving through Air* shows him poetically unsettled, bopping back and forth between Coastal influences with the abandon of Sal Paradise in *On the Road*. Before his next book would be published, however, his marriage to Waldman would end, he would leave New York, and, after briefly traveling in Europe, find himself back in California.

Warsh's 1969 itinerary is laid out in *Part of my History* (1972), a miscellany of sonnets, diaries, memoirs, photos, collaborations, annotated reading lists, and an unannotated list of favorite pop songs. Leaving New York, he went alone to Europe, returned briefly to New York, then travelled west, stopping briefly in Ann Arbor, Michigan, where Berrigan was residing, Chicago (for the opening of the Conspiracy Trial), and Iowa City, where he stayed with Ted's wife, Sandy, and their children. Arriving in San Francisco, he decided he "didn't want to live in the city, any city, at that time" (npl), and stayed only one night at Clark Coolidge's house before leaving for Bolinas, where he crashed briefly with Tom and Angelica Clark. After a number of temporary residences, he settled for the winter in "the house that Philip Whalen had spent the previous winter and that gave the place a certain amount of magic which I trusted, for some reason, as I found myself settling into Bolinas."

> A lot of time has passed. Bill Berkson visited over Xmas and spent two weeks here. Ted and Alice visited and it was great to be together with all of them, and Tom and Angelica, on New Years Eve. Also, on New Years, I spoke to Anne in New York, and Jon Cott, and later in the night saw Joanne and Jack and Ebbe. I write a lot of letters and read a lot of books and this book, however self-indulgent it seems to me at certain times, remains the clearest account of what's been happening recently in my life. (npl)

Part of my History is eclectic, intensely personal, and, as its author admits, self-indulgent. In 1970, when the quoted sentences were written, how many readers could be expected to recognize the above list of visitors and friends? Few will today. No matter. The identity of the friends is less important than the intoxication and self-congratulation the author feels in being among them. It was this youthful euphoria at discovering a company of sympathetic spirits that made this idiosyncratic and whimsical hodge-podge of observation, confession, gossip, collaboration, literary assemblage and snapshots a favorite among young Lower East Side poets in the late '70s, and continues to hold appeal for young readers in search of camaraderie.

The book intersperses poems by Warsh's friends among poems and clippings from George Meredith, Ford Madox Ford, *The New York Times* and *Tibetan Yoga & Secret Doctrines,* threatening conventional notions of authorship by incorporating entire poems by other authors, instead of merely alluding to them in literary fashion, and disdaining generic distinctions by printing lists of pop songs, diary entries, and occasional prose among poems and essays. Though in many ways the book prefigures the turn Warsh's books were to take twenty years later, Warsh himself has cited Spicer's "Heads of the Town up to the Aether" as its inspiration (*Poetry and Poetics in a New Millenium*, 153). Yet Warsh's poem strikes me as wilder and more circumstantial than Spicer's, far closer to Philip Whalen's shaggy compositions of poetic stanzas, lists, sketches, calligraphs, grumblings and quotations. That Warsh wrote parts of his book at the dining room table in the house Whalen had rented the year before may be its least surprising aspect.

FOR A MOMENT

Why doesn't the moment extend itself, I mean
the moment does, but you, changing through it, a
different person walks through the mirror, inside you
what is happening the day is beginning, you are
yourself, the parts of you everyone's seeing,
you are everyone you've ever been with for a moment.

(Dreaming as One, 71)

The most prominent and recurring friendly figures in *Part of my History* are Joanne Kyger, Tom Clark, and Bill Berkson. They are dedicatees of its poems and subjects of its diary entries. There are snapshots and sketches of them. Warsh even includes his introduction to a reading that Kyger and Clark give together. Oddly, the reputation of each, particularly at that time, owed much to their identification with a well-known mentor. Berkson was famously the protégé of Frank O'Hara, by any account the central figure in the New York School. Clark studied with Donald Hall and was chosen to succeed him as poetry editor of *The Paris Review*, where Clark began to publish many of the poets mentioned in Warsh's book. And David Meltzer's introduction to Kyger's *As Ever: Selected Poems* stresses her relation to Philip Whalen.

> Like her ally and mentor Philip Whalen, Kyger is an unorthodox American Buddhist. Heterodoxical yet profoundly traditional to the essence of the practice, deeply devoted to her own earned terms of spirit and self-awareness. Early influences were the grand mind lights of Robert Duncan and Jack Spicer, and no doubt William Carlos Williams. But the bridge is Philip Whalen, whose "mind graphs" allow, as they demonstrate, an expansive and nonauthoritarian attempt to write a distinctive yet unofficial poetry. Meditations that track the streams and strands of mind in its continuum and flight from captivity. (xvi)

Describing her own writing during the months she spent with "Warsh and Tom Clark in Bolinas within a flow of 1970s psychotropic and cannabis highs," Kyger says: "The 'individual' is swept out to sea, a group location identity, a place, takes precedence as voice" (*Angel Hair*, 590). The effects of such a voyage vary with each survivor. Though Warsh soon returned to the East Coast, where he has spent the years since, the "group location identity" that he experienced while in Bolinas remains a significant part of his history. His poems continue to respond to shifting landscapes and new circles of friends and readers, but his fealty to this Bolinas group identity remains a stubborn undercurrent throughout those shifts, manifesting with increasing strength as the poet ages and memory assumes a larger role in his imagination.

With the publication of his next book in 1974, Warsh was planted solidly on terra firma, specifically the streets of the Lower East Side. *Immediate Surrounding* consists of one 12-page poem charting the neighborhood's landscape through the eyes of a pedestrian and driver. The narrative manner might be described as "stream of consciousness," but each site on the itinerary remains discrete.

> A girl
> and boy in their
> teens talk to a policeman
> in the lobby

of the P.A.L.
building on the corner
of 10th and Avenue A.
In the old
Peace Eye Bookstore,
on Avenue A,
facing the park, some
Polish men sit around
a table, playing cards.
I decided not to walk
through the park. On
9th Street two kids sit
on the curb watching their
father change a tire, a rack
of tires in front of
a storefront, and a sign in the window
—black lettering on cardboard—
"Flats Fixed."

The poem is remarkable as a variant of the "I do this I do that" poem so named by Frank O'Hara and associated with him and Ted Berrigan (cf. Berkson, *Sal Mimeo 3*). Unlike O'Hara or Berrigan, however, Warsh's poem doesn't pulsate with restless energy or entertain with clever witticisms and in-jokes. It follows the bounces of the author's consciousness through the immediate surrounds, but at each stage the narrative is emotionally restrained and the description flat. Building to a small epiphany about Egyptian tombs and domestic possessions, the poem is a democratic marvel of the casual and accidental. Its subjects engage not because of any heightened import, but merely because those are the sites where the butterfly of consciousness temporarily alights. Though back in New York City and adopting a poetic strategy often considered quintessential New York School, Warsh resembles Kyger and Whalen more than Berrigan or O'Hara by subordinating personality to place. In his cruise through the neighborhood, he always seems on the verge of being "swept out to sea"—or at least to some oceanic, transpersonal consciousness.

"Immediate Surrounding" was reprinted in the collection *Blue Heaven*, published in 1978, where it is surrounded by similar democratic "mind graphs," among poems that are more generically conventional. In 1977, however, he published *The Maharajah's Son*, a collection of letters written to him by high school and college friends between 1960-65. I read it as an epistolary novel with a cast of predominantly adolescent characters who are bright, restless, self-dramatizing, often inadvertently self-parodying, and lacking sophistication—but with a charming veneer of existential, foreign cinema, and coffee house "culture." At the center is the Sphinx-like character Lewis, to whom all the letters are addressed, but from whom we never hear a reply. The book allows its author to collage the varied voices of his intimate acquaintances while permitting him to remain silent. In the context of this essay it's significant mainly as testament of Warsh's conception of writing as a communal activity in which correspondents explore potential identities, and where reading serves as beginning, not end, of composition by always inviting a reply. Most of the letter writers are distressed by unfulfilled desire and isolated by anxieties. They write not to exchange ideas (they seem strangely indifferent to the world beyond their circle), but to reassure themselves that someone is listening to them—and will respond.

Warsh published *The Maharajah's Son* and *Blue Heaven* while living in rural New England with poet Bernadette Mayer during a decade in which their three children were born. Both writers recorded the period extensively in journals and diaristic poems, culminating in Mayer's *Midwinter Day*, a domestic epic book-length poem recounting one day in their life in Lenox, Massachusetts. They also edited and published a literary magazine, *United Artists,* and Warsh began work on *Agnes and Sally*, which was to be his first published novel. The artistic collaboration and exchange between Mayer and Warsh deserves its own article. The intensity was extreme even for two artists coming to maturity in each other's daily presence. The effects on both writers' work are marked and incalculable. For a while both moved close to ventriloquism in their pursuit of a communal poetics. Mayer, noted for her conceptual experimentalism, began to write more narratively. Warsh, the Romantic autobiographer, moved toward the conceptual and impersonal.

Even a casual reading of *Blue Heaven* and the poems that follow reveal a poet constantly interrogating his own work, experimenting endlessly, sometimes subtly, sometimes radically. Early in *Blue Heaven* Warsh writes

All my poems

no center
everything scattered
many voices trailing off

> empty illusions
>   of emotions and thoughts
> incredible pipe dreams
> disappearing
>   beneath waves
>
> ("Single File," 20)

Yet most of the poems that appear early in the volume are centered on the poet, his memories and circumstances. The "many voices" is more prophetic than actual; the voice heard most consistently is his (in the narrowly autobiographical sense of the word).

The last 50 pages of the collection read more like a journal than independent poems. They add to a record of living in the Berkshires with small children—daily narratives of trips to the dump, washing baby clothes, buying cigarettes, chatting casually with friends and neighbors. Yet there is a through-line of self-interrogation, worry about over-intellectualizing domestic events and being caged within one's subjectivity, a conscious struggle to realize physical existence by latching onto common events and objects. Only two poems near book's end break free from this pattern. "The Secret Job" returns to the poet's youth in San Francisco when he held a job while hiding it from his friends—because it was too banal for an artist's biography, "a job / Any old lady could do."

> To feel embarrassed—everyone
> Knows what that's like. It's better
> To be poor, perhaps,
> Penniless, than to feel that.
>
> Who wants any of it. I don't know.
> A secret life for a Scorpio—I've had enough.
> I didn't want to do it all alone. ("The Secret Job," 127)

It's a poem that wouldn't fit within the romance of *Part of My History*, an effort by the older poet to amend his autobiography and render it more convincing to himself.

The second poem, "Footnote," considers the tensions between utopian ideals and the "trivial domestic labors" that are the "anguish and delight / of all domestic / relationship" through the distancing lens of biographies of Percy Shelley and Lou Salomé. Coming near the conclusion of this poetic journal of rural domesticity, the poem calls into question the pages that precede it by its skeptical, if tender, view of the persisting contradictions between selfless aspirations and personal desires.

> The light of radium
> in Madame Curie's eyes
>
> was to no one's benefit
> if despised by her children . . .
>
> Hogg's infatuation with
> Harriet forced Shelley
> to question
> his ideas about
> property . . . ("Footnote" 122)

Warsh invokes his infatuation with romantic biography to provoke consideration of his own tendencies toward romantic autobiography. His next three books dispense with the lyric persona altogether.

Self-published in Lenox in 1979, *Hives* is a 110-section poem about the habits of bees. The vocabulary is scientific, the diction impersonal, the structure fragmented and arbitrary. The technical subject allows Warsh to shift radically from the diaristic entries of *Blue Heaven*. Here are the first, fifth, and final stanzas.

> I
> In a colony in which
> a young gyne emerged
> but was not imprisoned,
> she attacked the old physogastric
> queen in about three hours,
> biting her abdomen
>
> V
> The invertase causes hydrolysis
> of the sucrose
>
> CX
> A bunch of grapes

Warsh followed *Hives* with four more conceptual poems using similarly technical subject matter and vocabulary and the same fragmented structure. Collected in *Methods of Birth Control*, the poems addressed the subjects of optics ("Eye Opener"), genetics ("The Genetic Ode"), electronic sound systems ("High Fidelity"), and birth control (the title poem).

> LV
> It may be necessary to perform
> an operation known as
> dacryocystorhinostomy
>
>   ("Eye Opener")

> II
> An individual heterozygous for 31 pairs of genes
> could produce more than 2 billion
> kinds of spermatozoa with different complements
>
>   ("The Genetic Ode")

> LXII
> The turnover point is the same
> for A and B, but A holds back
> its effect whereas B will produce
> a noticeable cut
>
>   ("High Fidelity")

These few but representative examples demonstrate the evenness of tone and treatment that characterize most of the volume. According to Warsh, he "didn't write a word of that book, it's all about choices, and the structuring of information in some new way. I was intentionally trying to keep myself out of it as much as possible. I figured that since I'd taken personal poetry to an extreme I might as well go in the opposite direction" (*Poetry and Poetics*, 153).

In "Partial Objects," an essay published in 1988, Warsh describes the process of composing this series of "parasitic monsters," which he says were inspired by Mayer's *Eruditio Ex Memoria*, transcriptions from her Catholic high school notebooks. He borrowed the "heavy, popeish looking" Roman numerals from Wallace Stevens to create an "illusion of order" (*Transfer* 79). "One of the guidelines I set for myself when putting together these works was that there be as little connection as possible between the subject and my life" (83). With the fourth poem, however, there's a shift. The charged subject resists the impersonal approach, even if the attitude introduced is merely ironic.

> II
> Herbal teas or other vegetable
> concoctions are usually harmless, unlike
> many common abortifacient
> potions that can be deadly
>
> XLVI
> *He* uses a condom
> *I* use the Pill
>
> LXXIX
> At the time of sexual enjoyment
> press your finger on the forepart
> of the testicle, turn your mind to
> other things, and hold your breath

It's a departure that persists through the last poem in the series, the book-length *The Corset*, which is prefaced by five rhymed editorial quatrains titled "To the Slaves of Fashion." Whereas the technical subjects and serial fragmentation of the first four poems in the series allow Warsh to escape the diaristic romanticism of *Blue Heaven* and to intervene in the poem only as composer, with the last poems in the series his personality begins to emerge again in point of view and tone. Though begun as conceptual works,

> . . . the impulse to write these poems coincides with some genuine reflection of the way I perceive things. I'm the subject of my own life, but I'm also on the periphery, looking in at a world that's a composite of all the myriad fragments that make up my or anyone's experience. And I'm not even the sum of these fragments—there's no center—but part of a spiral that radiates inward through memory into the present. My heart is broken into a thousand fragments. I have arms and legs, too, which seem to get me where I'm going. (*Transfer* 87)

With this paragraph Warsh recognizes the tensions that keep his work off-kilter and radically fragmented. There are echoes of Frank O'Hara at his most Romantic ("I'm the subject of my own life . . . part of a spiral that radiates inward through memory into the present. My heart is broken into a thousand fragments.") and at his most practical ("I have arms and legs, too, which seem to get me where I'm going.") Though eccentric and inconstant, it's "My heart," and the "genuine" is emphasized. Yet the passage also hearkens back to Kyger and Whalen, Spicer and Duncan, in that the poet is "also on the periphery, looking in at a world that's a composite of all the myriad fragments that make up my or anyone's experience." This isn't a profession of the Romantic imagination or the "Egotistical Sublime," but the graph of a mind that's faithful to fragments of experience, though making no proprietary or explanatory claims about that experience. Individual self-expression gives way to self-awareness; increased awareness calls into question the autonomy of the self.

While composing these poems from "found" material, Warsh was writing the novel *Agnes and Sally*, published between *Methods of Birth Control* and *The Corset* in 1984. But complicating any tale of poetic development, in 1987 he published *Information from the Surface of Venus*, a compilation of poems emphatically dated 1976-1982. The early poems in the volume, presumably written around the time of the publication of *Blue Heaven*, continue the methods of that book, but begin to seem contrivances, a way of composing at which Warsh has become so adept that it occasionally works for individual poems ("House of Horrors," "Past All Dishonor"), but begins to seem repetitive as the moves accrue. Near the end of the book, one encounters a note of urgency and loss of control foreign to its earlier, more measured poems. In "Heirloom" there is a note of risk and anxiety that is unsettling, in "Greed" a dark, almost panicky sarcasm. "Chain Reaction" continues the charge with despair rare to Warsh's contemplative sweetness. But it is "Korean Love Song" that signals the impending breakthrough in Warsh's method of composition. Written in the voice of a young female, the poem mourns the loss of love and uncomplicated desire, and expresses a wistful longing for another opportunity. It's rare to find among Warsh's poems of that era something other than a direct autobiographic lyric, one that expresses a degree of emotion more honed than that found in most of the poems in the book.

Warsh didn't publish another volume of poems until *Avenue of Escape* eight years later (1995). In the meantime he wrote and published a second novel, *A Free Man*. Though not published until 1991, Warsh listed the novel among his works in 1987—so presumably he finished writing it by that time. It's set on the Lower East Side of New York City, as will be most of the prose Warsh publishes over the ensuing ten years. Warsh returned with Mayer to the city in 1980, and they separated a few years later. Ostensibly *Avenue of Escape* picks up with poems composed following the last poems of *Information from the Surface of Venus*, but if I'm correct the earliest poems in the volume don't appear until its middle. From the first poem in the book ("Travelogue"), the departure in style and scope from *Venus* seems sharp. These poems have the novelist's epic social, rather than the lyricist's private voice. Instead of a contemplative continuum that spirals through the poem, lines are here juxtaposed without evident thematic or grammatical connection. Where Warsh's previous method might be called "stream of consciousness," these new poems read more like overheard fragments of conversation, reminiscent of Apollinaire's "Lundi rue Christine," if not so dramatic or colloquial.

> Nietzsche was fun to read in prison . . .
> What I saw when I looked down at the woman & her lover
>   was a reflection of the shadow of the heart broken
>   into shards
> The agency of the letter moves through the fabric of fate . . .
>
> ("Travelogue")

The second poem, "The Outer Banks," is also an accretion of individual lines, but there's a space between each, as if each line were a stanza. Three more poems in the book ("Entering Night," the title poem, and "Anyone But You") follow the same form as "The Outer Banks"—perhaps the accruing lines suggest an emotive gestalt, but any unifying concept or thrust remains elusive. As with much of Warsh's writing, erotic suggestion and obsession characterize a preponderance of the material, but the rambling structure permits any subject to be broached. It's a capacious new discovery that accommodates the poet's manifold vocabulary of moves and gestures, and permits an even wider range of voice.

It's the poem "Maybe You Can Define Love in Terms of What It Isn't," however, that seems to realize most fully a union of the many strands and possibilities within Warsh's previous writing. Harkening back to the inspirations of Spicer, Duncan and Whalen, Warsh here devises a form that collages stanzas reminiscent of his early lyrics, brief aperçus and aphorisms, prose memoirs and journal entries, anecdotes and even short stories in third person narrative, disparate lines wandering freely unto themselves, and quotations from letters (including correspondents from

The Maharajah's Son). Readers familiar with Warsh's work will probably identify the poet with the narrator of anecdotes about being locked in Bill Berkson's bathroom or taking LSD in Liam O'Gallagher's loft, taking a walk in Washington Square Park with his daughter Sofia, or teaching the class in which Mohammed is a student. The names and details are recalled from earlier autobiographical works, match known facts about Warsh's life, and provide a precise context to frame the rest of the poem. Interlaced with these first-person anecdotes are third person narratives about David, a bond trader, and Toni, a cosmetics exec, which reflect on ambiguities in acceptable sexual mores among young business travelers. Throughout, there is a great deal of talk about poetry, its worth and attendant anxieties. There are typical Warsh rhetorical plays ("in the face of a tirade / at the edge of the balustrade"). The final verse stanza follows a 4-1/2 page excerpt from letters addressed to "Dear Lewis," a character who—like the poet—is the author of a novel titled *Agnes and Sally*, from Allegra, one of the correspondents in *The Maharajah's Son*. After much talk about relationships and Allegra's enduring hope to experiment with group marriage, Allegra mentions that

> I really enjoyed *Agnes and Sally*. As always, your amazing talent for portraying what goes on inside the most intimate confines of the human mind carried me from beginning to end.
>
> In thinking about it afterwards I was trying to understand why I feel more fortunate than any of the 4 characters in the book, and I decided that the most obvious reason is that relationships are not the only passion in my life. A lot of time and energy and joy go into my dancing and singing. And I think it's true that one's art is a more durable and dependable soul alliance than most love affairs tend to be. Ours is an exception, I hope. (21)

In their apparent sincerity and in their ironic contradictions, the sentiments expressed by Allegra are not foreign to the author who appropriates them in his own poem. But he is only reading them, as are we.

> it might happen that you would
> consider someone else's feelings, and
> in that way learn something
> you didn't already know (14)

Of all Warsh's poems, "Maybe You Can Define Love in Terms of What It Isn't" seems the most perfect marriage of New York School poetics and those of the San Francisco/Bolinas poets mentioned above. Here he discovers a form that allows him to be as genuinely and capriciously personal as he desires, but in which "psychology, magic, history and dailiness exist in equal measure." Distinctions between lyric and epic, subjective and objective, seem superfluous. Self-awareness is but a fragment of awareness; "You are everyone you've ever been with for a moment."

Since *Avenue of Escape*, Warsh has published six books: two book-length serial poems, another volume of autobiography, a collection of short stories, a book that combines poems and stories, and an extended collection of poems. *Private Agenda*, a book-length poem in 19 parts, with drawings by Pamela Lawton interspersed, was published in 1996. The sentence is the unit of measure in most sections. Though often broken into shorter lines and even enjambed to form stanzas, the sentences are collaged or juxtaposed, rather than semantically connected. Three sections are brief narratives: one about the actor Montgomery Clift, another about a "convict" who seems to have been freed and is stalking a victim, the third about a man in love with his wife's younger sister.

Bustin's Island '68, a book of autobiographical writing, and *Money Under the Table*, seven stories, followed. In 2001, *Touch of the Whip* collected poems and prose, the prose including stories, autobiography, and prose poems. As I write that, it seems a betrayal of the book's spirit to categorize the contents, because Warsh moves so freely between genres, sometimes within a single piece. The two poems immediately recognizable as such are composed in the single-line form of "The Outer Banks" and "Avenue of Escape," though now most of the lines are sentences.

> You can only scratch the surface of what another person is like
> You scratch the surface of another person until you draw blood
> He gave up his life among people & became like a stone
> We could hear them talking about us out of the corners of their mouths
> The absent person is always present
>   ("We Wrote a Letter to Jesus")

So the distinction between them and what I've called the prose poems is largely a matter of arrangement. "Strike Anywhere," "Anonymous Donor," and "White Nights" are composed in single sentences also, but separated by punctuation instead of spacing.

It's better to live with other people, a family, than to live alone in a flophouse. It's better to be accepted as part of a family. The person I live with is not my mother. The tree outside my window is not a tree, but a picture painted on the landscape, backdrop for some play I've been acting in half my life. Feed me the lines, please: *I love you, I hate you, I never want to see you again.* How did I do? ("Anonymous Donor")

The contrast emphasizes the air in the poems, the progress of the prose.

The title poem hearkens back in form to "Maybe You Can Define Love in Terms of What It Isn't," and is thus more varied than most of those in his recent collections. Some sections are composed in the streaming enjambments of his early work, others in irregular stanzas, and some even in couplets. "Touch of the Whip" consists of seven sections, separated by asterisks. Some are in first person singular, others in first person plural or second person, and the poem ends with a third person narrative about the kidnapping and murder of an oil company executive by a New Jersey husband and wife. Sometimes the "I" seems to be Lewis Warsh (talking about his mother or his daughter Sophia) and sometimes it seems to represent a persona. Personality becomes increasingly slippery in Warsh's recent writing. Characters exchange loves and identities with frightening facility. Though oppressed by responsibilities and social demands, they exist in terrifying isolation. The executive dies alone in a box, but it's the distance between the ineptly criminal husband and wife that haunts.

The Origin of the World consists entirely of poems composed in the discrete line form that first appeared in *Avenue of Escape.* In fact, it reprints the five poems from that book written in discrete lines and adds twelve new poems written in the same form. Mysteriously, it doesn't include the two poems in that form from *Touch of the Whip* ("We Wrote a Letter to Jesus" or "The Gun in His Hand"), a decision perhaps owing to the recent availability of the previous book. In addition to the reprinted poems, the new poems contain echoes and even self-quotation from other works, e.g.,

> the woman directed the police to the place where the executive
>   was buried (47)

> She pushes the baby carriage up the steps of Grant's Tomb
>   that's part of my history (36)

> I told the psychiatrist at the army inductee center
> that I didn't like women, & he believed me (63)

> There was a rumor that many of Bertolt Brecht's most famous plays
> were written by his girlfriends (90)

The book concludes with "The Secret Police," a poem that provides a theme for those that precede it with its insistent focus on spying and informing, intrusion and expression, the inextricable entangling of personal and public. The poem's concluding lines are idyllic and ominous.

> We stare at the sun, into the sun, through the light of the sun & the sun going down over the horizon until the boats on the edge of the horizon resemble brothels on wheels

> We lie on a blanket near the ocean watching the sun disappear, islands of clouds dispersing on the horizon

> This is the time I like best, late evening, when the sun disappears, & there are no secrets (92)

Warsh's last book to date, *Reported Missing*, is, like *Private Agenda*, one poem in 19 sections. Sections 8 and 18 were published previously in *Touch of the Whip* as "Up Against the Ropes" and "Anonymous Donor." Here they are reprinted without titles. This disorienting recurrence of lines and sections in Warsh's latest work, always juxtaposed to new material, stresses the persistent power of memory to envelop and interpret new experience. Paul Goodman claimed that "as Freud deepened his explanation of the mental processes, he more and more gave up the contact of 'mind' and 'external world'; he tended toward a closed system, the individual acting out a mental drama on an isolated stage" (*Nature Heals*, 38). While recognizing the genius and necessity of Freud's investigations, Goodman resisted what he saw as the resignation of the later Freud by proclaiming the importance of the "new experimental try with a real person." Hope rests on the possibility of contacting and manipulating the environment. For Goodman, sexual liberation was a vital part of any successful political revolution.

From *Part of My History* through "Maybe You Can Define Love in Terms of What It Isn't," Lewis Warsh holds onto this hopeful Romantic possibility. Thirty years after Paul Goodman's death, however, it's difficult to mention social revolution without a sad smile, if not a smirk, of irony. In Warsh's most recent books, it's less clear that individuals have the power to choose between "the individual acting out a mental drama on an isolated stage" and the "new experimental try with a real person." Sometimes the persons in his poems and stories seem doomed to an incomprehensibly private destiny. Perhaps this reflects his imaginative response to yet another shift in the poetic and larger community around Warsh, as he and his artistic peers age into a post-9/11 ambiance that contrasts so dismally to the ebullience of their free-spirited 1960s youth. Yet in Warsh's work, even the private mental drama is many-voiced, and the courage for a new experimental try continues to hold the only promise for community—and for love. Warsh's writing moves beyond a conception of writing as self-expression to one of writing as what Goodman termed "the contact of 'mind' and 'external world.'" The results are unsettlingly democratic and contingent. Lewis Warsh leads us into territory where the ego cannot be distinguished from its entanglements. In contrast to the resurgent metaphysical tradition, where the individual soul seeks its own salvation, Warsh continues to engage a world where our fates are inextricably social. In that sense, the multiple voices in his poems resemble those in a Greek tragedy, where "psychology, magic, history and dailiness . . . exist in equal measure."

Works Cited

Allen, Donald M., ed. *The New American Poetry*. NY: Grove Press, 1960.

Berkson, Bill. "AIR AND SUCH: An Essay on *Biotherm*." NY: *Sal Mimeo* 3, (Spring 2003): n.p.

Blaser, Robin, ed. *The Collected Books of Jack Spicer*. Santa Barbara, CA: Black Sparrow Press, 1980.

Desnos, Robert. *Night of Loveless Nights*. Translated by Lewis Warsh. NY: The Ant's Forefoot 10, 1973.

Ellingham, Lewis and Kevin Killian. *Poet Be Like God: Jack Spicer and the San Francisco Renaissance*. Hanover & London: University Press of New England, 1998.

Foster, Edward, ed. *Poetry and Poetics in the New Millenium*. Jersey City, NJ: Talisman House, 2000.

Goodman, Paul. *Nature Heals: The Psychological Writings*, edited by Taylor Stoehr.

NY: Free Life Editions, 1978.

Kyger, Joanne. *As Ever: Selected Poems*. Introduction by David Meltzer. NY: Penguin, 2002.

Padgett, Ron and David Shapiro, ed. *An Anthology of New York Poets*. NY: Random House, 1970.

Waldman, Anne and Lewis Warsh, ed. *The Angel Hair Anthology*. NY: Granary Books, 2001.

Warsh, Lewis. *Agnes and Sally*. NY: Fiction Collective, 1984.

—. *Avenue of Escape*. Brooklyn, NY: Long News Books, 1995.

—. *Blue Heaven*. NY: Kulchur Foundation, 1978.

—. *The Corset*. Detroit, MI: In Camera, 1986.

—. *Dreaming as One*. NY: Corinth Books, 1971.

—. *A Free Man*. Los Angeles: Sun & Moon Press, 1991.

—. *Hives*. Lenox, MA: United Artists Books, 1979.

—. *Immediate Surrounding*. So. Lancaster, MA: Other Publications, 1974.

—. *Information from the Surface of Venus*. NY: United Artists Books, 1987.

—. *The Maharajah's Son*. Lenox, MA: Angel Hair Books, 1977.

—. *Methods of Birth Control*. Washington, DC and Philadelphia: Sun & Moon Press, 1983.

—. *Money Under the Table*. San Francisco, CA: Trip Street Press, 1997.

—. *The Origin of the World*. Berkeley, CA: Creative Arts, 2001.

—. *Part of My History*. Toronto: Coach House Press, 1972.

—. "Partial Objects." *Transfer*, Vol. 1, No. 2, Spring 1988, 78-87.

—. *Private Agenda*. Atlanta, GA: Hornswoggle Press, 1996.

—. *Reported Missing*. Brooklyn, NY: United Artists Books, 2002.

—. *Touch of the Whip*. Philadelphia, PA: Singing Horse Press, 2001.

The Pleasures of Elusiveness:
What Is In and Around Ron Padgett's Poetry

LORENZO THOMAS

I

Les mots sont plus lourds que le son
—Pierre Reverdy, "Patience"

This essay represents a modest attempt to examine one or two aspects of what goes into and around the making of Padgett's funny, poignant, and often astonishingly surprising poems. Clayton Eshleman has said that Padgett's poetry "ripples with immediacy—it is a poetry of primary colors"; adding that his often comic tone is "modulated by an austere, existential probing, and a keen sense of the liquid boundary between being and not being at all" (8). It might also be said that Padgett's poetry is simultaneously difficult and entirely accessible, employing everyday speech and arcane compositional gambits with equal facility. Much influenced by Kenneth Koch, who was one of his teachers at Columbia University, Padgett creates poetry that seems most carefully designed for our entertainment. But those who admonish us to seek nothing but delight from poetry also clearly imply that the purpose of the arts is to ameliorate an immiserating and brutalizing reality. This is obviously an aspect of Padgett's work.

While the energy of Padgett's imagination has not diminished, the poems collected in *You Never Know* (2001) seem to demonstrate that he is more than ever aware of the limitations of poetry. Standing in for Rilke, Padgett's "Advice to Young Writers" is alarmingly low key: "It's aright, students, not / to write. Do whatever you want. As long as you find / that unexpected something, or even if you don't" (4). On the other hand, he instructs us in "Exceptions to the Rule," one might just as unexpectedly be "the originator of a chain reaction / that sends a jagged love throughout the world and on" (*You Never Know* 48).

II

When we think or write about artists, too often it is as singular and isolated figures when, in fact, they are people whose work cannot be fully appreciated unless seen in the framework of their society and direct personal associations. Ron Padgett is a poet best understood in the context of a group of literary co-conspirators, the core of which includes childhood friends from Tulsa such as poet Dick Gallup and painter Joe Brainard who continued their association in New York.

Padgett was a brilliant student but public school in Tulsa, Oklahoma placed him in a milieu that required a kind of "aw shucks" matter of factness about good grades. He worked hard to appear unexceptional and certainly didn't want to be identified with the kids in the library who appeared to be "zealous demons engaged in research" ("Wilson '57," *New and Selected Poems* 59). Padgett was the kid in your science or social studies class who always knew the answers but thought it was tacky to raise his hand *all* the time. The kid it was smart to sit next to on the day of the test.

For all that, Padgett had sufficient interest in reading literature to get a part-time job in a bookstore and to begin publishing a little poetry magazine while he was still in high school. *The White Dove Review*, produced by Padgett with Gallup, Brainard, and other classmates, also included poems that he solicited from writers elsewhere in the country whose work frequently appeared in literary magazines. The magazine also brought Padgett into contact with a University of Tulsa student named Ted Berrigan. Studying for a master's degree on the GI Bill, Berrigan was a charismatic character. He was well read and, around 1960, interested in the poetry of John Ciardi and Kenneth Rexroth.

Ted Berrigan also exerted an influence on Padgett, and many others, as a Romantic model of what a poet should be. Berrigan, says David Lehman in *The Last Avant-Garde* (1998), "was determined to live the life of a poet twenty-four hours a day" (365). Moving to New York's Lower East Side at the beginning of the 1960s, Berrigan started publishing an idiosyncratic mimeographed poetry magazine and adopted a classic Bohemian lifestyle—arising in late afternoon, he stayed up all night reading, writing his book-length sequence *The Sonnets* (1963), roaming the city.

Padgett recalled:

> Ted's passion for writing was everyday and always. It wasn't something you did only in the depths of despair or on the heights of inspiration. It was something you did when you read the sports page or ate a donut. It was something you did when you sat at your desk and thought about the gods. It was something you did with scissors and Elmer's glue. (Ted 44)

And it was something that prevented getting a job.

Making sure to mention "my steady job, my jacket and tie," Phillip Lopate presented an entertaining analysis of the East Village poets. "Sometimes," he wrote, "they seemed like friars who had taken vows of poverty, dope, poetry, and family" (218). Lopate's fictionalized essay, "Lives of the Poets" (1981), focuses on the dismal circumstances of poet Greg Cannon and his family. Looking at Annie, Greg's frustrated wife, Lopate notes:

> She looked wrung out. It was a look that many of the wives of the poets had: a haggardness from having to answer demanding children and prepare meals in a tiny apartment and stretch the budget while some large white abstracted goofy American male sat at his desk, investigating the experimental properties of language. (224-225)

Compared to Lopate's glum scenario, Henry Mürger's gritty environs and Puccini's *La Bohème* seem positively jolly.

In this artistic milieu, Berrigan thrived. Ted was sociable and his personality charismatic. His East Side apartment became a sort of salon (or hangout) for a group of poets who were mostly six to ten years younger than he. Enthusiastically playing the rôle of accidental mentor and reluctantly gracious host, Berrigan enjoyed the flattery of his visitors. Within fifteen minutes of being in his presence, his visitors became an audience who began to imitate Berrigan's gestures and vocal mannerisms. If a group of people did that to me, it would probably scare me—but Berrigan accepted it as if he were a swing soloist and the guys in the room were Tommy Dorsey's band, catching his best notes and returning them as a riff.

Even though Berrigan's mimeographed *C* magazine was a publication on paper, the soirées in his apartment were an indispensable aspect of the project. Poetry was understood to be an *activity*, an attribute of *presence*. These poets rejected the position of academic critics who exalted poetry in dusty tomes and applied "the test of time" to buttress their pronouncements. In lines from "Tone Arm" that parallel a short poem of Berrigan's, Padgett peevishly declares

> You people of the future
> How I hate you
> You are alive and I'm not
> I don't care whether you read my poetry or not
> (*New and Selected Poems* 31)

Poetry as a form of sociable conversation suggests a reevaluation of art as *occasion* rather than as process or product because collaboration—either as joint authorship or as everyone's tacit agreement to write sonnets à la Berrigan—demands actual or virtual confrontation. This confrontation, if positive, can produce a sense of bonding and a shared style of communication, a cipher that denotes membership. Due to Berrigan's personality, the cadre that formed around his magazine quickly became a group of friends who shared an aesthetic that was initially most evident in Berrigan's own poems. Perceptively, Tom Clark wrote, "the real subject of *The Sonnets* was the grand clarity of the moment of creation, something 'stronger than alcohol, more great than song'" (*Late Returns* 23). The attraction of being in Berrigan's company was the excitement of sharing that "grand clarity."

C magazine's editorial policy was clearly stated—its pages contained "anything the editor likes." Similarly, the works that filled its pages quite unmistakably announced an aesthetic position. Within a short time, *C* was joined by a number of other literary journals that shared its orientation. Among the most interesting of these was *Mother*, founded by a group of students at Carleton College in Minnesota. Edited by a changing directorate including—at various times—David Moberg, Jeff Giles, Duncan McNaughton, and Peter Schjeldahl, *Mother* was a stimulating journal and eight issues appeared with startling regularity between 1964 and 1967. Other publishing efforts included short-lived mimeo magazines edited by John Perreault, Aram Saroyan, and Lewis MacAdams. *Nadada,* a journal edited by Timothy Baum with Gerard Malanga's assistance, included a number of poems by various hands that were based on Berrigan's sonnet permutations as well as texts generated by various idiosyncratic "mechanical" formulae. An issue of *Wagner Literary Magazine* edited by Malanga included more of these experiments. Almost all of the poets involved in these publications were also connected to some extent with *C* magazine.

Padgett's circle reveled in the kitsch of Americana—both old and new—the legend of Billy the Kid, Elvis Presley movies, bus station 25c photo booth portraits (cf, Wolf 103-104). Even more highly prized were those mundane metropolitan experiences that still had a raffish edge; for example hot dogs and draft beer at the Times Square stand-up deli counter called Grant's, a place frequented late at night by shift workers, junkies, and other shady characters (like poets).

What remains impressive from this period is the wide-ranging inventiveness of Padgett and his group. The widening circle of poets enthusiastically experimented with various surrealist gestures, "cut-ups" influenced by William Burroughs and Brion Gysin, and intriguing proto-Oulipian constraints.

A major theme in many of these experiments is the dissolution of personality—starting with the author. The group's exploration of anonymity extended to a season when everyone wrote Berrigan-style sonnets and, in fact, traded lines with each other. The notion of a *poem machine* was much discussed. It worked by generating poetic lines according to any number of arbitrary formulas and the desired end product was a 14-line poem that revealed neither authorship nor intentional meaning. Padgett's "Rain Dunce After Ted" (1963) takes this game to an extreme:

> This pinching prince nix! Some dumb fooze
> Glands oink to a dumb fooze, in the jerk blight.
> In the nookie of his moo (sic) the bunions have mated

These verses, generated by a strategically whimsical replacement of vowels and consonants, constitute a "phonetic mistranslation" of the opening lines of Berrigan's *The Sonnets*:

> His piercing pince-nez. Some dim frieze
> Hands point to a dim frieze, in the dark night.
> In the book of his music the corners have straightened:
> Which owe their presence to our sleeping hands,

Berrigan's closing couplet is influenced in its sonority by his avid study of F. T. Prince's elegant diction:

> We are the sleeping fragments of his sky,
> Wind giving presence to fragments. (Berrigan, *The Sonnets* 7)

In Padgett's parody, this becomes

> We are the beeping frogmens of his good-bye,
> Friends giving pup tents to frogmens. (85)

"Rain Dunce After Ted" and a number of other experiments by the *C* magazine group enlivened the *Wagner Literary Magazine* and similar work could be found in *Nadada*.

The "poem machines" that Gerard Malanga found interesting, like

Berrigan's various prose and verse collaborations (some of which involved plagiarizing popular paperback novels) also verged upon questionable identity or anonymity. In the tradition of King Talou's grand oration in Raymond Roussel's *Impression d'Afrique,* Jim Brodey's poem "Mswaki" (1964), published in *Nadada,* was guaranteed to mystify his Lower East Side audiences since it was written mostly in Swahili. John Giorno's *The American Book of the Dead* was drawn from newspaper articles about crimes and accidents retyped to resemble the lineation of poetry. Appropriately, Giorno's biographical note in *An Anthology of New York Poets* is actually Elvis Presley's resume (Padgett and Shapiro 557).

The avoidance of personality inscribed in these works must also be linked to the poets' playful emulation of Andy Warhol's non-ideas. Warhol was so disconnected from the Romantic stereotype of artistic egotism that any stray visitor to his factory might be invited to wield a squeegee on the Brillo boxes or life-size silver Elvises being prepared for his next gallery exhibition. Warhol, wrote Peter Schjeldahl, "had a steamrolling effect on the whole mental apparatus of Western cultural tradition" (101). Jacques Barzun and them might find this a bit overstated for much of the Western world, but Warhol was certainly a beacon to Padgett's pals.

In prose that mimics both Gertrude Stein and Warhol's own conversational manner, Joe Brainard wrote:

> As for Andy Warhol, yes, I do think so. As I said, Andy Warhol "dug deep." (Perhaps without digging at all!) At any rate, like I said, Andy Warhol "lets" you know what he's doing, but he doesn't "tell." If Andy Warhol "told" it would be telling about "what" he is doing. Or what he "did." Andy Warhol, he's got "courage" and he's got "ideas." Andy Warhol I think has creative ideas. Andy Warhol doesn't I don't think do creative paintings. Andy Warhol might not even do paintings at all! For all I know Andy Warhol might not even have "ideas" at all, but for me Andy Warhol has "ideas." Andy Warhol perhaps paints ideas, but if so, I sure do like the way his ideas look. Andy Warhol's ideas look great! Andy Warhol paints Andy Warhols. And I like that. (Lewallen 76)

Padgett liked it, too, and during this period, published a wide range of experimental poems including "The Andy of Andy the Warhol," which is constituted of random phrases that sometimes threaten to make sense:

> She had never returned to the dials
> While keeping a tight
> Hand on the lace
> Briefly before it becomes
> An epitaph for
> Himself of the ship of
> Photograph enthroned in a body

A clue to what's going on here might be found in the same 1965 issue of *Mother* where this poem appears. A full-page photograph of Joe Brainard's sculptural collage *St. Teresa*—an assemblage built-up with plastic flowers, marbles, rosary beads and other disparate items and scraps—suggests that Padgett and others might have been attempting to use words and fragments of sentences in a similar manner. As efforts that unmistakably derive from Duchamp's undoing of sculpture and painting in his *readymades,* similar deconstructions of the decorum (and recognizably standard syntax) that seemed appropriate to the academic poets of the 1940s and 1950s can be found in numerous productions from the *C* magazine circle. Much more direct, but to the same purpose, was Ted Berrigan's gesture when he grabbed a copy of *Nadada* out of my hands and, with a flourish, used his pen to black out the first three letters of the subtitle "Contemporary American Poets Issue." "There," Ted said. "Now it's accurate."

III

Padgett's enjoyment and understanding of poets who did not write in English was enhanced by his facility with languages, a skill that had not been particularly encouraged in his childhood. "When I was growing up, in the limited cultural atmosphere of blue-collar Oklahoma in the 1940s and '50s," he said in a 1981 talk at the Detroit Institute of Arts, "I used to laugh when I heard someone speaking a foreign language, especially an Asian one. To me foreign languages sounded 'funny,' in both senses of the word. Others thought they sounded funny in only the sense of odd or peculiar. In other words, *not like us.* I think my seeing foreign languages as both odd and amusing helped save me from this jingoist fate" (*The Straight Line* 25). He eventually became quite adept at languages, earning a fellowship to study in France when he graduated from Columbia University.

Padgett still managed to find amusement both in the *difference* another language presents and in our perception of it. "Falling in Love in Spain or Mexico" (1965), an extremely short play (probably about 2 minutes playing time), begins as "a handsome young man and a veiled woman enter." The man, José, begins speaking:

> I am happy to meet you. My name is José Gomez Carrillo. What is your name? This is my wife. I like your daughter very much. I think your sister is beautiful.

As he continues, it is evident that he is merely reciting lines from one-column of a Spanish-English tourist phrase book. "Falling in Love in Spain or Mexico" is delightfully funny, but it also points significantly to Padgett's fascination with our banal habits of anticipating syntactic counters in everyday speech and ordinary reading—activities that operate on the level of stored memory and logical structure. Padgett purposely disrupts such patterns.

Padgett's early interest in the poetry of Baudelaire and Rimbaud led to further studies of artists and writers of the early 20th-century avant-garde, especially Marcel Duchamp. Following Duchamp's bilingual word play, if you know enough French, might lead to Raymond Roussel, a writer who sidestepped making ordinary sense by inventing elaborate procedures by which "a readymade phrase was reduced to a similar-sounding string of fragments whose chance conjunctions became the basis for a narrative passage or tale" (Joselit 16). By the mid 1970s, following a trail blazed by Kenneth Koch, Padgett—along with Bill Zavatsky and Trevor Winkfield—was involved in careful study of Roussel.

In 1912, Duchamp—in the company of Francis and Gabrielle Picabia and Guillaume Apollinaire—attended a performance of Roussel's *Impressions d'Afrique* at the Théâtre Antoine in Paris and was immediately enraptured by the playwright's linguistic experiments (Mink 29-30; Ford 119-120, 218). Duchamp also became familiar with Roussel's poems and novels that described fanciful robots and Rube Goldberg-esque machines, inventions that directly influenced his own *The Bride Stripped Bare By Her Bachelors, Even* (Mink 32-33; Ford 116). Settling in New York in 1915 to avoid the war in Europe, Duchamp became part of the city's artistic vanguard. The controversial painting *Nude Descending a Staircase,* shown at the 1913 Armory Show, served as his letter of introduction. But instead of producing similar paintings, Duchamp began to create works he called "readymades" when he signed his name to a snow shovel purchased at a hardware store and titled it *In Advance of the Broken Arm* (Mink 51; Tomkins 154, 156-158).

According to Calvin Tomkins, the point of the readymade was the fact that the shovel was "a mass-produced, machine made object with no esthetic qualities whatsoever" and, therefore, beyond the categories of taste (157). Nevertheless, says Tomkins, a banal object possessed the *capacity* to become an artwork if it attracted Duchamp's attention:

> Only by giving it a title and an artist's signature could it attain the odd and endlessly provocative status of a readymade, a work of art created not by the hand or skill but by the mind and decision of the artist. (157)

IV

The possibility of creating a poetic *readymade*—a dadaistic exercise in purposeful plagiarism—advanced Padgett's project. The *C* magazine group frequently amused themselves producing poems and prose collaborations signed with pseudonyms; and sometimes with the names of other poets in their circle. An extensive practice of allusion and quotation based on texts by Frank O'Hara, John Ashbery, and each other, created an intertextuality that echoed models as disparate as Neoclassical verse and the Bebop jam session. These practices are also riddled with the peculiar humor and delight in practical jokes that the group enjoyed. Berrigan, says Reva Wolf, often "poked fun at authorship and artistic identity"; and Padgett told her that some of their collaborations were aimed at "making fun of the fear of plagiarism" (Wolf 104, 109).

An example of this assault on authorship might be Padgett's desire, confided to poet Aram Saroyan, to publish an expensive edition of Shakespeare's *A Midsummer Night's Dream* with T. S. Eliot listed as author. This nefarious scheme of mistaken identity puzzled Saroyan who admitted to being "intrigued by the idea of playing such quiet, low-key havoc with the world of letters" (33). An equally mischievous plot that was actually realized is represented by Padgett's poem "A Man Saw a Ball of Gold":

> A man saw a ball of gold in the sky;
> He climbed for it,
> And eventually he achieved it—
> It was gold.

Now this is the strange part:
When the man went to the earth
And looked again,
Lo, there was the ball of gold.
Now this is the strange part:
It was a ball of gold.
Ay, by the heavens, it was a ball of gold.

(*New and Selected Poems* 50)

If this outrageous gesture—first published in Padgett's debut 1963 chap-book *In Advance of the Broken Arm*—is an exercise in plagiarism, then it is a crime equivalent to stealing Polonius's purse. Padgett here copies Stephen Crane's "A Man Saw a Ball of Gold" almost word for word, digressing from the original only by replacing the last word in the first stanza (Crane's "clay") with his own word "gold."

Crane's "A Man Saw a Ball of Gold" was published in *The Black Riders and Other Lines* (1895), and has been admired chiefly by high school freshmen who discover it in anthologies—along with "A Man Said to the Universe" and the poem about the man in the desert eating his own heart—and marvel at Crane's profundity. When they go to the library to find more of his work, they see Crane's picture and immediately fall in love—either with him or with the notion that they, too, could become as profoundly handsome and menacingly cool.

Crane's poem, written when he was 21 years old, stands out in anthologies because it so flagrantly ignores the rhyme, meter, and poetic diction expected of late 19th century poetry in English. "When we read Crane's poems today," a critic wrote in 1964, "we need have no worry about their experiments in form. That struggle for freedom was won long ago, with his help" (McDonald x).

The message transmitted by Crane's poem might have attracted restlessly alienated readers in the Sixties, but his style is hardly as electrifying as the *vers libre* produced in the early 20th century by Amy Lowell, the Imagists, Carl Sandburg, and others (cf, Stallman 568-569). Actually, the unadorned directness of language in Crane's poem and the odd repetition of the line "Now this is the strange part" in the second stanza make the poem seem prosaic and rhetorically illogical. That Padgett would copy out this well-known poem and present it as his own work is an even greater affront than the lapse of literary taste (or at least sophistication) his choice of text reveals.

Even a Crane scholar such as Robert Wooster Stallman admits, "As unified wholes his poems are negligible, being chiefly fragments of unformed meaning" (575). In Crane's own day, Stallman adds, these works didn't even look like poems. Nor am I at all anxious about my assertion that Crane's poems appeal primarily to adolescents. That very fact, of course, endows these texts with a specific cultural value that interests a poet such as Padgett precisely because it is vulnerable to parody. I will argue, however, that Crane's text presents interesting complexities and that Padgett's engagement with this text involves a more serious purpose than the merely parodic.

Reviewers trashed or misinterpreted *The Black Riders* but, partly due to Crane's best-selling novel *The Red Badge of Courage* (1895), the book still enjoyed six printings in two years (Katz xxxiii-xxxiv; Stallman 567-568). "In rejecting the poetic conventions of his own time," commented Gerald D. McDonald in 1964, Stephen Crane "was writing, it may seem, for our own" (x). This, of course, is an illusion that flatters today's reader more than it documents Crane's literary contribution; but it may actually be a useful way to approach his poetry.

Stallman calls these works "epigrammatic parables" and argues that Crane's poems are about illusion and reality—"the theory or ideal being exploded by the facts of reality" (569). This is often presented in a poem by contrasting the same object viewed from different perspectives or vantages. Other poems in *The Black Riders* are structured as dialogues between differing points of view. As with a Zen *koan*, the juxtapositions sometimes suggest that a more extended discussion might be in order. An excellent example is a poem that seems to demand an examination of the deterministic philosophy implied in the genre of Literary Naturalism that Crane's novels helped make popular:

> A man said to the universe:
> "Sir, I exist!"
> "However," replied the universe,
> "The fact has not created in me
> A sense of obligation." (Crane, *Poems* 49)

That poem, from Crane's second collection *War is Kind* (1899), exemplifies what Stallman calls "a logic that contradicts 'logic'" (574).

By comparison, Crane's "A Man Saw a Ball of Gold" straightforwardly contrasts common sense and an idiosyncratic perception that might as easily be genius or madness.

There may be more to this paradox—both Crane's poem and Padgett's plagiarization—than first seems obvious. The man who sees "a ball of gold in the sky," even if that vision motivates him to great and ambitious effort, is mistakenly interpreting something that the rest of us quite simply and correctly recognize as the sun. We may, perhaps, choose to entertain the possibility that Crane is offering an inverted allusion to the myth of the cave in Plato's *Republic*. Still, if we believe—as Emerson and McLuhan did—that the artist or poet is that person who sees more clearly than the rest of us do, then we cannot simply dismiss the protagonist of the poem. Indeed, the second stanza of the poem suggests that—logic or no logic—he was right all along.

It is hard to guess precisely what recommended "A Man Saw a Ball of Gold" to Padgett, but Crane does have some affinities to 20th century avant-garde ideas. McDonald notes that Crane was interested in painting and sometimes called himself "an impressionist" (xi). It is possible that Padgett's appropriation of this particular poem is linked to his own serious interest in the so-called Cubist poetics of his favorite 20th century French writers. In a brief essay on Reverdy, Apollinaire, Cendrars, and Max Jacob, Padgett contends that their poems "exemplified the same play on appearance and reality as did Cubist collage: use of found materials and *trompe-l'oeil*—is it a newspaper clipping or a painting of one?—and play on words, which might be described as *trompe-l'esprit*." The stylized props of the Cubist *nature-mort* or still-life—guitar, wineglass, newspaper . . . the furnishings of a corner in the artist's studio or of a table in a café—are therefore paralleled in the medium of poetry by Reverdy's focus on "everyday objects and occurrences (including dreams)." This similarity was not just Padgett's perception. Reverdy himself admitted to an intensive study of the work of Georges Braque, Pablo Picasso, and Juan Gris between 1910 and 1914. He admired their geometric simplicity and declared, "I wanted to get that in literature" (Padgett, *The Straight Line* 33-34, 40).

There is another aspect of Stephen Crane's work that closely parallels avant-garde ideas in France. Interestingly enough, Crane composed his poetry in a manner that resembles the Surrealist practice of "automatic writing." Stopping by his friend Hamlin Garland's apartment one day, Crane feverishly wrote out perfect drafts of several poems that eventually were collected in *The Black Riders*. Garland himself thought the performance somewhat uncanny, "as if some alien spirit were delivering these lines through his hand as a medium." Crane wrote, Garland reported, "as if he were copying something already written and before his eyes" (quoted in Stallman 566). That, of course, is exactly how Padgett's poem *was* written.

On closer examination, though, it could be argued that Padgett's "A Man Saw a Ball of Gold" is not really plagiarism. Following the Cubist aesthetic, we might say that Stephen Crane's poem is, for Padgett, a *found object*. One must be very attentive, however, to notice that Padgett has purposely changed one of Crane's words. Thus, Padgett's poem follows the rules of Marcel Duchamp's *readymade*: the commercially available object—a snow shovel, a poem in a standard textbook anthology—is transformed into an artwork (and definitely *not* an *objet d'art*) when the artist *slightly alters it* with an evocative title, an unexpected placement, or his signature. In Duchamps's own most deliberately disruptive readymade, *Fountain* (1917), the artist underscores his point by affixing the bogus signature "R. Mutt."

We can now see "A Man Saw a Ball of Gold" as the exquisite artifice it is. In fact, by changing Crane's "clay" to "gold," Padgett reduces his version of Crane's clever paradox to repetitive tautology. When we hear the poem read aloud, or read it quickly, we respond to the Stephen Crane poem stored in our memory. It is only upon careful (i.e., *slower*) re-reading that we begin to see that Padgett has actually presented us with a poem that resembles a wall of identical (or almost identical) Warhol Marilyns—or, rather, the postcard-sized black and white photo reproduction of that wall as it would appear in a newspaper or magazine. Indeed, the sort of close concentration required here—which is not necessarily the same thing critics mean by the phrase *close reading*—is what generates many of Padgett's poems.

Padgett learned much indeed from Andy Warhol. "My favorite piece of sculpture," said Warhol, "is a solid wall with a hole in it to frame the space on the other side" (*Philosophy* 144). It is an interesting statement that is not merely about what art historians call "composition." Warhol claimed that he adored "empty spaces" and felt guilty because "I'm still making some art, I'm still making junk for people to put in their spaces that I believe should be empty; i.e., I'm helping people *waste* their space when what I really want to do is help them *empty* their space" (*Philosophy* 144).

Of course the only solution to Warhol's dilemma was that discovered by Marcel Duchamp, an artist who refused to make art. In fact, however, the works that Warhol did produce are exactly like his ideal hole in a wall: they have the effect of making people see the world in an entirely unexpected new perspective. Such a restructuring of the ordinary (and overlooked) is also the effect of Ron Padgett's poetry.

Ron Padgett is one of those who see poetry as the product of the inner life of the imagination; or, better, the process of imaginative living. There are ways to make sense of our presence in the world, and in society, other than the record of discontent and brutish conflict that we accept as history or news.

Poetry, for Padgett, is a different kind of news: the way the world could be—or might actually be—even if that's the way it isn't. What matters is that the art is good. And who is to say that because something has never been done quite this way before, that it will not work.

WORKS CITED

Ashbery, John. "The Invisible Avant-Garde." 1968. *Twentieth-Century American Poetics: Poets on the Art of Poetry.* Ed. Dana Gioia and others. New York: McGraw-Hill, 2004. 287-291.

Berrigan, Ted. *The Sonnets.* New York: Grove Press, 1964.

Brainard, Joe. "St. Teresa." *Mother: A Journal of New Literature,* no. 6. (February/March 1965): 12.

Clark, Tom. *Late Returns: A Memoir of Ted Berrigan.* Bolinas, California: Tombouctou Books, 1985.

Crane, Stephen. *Poems of Stephen Crane.* Ed. Gerald D. McDonald. New York: Thomas Y. Crowell, 1964.

Eshleman, Clayton. "Padgett the Collaborator." *Chicago Review* 43 (Spring 1997): 8-21.

Foley, Jack. "Unassimilable." Rev. of *The Complete Poems of Kenneth Rexroth.* Ed. Sam Hamill and Bradford Morrow. *Poetry Flash,* no. 292 (Winter/Spring 2004): 1, 21-25.

Ford, Mark. *Raymond Roussel and the Republic of Dreams.* Ithaca, New York: Cornell University Press, 2000.

Joselit, David. "Marcel Duchamp's 'Monte Carlo Bond' Machine." *October* 59 (Winter 1992): 8-26.

Kane, Daniel. *All Poets Welcome: The Lower East Side Poetry Scene in the 1960s.* Berkeley: University of California Press, 2003.

Lehman, David. *The Last Avant-Garde: The Making of the New York School of Poets.* New York: Doubleday, 1998.

Lewallen, Constance M. *Joe Brainard: A Retrospective.* Berkeley and New York: University of California, Berkeley Art Museum and Granary Books, 2001.

Lopate, Phillip. "Lives of the Poets." *Bachelorhood: Tales of the Metropolis.* Boston:

Little, Brown, 1981. 216-234.

McDonald, Gerald D. "For Truth Was to Me a Breath, a Wind, a Shadow." *Poems of Stephen Crane*. New York: Thomas Y. Crowell, 1964. vii-xiv.

Mink, Janis. *Marcel Duchamp* Cologne: Benedikt Taschen, 1995.

Nadada 1. August 1964.

Padgett, Ron. "The Andy of Andy the Warhol." *Mother: A Journal of New Literature*, 4. (February/March 1965): 16.

—. "Falling in Love in Spain or Mexico." *Mother: A Journal of NewLiterature*, no. 4 (February/March 1965): 17.

—. *In Advance of the Broken Arm*. New York: C Press, 1964.

—. "A Man Saw a Ball of Gold." *New and Selected Poems*. 50.

—. *New and Selected Poems*. Boston: David R. Godine, 1995.

—. *Oklahoma Tough: My Father, King of the Tulsa Bootleggers*. Norman: University of Oklahoma Press, 2003.

—. "Rain Dunce After Ted." *Wagner Literary Magazine*, no. 4 (1964): 85.

—. *The Straight Line: Writings on Poetry and Poets*. Ann Arbor: University of Michigan Press, 2000.

—. *Ted: A Personal Memoir of Ted Berrigan*. Great Barrington, Massachusetts: The Figures, 1993.

—. "We Are Gentiles." *Mother: A Journal of New Literature*, no. 3 (November/December 1964): 45.

—. *You Never Know*. Minneapolis: Coffee House Press, 2001.

Padgett, Ron, and David Shapiro, eds. *An Anthology of New York Poets*. New York: Random House, 1970.

Prince, F. T. *The Doors of Stone: Poems 1938-1962*. London: Rupert Hart-Davis, 1963.

Saroyan, Aram. *Friends in the World: The Education of a Writer*. Minneapolis: Coffee House Press, 1992.

Schjeldahl, Peter. "Andy Warhol." 1989. *The 7 Days Art Columns: 1988-1990*. Great Barrington, Massachusetts: The Figures, 1990. 101-104.

Stallman, Robert Wooster, ed. *Stephen Crane: An Omnibus*. 1952. New York: Alfred A. Knopf, 1961.

Tomkins, Calvin. *Duchamp*. New York: Henry Holt, 1996.

Waldman, Anne, ed. *Nice To See You: Homage to Ted Berrigan*. Minneapolis: Coffee House Press, 1991.

Warhol, Andy. *The Philosophy of Andy Warhol: From A to B and Back Again*. New York and London: Harcourt Brace Jovanovich, 1975.

Wolf, Reva. *Andy Warhol, Poetry, and Gossip in the 1960s*. Chicago and London: University of Chicago Press, 1997.

Charles North's Adventures in Poetry

Ange Mlinko

1.

In 2001, poet and editor Larry Fagin resurrected Adventures in Poetry, a Lower East Side imprint he presided over from 1968 to 1976. Of the books inaugurating the series, one was a reprint (John Ashbery's *100 Multiple Choice Questions,* from 1970) and one was a new poetry volume, *The Nearness of the Way You Look Tonight,* from a poet first published by AIP in 1974, Charles North.

It would be hard not to see this as a homecoming for North, especially since his previous book was a *New and Selected Poems* published by Sun and Moon Press. After a Selected, what does a poet do? In this case, he goes back to his roots. As a young poet on the fringes of The Poetry Project—or, let's say, a young poet in one of the microscenes that comprised the macroscene of The Poetry Project—North, for reasons that will unfold here, did not become one of the more famous "second-generation" members; he arrived on the scene too late to be included in Padgett and Shapiro's *An Anthology of New York Poets* (1970) nor has he been featured in the recent scholarship of the era. But North was clearly part of the generation that inherited the (literary) revolution: Donald Allen's *New American Poetry, 1945-1960* appeared when he would have been about 19. He studied at The New School with Kenneth Koch and sat in on a Poetry Project workshop led by Tony Towle. He co-edited the *BROADWAY* Poets and Painters Anthologies with James Schuyler. He wrote definitively in his "Statement for *Out of This World*": ". . . whatever sensibility I was forming when I began in the late '60s was certainly helped along by reading, hearing, and meeting a large group of other young poets who had gravitated in some fashion to St. Mark's. . . ." (*No Other Way* 86). And he published in their magazines and presses.

The history of the small presses that came out of the avant-garde in the '60s and '70s—sometimes referred to as the "mimeo revolution"—is well documented in *A Secret Location on the Lower East Side* and *All Poets Welcome*, two invaluable histories of the times. In the latter book Daniel Kane writes:

> Much of the poetry and associated commentary in the mimeos tended to emphasize and articulate both the poets' allegiances to a historical experimental tradition . . . as well as to a heightened sense of the poets' fraternity and their marginalized relationship to the society in which they wrote (59).

Adventures in Poetry was central to the scene, and when North's first book, *Elizabethan and Nova Scotian Music*, was published by AIP it joined a club that included John Ashbery and Frank O'Hara, Bill Berkson and Ted Berrigan, among many others. In 2001, after having published several books with other publishers, North once again collaborated with AIP to produce *The Nearness of the Way You Look Tonight*. Under the circumstances, it had a ready-made history and a context. Like other avant-gardists (in what may be the hallmark avant-garde gesture) North prepared the ground for the reception of his work. What he also succeeded in doing was showing, not just how a poet of that avant-garde *places* or *positions* himself in the space (ground) of reception, but creates an interval in *time*. While any "selected poems" may provide a career retrospective, few authors make their original publishers integral to the process of retrospection: Ashbery's reprinting of *100 Multiple Choice Questions* is one way to do it; the gathering of Bernadette Mayer's previously uncollected work in *Another Smashed Pinecone* (United Artists Books, 1998) is another. North did something slightly different: he wrote and arranged new poems in a slender volume that pointed back to his first book, *Elizabethan and Nova Scotian Music*, creating an echo chamber in which the utopias of "second-generation" New York School are warily re-examined. *The Nearness of the Way You Look Tonight* holds parallel dialogs with North's younger self and his peers, with whom he has, as they say, "grown up." It is this gesture that tethers him securely to the values of the "second-generation" New York School.

2.

Elizabethan and Nova Scotian Music, published in 1974 with drawings by Jane Freilicher, contained 19 poems, often addressed to or in homage of, various elders: John Ashbery, James Schuyler, Kenneth Koch, even Elizabeth

Bishop, whose name is invoked right in the title. Nowhere does the book lapse into imitation, even though it is saturated with the qualities of precursors. Then again, North is deeply engaged with the phenomenological conundrum of qualities (what are they and why are they so various?). In the list poem, "To the Book," qualities of poetry are enumerated and evaporated in the same line:

> Open poetry died with Whitman.
> Closed poetry died with Yeats.
> Natural poetry was born and died with Lorca
> And Clare, also with France's Jean de Meun. (n.p)

Continuing in this fashion, referencing poets from countries and times remote from New York City in the seventies, North wrapped up with the question: ". . . what qualities are dead / In you that will have their rebirth here?"

The rest of *Elizabethan and Nova Scotian Music* is an answer to this question. For North poses problems related to form without being a "formalist" in a narrow sense, and ultimately links form to qualities and thus to perception and ultimately, consciousness itself. This is where the original New York School influence is strongest: North picks up on the material innovations of Ashbery, Schuyler, O'Hara et al., and (with particular reference to painting) investigates the different qualities of representation. North is candid in his appreciations: "Some Versions of Reeds," for instance, is dedicated to Kenneth Koch, North's teacher at The New School. It uses a didactic form which Koch too lifted from tradition and used for Modern ends in such poems as *The Art of Love*. "Lights" is dedicated to James Schuyler, and employs his signature short-lined *plein air* mode. But these are merely touchstones in a book that moves skillfully and variously along several axes: long lines and short ones, didacticism and descriptions, breeziness and loftiness, giant-abstractionism and miniature-precisionism.

Here is an example of how North inventoried strategies of description. I quote his opening poem from *Elizabethan and Nova Scotian Music*, "Poem," in full:

> Now that I am seeing myself as a totally different person
> whose interests are like a street covered with slush
> and whose every word rings like the ear of a spaniel

night joins with its various egos, its tubeless containers
of islands being joined by the notion of paradise
and I am swept up in what it means to be drained, or

a little less like those pastels that hung around
sopping up every loose glove of moisture where the bay
wasn't defined by its shoreline. Yet that air and that sun

did us both good and the thieving bluejays were enjoyable
as dots on boards, beside rabbits, sparrows, and herrings
numerous trails each of which wound into the other's thicket

where it got new earths and new strengths, and flashed on the
screen, sparkling like corn as the sun went down each dusk. (n.p)

Contrast the panoramic view of this 14-line "Poem" with the concatenation of minutiae in the 184-line "Some Versions of Reeds." The latter begins:

If the box is tightly sealed, break it open.
(That is, tear through the gold opaque scotchtape.)
Twenty-five shafts of varying color—
Though all exist in a well-defined area
Somewhere between straw and wheat (cf. bamboo)
And shaped like wedges, approximately two
And one-half inches long and about two-fifths
Of an inch wide, flat on the underside . . . (n.p)

An instruction manual in the selection and use of clarinetists' reeds, interspersed with self-reflexive commentary on Modernist aesthetics, "Some Versions of Reeds" is a slow and dense poem. It breaks apart with the weight of realistic details ("gold opaque scotchtape," the exacting measurements of the wedges) until, with the help of its digressions, the reader forgets what the poem was supposed to be about in the first place. In contrast, for all the surface difficulty of the sonnet "Poem," it actually moves quickly, assuming connections between disjunctive but musical phrases, an impressionistic "nature scene" assembling itself in the wake of reading. Broad strokes in a short poem; fine detail in a long poem: North's experiments with description argue for an understanding of poetry as a

malleable means of investigation into the nature of perception, not a liter-
ary essence—the transcription of experience itself, say—stamped with the
poet's singular "breath" or "voice." This poetics bears a relation to, say,
Bernadette Mayer's and Clark Coolidge's procedural projects but would
have been somewhat at odds with the Beat and Black Mountain influences
of the day. For one thing, it worked to efface the poet's personality during
a time when big personalities (Ginsberg, Berrigan, Waldman) electrified
and expanded the community on several fronts: political action, cross-fer-
tilization with the art world, founding institutions like The Poetry Project
and The Jack Kerouac School of Disembodied Poetics.[1]

North's poetry correspondingly argued for writerliness as against oral-
ity. From Olson's theories on breath and voice to San Francisco "jazz
poetry" to the Lower East Side cafe scene, a central tenet of the avant-
garde was the privileging of the communal over the private, and hence of
the aural/oral over the written page. Jerome Rothenberg's "New Models,
New Visions: Some Notes Toward a Poetics of Performance" summarizes
this poetics. Drawing from the Dada movement, Cage, Olson and others,
he wrote in 1977:

> There is a move away from the idea of 'masterpiece' to one of tran-
> sientness. . . . The work past its moment becomes a document (mere
> history). . . . From this there follows a new sense of function in art,
> in which the value of a work isn't inherent in its formal or aesthetic
> characteristics . . . but in what it does, or what the artist or his surro-
> gate does with it, how he performs it in a given context (Rothenberg
> 642).

When, later, the Language Poets emerged against oral poetics while pre-
serving emphasis on the collective and the social, something else central
to North's poetics was lost: expressiveness.[2]

What, then, did North's poetics have in common with the fluctuating
mores of the avant-garde? An idea of utopia through language. "Work
your ass off to change the language & dont ever get famous," wrote Mayer
(author of *Utopia*) and by the evidence it looks like North would have
agreed. It is certainly apparent in "To the Book," where the sheer vari-
ety and abundance of poetics—Whitman's, Yeats's, Lorca's, Catullus's, et
al.—are invoked as pure dialectic. In "Madrigal: Another Life," paradise
has a superior language to which poetry on earth aspires:

> I like very much the notion that I will
> Appear in another life. I like
> The notion of another life with its cares
> Its concerts, its flamboyances
> Its caresses, its nouns and its words
> Which will take the place of nouns. (n.p)

The impulse to remake this world is caught in ". . . the periphrastic way / Of being other than we are not / Throughout the long afternoon of language . . ." ("Elizabethan and Nova Scotian Music" n.p.). Such utopias were part and parcel of the era, from Mac Low to Mayer to the Language Poets: utopia as bulwark against mortality; multiple language utopias foreshadowing the material one(s). Mayer: "The idea that real change . . . is not at the heart of experiment in which lies the chance for liberation, is the kind of scam where you might find the book you are reading grabbed from your hands" ("The Obfuscated Poem" 659). Silliman: "Among the several social functions of poetry is that of posing a model of unalienated work. . . ." ("Of Theory, Of Practice" 662). Hejinian: "The knowledge towards which we seem to be driven by language, or which language seems to promise, is inherently sacred as well as secular, redemptive as well as satisfying" (Hejinian 52).

North's utopia wasn't conceived as an exhortation to overthrow oppression, nor did it seek to break the bonds of signifier and signified in order to remake the world from the ground up. The poetics of *Elizabethan and Nova Scotian Music* worked to break down assumptions that kept the poet qua poet from *being free*. There was no duty to brand oneself through style; many styles could be accommodated. Neither realism nor literalism was essentialized; at the same time, language itself wasn't valorized over experience. The only sine qua non was imagination, which existed as a quality both in and for itself *and* for the envisioning of other, better worlds.

3.

Reading *The Nearness of the Way You Look Tonight*, published twenty-five years after *Elizabethan and Nova Scotian Music*, one hears echoes of the earlier book. It is as if the poet is in conversation with himself, sotto voce, even as he dedicates many of the poems to his peers and loved ones.

For every echo there is a slight and meaningful deviance.

Sine qua non of bed wetting
Sire of too-close recall, conquering mastiff

The one that got away, of obloquy,
Compressor of doubt into a herd of gold
　　　　("Air and Angels," *Elizabethan*, n.p)

... becomes:

Devoted dentist, darling chirugeon, beloved mailman,
dear critic, fragrant disciple,
esteemed second violinist, caring strip miner,
delightful bagman, wondrous instantiater, . . .
　　　　("Day After Day the Storm Mounted.
　　　　Then It Dismounted," *Nearness*, 23-4)

As kennings turn into epithets, the affect becomes more intimate; description converges with address. This is typical of the greater emotional warmth of *The Nearness of the Way You Look Tonight*. It is a more relaxed and conversational book:

Here you are a highly educated person. Hands, feet, chin, everything.
　　　　("Day After Day the Storm Mounted.
　　　　Then It Dismounted" 23)

The intimacy of direct address deflects any sense of the poet being alone or lonely—he speaks to his daughter Jill when he says "Actually the sky appears older than it is. It's 63 or 64 at most, not 75" ("The Philosophy of New Jersey" 13) and Trevor Winkfield when he writes, "The deer are practically pets. A few days ago, the small one that lay down to die got up when no one was looking" ("Landscape and Chardin" 48). To Marjorie Welish he exclaims, "Striding toward Eleusinian life have you noticed how much *detail* goes into paralleling the flow of earth / The last two summers were in fact quite nice" ("Attributes of Poetry" 43). It's the "striding" that reveals fleetingly the poet's darker awareness of age.

It is this darker awareness that informs the poet's conversations with younger self as well. It's difficult not to hear "Madrigal," the third section of "Philosophical Songs" as an update of the earlier "Madrigal: Another Life":

> Not border or pass—not quite
> > past either, post? postern? as
> in the past reaching around its
> turquoise plinth despite a coating of melted pine needles
> or are they melting meanwhile the landscape has turned
> > arrow-like to waste. (35)

If, in his early poem, he declared lightheartedly that "I like / The notion of another life . . . its words / Which will take the place of nouns" (n.p), by contrast now that he is closer to death it is not "another life" he looks to but the beloved landscape around him. And if it has turned to "waste," with melted pine needles, what words come to mind are not new, paradisical nouns but a stuttering; a reaching toward the past; the past a post blocking the backdoor view; a post-ness—as though the writer had become post-Charles North—right here on earth. Where once he had posited death as a leap into a new language, now he sees a "turquoise plinth" (referencing Wallace Stevens's description of our athiestic sky: "this dividing and indifferent blue") barring his way, the present landscape "waste" and the past unreachable. And when "Attributes of Poetry" begins "The Floridas of the soul / Not the mental Floridas the Floridas that happen to brush by on the street wearing musk and little else" (42), North further rejects his generation's earlier notion of utopia-through-language: Floridas, as in Wallace Stevens, stand for paradise on earth. The soul is nourished not by cerebral sex but the kind you get on the street. A utopia of mere language is insufficient.

Such a deflation is not merely a function of age, but of *the* age as well: in the years since North's first book appeared, the two avant-gardes of his generation—the second-generation New York School and the Language Poets—have entered history. In 1997 in New York City, the Segue Foundation sponsored a colloquium on Bob Perelman's *The Marginalization of Poetry*, an insider's history of the Language Poet movement. Ann Lauterbach, whose own work helped guide the avant-garde back to a poetics of the page, gently admonished Perelman for his, and his movement's, militancy against emotiveness:

> . . . but this brings me to ask an embarrassing question about the place of affect or feeling or spirit—there is a pervasive sense that, unless ironized or satirized to extinction . . . these are verboten. . . . It has to do with the objectification of feeling in such a way that structural or

formal aspects are foregrounded and the subjective or expressive self is eclipsed. . . . But is it possible that the bracketing of emotion along with constant emphasis on the present here nowness, materiality of language, resistance to narrativity and so forth might be a denial of mortality, literary as well as actual, a fundamental resistance to change? (18-20).[3]

Clearly, Language Poetry's austere attitudes toward personal emotion (part backlash against the previous generation, part Marxist rejection of bourgeois individualism in art) marginalized poets like North who by comparison seemed to offer a "softer" variant of avant-gardism: more lyrical, more expressive. Yet the achievements of Language Theory go hand in hand with its limitations. There is no way to grapple with the issues most at stake to the individual at the extremes of the human condition: love and mortality. These are the province of the lyric.

4.

North offers his own salute (think of Schuyler's "I salute that various field") to Language Poets in *The Nearness of the Way You Look Tonight*:

TYPING AND TYPING IN THE WANDERING COUNTRYSIDE

including the pond bitten down to its cuticles,
whatever you were doing pursuant to flatness

it doesn't mean we exist as writing.
What is flat is on trial for its flatness.
Whatever you were doing pursuant to flatness

is particular: it is its own witness.
While air billows and closes around the petal of evening

(whatever you were doing pursuant to flatness)
it doesn't mean we exist as writing
—fringed in charcoal and umber fields, loosestrife utterly
    mismanaged. (50).

Punning on Yeats's "Turning and turning in the widening gyre," from the eschatological "Second Coming," North rebuts the post-structuralist claim that "everything is language" by saying "it doesn't mean we exist as writing," while at the same time obfuscating the line between the countryside and the page. The last line is the punchline—for while we may not exist as writing, we may well exist as drawing. A landscape is being sketched here, but we don't know if the poem takes place in it or it takes place within the poem. There is no *outside* to it, and thus we remain trapped in the language of it—which is exactly what the poem claims to reject.

So, in fact, North evinces sympathy for the way what we do "pursuant to flatness"—writing, drawing, and otherwise representing the landscape ("representing" carrying the same connotation of legalese as "pursuant to" does)—ends up with our personhood reduced to what we did on paper. Is it life or loosestrife clumsily handled by the artist?

That this is the valedictory poem in *Nearness* begs comparison with the valedictory poem of *Elizabethan and Nova Scotian Music*:

NAMING COLORS

A perfect cream
               its middle reaches up
Wheaties ravishes the lower two-fifths
Geraniums thin as boxers' ears rip
The hem and catch light stars falling

And hair like a constellation of winter
Vegetables redeems the purple plain
Acorn squash, Idaho potatoes, philodendron,
Raw chestnut and grape ivy sweep the page

And become the pink and the lighter blue (n.p)

Like "Typing and Typing in the Wandering Countryside," this poem confuses life and art, landscape and "Landscape." They are both 10-line poems closing a slender volume. Was North writing an "answer poem" to his younger self? What resonates in the interval generated here? "Naming Colors" is an oblique ekphrasis, where "the page" seems to give us a point of orientation. "Typing and Typing" refuses to orient us. If "Typing and Typing" is a revision of his earlier poem, it was revised to be *even more indeterminate*.

It is difficult to separate the two poems once they are read together; together they function as a statement of the magical possibilities of language: that in the space of twenty-five years, one can work diligently on the confusion of art and life until one can't tell them apart: typing in the countryside, wandering on the page. Language thus acts as an elixir, in both senses of the word: the alchemical search for health as well as intoxicating pleasure.

What's the meaning of this? Does the intoxication build a bridge between two worlds, allowing us to slip into the painting through the fog? Are life and art really interchangeable? Might we really wander in the landscape of a poem, and breathe its healthful air?

One need only count the number of times "air" comes up in North's poetry. It shows up 11 times, by my count, in the 17 poems of *Nearness*, and that doesn't count the related references to sky, atmosphere, wind and breeze—which abound. In "Landscape and Chardin" he remarks "I like the idea that the air is too close to prove or disprove its existence, and that it has no stake whatever in the issue." Speaking of "Day After Day the Storm Mounted. Then It Dismounted," the 13-page centerpiece poem, North has stated that:

> I do recall that I had just reread The Iliad. As I look over the poem, it certainly doesn't seem very happy! There's death and darkness all over the place. It took me much longer to write than is apparent, I'm sure—again, not to get down what's there, but to decide that what I had was finished, that it proceeded in a way that seemed to me acceptable. And then when it was printed in Lingo I got depressed, because it looked small and squeezed together, when I had meant it to be roomy, have more air than I usually had. Does this illuminate anything? (Interview with the author)

There are a couple of things this passage illuminates: that "air" does exist in a poem, and that his process of writing a poem, in which decisions rest squarely on the shoulders of the poet and which he must feel his way out of, consists of a constant series of choices and decisions; it is not a deterministic relation, or one left up to chance. There were other formal paths North could have gone, after all. He could have gravitated to either of the two dominant materialist modes of the '70s and '80s—New Formalism and Language poetry—and he could have followed the Oulipian methods of the European avant-garde or the chance-generated ones of Cage following Mallarmé. But to submit to any of those processes would have been to introduce an element of the mechanical. How can the mechanical be *healthy*? The air in a North poem is not just a sign marshalled to behave a certain way among other signs. It stands for real air; breathing it brings health; the art of poetry *is* a path to health, life—possibly just a richer life on earth, but possibly the Eleusinian life too: "Striding toward Eleusinian life . . ." ". . . charismatic coroner, / self-abnegating occultist, glowing restorer . . ." Magical thinking infuses the formal structure of the poems as well: in one of the two "chain" poems in which the last syllable of a line is repeated in the first syllable of the next line, "Asterisks / Risks inside art" emblematizes the secret relation between syllables and risk: not the Mallarmé kind (chance-generated syllables/dice) but the Prospero kind (spells, magic, will). "Trio from Wang Wei," derived from an exercise in which North generated poems from Chinese ideograms on the basis of their visual appearance alone, can't help but invoke translation as a kind of transmutation.

Does North, philosopher of *qualia*, master of setting up and solving *poetic* problems, end up giving the reader real air to breathe through the magical risks of art? Let's say it's possible. Is it any *less* possible than the claim made by Bruce Andrews that his poetics

> . . . would be those of *subversion*: anti-systemic detonation of settled relations . . . The coherence between signifier and signified is conventional, after all—rather than skate past this fact, writing can rebel against it by breaking down that coherence, by negating the system itself (134).

Or is it any less fanciful than Diane di Prima declaring, in a lecture given at Naropa in 1975, that

> There are poems where the light actually comes *through* the page, the same way that it comes through the canvas in certain Flemish paintings, so that you're not seeing light reflected *off* the painting, but light that comes *through*, and I don't know the tricks that make this happen. But I know they're there and you can really tell when it's happening and when it's not (13).

In revisiting his early masterpiece, *Elizabethan and Nova Scotian Music*, 25 years later with *The Nearness of the Way You Look Tonight*, North revised it from a document of aesthetic invention into a documentary of time travel. He creates an interval (keep the musical titles in mind, and the reed instruments that appear passim) between younger and older selves, between artifice and magic, between utopia and elixir. Assumptions about language and image, reference and representation, register change in modality as clearly as Rembrandt in his self-portraits. Accordingly, he demonstrates the trajectory of an artist who begins as a "contemporary" and ends as a nonpareil. As a contemporary, North did not deal blows to his predecessors, found a school or advance a theory. Nor did other less social, more writerly poets of the second generation—and I think here of John Godfrey, Joseph Ceravolo, and William Corbett, among others—but they too will emerge from their still-shadowy history as poets who changed the language and didn't get famous.

WORKS CITED

Allen, Donald M., ed. *The New American Poetry: 1945-1960*. New York: Grove, 1960.

Ashbery, John. *100 Multiple Choice Questions*. New York: Adventures in Poetry, 2001.

Andrews, Bruce. "Writing Social Work and Political Practice." *The L=A=N=-G=U=A=G=E Book*, eds. Bruce Andrews and Charles Bernstein. Carbondale and Edwardsville: Southern Illinois University Press, 1984. 134.

Clay, Steven and Rodney Phillips. *A Secret Location on the Lower East Side: Adventures in Writing, 1960–1980*. New York: Granary Books, 1998.

di Prima, Diane, "Light/ and Keats." *Talking Poetics from Naropa Institute*, Volume 1, eds. Ann Waldman and Marilyn Webb. Boulder, CO: Shambhala, 1978. 13-37.

Hejinian, Lyn, *The Language of Inquiry*. Berkeley: University of California Press, 2000.

Kane, Daniel, *All Poets Welcome: The Lower East Side Poetry Scene of the 1960s*. Berkeley: University of California Press, 2003.

Koch, Kenneth. *The Art of Love*. New York: Random House, 1975.

Lauterbach, Anne. "Lines Written to Bob Perelman in the Margins of The Marginalization of Poetry." *The Impercipient Lecture Series* 1.4 (May 1997): 18-20.

Mayer, Bernadette. "The Obfuscated Poem." *Postmodern American Poetry*, ed. Paul Hoover. New York: W.W. Norton & Company, 1994. 659.

—. *Utopia*. Berkeley, CA: Small Press Distribution, 1984.

—. *Another Smashed Pinecone*. New York: United Artists Books, 1998.

North, Charles. "Attributes of Poetry." *The Nearness of the Way You Look Tonight*. New York: Adventures in Poetry, 2000. 42-44.

—. "Day After Day the Storm Mounted. Then It Dismounted." *The Nearness of the Way You Look Tonight*. New York: Adventures in Poetry, 2000. 20-32.

—. Interview with the author, *The Poetry Project Newsletter*, February/March 2001.

—. "Landscape and Chardin." *The Nearness of the Way You Look Tonight*. New York: Adventures in Poetry, 2000. 48-9.

—. "Madrigal: Another Life." *Elizabethan and Nova Scotian Music*. New York: Adventures in Poetry, 1974. N.p.

—. "Naming Colors." *Elizabethan and Nova Scotian Music*. New York: Adventures in Poetry, 1974. N.p.

—. *No Other Way: Selected Prose*. New York: Hanging Loose Press, 1998.

—. *New and Selected Poems*. Los Angeles: Sun and Moon Press, 1999.

—. "Philosophical Songs." *The Nearness of the Way You Look Tonight*. New York: Adventures in Poetry, 2000. 34-5.

—. "Poem." *Elizabethan and Nova Scotian Music*. New York: Adventures in Poetry, 1974. N.p.

—. "Some Versions of Reeds." *Elizabethan and Nova Scotian Music*. New York: Adventures in Poetry, 1974. N.p.

—. "The Philosophy of New Jersey." *The Nearness of the Way You Look Tonight*. New York: Adventures in Poetry, 2000. 13.

—. "To the Book." *Elizabethan and Nova Scotian Music*. New York: Adventures in Poetry, 1974. N.p.

—. "Trio from Wang Wei." *The Nearness of the Way You Look Tonight*. New York: Adventures in Poetry, 2000. 45.

—. "Typing And Typing In The Wandering Countryside." *The Nearness of the Way You Look Tonight*. New York: Adventures in Poetry, 2000. 50

Padgett, Ron and David Shapiro, eds. *An Anthology of New York Poets*. New York: Random House, 1970.

Rothenberg, Jerome. "New Models, New Visions: Some Notes Toward a Poetics of Performance." *Postmodern American Poetry*, ed. Paul Hoover. New York: W.W. Norton & Company, 1994.

Silliman, Ron, "Of Theory, Of Practice," in *Postmodern American Poetry*, ed. Paul Hoover. New York: W.W. Norton & Company, 1994. 662.

Waldman, Anne, ed. *Out of This World: An Anthology of the St. Mark's Poetry Project 1966-1991*. New York: Crown Books, 1991.

The Other Poet:
John Wieners, Frank O'Hara, Charles Olson[1]

ANDREA BRADY

If post-war American poetry is mapped onto localities, then John Wieners was a vagabond of style. From 1955 through the 1970s, he moved between the New York School, Black Mountain and San Francisco, before returning to Boston, city of his birth. From there, his writing expresses a longing for California and New York, havens of glamour and celebrity, tolerance and artistic company. Moving back to Boston signalled the absolute defeat of his ambitions:

> I feel like a jaded movie star
> who missed the big-time
> and ended up mopping floors (*Selected* 239)

His poetry from the early 1960s, before he rejoined Charles Olson at the State University of New York in Buffalo, was infused with a sense of displacement from geographical centres and from his cosmopolitan friends. Later, Boston became his beloved; until his death in 2002, Wieners's poetry archived the changing nature and landscape of the city. But the nostalgia which characterises his poems for friends, poets, former lovers and the "gay world" in the 1960s and '70s also extended to place. He remembered his "private residence on / West 8th" as a "shrine of devotion to Manhattan / Gotham shows mad weirdos and high-jinx"; but "Nothing like it is now on Beacon Hill" ("Biding in the Gloom," *Selected* 274). Put simply, Boston had "nothing to match New York's / excitement" ("Home-Duty," *Selected* 247).

Wieners was certainly drawn to these cities at crucial moments in his literary maturation, and he was gracious and self-deprecating in admitting the many poetic influences he found there. Among them are LeRoi Jones and Diane di Prima, who gave space to multiple revisions of his work in *Floating Bear*; di Prima also encouraged his participation in the Poets' Theatre, where his plays *Still Life* and *Asphodel in Hell's Despite* were staged. Allen Ginsberg may have influenced Wieners's graphic depictions of his sexual life, but his careful, mannerist prosody is distinct from Ginsberg's rhapsodic, spontaneously overflowing lines. Wieners's receptivity to drugs as a means of expanding consciousness and his affection for Eastern wisdoms could be associated with the poets of the San Francisco Renaissance; a participant in Jack Spicer's Magic Workshop, Wieners also believed in the occult powers of poetry and frequently used imagery from the tarot. But equally it could be argued that his itinerary through the major poetic locales of post-war America did not produce a related cosmopolitanism of style. His poetry retained its own distinctive character, and proved surprisingly resistant even to the influence of two very different mentors: Frank O'Hara and Charles Olson. Wieners's poems, correspondence and unpublished prose reveal the affection and admiration he had for both men, as well as their impact on his emerging sense of himself and his vocation. He associated them with an intellectual, artistic and social liberty that would rescue him from the conservatism of Boston. All the same, it is difficult to assign Wieners a place in either the New York School or the Black Mountain projectivist aesthetic. His similarities to and differences from O'Hara and Olson become especially apparent if we focus on three themes: the personal nature of his poetry, his veneration of celebrity, and his treatment of the past and present. These focuses will show how Wieners's poetry relished the immediate—both the poetic record of a transcendent present, and the idiosyncratic style not mediated by other writers. It will also allow us to establish the literary influences, and resolute independence, of one of the second-generation New York School's most loved poets, who has until now received almost no critical attention.

The Lure of Glamour

Wieners was a fundamentally personal poet, revealing in verse the most intimate, tender or appalling preoccupations of his insatiate heart. Perhaps this makes an association with O'Hara more instinctive than with Olson. Wieners had first encountered Charles Olson on "the night of hurricane Hazel" in 1954, when he passed the Charles Street Meeting House in Boston where Olson was reading. He got hold of a copy of the *Black Mountain Review* and afterwards wrote eagerly to the College Registrar:

> My age is twenty-one and I feel, in terms of my own development
> as a writer, that one to two years at Black Mountain College, "ham-
> mering form out of content" is the most worthwhile thing I could

do. I am eager to study under Mr. Charles Olson, having read his
poetry in *Origin*, *Four Winds*, and the *Black Mountain Review*, VI, No.
1, and also having heard him read his poems at the Charles Street
Meeting House in Boston last year. His essay, "Projective Verse" has
been the most important work I have read on the writing of poetry
in 1955.[2]

Olson invited Wieners to attend the college and offered him a loan cover-
ing tuition, room and board,[3] allowing Wieners to escape Boston at last.
When Black Mountain closed, he would begin the process of separating
himself from Olson by moving first to San Francisco in 1957 and then to
New York. Although his poetry (in particular *Behind the State Capitol*) is
sometimes read as an enactment of Olson's projectivist theories, from the
time he arrived in San Francisco and embraced the drug-impacted, alter-
native lifestyle of North Beach, Wieners avowed an autodidactic style. He
declared that "I must unlearn what has been taught me" (*Journal* 13), re-
jecting not only Olson's prosodic technique, but also Olson's epistemology
and his revision of intellectual and poetic history. Nonetheless, Olson's
description of himself as an "archaeologist of morning" remained influen-
tial to Wieners's conception of the work of poetry. As Olson elaborated,
"I find it awkward to call myself a poet or a writer. If there are no walls
there are no names. This is the morning, after the dispersion, and the
work of morning is methodology: how to use oneself, and on what" (*Col-
lected Prose* 206). Wieners's mystical understanding of the poetic vocation
had this in common with Olson: barriers between being a "writer" and
any other occupation must be pulled down, so that the self and his own
experiences of the instant could be *used*, to break through to truth.

Black Mountain had served as Wieners's initiation into the sacred and
magical mysteries of poetry. There, "Big Charles put his hand on me, and
ordained me a priest" (Wieners, "Youth," *Selected* 229). But Olson had a
problematic relationship with Wieners's natural idiom: personal poetry
(or, as Wieners would describe it, not confessional poetry but "obses-
sional"). Olson had told his students to become "personal revolutionar-
ies." The power of that instruction is especially evident in Wieners's two
early works, *The Hotel Wentley Poems* and *The Journal of John Wieners is to
be called 707 Scott Street for Billie Holiday 1959* (published in 1996). These
books take the observations of his "5 senses" as his material (*Journal*
13-14). They declare a commitment to writing as derangement of the self
and the processes in which that self encounters the present. Certainly in

Wieners's poetry that present is mottled by the shadows of the past. But it is *his* past, not America's or humanity's—his absent lovers, his melodrama. His poetry is produced out of isolation and private suffering, however much he depends on other writers for artistic, physical, and emotional sustenance. Wieners is a personal poet, but as he wrote to his fellow alumnus Ed Dorn, his were "not revolutionary sentiments; we leave each other alone / thinking we can take care of ourselves" ("For Ed Dorn," *Selected* 254). Despite such claims to independence, his poetry also acknowledges that from the beginning of his drug addiction in San Francisco, through his stoned and heartbroken days in New York, to his decades of mental illness, it was poetry and poets—and, to some extent, the celebrities of his imagination—who kept him alive. Michael Davidson argues the "unfashionable case" that "insularity is often necessary for the creation and survival *of* culture poetry" (Davidson xii). Wieners frequently confessed that the insular poetic community allowed not only his poetry, but himself, physically, to survive. In his poetry the literary and the personal, the aesthetic and the biographical, implicate each other fundamentally.

Frank O'Hara was one of the poets who took care of Wieners. Meeting O'Hara in Cambridge at the Poet's Theatre in 1956, after he returned from Black Mountain, Wieners was tantalised by this proxy for the excitements of the big city. O'Hara was acting in John Ashbery's play *The Compromise, or Queen of the Caribou*, and Wieners was stage manager. He memorialised a night with O'Hara and Jack Spicer in his "dreadful room infested with roaches": "while I read my poetry in the humid summer evening of Beacon Hill, the both of them wept through the incipient rain and electric-charged air" (*Cultural Affairs* 80). That O'Hara did admire Wieners's poetry is attested by his poem "To John Wieners':

> And one day weeks later the muffler grey and old
> for one so young unwraps its sheaf of poems
> heard already among the sets under the worklight
> a voice is heard though everyone was mumbling
> now so silent that the dark is all blown up (*Collected* 247)

O'Hara embodied something of the glamour which Wieners admired in the movie stars. Wieners was immediately drawn to O'Hara's irreverent humor, "his sophistication, his knowledgeability of the New York art world" (*Selected* 297). Wieners's poem "After Reading *Second Avenue*" (*Selected* 81) is full of admiration for O'Hara's "cosmopolitan incline" and "metropolitan tableaux." O'Hara was his first taste of New York life, "lox, & other delicacies," parties, satire and celebrity.

But where O'Hara had seemingly unlimited access to New York's mysteries, Wieners described himself as feeling excluded and unpresentable in his own brief periods of residence in the city. After treatment for drug addiction and mental illness, he moved to New York in 1961 with help from Allen Ginsberg's Poetry Foundation, and found work at the Eighth Street Bookshop. O'Hara and other members of the poetry community helped him settle in—O'Hara arranged for John Bernard Myers to include the poem "With Mr. J R Morton" in his magazine *Semi-Colon*, one of Wieners's first important publications. But other poems from this period, like "Tuesday 7:00 P.M." (*Selected* 81), are pæans to New York's bounded and exclusive spaces seen from outside. Gates are guarded by the "mastiff bitch," gardens are walled, windows curtained with "the hopes / of the poor." Another poem from "Autumn in New York" laments that only in "Dream" (*Selected* 85) and in poetry will Wieners dance "on the roof of the Waldorf Astoria" with a glamorous woman dressed in cocoa silk and pearls. Consequently, while O'Hara's poems explore the real freedoms offered by the city alongside the promises of the spectacle, Wieners's poems seem increasingly to split the real from the spectacular, with one as the domain of pain, slang and particularity, and the other as the haunt of unadulterated happiness, formal language and hazy abstractions.

The difficulty of negotiating between these two divided realms is articulated in his poems adulating the stars. Celebrities also dwell in restricted spaces, are the "dream" of the culture industry; but the tabloids and gossip columns raid their privacy, expose their limited interiority to public view. The stars are at once apotheosised and perfect, and vulnerable to exploitation and humiliation. Wieners uses a range of enthusiastic adjectives to describe their emotional lives: they are thrilled, elated, honoured by their experience of admiration; they are joyous, magnificent, ravishing, passing on their ecstasies to their admirers. In Wieners's poems, the lives and fortunes of Joan Crawford, Jane Fonda, Bette Davis or Barbara Hutton become mystical dramas of impossible perfection. Barbara Hutton is taken by train in a white silk crib to the White House with 500 devotees hanging on; she is not just materially privileged, but valued and loved by everyone around her (*Behind the State Capitol* 144). The stars return this devotion to the common people; they are joyous, effusive, grateful, they protect their fans. Marlene Dietrich moves "majestically down the avenue to guard over / the war torn refugees, waifs who lined the house"

("Youth," *Selected* 229); Barbara Stanwyck is "a watchful, ever-abundant woman, with the greatest sympathy for the sensitive, easily-oppressed individuals in our society," and Wieners—a Marian Catholic, who believed he had himself been visited by the Virgin—imagines himself 'surrounded by her devotion'" (*Superficial Estimation* 20-2).

Despite such florid raptures, Wieners recognizes the stars (and especially their perfection) as commodified spectacles. They live in the liminal space between total happiness, admiration, beauty and projected desire, and the tawdry realities of capitalist exploitation. In an unpublished modified sonnet "To Ross," it is O'Hara's tipsy heroine Lana Turner who speaks:

> I travelled fast, in a gold turban for the Eastman Jefferson Airplane
> to win not one Academy Award, but four snowy sedans gratis
> past *Le Place Vendôme*, at Julien's or Chicken-in-the-Basket
> where 3,000 glass imitations of my teats, suckled and craned
>
> Times Square, at Maxie's, Sardi's, Barney's, Andy's sneak
> preview, before the Grand Hotel, Le Belvedere Gardens, Albany,
>   Albermarle,
> and the big shots, the racketeers, chanteuses, off-Broadware cafe suites
> kept pace with my income, swept me off my feet, 300,000 dollars
>
> a year in taxes alone. I had to make films; *Cass Timberlane*, *Johnny Eager*,
> *The Postman Always Rings Twice* for Bugsy, Marion, Luana
> were in debt, needed some clothes, money to pay the rent, the legs'
>   stockings, beggar
>   their gems tonight, as they draw their gats to
>   put out this fury that tallies their totals meagre.[4]

Lana Turner, the tragic starlet who was embroiled in the murder of her lover Johnny Stompanato by her fourteen-year-old daughter, is brought to the collapse ironized by O'Hara by money and exploitation. Like the hero in O'Hara's "For James Dean" (*Collected* 228-30), she is preyed upon by racketeers and other opportunists—including the racketeer Bugsy Siegel, and possibly Wieners's own sister Marion. Wieners identified with the stars' vulnerability to threatening "inferiors"—jealous people, dependent on but also determined to wreck their beauty and success. In "Ailsa's LASt WILL and TESTAMENT," the speaker laments "A marriage that never existed, a death under investigation, / and a Fortune stolen from M a d women in custody of itinerants." This misfortune prompts him to ask: "Who could say wealth provides security, when the truth of one's income / lies upon inferiors," and is threatened by "truth serums," "innoculations," and jealousy (*Behind the State Capitol* 128). The celebrity poems are riddled with the vocabulary of hospitalisation, imprisonment, debt, war and political authority (one is signed Gerald Ford). They often include declarations of copyright, publication and performance. Such declarations licence them, give them formal status in systems of power which seek to extinguish them. But according to Wieners, the stars could also reconfigure reality around them. Their power could be read as a correlate of schizophrenic transitivism, projections of the individual's wishes, desires, and self-image onto the world which make the real unrecognizable. But these poems are more than just schizoid projections and paranoid effusions: like O'Hara's own poems for the stars, they explore the poet's wishes, contradictions, desires and aesthetics in terms which implicate the culture industry and class conflict.

Adorno and Horkheimer argue that "The paradise offered by the culture industry is the same old drudgery. Both escape and elopement are pre-designed to lead back to the starting point. Pleasure promotes the resignation which it ought to help to forget" (142). The culture industry militates against transformative pleasure, or against the possibility of any exit from the uniform, repressive pleasures which make a lifetime mopping floors barely tolerable. Though he worshiped at the movie theatres, Wieners admitted that "There is a condition of mankind dependent on hallucinations in place of imagination. A condition of parasitism in place of contribution" (*Behind the State Capitol* 153). He recognised the price he paid for his devotion to the "hallucinations":

> Of course, while associating with actors and artists, in tyrannizing innocence and intelligence, especially of amateur means, then one must realize that the false glamour they create is often a lure to the overworked and underpaid. The excess I speak of occurs in the fields of medicine and hospitalization, where traitors to the United States possess power to defraud and bungle the orthodox recognition of errors and illegality within the processes of maturation and self expression. (*Behind the State Capitol* 163)

This elaborate but fundamentally lucid statement reveals the falsity of the promise of glamour and the consequences of testing orthodoxy:

hospitalization. Those "traitors" who in the process of their own self-expression and maturation are lured to the excesses of glamour represented by actors and artists, "defraud" the system, and call into question the categories of truth and error, law and criminality. Consequently, they are punished. Throughout his work, Wieners speaks in the voices of celebrities, schizophrenia, poverty and addiction, dramatizing the difficulty of becoming a subject under the disciplinary regimes of late capitalism. This nexus of melancholic exaltation and depressed entrapment was, I will argue, partially sexual in origin. Horkheimer and Adorno also describe the representation of sexuality in the culture industry of the Hays Office era as "pornographic and prudish": "the mass production of the sexual automatically achieves its repression" (140). The endless prolongation of pleasure, never achieved on screen, fixes the spectator in a masochistic position. I will return to the masochism characteristic of both Wieners's and O'Hara's poetry later.

The poems O'Hara was writing shortly before his death—"At the Bottom of the Dump There's Some Sort of Bugle," "Here in New York We Are Having a Lot of Trouble with the World's Fair," "Should We Legalize Abortion," "The Bird Cage Theatre," "The Green Hornet," "The Jade Madonna," and "The Shoe Shine Boy"—are also a pastiche of Hollywood dialogue. They construct from semi-moral aphorisms and broad American casualness a portrait of the poet's wit and his familiarity with popular discourse. But his own thoughts, feelings, personality recede behind a stream of clichés which is most remarkable for its limitlessness. As in many of Wieners's poems, in this sequence of poems the possibility of critique and reflection is sequestered behind a streaming linearity of excerpts, each disconnected from any previous unit, each building not to an argument but to an impression of the vapid and ceaseless bounty spilling out of the culture industry—a bounty as lacking in value as the commodities whose manufacture such poems knowingly imitate. The stylistic features of this late work bear a striking resemblance to Wieners's later verse, and serve to remind us that its schizoid diction, style and versification make an important contribution to that work's cultural critique.

The Divine Trap: O'Hara and Wieners

Could Wieners be influenced by both O'Hara and Olson? In his sketch of the agonistic relationship between three "groups" in New York in the 1950s and '60s—the New York School, Black Mountain, and the coterie around Allen Ginsberg—Amiri Baraka suggests that he felt it necessary to choose an affiliation. He rejected the "Creeley-Olson types," "people who took an antipolitical or apolitical line (the Creeley types more so than Olson's followers—Olson's thing was always more political)" (Benston 306). For Baraka, membership in one group meant disavowing another. Not so for Wieners. Pressed by Robert von Hallberg to say if he felt closer to Olson and Creeley or to Ginsberg and O'Hara in the 1950s, Wieners would only say that "I felt close to most writers in the 1950s due to my own youth. Any writer qualified for total embracing" (*Selected* 291).

Although many critics have contrasted Olson's mythopoesis with O'Hara's excavations of sociability and personal feeling,[5] Olson himself, in writing to Wieners in 1964, complimented that "nice Frank O'Hara whom I met for the first time last week, here, and he read so that every word, etc."[6] Both Olson and O'Hara were fixated on the breath; Olson, taking a cue from Pound, believed breath to be the driving force of prosody, while O'Hara ended many of his poems with the intensity of breathing or held breath as a marker of intimacy and revelation. Olson was pleased to learn that O'Hara had grown up in nearby Grafton Massachusetts:

> This seemed too much, that he shd join us old-fashion New England city-type poets instead of all that higher literature of both the immediate past here & abroad. (I don't mean this, like, analytically, I mean that I was gratified he came of our own general sociology. For he was *the* other poet for all of us to have lived out the rest of this century by, simply that his tone and pitch was to be the lyre of this too, he was so capable of footing the measure once his feet were on the way. (*Homage* 178)

Olson was presumably referring to Pound in making O'Hara "*the* other poet" in this letter to Bill Berkson. He added, "In any case the thing he and so many of you stand for is in fact, & will be seen to be the track literally of two say tracks only which this time in a person like him he *so* made clear—oh Lord I hate the fact that he will not continue to be a master," again using the term of admiration, "master," he reserved for Pound (*Selected Letters* 373).[7] While their poetic "tracks" might have differed, Olson clearly admired O'Hara for making clear his own "way" and for his control of prosodic "measure."

Olson and O'Hara's work often appeared side by side. Both were published in Donald Allen's *The New American Poetry, 1945-1960* anthology, in *Floating Bear* and Ed Sanders's *Fuck You/A Magazine of the Arts*, among other magazines. Brad Gooch claims (278-9) that it was Wieners who had prompted O'Hara to revisit Olson's poetry, resulting in O'Hara's composition by field of poems from the early 1960s like "To a Young Poet." The letter from O'Hara included in Wieners's memoir "Chop-House Memories" also makes reference to O'Hara following up "your tip on Lawrence," an author Olson recommended in "The Present as Prologue" (*Collected Prose* 207).[8] O'Hara seems more skeptical about Olson, however, and writes cattily in "SUDDEN Snow" (1960) that "the snow like Charles Olson working on one of his ABC poems / is quietly and bitterly falling" (*Collected* 355). All the same, his question in "Hôtel Transylvanie" (*Collected* 351), "where will you find me, projective verse, since I will be gone?," shows his familiarity with Olson's essay, to which (Gooch again conjectures, 301-2) the "Personism" manifesto may have been a response. For all their differences, both O'Hara and Olson were articulating a new understanding of the poet's relation to the present—to the present tense as a marker of transformative activity, and to the instant as worthy of improvisatory reflection. This interest in the present, and "the immediate past," also affected Wieners.

Wieners's own poetry could be read as a kind of X-rated Personism. Like O'Hara, he wrote compulsively and spontaneously, dwelling on love, disappointment, and desire. He believed that the material provided by the personal must be absolutely, simultaneously and shamelessly recorded; nothing should be left out. This belief also reflects Olson's teaching at Black Mountain that "there are certain things which you hide from close friends and admit only to yourself; the task of the writer is to dig out those things which you will not admit to yourselves" (Duberman 371). Asked by Raymond Foye if he had a theory of poetics, Wieners answered "I try to write the most embarrassing thing I can think of" ("Introduction: Raymond Foye: A Visit with John Wieners," *Cultural Affairs* 15). In "Parking Lot" (*Cultural Affairs* 69) for example, he describes stealing $8 from Steve Jonas, which he pays to a man he blows, and then concludes, "Damned and cursed before all the world / That is what I want to be." His explicit depictions of sex are sometimes sweet or triumphant; sometimes, as in poems like "Memories of You" or "The Gay World Has Changed," they are filled with self-loathing. This is hardly surprising, given the social intolerance of homosexuality, and his Catholic family's condemnation of his sexual proclivities.[9] In an essay on "dangerous orgies and random, heedless sexual promiscuities of increasing despair upon a road to self-degradation," Wieners reveals how the repression of homoerotic urges prevents the poet from reflecting on his own life: "Usually a homosexual, since he has been a stigma or outcast freak for so long, does not have a chance to meditate upon himself, even as a 'straight' citizen, with their usual rights or opportunities" (*Behind the State Capitol* 88). The explicitness of his poetry could be read as an effort to subvert heterosexist monopolies on public self-reflection, to meditate not only on himself, but on himself as a gay man, a stigmatized or "outcast freak." But it could also be argued that the spectacle of the degraded self which he presented to "all the world" became another screen, a defenceless persona whose theatricality itself served as a form of defence.

O'Hara and Wieners shared this masochistic idiom; in their work, confessions of desire are often followed by fears of persecution, pain, and physical punishment. The comic aplomb of the runner in "Personism" may be a means of escape from traditional prosody, but for O'Hara and Wieners, writing often seems to feel like being chased down the street with a knife. O'Hara's depictions of his own sexuality were often entangled with forms of discipline and fear. In "Grand Central," the friend takes a "smoking muzzle in his soft blue mouth" (*Collected* 169); in "Hieronymus Bosch" (*Collected* 121), an allusion to fisting ("He puts his long / fingers into the wet mandolin precious with lotion / and stringy") is followed by an image of lynching: "they dried him out and hung him up. My, he swung." In his poem for Wieners, O'Hara describes the police following the strung-out poet, while jeering thugs and the "threats / of inferiors" frighten him like "a Negro choosing your own High School" (*Collected* 279). O'Hara aligns the persecution of his gay friend with other forms of discrimination, here using Wieners's own term for threatening and malicious hangers-on ("inferiors").[10] As Ben Friedlander has argued (131-2), fear of homophobic attacks informed many of O'Hara's references to race. O'Hara identified with victimised minorities, both in his experience of prejudice and in his desire to escape bourgeois mores. For him,

> The impulse, the, at times, compulsion, toward normalcy must be avoided, when its fulfillment is known to be unsatisfactory, and when the level of endeavor is, as it is by definition, inferior to that possible though idiosyncratic behavior. One must live in a way; we must channel, there is not time nor space, one must hurry, one must avoid the impediments, snares, detours; one must not be stifled in a closed

> social *or* artistic railway station waiting for the train; I've a long long
> way to go, and I'm late already. (*Early Writing* 101)

For O'Hara, prosodic and imaginative speed are a means of avoiding entrapment and danger.

Wieners was infamous for the idiosyncratic behavior which O'Hara praises in this passage. In "Les Luths," O'Hara publicises his admiration for Wieners's work: "everybody here is running around after dull pleasantries and / wondering if *The Hotel Wentley Poems* is as great as I say it is" (*Collected* 343). Wieners, shy but outrageous, was not prone to producing dull pleasantries.[11] Barbara Guest wrote that "I think Wieners had a special appeal for Frank, especially his madness" (Gooch 279). That appeal is apparent in "A Young Poet," where O'Hara memorialized a visit by Wieners to New York. Strung out on benzadrine in the library, Wieners had become paranoid after spending "8 hrs with near every book S Noah-Kramer ever wrote" (a reading program notably influenced by Olson).[12] O'Hara may be remembering their meeting in 1956, and the publication of *Hotel Wentley* in 1958, when he writes:

> Two years later he has possessed
> his beautiful style,
> the meaning of which draws him further down
> into passion
> and up in the staring regard of his intuitions. (*Collected* 278)

The poem makes two references to "the divine": both the "divine trap" of poetic inspiration in which all Wieners's admirers are compelled to believe, and the "divine prosecutor" (279), who might dictate to Wieners his elegies. Again, the act of composition imperils the poet, "trapping" him and "prosecuting" him for his crimes. O'Hara attributes to Wieners a kind of vatic authority through his madness itself, reminiscent of the ancient Platonic concept of poetic fury. But he also predicts that Wieners, a poet whose intuitions included the psychoses of drug abuse and schizophrenia, would eventually be "exhausted by / the insight which comes as a kiss / and follows as a curse" (279). The erotic pleasure of creation first seduces the poet sweetly, but becomes "cursed" when it exposes the poet to the cruelty of the world, or when it abandons him.

For both O'Hara and Wieners, the maddening commitment to poetry must end in death. Both poets fantasised about death, how it would unveil the extremity of their commitments to poetry, and punish them for their infractions against decorum, morality, or bourgeois taste. As his elegies for James Dean show, O'Hara was excited by the mythology of the fast-living, self-consuming icon, martyred by his own excellence, "racing" towards the heights of the gods (*Collected* 228). In another poem, O'Hara asks to borrow a "forty-five" and a silver bullet, the weapon that kills werewolves—men who turn by night into beasts. He then observes that "if you can't be interesting at least you can be a legend" (*Collected* 430). Wieners clearly shared O'Hara's live-fast-die-young aesthetic. In "Chop-House Memories," he recalls accompanying O'Hara to Provincetown on the ferry to visit Edwin Denby. Both he and O'Hara "thought of suicide as the final resolution of our desire as we stood again below deck by the hectic Atlantic cutting at our feet, speaking of Hart Crane and the last words we would have in our mouths at that moment of surrender" (*Cultural Affairs* 80). It is notable that Wieners focuses on life as "desire," and suicide as eliciting language ("last words"), in this pledge to enter the great tradition of self-destructive literary types. But the bravura of this conversation does not sustain Wieners in the truly suicidal moments memorialised in some of his poems. Although Wieners sometimes expressed a grandiose belief that "There is no age for a poet, that he exists outside of time, and is its watchdog" (*Cultural Affairs* 106), he more often worried that the moment of surrender was imminent, and that he with his experiences will be obliterated. "What one knows today will be gone tomorrow. / One reason to write" (*Selected* 73). As a justification for writing this is highly conventional: poetry outlasts brass monuments, is a deep mnemonic reservoir of all that eludes the biographical record. But Wieners has an additional anxiety prompting him to dwell on death: his experience of a generation that destroyed themselves with drugs. The future may hold imprisonment, hospitalization, or death by overdose; so "Do not think of the future; there is none. / But the formula all great art is made of" ("The Acts of Youth," *Selected* 62) Wieners legitimates his refusal to contemplate the future through an artistic tradition which values immediacy, as well as the suicidal self-destructiveness which he shared with O'Hara.

Wieners began seriously to court self-destruction when he moved to San Francisco in 1956. Raymond Foye suggests that heroin became widespread in North Beach that year, and notes that "Nobody had ever seen anyone throw themselves into the abyss the way John did." Foye continues, "By the time of the *Wentley* poems Wieners himself is very heavily into drugs, taking grass, crystal meth, heroin, belladonna and a few other things, on a daily basis. According to Ginsberg, Wieners was intent on alienating himself from reality, with a vengeance; and, Allen claims, by 1959 W. had pretty much 'blown his mind.'"[13] Poetically, it was a productive time; Wieners regularly wrote during or about drug-induced hallucinations or described his interactions with drug users. Asserting that the deepest truths are available only to the unconscious and that the unconscious was accessible through drugs, Wieners recommended the altered states of drug hallucination or magical intuition as conditions for writing. The poet should wait for the words of the poem to arise "in middle of dream / opium shadow curtains hang / off eyelids, lips parched" (*Cultural Affairs* 52). Wieners cultivated this state of susceptibility, "drowsy and half-awake to the world / from which all things flow" ("Feminine Soliloquy," *Selected* 159). But after an initial period of idealism about drug use, he became suspicious of such trance aesthetics. He found it "very hard" to review Clive Matson's *Poems* for *Floating Bear*,

> cause (his poetry springs out of a "narcotic" experience, or milieu, I mean it's toughness, that isn't natural to him, and which he has gone to junk for.) [. . .] (I got thrown into junk for glamour and pain yes, because it led to new experience, and because the people I loved were using it, and the nature of "evil" is such, that it is contagious and infectious.) Can I say that? (But to take on the pain of the world, is not right. One should obiate [*sic*], or obviate suffering, not induce it.) Don't you think?[14]

He was drawn to junk for the same reason he was drawn to the stars: "for glamour and pain." Once rehabilitated, he recognized it as "evil," an infection, which exposed the poet to the pain of the whole world.

Although Wieners eventually broke his drug addiction, he became chronically afflicted by mental illness. After an opium- and benzadrine-fuelled roadtrip from San Francisco via Washington and New York in 1959, he found his way back to his family home in Massachusetts. He was then hospitalized from January to July 1960 at Medfield State, and from March to August 1961 in the Metropolitan State Hospital, where he was treated with electric shock therapy.[15] The poem "Untitled" (*Selected* 226) says that his parents borrowed $900 for this painful and ineffective procedure in a private sanatorium. Wieners described himself as

> Pierced with a miniature electric track
> on which no trains run
> our back against the wall
> this shock treatment does not cure
> as it's supposed to
> Only reduces sustained intellectual effort
> and turns poets into dogs.

After he had recuperated, he moved to New York in 1961. Diane di Prima writes, "Irving Rosenthal brought him over I recall, and we hit it off. John's story was tragic, but familiar, too. His Boston Catholic family had had him committed for being gay, and using dope, maybe junk, now, all those shock treatments later, he was more than a little crazy"(272-3). If di Prima thought the treatment had made him "crazy," Wieners himself worried that it had killed off his poetic abilities. Depressed, lonely and living with his parents in 1965, Wieners confirms that "Now that life no longer provides means for poetry, I am caught within my mind. And it is not enough. With the shock-treatments and drugs. It never was, even before."[16] For a poet who believed that poetry emerged from the magical subvention of reality, the deadened consciousness maintained by pharmaceutical treatment and electric shock was more frightening than the delusions of dope and madness.

In San Francisco, Wieners had picked up not only a heroin habit, but also a magic vocabulary to describe the effects of his variously transformed consciousness. For Wieners, poetry was like the tarot, junk or schizoid delusions in its power to radically transform the world. A statement "written for Robert Creeley's class of August 17/72" describes poetry in terms similar to his description of the Marian movie star: poetry is "the most magical of all the arts. Creating a life-style for its practitioners, that safeguards and supports them" (*Cultural Affairs* 106). In one poem in *Floating Bear* 10, Wieners directs a magic ritual to bless his bond with O'Hara. He invites O'Hara to join an occult ceremony which starts with a public declaration of affection and invokes blood, astrology, dream and "freedom":

> We hold hands on the street in the dream I never passed
> the sun stone to you. Who stomps for freedom and the
> rites? Three times right around the stone (only a capricorn's
> blood can break) it's yours. ("For Frank O'Hara," *Floating Bear* 10)

Holding hands, they declare their affection publicly; they are both "free" to show their love and bound by an esoteric "rite," which closes their relationship to the rest of the world. Wieners marries O'Hara to himself, replacing the orthodox ceremonies of commitment with his own magic vocabulary.

This desire to establish a bond with O'Hara is understandable, given Wieners's frequent references in his poetry to the sorrow of abandonment and the unreliability of his relationships. Often he attributes this to his lovers being kept away from him by their families; consequently, he not only wants a wife; he wants to *be* one. The bond of marriage is, he says, a kind of sacred ownership. In "Gardenias," he confesses that after "two decades of drunken futility"

> still some loneliness lingers as sickness's vapor—
> is it jazz, or late-night musings by the harbor,
> unemployment with an empty head in the library
> merely only poverty, or could it be the inability
>
> to hold a man, or woman as my own property?
> (*Behind the State Capitol* 62)

Whatever the answer, "I am sick of sickness in the heart, / having no part in the world, being only a victim / to time, money, and machines made by men other than I." He is excluded from marriage, the one form of property relations which will liberate him from hunger, loneliness, and exploitation. "Forthcoming" (*Selected* 110) laments that

> I died in loneliness
> for no one cared for me enough
> to become a woman for them
> that was not my only thought
> and with a woman
> she wanted another one.

The concluding reference is probably to Panna Grady, whose shattering effect on Wieners is described below. But he also regrets that his lovers have not asked him to become a woman—to dress up for them, nurture them, be at home when they return, enacting the rites of bourgeois family life.

"I have a woman's / mind in a man's body" (*Cultural Affairs* 59), he repeatedly affirmed. The feminized persona allowed Wieners to express both his relative powerlessness as a lover or as a "mentally ill person," and his desire for power through beauty which he associated with stars like "The Garbos and the Dietrichs." The big screen celebrity never has to experience material or emotional lack; she can avoid tedium, loneliness, ugliness. She lives thoroughly and permanently in a condition of emotional and aesthetic intensity which Wieners himself can only *recollect*, her powerfulness accentuated by her distance from her admirers, her image mediated by print, film and magazines. His own fantasised position relative to these Hollywood beauties is both intimate and masochistic. Wieners wishes to be "a gossip, a behind-the-scenes man who knew all the stars, was able to enjoy their carryings-on, and to participate in the difficulties of experience in our contemporary society" (*A Superficial Estimation* 12-13); he is hypnotised by Rita Hayworth, who generates "unending desire" in him, and turns him into "a passive slave to her wishes, knowing I'm unnecessary to her" (*A Superficial Estimation* 16). He is also personally related to them: he is Elizabeth Taylor's sister, Barbara Stanwyck's neighbour, Bette Davis's daughter. Unlike some of the starlet poems of *Behind the State Capitol*, where the addition of the star's name at the end of the poem attributes the poem's extravagant claims to an extravagant persona as a kind of comic detournement, these poems adopt the celebrity identity as part of a mundane, domesticated or familial fantasy. He sees Elizabeth Taylor in a bookshop; "Never once in the thousand times we have met" has she refused him anything (*A Superficial Estimation* 2). Rita Hayworth meets the "inexorable" demands of stardom and the speaker's "attempts to conduct myself as an adult" with patience as they move around town together (*A Superficial Estimation* 13-14).

His poems written in the voice of Lana Turner or Elizabeth Taylor bear formal similarities to O'Hara's poems "Portrait of Grace" and "Jane at Twelve." In a technique which Wieners himself would adopt, O'Hara punctuates the baroque formality of hortatory lines like "Let not that firebrand / stolen from the summits mark her brow" with more earthy descriptions of a woman "decisive as a lightbulb" (*Collected* 88). But where Wieners inhabits the female personae of his poetic fantasies, O'Hara renders these idealised females in violent, surrealist terms. The poems alternate between the declarative powerfulness of a male poet describing an otherworldly "she," and that she being given leave to speak of her own experience from the perspective of an "I," in terms whose very syntax and diction corroborate the original assertions of the male voice. What differentiates Wieners's poems about the stars from O'Hara's is the quality of their sympathy. Lana Turner may have collapsed, but for O'Hara the tribulations of Hollywood are mostly available to comic speculation. His benedictions—"may the money of the world glitteringly cover you / as you rest after a long day under the klieg lights with your faces / in packs for our edification" ("To the Film Industry in Crisis," *Collected* 232-3)—are sprinkled from on high. By contrast, Wieners's increasing tendency to identify with the stars has to be read in the context of his depictions of, and identification with, the underclass who serve as their foils.

Wieners's Hollywood poems express his desire for freedom, for the liberty to travel and to act, as well as empathy for the restraints and exposure which a celebrity lifestyle imposes. His flamboyant resistance to respectable bourgeois mediocrity was expressed in his dress, his conversation, and his desire for absolute relationships both with his lovers and his poetic mentors. That resistance—a dramatic enactment of the desire to be seen as unique and differentiated—takes on a political character in the context of his frequent hospitalization. People, he told Charles Shively, "are in those institutions just because we have created stereotyped roles of what people should look like; what they should wear; how they should converse." The patients' failure to abide by those stereotypes "would probably imperil the ordinary citizen on the street" whose identities are manufactured out of conformity with the stereotypes, and leads to their incarceration (*Selected* 293). Wieners implicates his own appearance alongside the

> dwarfs, who cannot stand up straight with crushed skulls,
> diseases on their legs and feet unshaven faces and women,
> worn humped backs, deformed necks, hare lips, obese arms

described in "Children of the Working Class" (*Behind the State Capitol* 35-6). In this blazon, the deformed citizens of a society which values glamour are subject to the poet's gaze, just like the stars who grace the pages of women's magazines. Beauty and monstrosity, conformity and nonconformity are alternate and equivalent disciplines.

That Wieners's poetry rotated between such idealized and negative realities may express something of the psychic conflict which his sexuality produced, in his family and himself. Wieners venerates the "wrapped up romance" and refreshment of a gay bar in "The Gay World Has

Changed" (*Selected* 248), but he still must insist that

> The men, normal looking enough, you'd never know,
> are not degenerates, good clothes with intelligent con-
> versation

against the voice in his head which hisses: "you're a faggot, a faggot, you're nothing but a homosexual, / nothing more; sex, sex, Sex and sex." However well they and he observed decorum and style, a voice of normalizing morality keeps insisting on their "degeneracy" and "dirtiness." By contrast, the movie star constantly obeys decorum. "How Perfect, How Quintessential!" (*Selected* 251) describes Ava Gardner's living room in Madrid in the language of the glossy celebrity profile. The room has "the proper paintings, the correct books," observes a disciplined and appropriate aesthetics. But why should such conformity appeal to a writer who himself cultivated the inappropriate, the indecorous, and the maladjusted? "Unsterile, who would this photograph have been taken for, / if not to titillate our collages in the frames, our poverty-starved suites," he concludes. Wieners's poetry plays in the gap between poverty and wealth, between his messy collages and their tidy, controlled source images. He was aware of the penalties for misappropriating the glamour possessed by the stars: he had even been arrested for impersonating Ethel Kennedy at an airport.

Wieners wrote that Lana Turner "travelled fast." As for O'Hara, speed was an expression of ultimate freedom. Travelling fast was not only a condition of physical and social escape, but also a poetic impulse. After the syntactic and lexical economies of *Nerves*, many of Wieners's later poems, such as "Maria Gouverneur" in *Behind the State Capitol*, are dominated by polysyllabic words and convoluted syntax ("Attic coiffure admonitioner / supreme Parisian commissioner / unblemished saviour's listener," for example). In such lines, the clutter or collage of sound and sense is produced from a superabundance of free language. While psychologists identify schizophrenic speech as highly rhythmic and rhyming, with a tendency to perseveration (Cohen 18), such syllabic pile-ups in Wieners's poems share with readers the complex semantic possibilities and luxuriant aural properties of language, made available when the ratiocinating consciousness lets go. It cannot be overemphasised that what might be diagnosed as perseveration in a poet known to suffer from schizophrenia is often revered as complex and artful play with the texture and sound of words in the work of Wieners's contemporaries. In many of Wieners's later poems polysyllabic words tumble out with little apparent semantic logic; personal pronouns are avoided; asyndeton emphasizes the sonic textures of his diction, especially the similar suffixes or rough consonance which hook individual words to each other. This work shares many character- istics with a poem like Ashbery's "Europe," but for that poem's sequence of prominent lacunae Wieners would always substitute a tangle of nouns and attributes selected for their jarring or consonant sounds. It also bears comparison to poems by O'Hara such as "Dido," where parataxis feeds the flood of consciousness, words urgently vault over the absent syntactic or semantic connectives to produce a sense of urgency. The frenzied pace of O'Hara's prose poem, its associative structure and sociability combined with its morbidity, resembles Wieners's techniques. So, too, does the camp feminized persona:

> I could find some rallying ground like pornography or religious ex- ercise, but really, I say to myself, you are too serious a girl for that [. . .] If, when my cerise muslin sweeps across the agora, I hear no whispers even if they're really echoes, I know they think I'm on my last legs, "She's just bought a new racing car" they say, or "She's using mercurochrome on her nipples." [. . .] But if this doesn't cost me the supreme purse, my very talent, I'm not the starlet I thought I was. I've been advertising in the Post Office lately. Somebody's got to ruin the queen, my ship's just got to come in. (*Collected* 74-5)

The starlet is down on her luck. Listening for whispers of admiration as she walks through the marketplace but hearing none, she turns to consumption (buying a racing car) to contradict rumors of her decline. The use of the first person invites readers to consider how O'Hara is "advertising" himself, his talents and his looks, in the office of letters; and how the abundance of ideas, phrases and images in this poem is a kind of conspicuous consumption to stave off rumors of his own defeat.

Many of Wieners's early poems use ornate, formal diction and convo- luted syntax, but (as we have seen) his tendency to adopt celebrity per- sonae and associative patterns of speech and imagination increased in his later work. It may seem surprising, given his experience of street life, drug use and the gay subculture and of their vocabularies, that Wien- ers so often used archaic idioms. His ornate formality was partly camp. Many of his poems modulate between antique, deluxe idiom and slang or concrete detail; slang differentiates real, nasty life from fantasy, brings the poem tumbling back down to earth. In "The Waning of the Harvest Moon," for example, the unspecific and formal address to "daughter my soul" is broken suddenly and effectively with a confession of violence and covetous poverty: "I want to go out and rob a grocery store" (*Selected* 58). Such modulation is generally not a declaration of equivalency between fantasy and reality, but of the conflict between imagination and instrumental reason. In "A poem for cocksuckers" (*Selected* 36), the queer bar is a utopian space within a city where hostility to homosexuality is still the norm; that utopia is defined through the poem's own remastery of abusive language ("niggers," "fairies," "cocksuckers"). By placing such words in the frame of camp or ornate language, he neuters them. The poem moves away from violent slang and the detailed, specific interior of the bar to a fantastic pastoral realm of fountains, rivers, mountains and springs. Wieners concludes that it is only by abandoning the specific for an idealised landscape produced through associations that the poem can fully express the "gifts" possessed by those around him.

His syntax itself is fraught with this clash between idealism and realism. Though Olson advised him early on that "I'd put back yr original straightness of syntax,"[17] Wieners regularly uses archaic grammatical forms to call attention to the artificiality and insufficiency of his idealized wishes. "When green was the bed my love / and I laid down upon," he writes in "A poem for Painters" (*Selected* 31). The compound preposition "upon" is one of his favourites, used three times in this stanza alone. Such poems are also consistent with this veneration of the stars: they provide luxury at the syntactic level. Where shifts between outdated diction and contemporary slang highlight the gulf between fantastic alternatives and grim reality, this luxurious syntax provides a poetic architecture similar to the bountiful and inaccessible realms of the cinema stars. Antique language also locates an idealized past within poems which celebrate immediacy. Though Wieners embraces the sexual liberties achieved by changing social conditions and the gay rights movement, he is also a poet who regularly expresses his desire for failed marital archetypes. The archaisms of his diction and syntax, by evoking older kinds of discourse, also appeal for the older, more genteel relations established within those discourses.[18]

The Present as Prologue: Wieners and Olson

Despite his use of old-fashioned language, Wieners declared himself to be a poet of the present—of the instant unmediated by scholarly reflection, an oppressive sense of literary history or even concerns for the future which might necessitate planning (of his life or his writing). Here, he may resemble O'Hara; but just as it would be reductive to understand O'Hara's poetics of the present as a simple "I do this, I do that" formula, so Wieners regarded simple "description" of the moment as "a deceit. An easy / trap to fall into" (*Selected* 70). In "Confession" (*Selected* 74), he writes

> I remember
> Wednesday afternoon when we walked
>
> in the sun and heard the girl sing
> *Stormy Weather.* Mere description
> but spirit of the night, teach us
> to bear despair.

The almost guilty shift from "mere description" of the O'Hara-style peram-bulatory opening, through the short conjunction "but" shows how close to the skin this despair lurks—any poetic occasion can trigger it. But it also suggests that Wieners is poetically and emotionally habituated to invoking that despair: it is the ruling topos of his literary and psychic life. Wieners's attitude to both description and despair is conditioned by his understanding of the present. As he writes in "A poem for record players," the effluvium of life is its "dull details / I can only describe to you, / but which are here and / I hear and shall never / give up again" (*Selected* 27). The excruciating beauties of the present, if they are not shared, can only be *described*, though they remain in the memory of those who experience them as a site constantly to be revisited. Wieners was certainly aware of Olson's insistence on regarding the present as "prologue" to a future deter-mined by the activities especially of poets. But unlike Olson, who sought to recover the past through creative scholarship, Wieners regarded the past as "a vapor that escapes / from the mind in impatience" (*Selected* 156). Like O'Hara and other New York School writers, he had limited interest in Olson's serious projects to excavate the past. O'Hara himself describes the past as "really something" ("Biotherm (for Bill Berkson)," *Collected* 446) because you can remember it honestly or "you can / lie about everything." In this sense, the past is poetic—O'Hara may be remembering Plato's description of the poet as a bad liar in *Republic* book 2. Later in the poem O'Hara contemplates the "long history of populations" but quickly turns to making fun of scholars who misidentify German-language books as

"SANSKRIT or Urdu" and end up brawling while "the dark was going on and on" outside. In what could be read as a poke at Olson, this teasing eventually turns into a pseudo-etymology of English.

Wieners found in O'Hara's glorification of the present an alternative to Olson's intellectual scrutiny of the past. In his statement for Donald Allen's *New American Poetry* anthology, Wieners advised that "one cannot avoid the / days. They have to parade by in all their carnage" (Allen 426). O'Hara was a poet who watched that parade of days, not shrinking from their carnage or retreating into academic speculation. In an essay he sent to Olson, Wieners clearly identifies his own poetic vocation with what he awkwardly calls O'Hara's "triumph of will" over those persecuting forces which seek to "dominate his imagination" or his existence.

> The world of the intellect or sensibility is excruciated. The poems of Frank O'Hara seem as valid testimony in the face of this <violet crushed against a skyscraper>. All poets do their work is a triumph of the will over those who seek to dominate <their imagination> or limit their potentiality possibility of existing, all day.[19]

O'Hara's will to work among the skyscrapers which would "crush" his delicacy, represents for Wieners the possible triumph of imagination over the grim conditions of modernity. His "triumph" is his capacity to exist, "all day," wholly in the present, as exemplified by Wieners's unironic reference to Leni Riefenstahl's film. Charles Altieri has described O'Hara as depicting "the present as landscape without depth": "And if the present is without depth, whatever vital qualities it has depend entirely on the energies and capacities of the consciousness encountering it" (Altieri 110). But where for O'Hara that present-as-cityscape is a constantly changing, exuberant superficiality against which a variety of transient subjectivities can play, for Wieners the depth of the present is filled with memories, patterns of loss in which his subjectivity is pathetically fixed, despite the many characters he plays. Those characters seem chosen precisely for their unsustainability, to mark the alienation and lack which stain his private life. Despite his valorisation of the present through occasionally paranoid or mystical sense of immediacy, he cannot abjure the past completely.

If his acknowledgement of the past were limited only to personal memories and anachronistic diction or syntax, then Wieners would owe little to Olson and much more to O'Hara's poetry of specificity. But he explains his real debt this way: "Before Charles, I practised a hands-off policy in terms of my experience . . . I was looking inwards, rather than gazing out" ("Twenty Hour Ballet," *Cultural Affairs* 135). Wieners simplified Olson's argument—that the personal and the impersonal, the world and the self, context and soul are both *spaces* which can interpenetrate each other[20]—via LSD and opium into a negation of the importance of distinctions between the real and the imaginary, materialism and idealism. While Olson's art implicated his own life in the epic of history, Wieners's elision between poetry and the "estates of being around us" became a chronicle of collapse into schizophrenia. Olson recommended "objectism," defined as "getting rid of the lyrical interference of the individual as ego, of the 'subject' and his soul" and listening to the identity between himself and the world (*Collected Prose* 247). Wieners did engage in such listening for the "secrets objects share," but through the magnification of his own ego's lyrical interference, not its obliteration. In fact, in addition to being a ripe poetical technique, collapsing the boundaries between "himself and world" is, according to Kleinian psychoanalysis, part of the faulty process of projection and introjection inherent to schizophrenia.

Olson believed that Wieners was always in danger of being too personal, relying on the insights of his occultized inner life rather than the deliberated products of study. Sometimes Olson spun it, as Robert Creeley remembered his talk at SUNY Cortland, as a distinction between the poetry of art and the poetry of affect.

> He spoke of such poets as Wieners   John Wieners   as
> being poets of *affect* in   so far as the daily life   daily lived
> and its im   agination   it wasn't simply stuck with that   but
> it did not   metaphysically propose a conclusion. It wasn't
> working towards an end   in mind.   The mind was used to
> make   the mind was used to   not merely to record but to
> work on what is. (Spanos 16)

Wieners did not write through the mediation of precepts, or of systems for comprehending history and language; his poetry translates, with sometimes unbearable immediacy, the events and non-events of present personal life into a sustained argument about the alienation and loneliness intrinsic to a fallen human condition. It reads the body as a map of such moral convictions. In this way, his were eminently metaphysical concerns.

Perhaps this reflects the symbolic repertoire provided by his Catholic upbringing. The secularist Olson challenged Wieners's occult and mystical obsessions, but he was also sensitive to the hardships Wieners faced. His essay "The Present Is Prologue" acknowledges that how any of us "make ourself fit instruments for use" is affected by the family (both immediate and historical): "what strikes me . . . is, the depth to which the parents who live in us (they are not the same) are our definers. And that the work of each of us is to find out the true lineaments of ourselves by facing up to the primal features of these founders who lie buried in us" (*Collected Prose* 205-6). Olson wrote about one of Wieners's poems in 1957, "I feel defenses here which, I took it, the spring was the time to dissuade. (I dare say it is the environment?" (Boston College MS.f. 12. Charles Olson to John Wieners, Aug 19 [1957]) This surmise—that Wieners's poetry was defensive on account of the hostility of his family—is corroborated by many of Wieners's own journal entries and poems including "Two barbarians" (*Selected* 240-241). At the same time, Olson symbolised for Wieners the challenge of repudiating the immediately available knowledge of the heart. With reference to "The Present Is Prologue," Wieners describes his "master" as being

> the first to recognize
> and save me from the self condemnation I practiced
> Let me know the chambers of my soul. (*Journal* 50)

Olson's poetics legitimated the dissociative patterns that increasingly affected Wieners's thinking. Wieners was still citing the "Projective Verse" imperative that "one perception must immediately and directly lead to a further perception" in a letter to Hank Chapin in 1962,[21] and in the poem "Ma's Deck Chairs" from *Behind the State Capitol* (9). He described himself and Olson as "different sides of a coin, reversed in spirits" (*Selected* 292). He was faithful to Olson's emphasis on "feeling and desires and breath" as "the cause of the words coming into existence / ahead of them" (Olson, "Human Universe," *Collected Prose* 202). His review of Matson celebrates

> Breath, and the practice of it. Form is not of the question here.
> Jazz, and its mainline to the heart.

While the first occasion for celebration is typically Olsonian, the second is closer to both New York writers and the Beats. As he explained about his poetry's rhythms, "the gauge is intellectual," not respiratory: he rejects Olson's veneration of the breath, because "the breath is so relative" (*Selected* 290).

Despite the debt he owed to Olson, Wieners sought to differentiate himself from his "master" the "sage." After leaving Black Mountain, he wrote in gratitude to Olson, "somebody like me doesn't get what those three months gave, and walks away to a less-kind of world. He walks with it between him and the ground."[22] But soon after, he resolved—just as Olson had overcome his own "master" Pound—"Damn the references to my lords, I must set myself up as absolute" (*Journal* 62). When *The Hotel Wentley Poems* was published, Olson praised its "*delicious* recked exciting split seconds throughout."[23] A series of poems written over the course of a week in a flophouse, *Hotel Wentley* showed a command of the short and regular line which owes little to Olson's projectivist prosody. Although the stanza beginning "south of Mission" in "A poem for Painters" evokes Olson in its panegyric to the rolling American landscape, these poems are about the introverted subject, not about the heroic destiny of Americans as a first people. Rather, they take an inward voyage into "the Place / of the heart where man / is afraid to go" (*Selected* 34) but which the drug sub-culture makes inhabitable, the "dark places" of a primordial self. Nonetheless, Olson admired the book as "really on, in a French way which lighted up his natural sensational Irish powers so the plums stayed on trees, instead of falling off and rotting all over the ground (no matter what fine grass I thought that made, the next season, anyway!)" (*Selected Letters* 263). By their "French way" Olson probably meant their imitation of Rimbaud. In a notebook entry written around 1965, Wieners resolved to "be the new Rimbaud, and not die at 37 but set the record straight, new words to music, <nor Hart Crane either,> the key to existence."[24] Rimbaud's famous dictum "*Je est un autre*" epitomizes the violent estrangement from a sentimental self which also characterizes many of Wieners's drug poems. Olson had recommended Rimbaud to Wieners at Black Mountain, as a poet who restored the law laid down by Heraclitus and "vitiated by Socrates": "that man is estranged from that which he is most familiar, that like Rimbaud said we are all niggers, and, as I added, we treat ourselves cheap."[25]

After Black Mountain, Wieners and Olson lost touch; but they renewed their friendship at the Berkeley Poetics Conference, and Olson invited Wieners to join him at SUNY Buffalo as a teaching assistant in 1965. The year in Buffalo was in some ways productive for Wieners. He was part of an active writing community, and looked forward to the Spring Arts Festival, whose participants included Jean-Luc Godard, Nam June Paik, Michael McClure, and Taylor Mead. But he revealed his mounting paranoia in a letter to publisher George Minkoff:

I have all kinds of irritants here; the drug-addicted undergraduates at the State University fill every evening with pain, screaming and offal. As a descendant of the original designer of the town, I am horrified at their behavior, ex-convicts and thieves particularly from Long Island and the Bronx. I have been persecuted by them for twenty-five years, so desperately turned to poetry as a means of revenge. [. . .] To have these undesirables in town hinders mobility at the theatre, museum or concert hall, but I still attend, and if I could afford would purchase season tickets for all three. Someday that will be my usual activity. As it is now, the air is rent with parasites and I look to these opportunities for relief.[26]

Wieners relied on Olson's friendship as well as the theatre, museum and concert hall; but he later wrote "I fear that I drove him out of Buffalo with my obsessive attention. We seldom allow what is beneath our dignity. I was pretty low class at that time, rooming above a clothing store, using Mister Olson for many things" ("Hanging on" 23). At this point, Olson's relation to Wieners was not entirely supportive and benign either. After the pleasantries of their trip to Spoleto, Italy, together, Olson and Wieners fell out in 1966. Wieners had set up house with Panna Grady and her daughter Ella in Annasquam, Massachusetts. Olson wrote to them as *"Romeo und Julia auf dem Dorfe"* from Gloucester on 26 June 1966: "Please send the following message to your newly weds—the fullest & deepest realizations of the joys and fruits of the marriage ceremony." Though they were not married, the fruits of the ceremony were planted; Grady was pregnant. She decided to return to New York for an abortion. Wieners was devastated, describing that event with uncharacteristic violence in "Alcohol doesn't see . . . ," "Sunset," and "Maine."[27] His long-held wish for "a wife and home" ("Supplication," *Selected* 125) seemed unlikely ever to be satisfied; and the beautiful heiress, who had temporarily fulfilled his fantasies of the glamorous woman, had betrayed him. The misogynist aggression of a poem like "The Garbos and Dietrichs" (*Selected* 101), with its reference to "odd pregnancies / abortions are not counted," shows how all his former goddesses were degraded by these events. His journal from this period is filled with rambling, violent improvisations on his unhappiness and Grady's treachery.

The last poem in the journal is "Billie" (*Selected* 130). The man who "as a god / stepped out of eternal dream" to steal his girl was none other than Olson himself. The next letter from Olson (18 November 1966) found

Wieners in Buffalo, and his mentor "two weeks here in London on Piccadilly no less until things clear; Panna purposeful to finish London—& I as you know determined to spend the winter in *healthy* climate: England's too cold for me!" The cheerful weather report did little to disguise Olson's betrayal. When he returned to SUNY Cortland to give the lecture discussed by Creeley above, Olson wrote to Harvey Brown about his nervousness at seeing Wieners again:

> Off today to do that stint before 70 New York State (College I suppose poets—including I hear one John Wieners. So hold your breath—I'm not sure I shldn't have you along as my bodyguard, at least to frisk him unnoticeably! (*Letters* 389)

Later, he reports with relief, "saw John & he was just as usual too much. Read marvelously—& was more than ever my Admired One! Though his hair is now Henna Bardol I mean Clairon I mean Neponset Bleach—& there are three teeth hanging in his front mouth.—He *is* sharp-tongued & swollen with hurt-pain & feeling, but anybody who can't see he is quicker & more profound than ever are themselves fools!" (390). Wieners also wrote enthusiastically about the meeting,

> It was so fabulous to meet after a year when I thought—all love I had told him my years as a student were over, 12 in all, last summer 1966. Now our friendship may start. It was never that before as I was in such awe, I could never contribute anything but audience. Last weekend held delight—maturity, sophistication. Expect to honor his birth this December as always.[28]

Later, in a memorial to Olson, he wrote magnanimously that "I came to Gloucester with a girl, Panna Grady, who has since become Mrs. William van O'Connor in Paris. She studied his work as well as I and he came to call on us frequently that summer of 1966, until they sailed for London on the *Empress of Canada* in the Fall from, I believe, Montreal. It was not an unhappy time, I see in retrospect, for any of us" ("Hanging on" 23).

Although the letters to Olson in the late 1950s and early '60s employ many of the older poet's idiosyncracies of lineation, syntax and punctuation, after the sorrows of 1966 Wieners found his own independent style in both correspondence and poetry. The memorial "Hanging on for Dear Life" explains its admiration for the older poet negatively: "Charles

Olson has not for me since his death, become a colossal bore" (*Behind the State Capitol* 14). It praises Olson for "his navigator's tools or pilot's compass for charting the depths of unfathomed waters, see[k]ing to steer a man straight. I am not going to make the compromise of seeking love on strange shores, just because it's available. It doesn't of necessity follow that available means are the most satisfactory." This ambiguous statement at once indicates the value of Olson's "tools" for poetic discovery, and the usefulness of more than "available means"; but it also rejects the "compromise" of exploratory poetics, choosing instead love and familiarity. While Wieners's gratitude to his mentor resonates in many such commemorative statements, this ambivalence also indicates that Olson's betrayal had given Wieners an opportunity to escape the teacher-student relationship for one of greater self-assurance and equality. When Olson died, he composed an elegy "Charles' Death" (*Selected 237)*, which concludes

> I could not believe he would die
> even though my dream had come true
> and he had fulfilled so many.

Is "my dream" partially the fantasy of Olson's death itself? The edgy narcissism of this tribute—that Olson's mortality was incredible *even though* he had in a sense completed his work by fulfilling the dreams of Wieners and other poets—suggests that such ambivalence remained even after his death.

I have characterised the relationship between Wieners and O'Hara and Wieners and Olson as (mostly) sympathetic friendships, with O'Hara's cosmopolitanism and humour taken to extremes in Wieners's obsession with Hollywood and camp melodramatics, and Olson's emphasis on the present and the personal providing the springboard for Wieners's early Rimbaudian writing. These are just two of the vectors of influence and collaboration which can be drawn from Wieners's writing, and I hope this essay will encourage other critics to look again at this work. It is too easy to take the poetry of John Wieners for granted, sketching its trajectory as a drug-induced shift from the occasionally overblown formalism and luxuriating archaisms of the early works to the schizoid associations and chaotic referentiality of the late. Along the way, despite the careful prosodic controls of the volume *Nerves*, Wieners might be seen as an introvert who is redeemed from ultimate narcissism mostly by the sordidness of what he is willing to reveal about his own desires. He has been described by Ginsberg and Creeley as magically gifted by his own drug psychosis and mental illness. In his foreword to the *Selected Poems* (15), Ginsberg plays Shelley to Wieners's "Keatsian eloquence, pathos, substantiality, the sound of Immortality in auto exhaust same as nightingale." Creeley likewise described his poetry as "in the process of a life being lived, literally, as Keats's was, or Hart Crane's, or Olson's own" ("Preface," *Cultural Affairs* 11). While some of the features of Wieners's writing can be attributed to his derangement of the senses through drugs and later his mental illness, these features are above all filled with critical artistry which draws on currents in contemporary writing and aesthetics. It is only by reinterpreting such diagnostics within the larger field of his technical and thematic experimentation that we can really understand the poetry of John Wieners as more than torch-songs by an original who jeopardized everything for his art. His dramatic self-presentation owes something to O'Hara, though his poems can lack the improvisational comedy of O'Hara's *Meditations in an Emergency*. And while his engagement with his own past lacks the complex historical sweep which gives Olson's work its epic grandeur, it nonetheless exemplifies the "mind, that worker on what is" in ways Olson might never have anticipated. But I hope these similarities do more to situate Wieners's controlled artistic intelligence than to limit his achievement. As a chronicler of the ups and downs of the early gay rights movement, as an aficionado of the culture industry, as an incisive critic of state institutions and social perceptions of mental illness, and as an artificer whose syntax and diction expressed the profoundest state of alienation and profoundest hope for love, his poetry stands alone.

Works Cited

Allen, Donald, ed. *The New American Poetry, 1945-1960*. Berkeley, Los Angeles and London: University of California Press, 1960.

Altieri, Charles. *Enlarging the Temple: New Directions in American Poetry During the 1960s*. Lewisburg, PA: Bucknell UP, 1979.

Benston, Kimberly W. "Amiri Baraka: An Interview." *boundary 2* 6.2 (1978): 303-318.

Berkson, Bill and Joe LeSueur, eds. *Homage to Frank O'Hara*. Berkeley, CA: Creative Arts, 1980.

Cohen, Bertram D. "Referent Communication Disturbances in Schizophrenia."

Language and Cognition in Schizophrenia. Ed. Steven Schwartz. Hillsdale, NJ: Lawrence Erlbaum, 1978.

Davidson, Michael. *The San Francisco Renaissance: Poetics and Community at Mid-century.* Cambridge: Cambridge UP, 1989.

di Prima, Diane. *Recollections of My Life as a Woman: The New York Years.* New York: Viking, 2001.

Duberman, Martin. *Black Mountain: An Exploration in Community.* London: Wildwood House, 1972.

Friedlander, Benjamin. "Strange Fruit: O'Hara, Race and the Color of Time." *The Scene of My Selves: New Work on New York School Poets.* Ed. Terence Diggory and Stephen Paul Miller. Orono, ME: National Poetry Foundation, 2001.

Gooch, Brad. *City Poet: the Life and Times of Frank O'Hara.* New York: Harper Perennial, 1993.

Horkheimer, Max and Theodor W. Adorno. *Dialectic of Enlightenment.* Trans. John Cumming. New York: Continuum, 1994.

Meyer, Thomas. "Glistening Torsos, Sandwiches, and Coca-Cola." Review of *Early Writing* and *Poems Retrieved. Parnassus* 6 (Fall-Winter 1977): 241-57.

O'Hara, Frank. *The Collected Poems.* Ed. Donald Allen. Berkeley, Los Angeles and London: U of California P, 1971.

—. *Early Writing.* Ed. Donald Allen. Bolinas, CA: Grey Fox, 1977.

Olson, Charles. *Collected Prose.* Ed. Donald Allen and Benjamin Friedlander. Berkeley, Los Angeles and London: U of California P, 1997.

—. *Selected Letters.* Ed. Ralph Maud. Berkeley and Los Angeles: U of California P, 2000.

Spanos, William V. "Talking with Robert Creeley." *boundary 2* 6.3 (Spring-Autumn 1978): 11-76.

Wieners, John. *Behind the State Capitol or Cincinnati Pike.* Boston: The Good Gay Poets, 1975.

—. *Cultural Affairs in Boston: Poetry and Prose 1956-1985.* Ed. Raymond Foye. Santa Rosa: Black Sparrow, 1988.

—. "Hanging on for Dear Life." *boundary 2* 2.1/2 (Autumn 1973-Winter 1974).

—. *The Journal of John Wieners is to be called 707 Scott Street for Billie Holiday 1959.* Los Angeles: Sun and Moon, 1996.

—. *Selected Poems 1958-1984.* Ed. Raymond Foye. Santa Barbara, CA: Black Sparrow, 1998.

—. *A Superficial Estimation.* Madras and New York: Hanuman Books, 1986.

Wilkinson, John. "A Tour of the State Capitol: Introducing the poems of John Wieners." *Edinburgh Review* 114 (2004): 96-125.

"Against the Speech of Friends"

[1] William J. Harris usefully draws attention to Baraka's interest in "the concept of turning—even the verb *to turn*" (21). However, for Harris, whose study focuses on what he calls Baraka's "jazz aesthetic" and its practice of reversing or inverting "white" forms and making them "blacker," "turning" is linked to Baraka's habit of "taking a white stereotype of blacks . . . and transforming it into a symbol of its opposite." In contrast, I argue that for Baraka "turning" is a more general process of troping, departing, or pushing away from that which is constraining with dramatic social, psychological, and aesthetic effects, and that this concept is absolutely essential to Baraka's aesthetic (21).

[2] The name "New American Poetry," which was further solidified by a second anthology of prose writings, *The Poetics of the New American Poetry*, is still used to refer to the diverse experimental poets of the 1950s and 1960s who grew out of the Whitman/Pound/Williams/Stein/Dada/Surrealism traditions, and I will be using it in this sense. For a helpful and well-researched essay on the context from which *The New American Poetry* arose—Donald Allen's editorial decisions, the literary politics of the era, the diverse voices and rivalries within and between poetic communities—see Alan Golding, "*The New American Poetry* Revisited, Again." Golding's essay stresses the epoch-shaping power of this anthology, noting its "central place in most readings or structurings of postwar literary history" and arguing that it "helped promote and canonize ideas of field composition based on Charles Olson's 'Projective Verse'; a (re)definition of poetic form as immanent and processual; a poetics of dailiness and of the personal (as distinct from the confessional); and a poetry of humor and play (as distinct from wit)" (180-1).

[3] The poem appears in *Nice to See You: Homage to Ted Berrigan*.

[4] The story's trajectory is of course a familiar one: in the early 1960s Baraka grew more and more dissatisfied with the downtown New York poetry scene, and with his own interracial marriage to Hettie Jones, increasingly uncomfortable about his entanglement with the white world and the, to his eyes, apolitical stance of the bohemian avant-garde. This extended transitional moment ended

abruptly in 1965 when Baraka left his wife and children, cut off all ties with his former companions, and physically left the Lower East Side behind to move uptown to Harlem, and then to Newark, where he helped found the Black Arts movement. He quickly adopted a much more essentialist, race-based concept of identity, rejected integration as a failed liberal fantasy in favor of separatism, and became a spokesman for black cultural nationalism and a political organizer and leader.

[5] See, for example, book-length studies of Baraka by Werner Sollors, Kimberly W. Benston, William J. Harris, and Theodore Hudson, which tend to treat Baraka's so-called "Beat" period as a mistaken and temporary pit-stop on his way to arriving at his distinctive genius and political and racial clarity. Although these books have contributed a great deal to our understanding of Baraka's interactions with the white avant-garde, the emphases of their studies (and, to some extent, their introductory nature) often detract from an understanding of the specifics and the scope of those dialogues.

[6] Some important exceptions to the general neglect of such overlapping spaces can be found in the critical works of Aldon Lynn Nielsen and Nathaniel Mackey. See Nielsen's *Writing Between the Lines: Race and Intertextuality*, which argues that "rather than segregating our readings of African-American literary creations, we must, as the very name African-American literature implies, read black texts in their fulsome implication in all English writing" (23) and his *Black Chant*, which admirably recovers an extensive postwar African-American poetic avant-garde that existed side by side and was intertwined with the New American Poetry. See also Mackey's *Discrepant Engagement*, which rejects rigid categories and rubrics of recent literary history and deliberately places writers from across racial and cultural boundaries in dialogue with one another—most centrally African-American writers (including Baraka), white projectivist poets, and Caribbean writers.

[7] My intention here is to argue that the early Baraka exemplifies the longstanding intertwining of African-American and pragmatist thought, as well as some of the tensions inherent in that conversation. Ross Posnock provocatively illuminates this fascinating cross-racial dialogue in his study *Color and Culture* (1998), where he traces the rejection of essentialism and embrace of cosmopolitanism in the African-American intellectual tradition by convincingly demonstrating the profound connections between this tradition and pragmatism. Posnock usefully includes the early Baraka in his canon of African-American pragmatist-inspired intellectuals. In addition to Posnock, for other pioneering studies that have focused on this intersection, see Cornel West's *American Evasion of Philosophy*, Nancy Fraser's essay "Another Pragmatism: Alain Locke, Criti-

cal 'Race' Theory, and the Politics of Culture," in Dickstein's *Revival* (157-175), Mark Sanders's study of Sterling Brown, and James Albrecht's essay on Ellison, Emerson, and pragmatism.

[8] The idea that poets of the 1950s and 1960s like Allen Ginsberg, Frank O'Hara, John Ashbery, Charles Olson, Robert Creeley, and Amiri Baraka led an avant-garde rebellion against the stultifying aesthetic, social, and political mores of the postwar period is ubiquitous in poetry criticism. See, for example, James Breslin's *From Modern to Contemporary*, David Perkins's *History of Modern Poetry*, Michael Davidson's *San Francisco Renaissance*, Charles Altieri's *Englarging the Temple*, Alan Golding's *From Outlaw to Classic*, Daniel Kane's *All Poets Welcome*, and Marjorie Perloff's *Frank O'Hara* and *The Dance of the Intellect*. Such discussions, like David Lehman's forceful case for O'Hara's enthusiastic participation in a dramatic avant-garde enterprise in *The Last Avant-Garde*, often stress how these poets were "zealously undertaking some crucial avant-garde mission," as O'Hara's biographer Brad Gooch claims he was. My point is not to dispute whether these poets overturned existing paradigms and radically altered the course of literary history (they did), but rather to emphasize that poets like O'Hara and Baraka are profoundly ambivalent about the avant-garde as a project, and frequently resist the idea of a "New York," "Beat," or any other "school"; furthermore, they seem perpetually caught on, and fascinated by, the horns of the avant-garde dilemma (Gooch 188).

[9] *The Toilet* was first published in *Kulchur* 3, no. 9 (Spring 1963), but according to Sollors, it was written in 1961. The Grove Press edition of the play indicates that it was first performed on December 16, 1964, at the St. Marks Playhouse, New York, with a set by Baraka's (and O'Hara's) friend Larry Rivers, but Sollors points out that although this production "is often referred to as 'first,'" the play was "first performed by the Playwright's Unit of the Actor's Studio in 1962" (282, n. 25).

[10] Baraka's words are from his "introduction" to the play, quoted in Sollors, 110. Sollors explains that this introduction was printed on the playbill "of the famous 1964 production" (282, n.25).

[11] Sollors observes that "while Foots denotes a 'lower' kind of 'plebian' existence, that is closer to the ethnic roots and the soil, 'Ray' suggests a more spiritual personality," while also resembling the name "Roi." He points out that the protagonist must choose between "his generic identity as 'Foots' and his individual peculiarity as 'Ray'" (109).

[12] See Benston, who points out that "The basic root of the pathos in *The Toilet*, especially as it relates to Ray, is twofold: first, his inability to articulate any aspect of his own tragic dilemma; and second his exclusion from the social

groups (black gang, white friendship) to which he is trying to belong" (*Baraka* 193).

[13] Two of Baraka's major plays feature sympathetic gay characters (*The Baptism*'s "Homosexual" and James Karolis in *The Toilet*), and at the very heart of his only novel, *The System of Dante's Hell*, is a vexed relationship with homosexuality that most of the novel's readers have skirted around. Unfortunately, the scope of the present essay prevents a fuller discussion of the complexity of Baraka's feelings about and nuanced treatment of homosexuality in his earlier work. Although it is a subject that has remained largely unexplored, Posnock's chapter on Baraka in *Color and Culture* usefully argues that Baraka conflates "intellectual" and "homosexual" in such works as *The Toilet* and *The System of Dante's Hell* and that these texts are filled with ambivalence about both identities. For a fuller discussion, see my study *Beautiful Enemies: Freindship and Postwar American Poetry*.

[14] In a later (1978) interview, Baraka claims that he "tacked on" the ending because "it actually invokes my own social situation at the time—not so much the event that I used to build the play on . . . there was a question of wanting to offer that kind of friendship that existed across traditional social lines. At the time I was married to a white woman, and most of the friends I had were white, on the Lower East Side." He also says "when I think of *The Toilet* I just think of it as the product of a particular time and place and condition as far as my own development was concerned, and I think it is a legitimate play, even though the ending was tacked on. If you ever look at the manuscript you'll see that the manuscript stops at the end of the fight. But then I sat there for a while thinking, was that really the way it had to end?" (*Conversations* 131). See also his very similar comments in 1981—"and then I tacked it on, I guess, as some kind of attempt to show some kind of, you know, reconciliation, or something like that. And I think that's where I was at that time" (*Conversations* 217).

[15] See Gooch's biography of O'Hara for a colorful discussion of the entire incident (322-24). O'Hara's side of the story is reported in a terrific letter to Ashbery (16 March 1959). A transcription of this letter can be found in "Frank O'Hara Letters Vols. 1 and 2," Donald Allen collection, Boxes 2 and 3, at the Archives and Special Collections Department, Thomas J. Dodd Research Center, University of Connecticut Libraries.

[16] In Joe LeSueur's recently published memoir about Frank O'Hara, he also suggests that this friendship was at times more than platonic, relating that Baraka would frequently drop by the apartment LeSueur shared with O'Hara, "sometimes staying over and sharing Frank's bed, while I, the very soul of discretion,

was in my own bed, minding my own business, never asking questions, never saying a word to anyone about what I thought might be going on, Roi being a married man, a father, a stud, a sexist, a *heterosexual*!" (246).

"As Radical As Society Demands the Truth to Be"

[1] Primary among these are extended published accounts by Lorenzo Thomas, Michel Oren, Eugene Redmond, Aldon Nielsen, and Daniel Kane, and also shorter but significant pieces by such Umbra members as Tom Dent, Calvin C. Hernton, and Rashidah Ismaili-Abu-Bakr.

[2] Let me make clear that Smith doesn't apply this taxonomy to the Black Arts movement and Umbra as such; his is a more general point about blackness and culture.

[3] One has only to read Calvin C. Hernton's essay on the March on Washington to get a sense of this alternate perspective on the day's events: "As I stepped from the train, walking with the crowd through the station, out into the city of Washington, a terrible dread—an ominous presence—settled upon me. Forbodedom! Not so much for the march per se, or any single thing by itself, but for a total civilization" (Hernton *White Papers* 150).

[4] Significantly, Bond was at the time communications director of SNCC; he later became well known as a Georgia state representative and senator. Both Bennett and Gore were also closely associated with the civil rights movement, Bennett as an editor at *Ebony* and Gore as a member of CORE

[5] In his autobiography, he tells the story of meeting Ishmael Reed and Calvin Hernton, who, he says, confronted him as though they were issuing "some challenge," telling him that though they liked his prose, they didn't care for his poetry (Baraka 182).

[6] It may also be due to the fact that Umbra's nominal leader, Tom Dent, was publicity director the NAACP's Legal Defense Fund at the time of the group's creation.

[7] In addition to the black-white tension mentioned earlier, this principle became especially contentious later on and perhaps contributed to the dissolution of the group: in 1964, poet Ray Durem contributed a poem titled "A Decoration for the President," which some members believed was too insensitive so soon after Kennedy's assassination.

[8] Seven of the sixteen poets are members or future members and two were very closely associated with the group although never listed as official members; fourteen (nineteen if you include the poems of unofficial members) of the issue's thirty-two poem were written by the members.

[9] Apparently, there was also a fifth issue titled *Umbra's Latin/Soul,* but I have been unable to find a copy.

"The New York School is a Joke"

[1] See Libbie Rifkin, *Career Moves: Olson, Creely, Zukofsky, Berrigan, and the American Avant-Garde* (Madison: University of Wisconsin Press, 2000), 128-135, and Daniel Kane, *All Poets Welcome: The Lower East Side Poetry Scene in the 1960s.* Berkley: The University of California Press, 2003), 100 -122

[2] See, for example, David Lehman, *The Last Avant Garde* (New York: Doubleday, 1998), 363.

[3] In the same interview that the above quotation is taken from, Berrigan showed his awareness of the relationship between poetic groups and "little magazines" by saying "that's how you get a group, I think, you start a magazine." Interestingly, Berrigan initially names *C* as his group magazine but then immediately takes back this comment by saying that *C* was not representative of any group of poets.

[4] Unpublished interview with Padgett, 8/22/03

[5] *C*'s size also allowed Berrigan to place poems by different authors on the same page, a tactic he sometimes employed in order to highlight contrasts.

[6] As Rifkin points out, O'Hara did in fact defend the cover of *C* (4) by saying to Berrigan, "if poetry can't survive a little faggotism then I don't know what can." However, O'Hara's comment is more of a defense of the representation of homoeroticism than it is of Warhol's artistic philosophy.

[7] The poem is probably set in Tangiers—a setting that evokes the work of William Burroughs who would also appear in later issues of *C.*

[8] William Burroughs, "Traced from the format of Newsweek, July 6, 1964 page 37," *C* (9).

[9] See Notley's introduction to Berrigan's *The Sonnets* (New York: Penguin, 2000), ix.

[10] In an interview, Berrigan made fun of overly simplistic conceptions of the New York School by saying, "I used to tell people they could join for five dollars. And they would all write a certain type of poem." See Ratcliffe and Scalapino, *Talking in Tranquility,* 91.

Angel Hair *Magazine, The Second-Generation New York School, and The Poetics of Sociability*

[1] I use the phrase "so-called second-generation New York School" both to capture the casualness of the era and the general hostility towards classification, as

well as to allow for Anne Waldman's and Lewis Warsh's ambivalent use of the moniker. Waldman writes, "Obviously, a major consequence of Angel Hair's publishing debut books and pamphlets and other items was the launching of an array of young experimental writers, including ourselves, onto the scene and into the official annals as second-generation New York School poets. A handy moniker, it doesn't cover the entire territory. Of course the magazine was a project of friendships, artistic collaboration, which are defining qualities of 'New York School.' Yet our project mixed up East and West coast scenes and juxtaposed them in an unusual and appealing context." Anne Waldman, introduction to *The Angel Hair Anthology*, xxvi.

[2] While Black Mountain and Beat poets certainly privileged the public poetry reading, the distinction is not so much difference as it is scale. Second-generation figures including Anne Waldman (who served as director of the still-extant St. Mark's Poetry Project), Ted Berrigan, Bill Berkson and Lewis Warsh were crucial in extending the social conditions that allowed for thrice-weekly poetry readings and parties to become the norm within the poetic community.

[3] Importantly, *The Angel Hair Anthology* shows how Waldman and Warsh were active in at once participating in and productively complicating the relatively established Lower East Side literary scene epitomized by publications including *C* and *Fuck You/a magazine of the arts*. While Ted Berrigan's *C* magazine—with its publication of second-generation figures including Ron Padgett, Joe Brainard and Dick Gallup—is perhaps the most obvious model for *Angel Hair*, as we will see Waldman and Warsh can nevertheless claim to have advanced on Berrigan's style through their more inclusive editorial policies and more overtly political sensibilities. For more information on *C* magazine, *Fuck you*, and the little magazine culture of the Lower East Side generally, see Kane; Clay and Phillips; Anderson and Kinzie.

[4] However, I should add that *literal* knowledge of the actors named in the poems isn't a prerequisite to reading the poems. The work is there as much to serve as an incitement to "crash" the second-generation world—to imagine our own Ted, Bill, Ron, and so on—as it is an enticement to gain actual knowledge of the main players in the scene.

[5] See Georges Ribemont-Dessaignes's "History of Dada," 102.

[6] In an interview published in *The Little Magazine in America*, Anne Waldman said, "When you come right down to it, it's the particular piece of writing (and not the writer) that's primary. Forget about the scene—and gossip! Interesting sometimes but, finally, irrelevant" ("Discussion of Little Magazines and Related Topics" 509). In light of such a comment, the use of words like "communal" might appear inappropriate. However, such a comment—made in 1976 after

the geographical dispersion of the scene—should be taken with the proverbial grain of salt. Despite Waldman's understandable effort to privilege individual work after the fact, we should note that in the many interviews she's held over the decades Waldman almost always speaks about the value of community in relationship to poetry.

[7] Daniel Belgrad insists that "The poetry of the [first-generation] New York School poets was spontaneous and subjective, but it lacked the radical impetus that these qualities were supposed to ensure" (255). This is certainly a debatable position. In "Tribes of New York," Michael Magee argues convincingly for a reading of O'Hara's poetry as determinedly progressive and political, and supports his position by pointing to the valences between O'Hara's poetics and the enactments of spontaneity in jazz. Nevertheless, Belgrad's book is useful in terms of helping us historicize the second-generation scene within an overall American 20th century avant-garde culture. Belgrad argues that this avant-garde promoted ideals of communal spontaneity and "nowness" as part of a dissident stance directed against a loathed academic scene and related conservative rationalism. As Belgrad writes, "The culture of spontaneity developed an oppositional version of humanism, rooted in an alternative metaphysics embodied in artistic forms. The basic attributes of this alternative metaphysics can be summarized as intersubjectivity and body-mind holism [. . .] [S]pontaneity posed intersubjectivity, in which 'reality' was understood to emerge through a conversational dynamic" (5). Belgrad adds: "By 1960, the culture of spontaneity was poised to have a powerful impact on American society. It embodied a cohesive set of values distinctly divergent from the culture of corporate liberalism. Its tenets and practices offered a template for expressions of social dissent" (247).

[8] In light of this resistance to outsider academic discourse, we should consider that Waldman's collection of essays, writings and manifestoes is entitled *Vow to Poetry* (2001). The religious and communal associations attached to the word "Vow" can be related to Warsh's and other affiliated poets' distrust of critical discourse as it relates to their poetry. The academic, in the context of a group poetics, is a social outcast feeding off the work of a community bound by a vow to unmediated and uncritically joyful reception. Unsanctioned by and independent of the community, the academic helps define future reception of the work via a loathed theoretically determined language, a language that, had Waldman, Warsh and others had their say, would never have made an appearance alongside the group's work.

[9] See chapter 4 in Kane for a discussion of the ways in which the Poetry Project at St. Mark's Church dealt with the often-thorny issues brought up by federal funding.

[10] Again, though, it would be disingenuous to assert that *Angel Hair* contributors were willfully devoted to remaining in the "underground." For example, all issues of *Angel Hair* were officially copyrighted. Poems originally published in *Angel Hair* were represented in Volume 1, 2 and 3 of *The American Literary Anthology* (Plimpton and Ardery). Other magazines featured in these volumes included a real mix of "academic" and "underground" journals including *The Denver Quarterly, The Genre of Silence, Prairie Schooner, Partisan Revue, Southern Review, Western Humanities Review, Poetry, Virginia Quarterly Review, Floating Bear,* and the *Massachusetts Review.* Additionally, in a letter from Ted Berrigan to Anne Waldman, Berrigan wrote that he was pulling a poem intended for *Angel Hair* because Tom Clark accepted it for publication in the more prestigious *The Paris Review.*

[11] As Bruce Andrews states, "I remember getting a hold of the Paul Carroll anthology [featuring many second-generation stalwarts] [. . .] I had no idea there were people my age who were doing this. [. . .] I remember getting a hold of *0-9,* I remember getting a hold of the *Paris Review* when it was edited by Tom Clark—the *Review* was publishing people like *0-9* editor Vito Acconci, and Clark Coolidge" (qtd. in Kane 197).

[12] I am inspired to use the phrase "owned the machines" by Libbie Rifkin's quotation of Waldman's line "I know how to work the machines!," from the poem "Fast Speaking Woman" (qtd. in "My Little World Goes On St. Mark's Place').

[13] Initially based in New York City, "Fluxus" was the name given to a loose confederacy of artists including Yoko Ono, George Maciunas, Dick Higgins, Nam June Paik and La Monte Young. Members of Fluxus were known for engaging in chance-operation procedures, "Happenings," concept art, installation, performance art, intermedia and video.

[14] In the original *Angel Hair* issue, three pages separate the Mayer and Anderson poems.

[15] Practically all the second-generation poets under consideration here had close relationships with Ashbery, O'Hara and Koch, either by taking classes with Koch at the New School and Columbia University, sharing readings at the Poetry Project or related venues, or simply participating in mutual publications ventures. Ashbery, Koch and Schuyler, for example, often published the work of Ted Berrigan, Ron Padgett, and Gerard Malanga, to name just a few examples.

[16] Poetry collaborations by Ashbery and affiliated writers are difficult to find outside of the special collaborative issue of the Paris-based magazine *Locus Solus* edited by Kenneth Koch, and early collaborative publications published through

the auspices of the Tibor de Nagy gallery. Nevertheless, the legend of the New York School as especially given to producing collaborative poems persists.

[17] Linda Russo quotes from her interviews with Maureen Owen and Alice Notley regarding the significance of Waldman and the Poetry Project to future experimental women's writing:

> The Poetry Project had a "matriarchal kindliness and openness to all poets, women and men," and has "stayed woman-strong" because Waldman's influence "lasted a long time both literally and imaginatively." Waldman had sought out many poets in New York during the 1960s, including Diane di Prima, Mayer, Notley and Hannah Weiner because "the sense of other women engaged in the same demanding act of writing & being a poet in what was basically, at that time, a man's world, was inspiring, encouraging" (261).

[18] *How(ever)* was first published in 1983 as an alternative to hegemonic feminism and feminist-affiliated poetry.

Poetics of Adjacency

[1] See Kane 163-164.

[2] This period in small press publishing is characterized by the prevalence of male contributors. Of the several magazines being published in connection with the second-generation New York School at this time, including *Fuck You / a magazine of the arts* (ed. Ed Sanders, 1962-65), *'C'* (ed. Ted Berrigan, 1963-66), *Adventures in Poetry* (ed. Larry Fagin, 1968-76), and *Angel Hair* (ed. Anne Waldman and Lewis Warsh, 1966-69), only the latter was co-edited by a woman.

[3] *The World* appeared every month or so throughout the late 1960s and regularly featured poetry and collaborations by then-editors Warsh and Waldman, Berrigan, Joel Oppenheimer, Ron Padgett and others. A few of Weiner's Code Poems, marking her only other appearance in the magazine, were published in *The World 11* (April 1968).

[4] Here I mean to invoke not only the first- and second-generation New York School poems that cohered through a concept of voice, but those of other poets who lived in or frequented the Lower East Side as well, those who arrived in the late 1950s or soon after (Allen Ginsberg, John Wieners, Diane di Prima) and those who activated community just prior to the founding of the Poetry Project (Paul Blackburn, Carol Bergé).

[5] Andrews, who had also encountered her writing in *0-9*, wrote to Mayer requesting work for an issue of Michael Water's magazine *Toothpick* that he was co-editing in 1973. On July 3 he wrote to Mayer: "I've gotten 3 people

turned onto your *Moving* & all have been very impressed & pleased—it's a fine book." Watten wrote to Mayer as early as 1974 seeking submissions for *This*, a magazine he co-edited with Robert Grenier and in which her clairvoyant work debuted. Mandeville Collection, UCSD, MSS 420. Weiner's "Big Words," an early clairvoyantly-composed journal, debuted in *This* in 1975.

[6] Undoubtedly conflicts arise from the gendered practice of theory; Mayer and Weiner didn't theorize their writing for their poetic community. As a result, Mayer has continually protested her "status" as a Language poet. Weiner's work occasionally reveals her sometimes ambivalent feelings about her association with and relationship to the "language boys," as she dubs them.

[7] See Bernstein's confrontation with and attempt to discount the notion that there is a "natchural" mode of writing in his essay "Stray Straws and Straw Men." All writing, he points out, is artifice and artifact, styled and constructed, the result of procedural decisions regarding the conditions under which writing is undertaken and the various rules of grammar, syntax, and vocabulary it may reproduce; many of these, his work would argue, are unconsciously-made decisions.

[8] Bernstein letter to Silliman, Mandeville Collection, UCSD, MSS 075.

[9] By "performative" I refer to the active visual dimension of texts; by "performance-oriented" I refer to texts documenting or scoring performed activities or events.

[10] For a description of this event and Cage's commentary, see Duberman 350-58. For yet another, perhaps more thorough description, see pp. 52-53 of "An Interview with John Cage" conducted by Michael Kirby and Richard Schechner in Sanford.

[11] See Goldberg.

[12] Kirby, "The New Theatre," in Sanford, p. 33.

[13] See Emmett Williams's *Anthology of Concrete Poetry* (Something Else Press, 1967).

[14] Rothenberg's translations of Seneca songs appeared in *0-9* no. 5 (January 1969). These attempted to capture the oral or "analphabetic" quality of these songs, to resist the fixity of text through repetition, creative "vowelization" and other effects.

[15] See Clay and Phillips. As committed as *A Secret Location on the Lower East Side* is to a representation of literary production as a diversely-gendered field, in the entry on *0-9* Clay and Philips focus almost exclusively on the role of the magazine in the development Acconci's art.

[16] Mayer planned for this event in great anticipation, writing to her sister Rosemary, "everybody is doing very stiff things like labeling building poems or advertisements poems I'm going to label buildings advertisements . . . i'm going

to solicit anyone in uniform or sell streets for the price of a chestnut exchange all the painting in the museum of modern art for the paintings [*sic*] in the metropolitan museum and the whitney for the ny historical society then replace those buildings around their correct paintings . . ." Mandeville Collection, UCSD, MSS 520.

[17] What I've presented here is not comprehensive historical documentation, but a sampling of events from all three Street Works as described in the *0-9* supplement, Perreault's columns, and Mayer's correspondence at UCSD. For a brief contemporary account of this event, see John Perreault's ARTOPIA at www.artsjournal.com/artopia/archives20051101.shtml.

[18] Mayer taught from 1971-75 and intermittently through the succeeding decades. See Kane, chapter six, "Bernadette Mayer and 'Language' in the Poetry Project."

[19] Much of these early proposals falls to the wayside in the ongoing collaboration of the Experiments List—a blending of ideas that is characteristic of Mayer, who no doubt introduced her concepts to the Poetry Project workshop in the spirit of contributing to and not definitively shaping or marking the production of new writing.

[20] Lyn Hejinian wrote Mayer from Berkeley: "So now [February 1979] Charles Bernstein is in town, bringing copies of *Clairvoyant Journal* from Hannah and copies of *United Artists*." Mandeville Collection, UCSD, MSS 420.

[21] Interview with the author, November 25, 2003. Hereafter cited in-text as "Interview."

[22] Rifkin points out that "deriving his poetic material (even his identity) from that of his friends and colleagues, he had a personal stake in facilitating their success" (129).

[23] In response to a phone call protesting a prose sample she'd sent in support of her application for a grant in poetry, Mayer replied: "turn the page twice and it'll be poetry." Interview with the author, November 25, 2003.

[24] See for example Larry Fagin's "32 Girls I'd like to Fuck," Anne Waldman's poem "Sick" with its "sick list" in *O My Life* (Angel Hair, 1969), and Joe Brainard's *I Remember* (Angel Hair 1970).

[25] Berrigan and Padgett would continue to submit their work even while Mayer would continue to reject it.

[26] "Long Poem for Roy Lichtenstein" was one of only two art objects Weiner showed during this period; the other is a "wheel" to accompany the code poems, shown as part of "Language II" at the Dwan Gallery in 1968 and again in 1969 at Gain Ground.

[27] At the annual Avant-Garde Festival in New York in 1965, Weiner performed

Code Poems employing flags and semaphore signalmen, and in the 1966 Festival parade she joined Giorno, Mac Low and others on the "poets truck" (a mobile stage) to perform with a bullhorn. She organized Tiny Events (1968), which included short events by several *0-9* contributors, at the Longview Country Club.

[28] The event was part of the Spring Gallery Concerts. Her first event for voices foreshadows the 1974 performance of *Clairvoyant Journal* with Sharon Matlin and Margeret DeCoursey.

[29] In "Mostly About the Sentence"(1986), Weiner identifies *Code Poems* as a significant breakthrough in her thinking about gender and language. Her use of International Flag Code, which regularly proposes he/she/it/blank as subject or predicate, led her to the use of alternating pronouns as a means of de-sexualizing language. She could also avoid invoking the habitual masculine as the indefinite pronoun. It's notable that this realization arose while women Language Poets were addressing gender and language (*Poetics Journal*, ed. Lyn Hejinian and Barrett Watten, published a "gender and language" issue in 1984 (vol.1, no. 4)); that is to say, Weiner is both precursor and beneficiary of the poetics and politics of Language Poetry.

[30] *0-9* no. 6 (June 1969), p. 102.

[31] Ibid., p. 100.

[32] Bernstein includes Wiener's comments as part of a "forum" of four brief essays in *The Politics of Poetic Form* (NY: Roof Books, 1990), taking the occasion of her comments on disjunctive writing and consciousness to raise the question of the politics of form that she decidedly fails to address. This fascinating exchange illustrates why Weiner is not a "Language poet" but a crucial precursor, firmly of her generation and very unlike Bernstein for whom any instance of language use is political but can only be acknowledged as such when it is "denaturalized," or exposed in light of the frame in which it operates. Even after Bernstein stresses that the political question is that of "the *mind in action*, in [social] context, not the brain as receptor" (227), Weiner's touché returns to the discourse of "consciousness" in the abstract.

[33] Her subsequent interest in knowledge and "silent teaching" and the plight of Native Americans suggests that she came to realize that even the International Code of Signals for the Use of All Nations fails to address the fact that all senders and receivers are not created equal. See Vickery (210-211) and Damon.

[34] Unpublished mss. Mandeville Collection, UCSD, MSS 420.

[35] In "The New Theatre" Kirby uses this term to describe meaning in de-matrixed performance structures. See Sanford, p.33.

[36] My account of the fusion of poetry and conceptual art contrasts sharply

with that of Henry Sayre, who finds in the performance-oriented oral poetics of Ginsberg, Rothenberg and Antin an Olsonian proposition of words-as-event in which the poem-as-aesthetic-object gives way "to the voice of the poet speaking"(99) and it is this dematerialization of text that links the oral poetics of the 1970s avant-garde to the conceptualization and "de-objectification" of art. For Sayre, oral poetics as a form of social praxis unites performer and audience and engages community in the working through of either the "common cognitive" dilemma of narrative to the "overtly social" dilemma of ritual. In contrast, I would argue, Mayer's and Weiner's conceptual writing addresses a "dilemma" that is *both* cognitive and social.

[37] Mandeville Collection, UCSD, MSS 420.

[38] Ibid.

[39] Apparently Mayer showed considerable promise as an artist; Lucy R. Lippard included a smaller version of *Memory* in 'c. 7,500,' an exhibition of women conceptual artists that showed in several colleges and art galleries from May 1973-February 1974.

[40] Mandeville Collection, UCSD, MSS 420.

[41] These terms are from Juliana Spahr, *Everybody's Autonomy: Connective Reading and Collective Identity*, a study of "the sorts of communities [literary] works encourage"(5). She refers to the effects of poetry that encourage dynamic participation and in which reading is a form of co-production that requires (and enables) reader autonomy in an exchange of (rather than in submission to) meaning.

[42] Interview from mid-1980s with unknown. Mandeville Collection, UCSD, MSS 420.

[43] Jaynes's *The Origin of Consciousness in the Breakdown of the Bicameral Mind* (1976) begins with the assumption that in Ancient, pre-literate cultures human nature was "split" into god (executor of orders) and man (follower of orders) so that individuals did not "think" but acted "unconsciously" on the command of familiar voices or gods. Jaynes continues by addressing schizophrenia as a modern manifestation of bicamerality. Weiner wrote to Charles Bernstein on March 18, 1977, that Jaynes's work was "*a brilliant structural analysis of the brain*," explaining that in the bicameral mind of preconscious man the right hemisphere spoke, the left heard and obeyed. Mandeville Collection, UCSD, MSS 519.

[44] Letter to Bernstein, Mandeville Collection, UCSD, MSS 519.

[45] In "Mostly About the Sentence," she explains how due to the typewriter's constraints and her own limitations, she told these words they would "have to settle [themselves] in three different prints." In its published form, the typewritten underlined words of *Clairvoyant Journal* appear in italics.

[46] Weiner addresses the limits of language as socially constituted; it is this fact that makes her work a crucial link between conceptual art of the late 1960s and Language Poetry.

[47] Mandeville Collection, UCSD, MSS 519.

[48] In this sense Weiner's invocation of oral literature, based on Jaynes's scientific theories, contrasts interestingly with Olson's idealized form of subjectivity, as the figure of Maximus suggests.

Faulting Description

[1] Further references to this text will be marked parenthetically with AS.

[2] Future citations, marked parenthetically by C, are to a manuscript copy generously provided to me by Marcella Durand. The first number indicates the section; the second the page number within that section. The sections are: (1) Coolidge, "The Trip to Eldon's Cave"; (2) Mayer, "Modular?"; (3) Coolidge, "Karstarts"; (4) Mayer, "Attention to Pain or Piano"; (5) Coolidge, "Only Passage to Drain Attention within a Cell of Ordering Shortening"; (6) Mayer, "A Passage to Drain Attention or an Intermission"; (7) Coolidge, "Passage or Abruptness"; (8) Mayer, "Cave of Metonymy"; (9) Coolidge, "Sam and Floyd, Purgatory Again"; (10) Mayer, "Clark and Bernadette in the Paradise of the Last Passage"; (11) Coolidge, "Poem."

[3] The critique of description certainly has precedents in poetry. In a 1953 statement called "To Define" Robert Creeley writes that "A poetry denies its end in any *descriptive* act, I mean any act which leaves the attention outside the poem" (reprinted in *A Quick Graph: Collected Notes and Essays* [San Francisco: Four Seasons, 1970), 23. Citing this very passage in his essay "Of Theory, To Practice," Ron Silliman argues that Coolidge's early poetry "carries this to a logical conclusion" (*The New Sentence* [New York: Roof, 1987]), 58; future references to this text will be parenthetical, marked by NS.

[4] In his lecture, "Arrangement," Coolidge describes how he "became a cave explorer"(*Talking Poetics from Naropa Institute,* vol. 1. eds. Anne Waldman and Marilyn Webb [Boulder: Shambhala, 1979]), 152; future citations of this lecture will be marked parenthetically by AR. Coolidge later studied geology at Brown for two years before being turned off by the daily lives of scientists: "I remember this one guy, he was an expert on foraminifera, tiny little—they call them forams, maybe some of you know them. Tiny shelled creatures that lived in the early Paleozoic time. He went down to the basement all the time and he took these rocks and he smashed them up with a hammer and took these tiny things out and put them in trays, classifying them. That's all he did. He

didn't read the newspapers or anything. He wore gum shoes that made a funny sticking sound when he walked by" (AR, 149). But, as I will describe in what follows, Coolodge's practice as a writer will come oddly to resemble that of the basement researcher.

[5] When Coolidge suggests in "Arrangement" that "geologists *read* rocks" (AR, 154), he does not mean that this is simply a textual experience, but rather a complicated interpretation of the material world involving "the identification of mineral or fossil components, the making of a chronology of strata, a reconstruction of the original structures from the often pretty chaotic physical (sited) evidence" (Letter to the author, November 19, 2003).

[6] This is not to say that postwar American poets were not engaged with science: there is Robert Duncan's critique from the position of the hermetic tradition, as well as a whole range of Black Mountain and ecopoetic cultivations of anthropology, archaeology and biology. My point is rather that it is not until the late 1960s, with the linguistic turn in the humanities, that the linguistic bases of scientific authority become a more explicit concern for American poets.

[7] Further references to this text will be parenthetically marked with RS.

[8] In 1974 Coolidge read his unpublished "Long Prose Work" for three nights at New Langton Arts. While it is certainly arguable that Coolidge's prose was a major influence on Ron Silliman's books such as *Ketjak* and *Tjanting*, and on his concept of "the new sentence," Silliman argues that Coolidge's emphasis on the "phrase and clause" render his prose "not an example of the new sentence because it works primarily below the level of the sentence." Calling his sentences "decontextualized," Silliman claims that "Coolidge refuses to carve connotative domains from words" (NS, 88).

[9] The Authors' Page at the Electronic Poetry Center (epc.buffalo.edu/authors/coolidge) has both indexed and prepared many PDF files of Coolidge's vast amount of unpublished work; unfortunately no similar project has been undertaken as yet with Mayer's unpublished manuscripts.

[10] The very fact of these parallels works to undercut a claim, like Ann Vickery's, that gender is the only determinant in Mayer's slow reception. See *Leaving Lines of Gender: A Feminist Genealogy of Language Writing* (Hanover: Wesleyan University Press, 2000): 150-166.

[11] May 31, 1975 (Bernadette Mayer Archive, Mandeville Special Collections, University of California, San Diego).

[12] Both appear in Ron Silliman's 1986 Language writing anthology *In the American Tree*. Both were also sought out by the Language writers in the early 1970s. Bruce Andrews, for instance, begins writing to Mayer in 1973. In a June 7, 1976

letter he writes: "Am reading *Studying Hunger*—which remains a real inspiration, as illuminating as anything anybody is writing. I'm glad to be able to read it." (Bernadette Mayer Archive, Mandeville Special Collections, University of California, San Diego).

[13] Consider Lyn Hejinian's remarks in a December 15, 1983 letter to Coolidge: "I discover in myself (and I hear it from time to time in other people) a tendency to guard, as if jealously, my reading of your work—as if only *I* "got it," whatever that means. That's the best and the worst a writer can hope for, I suppose. I mean, one does hope each reader will be the single intense reader, but of course one wants there to be many of those (not millions but many)." Coolidge's response is also of interest: "Can this be largely true? And if so, what?? I hope this might mean that my work is immediately taken into that interior 'condition of writing' you speak of, instead of remaining in a more exterior state where texts are quickly exhausted in opinion etc. I hope" (December 29, 1983; Lyn Hejinian Archive, Mandeville Special Collections, University of California, San Diego).

[14] In a November 19, 2003 letter to the author Coolidge writes: "Most writing probably relates to 'place' in some way, no? I think Place got blown out of proportion, due to various academic uses of Olson in particular. Suddenly everyone was claiming 'place' for the authenticity of their poems etc."

[15] *Dictionary of Literary Biography*, ed. Joseph Conte, Vol. 193 (Detroit: Gayle Research, 1996); hereafter cited parenthetically as DB. Another useful essay is Michael Golston's "At Clark Coolidge."

[16] Mayer's work after *Studying Hunger* and *Eruditio* was generally less well received (though *The Desires of Mothers* may be an exception). While it's true, as Ann Vickery remarks, that many Language writers did see Mayer's later work as turning the domestic into a less radical "romance" (the term is Hejinian's), these writers were not alone in their reaction. Coolidge complains of "too much untransformed dailiness" (letter to Henjinian, April 21, 1983), and Howe thinks the present work "far less powerful" (letter to Hejinian, July 25, 1979).

[17] For arguments locating the turn to a relational aesthetic in Minimalism, rather than after it, see Rosalind Krauss's chapter on Minimalism in *Passages in Modern Sculpture* (Cambridge: MIT UP, 1977) and Hal Foster's essay, "The Crux of Minimalism," in *Individuals: a Selected History of Contemporary Art, 1945-1986* (New York: Abbeville, 1986).

[18] For a good history of this movement see Miwon Kwon, *One Place After Another: Site Specificity and Locational Identity* (Cambridge: MIT UP, 2002).

[19] Coolidge and Mayer were certainly not alone in their shift from the poem to

the book. Most of the Objectivists worked serially in ways that foregrounded the book as a frame; Jack Spicer, too, wrote and theorized the serial poem, as did Charles Olson.

[20] In fact it is primarily Mayer and Coolidge's insistence on working on experimental book-projects (often several hundred pages long, and in one case, in collaboration between the two) rather than on short poems that can be grouped together into collections that has kept such a large proportion of their work unpublished.

[21] Coolidge was involved with artists in a variety of ways; his magazine *Joglars* published works by Bruce Conner, Stan Brakhage, John Cage and Ian Hamilton Finlay, among others. The magazine ran 3 issues from 1964 to 1966; the first two were co-edited with Michael Palmer. Coolidge also had covers for his early books done by Jasper Johns, Brice Marden and Philip Guston, with whom Coolidge also collaborated on the book *Baffling Means*.

[22] This comes in response to Tom Orange's question, *Have you ever thought of your work in terms of conceptual art?* Coolidge's first two sentences in the response, before seeming to answer quite positively, are, however: "Not really, no. I had a brief interest in it for a while in the sixties, or was it the early seventies." Given the explicitly stated interest in Smithson, one might take the initial negation as a reluctance to have the specificity of his own work swallowed within a pre-existing discourse. See Orange's interview in *Jacket* 13.

[23] Conversation with the author, 1998.

[24] Writers included Jackson Mac Low, Harry Mathews, Jerome Rothenberg, Dick Higgins, Clark Coolidge, and both of the editors.

[25] For an account of Acconci's own writing, see Craig Dworkin's "Fugitive Signs" (*October* 95 [Winter 2001]), 91-113; more recently, Dworkin has edited *Language to Cover a Page: The Early Writings of Vito Acconci*.

[26] Kate Linker writes that "for Acconci, as for innumerable others, the appeal of the photograph lay not only in its role as a record but also in its disciplined and unsentimental manner of reporting, which accorded with a vision of the self increasingly common to contemporary art" (*Vito Acconci* [New York: Rizzoli, 1994]), 18.

[27] Further references to this work will be parenthetical, marked by M.

[28] For a chronology of Acconci's work, see Linker or *Vito Acconci*, ed. Gloria Moure (Barcelona: Ediciones Polígraga, 2001).

[29] In an August 24, 1976 letter to Jackson Mac Low, Mayer writes: "I'm teaching myself how to write a direct sentence, simple communication. Sometimes it's boring but mostly to me it's as much an experiment as anything I've ever done. I wish for feedback about my books, money and fame. So what?" (Bernadette

Mayer Archive, Mandeville Special Collections, University of California, San Diego).

30 Advocating "creating without creating a thing," the artist Michael Heizer, for instance, claims that "the position of art as malleable barter-exchange item falters as the cumulative economic structure gluts. The museums and collections are stuffed, the floors are sagging, but the real space still exists." Quoted in John Beardsley's "Introduction" to *Probing the Earth: Contemporary Land Projects* (Washington: Smithsonian, 1977), 10.

31 And while clearly the art world proved capable of recuperating seemingly non-aesthetic strategies like photography, that "contradiction" can too easily buttress a kind of cynical and inaccurate leveling of the social implications of all artistic practices.

32 It would be inaccurate, however, to understand a move toward dematerialization, emerging from a critique of art's status as a commodity, as a kind of one-way determinant in the history of the avant-garde. This is because the opposite critique, that art works of the recent past *are not material enough*—that they elide their physical basis or conditions of production—has also driven a broad range of practices, from Courbet's brush strokes to Jackson Pollock's drips; from David Smith's use of industrial fabrication methods to Robert Smithson's use of dirt and rocks.

33 Charles Bernstein's version of this tends to posit an experience of the substance of language as itself liberating; his essay "Maintaining Space: Clark Coolidge's Early Work" would be one central example: "These words take on the texture, the complexion, the materiality, the physicality of it—of language" (*Content's Dream* [Los Angeles: Sun and Moon, 1986]), 264. Bruce Andrews, on the other hand, always understands linguistic materiality within social frameworks. He writes, for instance, in "Poetry as Explanation, Poetry as Praxis": "There is nothing to explain about the words, there is nothing to explain the words. Writing makes explanation superfluous because it *is* explanation. It positions words carefully within the horizon of some outer social world. How to create an *adequacy;* how to be 'true to form'? By eliciting praxis—to carry out language's demand for prescriptions; for the Anti-Obvious. By actively pressing the 'network of differentials' in the writing itself. How to disclose & unclothe the social world: moving outward through these broader & broader layers & concentric circles of intelligibility. By a writing that counter-occludes, or counter-disguises; that politicizes by repositioning its involvement in, its intersection with, a nexus of historical relations—that is, contingent social relations, an edifice of power—which otherwise 'ceaselessly governs' it. It rewrites its material—in this case: the raw materials of a society, a collection of practices &

avowals & disavowals, governed by discourse" (*Paradise and Method: Poetics and Praxis* [Evanston: Northwestern UP, 1996]), 55.

[34] By comparison, one might consider both the conceptual clarity and the social codings Ron Silliman attributes to formal structures that underlie a book like his 1981 *Tjanting*. I discuss this work in my essay "The Labor of Repitition: Silliman's 'Quips' and Politics of Intertextuality" (in *Ron Silliman and the Alphabet* [*Quarry West* 34], 1998). Coolidge remains distant both from any consistent and programmatic use of formal devices and from Silliman's understanding of form's social coding. In a 2001 interview with Tyler Doherty (published on-line in *Jacket* 22), Coolidge advocates "the idea, probably out of Cage but also free-jazz, that you can have those blurs, you can have stuff that's in between the pitches, that's more like what they used to call noise than music. If the work lacks that I find it misses some . . . it feels like it's missing something to me. That would be one thing I would be critical I guess of with Silliman, in that it's a little too clean for me, it's a little too demarcated and has that kind of evenness to it. Sometimes it looks like a whole page of that is the same color . . . . I lose purchase on that surface. I just can't stay with it. To me it has to be full of more dirt or . . ."

[35] In Mayer's correspondence with Coolidge, the two continually evoke Godard. Both seem to identify with Godard's ability to immerse his entire life in his work. In a letter to Ed Bowes, from early 1970s, Mayer writes: "The problem with the auteur theory of movies is that in its attempt to get away from sociological views of movies it goes only halfway towards seeing movies as movies by seeing them as an art, as a personal statement by their directors and denies—not completely—their collaborativeness which is what makes them so able to tend to be not art but movies which is what they should be." (Bernadette Mayer Archive, Mandeville Special Collections, University of California, San Diego).

[36] In an October 12, 1986 letter to Nada Gordon, Mayer writes: "I did once consider publishing an edition of *Memory* with all the photos (over 1200 of them) but that is a funny story. A man from Praeger came by my house and said he could publish it (Praeger would) if only I would make love to him. I knew him from the art world a bit and he was quite attractive too, an Italian boy in a black leather jacket, etc. I told him I would love to make love to him but only if he wouldnt publish my book, and then I'm afraid I asked him to leave, so then *Memory* with all the photographs never did get published." Quoted in Gordon's *Form's Life: An Exploration of the Works of Bernadette Mayer*. This manuscript was Gordon's 1986 MA thesis at San Francisco State University. It has now been published on line at Readme.com.

[37] As Nada Gordon writes, "Mayer is observing not the past in itself but the way her emotions create the past in the present." This excerpt comes from page 2 of Gordon's chapter on *Memory* in *Form's Life*.

[38] For a wider account of conceptual art one might consult Alexander Alberro's, "Reconsidering Conceptual Art, 1966-1977." Alberro writes: "In its broadest possible definition, then, the conceptual in art means an expanded critique of the cohesiveness and materiality of the art object, a growing wariness toward definitions of artistic practice as purely visual, a fusion of the work with its site and context of display, and an increased emphasis on the possibilities of public-ness and distribution" (*Conceptual Art: A Critical Anthology,* eds. Alexander Alberro and Blake Stimson [Cambridge, MIT UP, 1999]), xvii. Smithson, however, was critical of the idea of conceptual art. In his essay "Production for Production's Sake" he writes: "Gallery development starting in the late '50s and early '60s has given rise to a cultural economics that feeds on objects and ideas through a random market. The 'market place of ideas' removes ideas from any physical reality. Because galleries and museums have been victims of 'cut-backs,' they need a cheaper product—objects are thus reduced to 'ideas,' and as a result we get 'Conceptual Art'" (RS, 378).

[39] She provides a brief overview of some procedures in "From: A Lecture at Naropa" in *Disembodied Poetics: Annals of the Jack Kerouac School* (Albuquerque: University of New Mexico Press, 1994). Further references to this text will be parenthetically marked with LN.

[40] But if desire and the social world enter the pursuit of "knowledge" in ex-perimental ways (making this an "emotional science project") Mayer's goal is not merely that of rendering science somehow subjective. Fascinated, for instance, by the fact that Albert Einstein's autobiography contains "little about his personal life" and much more "about the history of the development of the ideas that led to" (AS, 58) Einstein's own, Mayer elsewhere suggests that "it would be interesting to write about what you know and leave out the self" (LN, 101).

[41] Campbell: "Coolidge begins as a gestural painter in the tradition of the New York poets and the painters of Abstract Expressionism . . . becomes in the mid 1970s more of a Constructivist poet, only to resemble, since the early 1980s, a meditative-philosophical poet" (55).

[42] Not surprisingly the *yield* and afterlife of Coolidge's basement mining opera-tions are a frequent concern in his letters. Like Mayer, he yearns for a culture that would value and distribute his product, and often discusses musicians, filmmakers and artists by way of contrast. Responding to a question from Lyn Hejinian about why he had named his third chapbook *Clark Coolidge*, he writes:

"By the way, that CLARK COOLIDGE title came from thinking about paint-
ers' show catalogs, how they would usually have only the painter's name on the
cover and why couldn't poets do the same (?) I still admire the way painters get
to have a yearly show of the work as it develops, seems to make more sense than
poets' occasional and often rearranged volumes." (May 3, 1982; Lyn Hejinian
Archive, Mandeville Special Collections, University of California, San Diego.)
[43] Coolidge continues: "But, after ten years in this house on this tattered hill-
side I do feel like just picking up and going to live on Corfu or somewhere
improbable but famous in charm. . . . But I have all this work to do, more plans
that way than ever actually, and should hold onto a place of reasonable quiet/
non-distraction." (Bernadette Mayer Archive, Mandeville Special Collections,
University of California, San Diego.)
[44] In "Arrangement," Coolidge writes: "All right, the word 'arrangement'—hear
the word 'range' in that word—a field which I think we've been given as artists
since the fifties in this country by men as diverse as Charles Olson and John
Cage, from two sides. You might even think of them as positive and negative"
(AR, 144). Coolidge also describes his early trip to the Boston Museum of Natu-
ral History: "it was a marvelous place, a great big old red brownstone building
with dark rooms. I see them as if they were covered in black velvet inside,
and with beautiful glass cases with buttons that you push and lights come on
and wonderful objects inside. Imagine, six years old, and there it is—minerals!
Crystals, quartz, calcite, agates, opals—things; I didn't know what they were.
Push the button and see the arrangement. And the minerals themselves as an
arrangement of molecules" (AR, 147).
[45] Further references to this text will be parenthetical, marked by SD.
[46] In the 1967 essay, "Language to be Looked at and/or Things to be Read,"
Smithson writes: "An emotion is suggested and demolished in one glance by cer-
tain words. Other words constantly shift or invert themselves without ending,
these could be called 'suspended words'" (RS, 61).
[47] While Coolidge in particular often figures "discourse" as that which would
stifle poetry's unpredictable energy ("Letters so much copies they make dis-
course" [*Research*]), much of his work nonetheless relies on an idea of dis-
course—be it geological, science-fictional or art critical—as a kind of tonal
ground out of which to mine or carve exceptions, as a "straight" field to parasit-
ize and deform. Which is to agree with Coolidge that his work, like Mayer's,
is more properly described as meta-discursive, rather than simply discursive.
In a section from his notebooks published in *Code of Signals*, Coolidge writes:
"It has always puzzled me when a poet, who must / primarily expend so much
energy transforming / the common language into an irreducible variation, /

then immediately wants to break down what / he has made into the common tongue again. / As if fear of the unknown were / the mother of discourse." (177) In his book *Research* Coolidge writes: "There is never one word, there is never one image / Sound too is loose / The control of a notion / The noise of poetry" (op. cit; unpaginated).

[48] "[Judd's] own writing style has much in common with the terse, factual descriptions one finds in his collection of geology books" (RS, 18); "Judd's syntax is abyssal—it is a language that ebbs from the mind into an ocean of words. A brooding depth of gleaming surfaces—placid but dismal" (RS, 80).

[49] This passage in Judd reads: "Quite a few of my pieces have been worn out in shows, leaving me and the Castelli Gallery with the construction cost. Mostly it's accumulated damage. A few have been destroyed. A large anodized aluminum piece that was in my show at the Whitney, which cost seven thousand to make, was sent to the 4th Documenta. It was braced with wood for moving but after it arrived in Kassel, they took the wood out and moved it again, breaking most of the welds. They couldn't show it and sent it to Van der Net's factory in Holland. The factory left it outside for two years, ruined the surface, then loosely and crookedly welded it again and sprayed it with aluminum paint. It had to be destroyed. Documenta was never interested. It was awful this time too. They sent a letter that seemed to be missing its first half informing me that some small unspecified piece would be in the show and ordering me to check a bundle of papers they had sent" (DJ, 209).

[50] Judd continues: "Shows are often full of people, a few of whom are idiots. You can only stand and look, usually past someone else. No space, no privacy, no sitting or lying down, no drinking, or eating, no thinking, no living. It's all a show. It's just information. Art is kept isolated and half visible. . . . At the opening of a show I had at the Pasadena Museum I counted sixty-four mistakes in the catalogue" (DJ, 210).

[51] From correspondence it appears that Coolidge and Mayer first came into contact in 1965 when Mayer sent Coolidge work for his magazine *Joglars*, which ran 3 issues between 1964 and 1966. In a letter dated Nov 28, that begins "Dear Bernadette Mayer" and thus seems to initiate Coolidge's end of what would be a rich and extensive correspondence, he writes: "Thanks for sending poems & thanks for waiting! I like them, and will select one or two for use in Jog#3. Hope to let you know definitely by Xmas and send back what I don't use" (UCSD). Mayer's chronology of her life in *Studying Hunger* lists her actual meeting with Coolidge as occurring in 1968. By the late 1970s the two wrote to each other weekly, Coolidge's letters almost always taking up the entirety of two small margin pages, front and back.

[52] The only published sections are Coolidge's "Karstarts," the third piece, and Mayer's "The Cave of Metonymy," the eighth. Mayer's piece was published in Alan Davies's *Oculist Witnesses,* (#3, 1976). "Kartsarts" was published in Barrett Watten and Robert Grenier's *this* 5, 1974.

[53] Mayer writes: "the reason I didnt enter the cave was that i suffered from an overwhelming fear & clark found out later in his readings (though he never mentions it 'in public' that women who have their periods, as i did) are enjoined from entering caves, i was bleeding profusely[.]" (December 6, 2003 letter to the author). Inside, Susan and Celia turn back (after discussion about Celia possibly getting too tired), and then eventually Ed and Clark fear that their lights may go out and so turn around before reaching the end: "No good to get stuck without some kind of light in here. Ed says he feels a bit tired & claustrophobic at this juncture so we decide to turn back" (C, 1:3).

[54] It's important to note that, despite their consistent project of destabilizing description, both cared a great deal about accuracy. Coolidge would write, for instance, a few years after their Cave project, and seemingly in response to something Mayer had said about *Smithsonian Depositions*: "Pardon a pickish mineralogical correction? Smithsonite is zinc carbonate, not silicate" (Aug 21, 1980, Bernadette Mayer Archive; Mandeville Special Collections, University of California, San Diego).

[55] The title is a representative collision of mechanics and geology in language; audibly it evokes "car starts," a scene of ignition—a sense which extends meta-poetically, but also paradoxically, into the idea of the cave (which must be visited on foot or even on one's hands and knees) as an area of fascination that would seem to power Coolidge's poetic cylinders. But the title also references the poem's geological foundations more explicitly, since the project itself makes *art* out of a "karst," which, as Webster's tells us, is an "area of irregular limestone in which erosion has produced fissures, sinkholes, underground streams, and caverns." Such a list quickens Coolidge's pulse. Exploring such an underground cavern, confronting its alterity with a language whose descriptive moment frequently turns back on the almost geologic substance and foreign-ness of its own terms, is the "karst art" of the poem. And yet it is important to the semantic complex that Coolidge creates through his neologism that neither "car starts" nor "karst arts" is clear visually. Instead, Coolidge insists both on an oscillation between the two senses and, through the slight graphic and sonic alterity of the mined non-word, a kind of sedimentary remainder that keeps the title from reducing itself seamlessly into what he would call "discourse."

[56] Coolidge writes: "Multiplied expressions enclose ordinary language. Impon-derable roofs precipitate chalks. Office cracks, both perfectly preserved and

performed, older than our heads conflict" (C, 5:7).

[57] In "Karstarts," for instance, Coolidge references phrases of Mayer's including "swells of being" (C, 3:7); "we have lotsa money" (C, 3:6); "the pleasure of denial" (ibid.); "iron feldspar" (C, 3:9); and "The trouble with style is an endless surround" (C, 3:10). The quotational quality of this phrase accumulation is crucial to the development of *The Cave:* in fact, it is through the series of appropriations and substitutions that the two authors produce less a collaboration *about* a cave than a collaboration *as* a cave. As Coolidge writes: "Geologists say the Taconics were composed of letters from a to z. Some fields get fired up. Some chickens were originally laid down. Pages were pushed up and over them" (C, 3:19). Enclosed by a series of pages "pushed up and over them," this "passage" becomes a kind of geological/literary space that figuratively encloses the poets, constructed out of their own texts, which keep poking through and becoming the surface. This play on "passage" is mobilized throughout the manuscript: "Only the passage that is defined is in pain" (C, 4:4).

[58] As Mayer writes: "We'll call it impossible to use leaves as you show movement you slide the cave down the solutions to mathematical problems as they stand in relation to the context & ground of their formulation" (C, 4:3). Presenting itself initially as a claim about the impossibility of showing movement in language, this sentence moves from the more distanced stance of calling the description of movement impossible to a more impacted linguistic analogy for this impossibility.

[59] But it is not only phrases and words that provide the raw material for Coolidge and Mayer's cave. In fact, the two shift syntactical patterns as a way to respond to previous stages: Coolidge moves, for instance, from narrative to his new sentence-like abstraction, to a kind of run-on inclusive syntax that plays off Mayer's, eventually to dialog. This final shift is a response to Mayer's introduction of dialog in section seven—one of the most striking shifts, or new "passages," in *The Cave.* Here, Mayer has Herman Melville and Nathaniel Hawthorne debate about Coolidge's sentences. Responding to Melville's recitation, Hawthorne complains that Melville is "just picking out all the abstractions" (C, 8:5) and citing the lines—"Give your codpieces, every one of them, a real demonstration" and "Wittgenstein tossed & turned"—proposes that Coolidge "likes sex more, or even anguish" (ibid.). After Melville calls Hawthorne "naïve" and the latter retorts that Melville is being too "sociological" (C, 8:6), Mayer's daughter Sophie comes in (along with Louis Malle) to resolve the argument, Sophie glossing Wittgenstein as "the great progenitor of all real interpretation, scientific *and* literary" and "the fine & generous restorer

here of the famous 'endless room' referred to in the work" (C, 8:7). Coolidge first responds with a similarly bizarre dialog between the cave explorer Floyd Collins and Beckett.

Anne Waldman

[1] "Women's mobility is an important means through which the reconfigurations of the modern female subject are textually represented: modern women may 'move dangerously,' but their journeys situate women at the heart of modernity and remind us that, as [Ernst] Bloch wrote 'one has one's time according to where one stands corporeally.'" This is cited from and article by Wendy Parkins, whose interest in women defining modernity has been influenced by Rita Felski.

[2] This essay is published in the book *100 Days*, a title that refers to the first 100 days of the Bush appointed-presidency.

[3] Charles Olson, in *Charles Olson and Ezra Pound: An Encounter at St. Elizabeths*. Olson means this as apart from "the vomit of his conclusions," 18.

[4] I am assimilating the terms merriness and chiaroscuro from Rosi Braidotti, *Nomadic Subjects: Embodiment and Sexual Difference in Contemporary Feminist Theory*, New York: Columbia University Press, 1994, 167.

[5] And another thing going on right now: over the past 25-35 years, a tremendous input in women, of a variety of opinions, writing very very long book-length poems. Here is a partial list: Diane di Prima, *Loba*, Diane Wakoski, *Greed*; Bernadette Mayer, *Midwinter Day*; Sharon Doubiago, *Hard Country*; Susan Howe, *The Liberties*; Beverly Dahlen, *A Reading*; Susan Griffin, *Women and Nature: The Roaring Inside Her*; Alice Notley, *The Descent of Alette*; Lyn Hejinian, *My Life* (and *Oxota*), Anne Waldman, *Iovis*; Harryette Mullen, *Muse and Drudge*; Rachel Blau DuPlessis, *Drafts*.

[6] There is no doubt these works are linked. Notley's thinking on epic, her narrative strategies within the mythopoetic, her desire for a world-transformative analysis of patriarchy links and interwines with Waldman's thinking on epic, her encyclopedic strategies for the mythopoetic, her analysis of patriarchy. Notley also produced a subtle, apt, discerning, empathetic study of Iovis in *Chicago Review*. There is a further link, a deep curiosity of literary history. Frances Boldereff, by the force of her enthusiasm and knowledge, made Charles Olson look at Sumerian materials from Samuel Noah Kramer, the great archeologist and historian. Some of that material involved *Inanna*, the mother goddess epic, one of the great poems of world literature with a female quester. Under the influence of feminist desire and curiosity, about thirty-five years later, a

stunning retelling of *Inanna* was published (in 1983) by Diane Wolkstein, based on Kramer's scholarship. This was rather fervently read; indeed, this epic of female quest was highly influential. Of these long poems, it influenced Grahn, Notley, and Waldman.

[7] One can point, now, to a strong set of collected essays by poets, critical books (all or parts) and special issues working on the reception of women "experimental" writers of all kinds, books including Kathleen Fraser, *Translating the Unspeakable: Poetry and the Innovative Necessity*. Tuscaloosa: University of Alabama Press, 2000; Lyn Hejinian, *The Language of Inquiry*. Berkeley: University of California Press, 2000. Joan Retallack, *The Poethical Wager*, Berkeley: University of California Press, 2003; Rachel Blau DuPlessis, *The Pink Guitar: Writing as Feminist Practice*. New York: Routledge, 1990 and the forthcoming *Blue Studios: Poetry and Its Cultural Work*; Lynn Keller, *Forms of Expansion: Recent Long Poems by Women*. University of Chicago Press, 1997; Ann Vickery, *Leaving Lines of Gender: A Feminist Genealogy of Language Writing*. Wesleyan/ New England, 2000; Linda A. Kinnahan, *Lyric Interventions: Feminism, Experimental Poetry, and Contemporary Discourse*. University of Iowa Press, 2004; Elisabeth A. Frost, *The Feminist Avant-Garde in American Poetry*. University of Iowa Press, 2003; Laura Hinton and Cynthia Hogue, eds., *We Who Love to Be Astonished: Experimental Women's Writing and Performance Poetics*. Tuscaloosa: University of Alabama Press, 2002; Steve Evans, ed. *differences* 12. 2 (Summer 2001), special issue: *After Patriarchal Poetry: Feminism and the Contemporary Avant-Garde;* Patricia Dienstfrey and Brenda Hillman, eds., *The Grand Permission: New Writings on Poetics and Motherhood*. Middletown, CT: Wesleyan University Press, 2003.

[8] See DuPlessis, *H.D.: The Career of that Struggle*, 1986. H.D.'s "epic" clearly had an impact on Waldman's conception of *Iovis*. Along with the encyclopedaism (alluding to Pound, Williams and Olson), Waldman has made several key allusions to H.D.'s *Helen in Egypt*. Stylistically the poems are exceedingly different—even opposite, as H.D.'s is a centered, dreamlike but narrative-meditative reflection on one central myth of Western culture: the fault of Helen of Troy in triggering one of the key culturally and politically formative wars in our tradition. H.D.'s poem is centered, regular and, while spiritual, non-vatic. But Waldman learned from and alluded to several specific elements of H.D.'s poem. One is in the general reflection on women in a mythologically charged site. Another is the creation of a quester speaker who is a thamaturge, responsible for rites of naming and envisioning. Another is a specific rhetorical strategy that is very clarifying: of having a headnote, a box of italicized information, that explains the work of the canto to come, doubling its argument in allusive prose and then in poetry.

[9] My analysis in *Writing Beyond the Ending*, that in kunstlerromans, female heroes often complete the incompleted work of thwarted parents seems germane here.

[10] About the operatic, one may link this, pertinently, to the computer. Waldman feels with *Iovis* the impact of the computer; she says "it is like a theater, a magic movie screen. You have all of these little players to move around [referring to sections of poems]. It is like an opera." (*AWP Chronicle* interview with Lee Christopher, 4)

[11] Given the breadth of materials and of years over which such a poem is composed, one might find some of its genres are conflictual (narrative and notes; sequence and collage; sestina and letter). The absorption and transcending of conflicts in this poem's space would be this poem's method. A writer may throw out a variety of analogies for the work of encyclopedic form, analogies that are always right, of course, but always incomplete. Despite the fiercely febrile performativeness of the work, Waldman has also called it a temple ("Go Between Between") meaning a plurality of nooks and crannies, a "catholic" space in which the sacred dwells in every spot—and in which worship and exorcism can occur. There are other analogies besides shrine or temple. In a lecture in 1996, she calls *Iovis* a totem pole. This last analogy is appealing in its frank phallicism—and in its quasi-Jungian cast of poised characters stacked like masks on the pole. Both these analogies are very spatialized and at interplay with the performative, aria/cantata sense of a poem cut into time for performance.

[12] A little touch of Marjorie Perloff in her Futurist book, but I am mainly drawing on Janet Lyon's *Manifestoes: Provocations of the Modern*, 16.

[13] People sometimes call these poems epics. This is the subject of a very important comment made by Alice Notley on the matter of *Iovis*, that does have epic themes (love and war). Notley makes two propositions. She says that it is conventional to call Olson's, Pound's and Williams's work Epic (as a metaphor), and therefore Waldman must be accorded the same rights, as she emphatically works in this tradition. But Notley suggests (and I have long agreed) that a strict definition of the term epic would exclude these modern long poems, though not the work of H.D.: the definition of Notley is that it is a narrative that does cultural service. By the way, this implicitly makes *The Descent of Alette* an epic moment—that is using the "desent to the underworld" part of epics—the nekuia—as the whole story.

[14]
> I use words as my table, as a kind of shrine
> I sweep over the care of the words
> They take care of themselves
> I sweep them under my demand (*Iovis* I 119)

Scope is here in conflict with being through-composed. This is the challenge, par excellence, for the writer of the long poem.

"fucking / me across the decades like we / poets like"

[1] It should be said, however, that the Langton venue was occasionally the site where incipient Language poetic practices bumped against other practices. I'm thinking especially of the talk David Antin gave in the Talk Series I curated. At that event, uniquely as far as I know, his talk piece morphed into a large argumentative interchange with the audience. I discuss this in "Speech Effects: the Talk as a Genre," in *Close Listening: Poetry and the Performed Word*, edited by Charles Bernstein. Oxford: Oxford UP, 1998.

[2] Thanks to Daniel Kane for reminding me of such points.

[3] I take this citation from Matt Hart's dissertation, "Synthetic Vernacular and Transatlantic Modernism."

[4] Incidentally, I suspect that Alice B. Toklas stitched "A rose is a rose is a rose" in a circle on Stein's panties. At least that is the salacious undertone I read in Toklas's statement: "Speaking of the device of rose is a rose is a rose is a rose, it was I who found it in one of Gertrude Stein's manuscripts and insisted upon putting it as a device on the letter paper, on the table linen and anywhere that she would permit that I would put it." [*Autobiography*, 130]

[5] I ask (or, more precisely, I have an imagined Roland Barthes ask) a similar question concerning the statement made by "the narrator" in "Une Journée be Juillet": "I suck off every man in the Manhattan Storage Warehouse." See my *Marginalization of Poetry*, 163-4.

'A generous time'

[1] The author would like to express thanks to Sandy Berrigan, Anne Waldman, Lewis Warsh, and—especially—Lee Harwood, for their detailed, illuminating and generous responses to my many questions about the New York poetry scene in the mid-late 1960s.

[2] Harwood, letter to author, 7th April 2004.

[3] "In the early summer of 1965 . . . I was filled with French poetry—Tristan Tzara, Max Jacob, the Dadaists, Alfred Jarry, Rimbaud." Harwood had visited Tzara in Paris in 1963, and translated his poetry.

[4] "New York will welcome me" is an earlier poem than "Summer," which is dated "london aug 65" in *The Man With Blue Eyes*.

[5] David Herd has noted how "The Instruction Manual" is a poem that introduces

"the reader to a place the writer has never visited" in his *John Ashbery and American Poetry* (48). John Shoptaw's *On The Outside Looking Out: John Ashbery's Poetry* (39), notes the Americanness of this poem and quotes Ashbery describing the poem's long lines as being like the easygoingness of Walt Whitman.

[6] The poem is untitled in *The Man With Blue Eyes*; its first line provides its "title" here. Though it is the opening poem of the collection it is dated significantly later—"london 11-21 oct 65"—than all but the final five poems of the collection. Robert Sheppard, *Some Aspects of Contemporary British Poetry: With Particular Reference to the Works of Roy Fisher and Lee Harwood* (329) has noted that this is Harwood's "first mature poem."

[7] Olson's essay "Equal, That Is, To the Real Itself," appears in his *Selected Prose*, pp. 46-52.

[8] Harwood has noted the importance of Ashbery's magazine *Locus Solus* on his early poetic development. For more information on *Locus Solus*, see Mark Ford's *John Ashbery in Conversation with Mark Ford* , pp. 45-6.

[9] John Ashbery's dust-wrapper blurb for *The White Room* (London: Fulcrum, 1968).

[10] Ashbery, ibid.

[11] See "Harwood Bibliography," *Poetry Info*, 14 (Autumn-Winter, 1975), pp. 17-18; and Harwood (1994), p. 143.

[12] Lewis Warsh, in an email to the author, 3rd April, 2004, noted, "Anne [Waldman] and I started *Angel Hair* magazine in 1966, & quickly began contemplating publishing books. MWBE was the first book we did. It was supposed to be done by Peter Schjeldahl's Mother Books but I think Peter was losing interest in being a publisher. So there was the mss., and Lee came to New York, we met him, & decided to do the book. Joe [Brainard] did many covers for many of the small press books in New York in the '60s & '70s, and I'm sure he had met Lee. We did the cover on the same Fabriano paper we used for *Angel Hair* magazine but Joe was surprised (despite the title) that we printed his cover on blue paper. It was our first book so we were experimenting with everything."

[13] This is reiterated in a letter to the author, 7th April, 2004, where Harwood states, "what Ashbery showed me was a whole approach and perspective in writing that was an immense release for me. A 'Yes!' The idea of creating a text that readers could pick up and use and wander around in. A text that didn't depend on the writer's own life, but was a real creation. A collage like poem that could pull in or push out whatever it liked, and in a way leaving the reader to sort out a lot of the material, to be involved in the process of writing, the creating."

[14] John Shoptaw notes that Ashbery composed this poem between 'the fall of 1963 and the spring of 1964' and that it "first appeared in the fall of 1964 in *Art and Literature.*" Shoptaw, p. 89. The poem subsequently appeared in the collection *Rivers and Mountains* (1966). David Herd discusses the poem, pp. 109-113; and Bonnie Costello analyses it in terms of ideas of Landscape in her essay "John Ashbery's Landscapes," in *The Tribe of John: Ashbery and Contemporary Poetry.*

[15] This poem was reprinted in Harwood's *Landscapes*, pp. 12-13.

[16] Benjamin Friedlander's excellent essay, "Strange Fruit: O'Hara, Race and the Color of Time," is the first reading of this poem that seriously engages the issue of colour and race in relation to O'Hara's "profound jest" over the colour "orange" in this poem.

[17] "When The Geography Was Fixed," first appeared in *The White Room*, pp. 90-1.

[18] Ibid, p. 22.

[19] See also Weatherhead, p. 178 who comments on the "throwaway" nature of this line.

[20] In a letter to the author (7th May, 2005) Harwood notes: "The lay-out of these poems in *Landscapes* was suggested by—besides the experiments with lay-out used by Pound and other 'Modernists' as well as Dada poets such as Tzara—the work of the poet Joseph Ceravolo. In his first book, *Fits of Dawn*, published by Ted Berrigan's C Press in 1965 and in later poems in mags and books he used this lay-out that I also used in the 'Question of Geography' poem."

[21] See also Sheppard, unpublished thesis, p. 338.

[22] See Sheppard, unpublished thesis, where Harwood notes, "The war in Vietnam didn't seem to be a major preoccupation of the poets on the New York 'scene' then. (And here I'm only talking about poets associated with the New York School, St. Marks Poetry project, etc.) But it was always there in the background and I think everyone was very aware of it, but it just didn't show up in the actual poems. The general feeling was against directly political poetry. But in practical matters it was there in things like being called up for the draft board. I remember Peter Schjeldahl and Joe Brainard and other friends having to report and all trying different ways to be rejected" (338). The chapter "Forms of Action" in David Herd's *John Ashbery and American Poetry* is a fascinating and subtle analysis of the political commitments of New York poetry in the face of the conflict in Vietnam. Like Harwood, he perceives a gap between the general sense of the war being always there in the background and a "directly political poetry." He invokes George Oppen's distinction between "the action of poetry and the action of protest" as a means of clarifying how the war occasioned a

troubled negotiation amongst various New York school poets of the gap between aesthetic demands and political pressures (esp. pp. 93-100).

[23] See Herd, pp. 93-100.

[24] The poem appears in *Landscapes*, pp. 25-7.

Spring in This World of Mad Angels

[1] There are a number of non-scholarly essays about Ceravolo, among them essays by Lita Hornick, Charles North, and Ron Silliman (see Works Cited).

[2] We regret, in particular, that the person who knew him best, Rosemary Ceravolo, declined our request for an interview. For the purposes of this essay, David Shapiro, Ron Padgett, and Paul Violi were interviewed in March and April of 2003.

[3] For more on this, see Libbie Rifkin's account of Berrigan and "C" Press in *Career Moves*, p. 132.

[4] Nevertheless, issues of coterie affiliation are always tricky. For example, a letter to the editor written by John Bernard Myers, correcting Stephen Koch's use of the phrase "The New York School of Poets," situates Ceravolo within the first-generation nexus: "As discoverer, editor and publisher of the entire group which consists also of Barbara Guest, Kenward Elmslie, James Schuyler, Bill Berkson, Frank Lima, Joseph Ceravolo and Tony Towle I have been careful not to call them by this name, and use instead the Poets of the New York School" (22).

[5] It should be noted, particularly in the context of *Transmigration Solo*, that it is often difficult to date Ceravolo's published poems. *The Green Lake is Awake* selection complicates this problem by observing no recognizable chronology with respect to Ceravolo's poems. Nonetheless, we can be fairly certain that the poems in *Transmigration Solo* are the earliest published Ceravolo poems that we have. Ceravolo, when he did date his poems, also sometimes misdated them, and we know that Ceravolo revised some of his poems over long periods of time. There are at least two substantially divergent published versions of "Ho Ho Ho Caribou," for instance. The best known version of "Ho Ho Ho Caribou" is printed in *Spring in This World of Poor Mutts*; this version is also included in *The Paris Review* (see Works Cited). Another version of the poem titled "Leaped at the Caribou . . ." appears in the Tom Clark-edited journal *Slice*. Advertised as "a one shot magazine" with "no copyright no nothing," *Slice* is undated, but most likely dates from 1965 or 1966. For more on Clark's Once series, see Clay and Phillips (191). A notable example of misdating occurs with Ceravolo's long poem "Apollo in the Night," which appears in the 1982 *Millennium Dust* (73-81). Ceravolo gives the dates of composition as being 1964/1972; however, a signifi-

cantly different version of the poem appears in *Adventures in Poetry #11* (Spring 1974) under the title "Water Over Stones" (unpaginated).

[6] Book III of *Fits of Dawn*, which is significantly more approachable, is included in *The Green Lake is Awake*. "The Green Lake is Awake," it should be noted, is a title that Ceravolo himself recycled. The title appears alone on its own page at the opening of Book III of *Fits of Dawn*, but it is also the title of a completely unrelated poem in *Spring in This World of Poor Mutts*.

[7] Ron Padgett and Paul Violi recall that Ceravolo once puzzled an audience at a 92nd St Y reading by handing out worksheets and diagrams for the construction of highways and viaducts. This likely had more to do with Rosemary Ceravolo's performance art than with Ceravolo's poetry.

[8] Ron Padgett recalls that he, Ted Berrigan, and Ceravolo (along with members of their respective families) made a pilgrimage to the Williams's home not long after his death, and were invited in for tea by Flossie Williams.

[9] Five Frank O'Hara Award books were published in all, beginning with *Spring in This World*. Columbia University Press would issue a Frank O'Hara Award book a year for the next three years: Michael Brownstein's *Highway to the Sky*, Tony Towle's *North*, and Kenward Elmslie's *Motor Disturbance*. The last prize was awarded in 1973, going to John Koethe for his book *Domes*. All five books were to have been reissued by Full Court Press in the late seventies, but the project never materialized.

[10] Epstein argues this particularly in the context of O'Hara, Ashbery, and Baraka. See *Against Fixity: Individualism and Friendship in Twentieth-Century American Poetry* (PhD Dissertation, Columbia University, 2001).

[11] The first sentence of Lehman's book is: "The story of the New York School of poets is a study in friendship, artistic collaboration, and the bliss of being alive and young at a moment of maximum creative ferment" (1).

[12] Originally included on an LP in the journal *Mother 9* (Spring 1968), this recording is now available on the companion CD to Daniel Kane's *All Poets Welcome*.

Charles North's Adventures in Poetry

[1] See Kane for an in-depth look at how individual personalities like Waldman, Mayer, and Bob Holman galvanized other writers into action.

[2] See Kane, chapter 6: "Bernadette Mayer and 'Language' in the Poetry Project" for a discussion of some Language Poets' goals and their rejection of lyric expressivism and the personal.

[3] Originally written in couplets, this text appears here without virgules for easier reading.

The Other Poet

[1] Thanks to John Wilkinson, John Temple and Jim Dunn for their comments on earlier versions of this essay.

[2] John Wieners, letter to the Black Mountain College Registrar, 1955, Charles Olson–John Wieners Papers 1952–1968, f. 45, John J. Burns lib., Boston College.

[3] Charles Olson, telegram to John Wieners, 30 March 1955, Charles Olson–John Wieners Papers 1952–1968, f. 6, John J. Burns lib., Boston College.

[4] John Wieners, "To Ross" (unpublished poem), John Wieners Papers Series I f. 9, Thomas J. Dodd Research Center, University of Connecticut, Storrs, CT.

[5] See for example Meyer, 241-57.

[6] Charles Olson, letter to John Wieners, 6 Oct. 1964, Charles Olson–John Wieners Papers 1952–1968, f. 21, John J. Burns lib., Boston College.

[7] In a testimonial which Berkson solicited and Olson dated 26 April 1969, Olson said "I believe it was Frank who was chiefly responsible that I was invited to read at Spoleto, the following summer–and himself didn't go" (Berkson and LeSueur 178).

[8] Olson notes in a letter: "Lawrence, e.g., is clearer on this point: he was *psychically* serious. Civ'n? well, sd DHL, ok. *After*. But 1st, le soleil de la flesh. As Rimbaud." Charles Olson, letter, 23 Dec. 1956, Charles Olson Research Collection Series II, Thomas J. Dodd Research Center, University of Connecticut, Storrs, CT.

[9] Wieners says that in his youth he had to choose between homosexual pleasure and "organized religion and a possible salvation after death." But he decided "even to lose that–my salvation–I decided I would forego it–for the sake of being frequently in the company of persons who qualified as professionally competent" (*Selected* 299).

[10] Wieners's "Letters" (*Behind the State Capitol* 79) offers a distinctly paranoid account of playing "copus superlative robbers up and down NY STS", as he tried not to lead the goons following him "back to Poet Frank and Joseph O'Hara's [*sic*]", where he arrives "out of my wits, consult. eager colloquy" with O'Hara and LeSeur [*sic*]."

[11] Asked by Bockris-Wylie if he "dressed the part," Wieners promised that "If I had more money, I wouldn't be allowed to go out on the streets" (*Cultural Affairs* 139). Raymond Foye described his appearance at a class on Olson taught by Bill Corbett: "On the day of the lecture, he arrived wearing red high heels, pink hotpants, a ladies 1940s tuxedo jacket w. rhinestone buttons, white Brooks Brothers shirt & bow tie, & a Nehru cap. And red lipstick. He lectured in won-

derfully erudite manner for about an hour, and then answered questions from the students. When one student asked why he was dressed this way, he simply replied, "It's an experiment," & moved on to the next question." Raymond Foye, letter to Neeli, 1984, John Wieners Papers, Series II f. 1, Thomas J. Dodd Research Center, University of Connecticut, Storrs, CT.

[12] John Wieners, letter to Charles Olson, 22 Sept. 1957, Charles Olson Research Collection Series II, Thomas J. Dodd Research Center, University of Connecticut, Storrs, CT.

[13] Raymond Foye, letter to Kevin Killian, 10 Nov. 1984, John Wieners Papers, Series II f. 1, Thomas J. Dodd Research Center, University of Connecticut, Storrs, CT.

[14] John Wieners, letter to Diane di Prima, 16 Feb. 1966, John Wieners Papers, MS 138 Series I f. 2, University of Delaware lib., Newark, DE.

[15] In the 1950s, electro-shock therapy, insulin comas, and barbiturates were the few methods used to treat schizophrenia, before the inception of chlorpromazine and other phenothiazines (neuroleptic drugs).

[16] John Wieners, diary entry, 27 Sept. 1965, John Wieners Papers, MS 138 Series I f. 6, University of Delaware lib., Newark, DE.

[17] Charles Olson, letter to John Wieners, 13 March 1958, Charles Olson–John Wieners Papers 1952–1968, f. 15, John J. Burns lib., Boston College.

[18] For the influence on Wieners of such older poets as Sara Teasdale and Edna St. Vincent Millay, see Wilkinson.

[19] John Wieners, diary entry, John Wieners Papers, MS 138 Series I f. 6, University of Delaware lib., Newark, DE.

[20] Charles Olson, letter to Michael Rumaker, 23 Dec. 1956, Charles Olson Research Collection Series II, Thomas J. Dodd Research Center, University of Connecticut, Storrs, CT.

[21] John Wieners, letter to Hank Chapin, 1 April 1962, John Wieners Papers, Series II f. 14, Thomas J. Dodd Research Center, University of Connecticut, Storrs, CT.

[22] John Wieners, unsent letter to Charles Olson, 8 Feb. 1956, Charles Olson–John Wieners Papers 1952–1968, f. 46, John J. Burns lib., Boston College.

[23] Charles Olson, letter to John Wieners, 14 Feb. 1959, Charles Olson–John Wieners Papers 1952–1968, f. 16, John J. Burns lib., Boston College.

[24] John Wieners, diary entry, John Wieners Papers, MS 138 Series I f. 6, University of Delaware lib., Newark, DE.

[25] Perhaps this remark was in Wieners's ear when he wrote in "A poem for cocksuckers" that "it's a nigger's world/ and we retain strength" (*Selected* 36).

[26] John Wieners, letter to George Minkoff, 20 Nov. 1968, John Wieners Papers,

Series II f. 11, Thomas J. Dodd Research Center, University of Connecticut, Storrs, CT.

[27] He revised these poems to suppress some of their violence, changing "and then the knife" to "and then the night," for example. John Wieners, journal, John Wieners Papers, MS 138 Series I f. 6, University of Delaware lib., Newark, DE; "Alcohol doesn't ease the pain nor . . .", *Selected* 223.

[28] John Wieners, letter to Bill, 28 Oct. 1967, Charles Olson–John Wieners Papers 1952–1968, f. 56, John J. Burns lib., Boston College.

Rachel Blau DuPlessis, Professor at Temple University, is a feminist critic and scholar with a special interest in modern and contemporary poetry, a poet and an essayist. Recent critical books by DuPlessis are *Genders, Races, and Religious Cultures in Modern American Poetry, 1908-1934* (Cambridge University Press, 2001) and *Blue Studios: Poetry and Its Cultural Work* (University of Alabama Press, 2006); Alabama also reprinted DuPlessis's classic work *The Pink Guitar* in 2006. Her recent books of poetry are *Drafts 1-38, Toll* (Wesleyan University Press, 2001) and *DRAFTS. Drafts 39-57, Pledge with Draft, Unnumbered: Précis* (Salt Publishing, 2004). *Torques: Drafts 58-76* is forthcoming.

Andrea Brady is a lecturer at Brunel University, and a specialist in early modern elegy, ritual, and the poetry of the seventeenth century. Her book *English Funerary Elegy in the Seventeenth Century* was published by Palgrave Macmillan in 2006. She also writes about contemporary innovative poetry of the US and UK, and has published and performed her own poetry widely; in addition, she runs a small poetry press, Barque.

Andrew Epstein is the author of *Beautiful Enemies: Friendship and Postwar American Poetry* (Oxford University Press, 2006), which focuses on Frank O'Hara, Amiri Baraka, and John Ashbery. He received his Ph.D. from Columbia University and is currently an Assistant Professor at Florida State University. His essays, reviews, and poems have appeared in various journals, including *Contemporary Literature, Lingua Franca, Verse,* and *Raritan.*

Daniel Kane is Lecturer in American Literature at the University of East Anglia. He is the author of *All Poets Welcome: The Lower East Side Poetry Scene in the 1960s* (University of California, 2003) and *What is Poetry: Conversations with the American Avant-Garde* (Teachers & Writers, 2003). He has contributed essays, reviews and poems to journals including *Contemporary Literature, The Poetry Project Newsletter, The Denver Quarterly, Fence,* and *TriQuarterly.*

Gary Lenhart is the author of five collections of poetry, including *Father and Son Night* (Hanging Loose, 1999), and *Light Heart* (Hanging Loose, 1991). His most recent book is *The Stamp of Class: Reflections on Poetry and Social Class* (U. of Michigan Press, 2006). He has contributed poems, essays, and reviews to many magazines and anthologies, and edited the magazines *Mag City* and *Transfer*. He also edited *Clinch: Selected Poems of Michael Scholnick* (Coffee House, 1998), *The Teachers &Writers Guide to William Carlos Williams* (1998), and *The T&W Guide to Classic American Literature* (2001).

Patrick Masterson was born in Louisville, KY and studied at Bard College and Columbia University. A Windgate Fellow in the book arts, he currently attends the University of Alabama and prints and edits *The Rest*.

Jon Panish is the author of *The Color of Jazz: Race and Representation in Postwar American Culture* (University of Mississippi, 1997). He teaches English at Palomar College in San Marcos, California.

Bob Perelman has published 16 books of poetry, including *Ten to One: Selected Poems* (Wesleyan), *The Future of Memory* (Roof), and a painting/poem collaboration with Francie Shaw, *Playing Bodies* (Granary Books); *In a Mean Time* will be published by Roof in 2006. His critical books are *The Trouble With Genius: Reading Pound, Joyce, Stein and Zukofsky* (California) and *The Marginalization of Poetry: Language Writing and Literary History* (Princeton). He has edited two collections of poets' talks: *Hills Talks* and *Writing/Talks* (Southern Illinois). He teaches at the University of Pennsylvania.

Jed Rasula is the Helen S. Lanier Distinguished Professor of English at the University of Georgia. Among his books are *Syncopations: The Stress Of Innovation In Contemporary American Poetry* (2004), *The American Poetry Wax Museum* (1996), *And This Compost: Ecological Imperatives In American Poetry* (2002).

Linda Russo is a graduate of the Poetics Program at the University at Buffalo and a contributing editor of *HOW2*, a journal of experimental writing by women. She is the author of several chapbooks of poetry including *Solvency* (publisher unknown, 2005) and *o going out* (potes and poets, 1999). She teaches at The University of Oklahoma.

Nick Selby is Lecturer in American Literature at the University of Glasgow. He has written widely on American literature and poetry and is the author of *From Modernism to Fascism: Poetics of Loss in The Cantos of Ezra Pound* (Edwin Mellen Press, 2005). His book, *Dazzling Geographies: American Poetics in Ezra Pound, Gary Snyder and Jorie Graham* is forthcoming. He is Director of the Andrew Hook Centre for American Studies in Glasgow.

Lytle Shaw is author of the poetry books *Cable Factory 20* (Atelos, 1999), *The Lobe* (2002) as well as the critical study, *Frank O'Hara: The Poetics of Coterie* (Iowa University Press, 2006). He lives in New York City and teaches American literature at New York University.

Paul Stephens lives in New York City, where he recently earned a PhD in English at Columbia University. He teaches at Bard College.

Lorenzo Thomas was born in Panama and grew up in New York City, where he studied at Queens College. Thomas was a founding member of the *Umbra* writing collective. He served in the Vietnam War, and later worked as a professor at the University of Houston-Downtown. Lorenzo was a widely published poet and critic whose works appeared in many journals including *Umbra, African American Review, Living Blues, Partisan Review,* and *Ploughshares.* His poetry books include *Chances Are Few, The Bathers,* and *Dancing on Main Street*; he also edited the Teachers & Writers Collaborative book *Sing the Sun Up: Creative Writing Ideas from African American Literature.* He was an Associate Professor of English at the University of Houston-Downtown for many years. He died on the Fourth of July, 2005.

Harry Thorne teaches English at the College of Staten Island. He has published essays, reviews and poems in a number of publications including *Textual Practice, How2, Jacket* and *Chain.*

SELECTED DALKEY ARCHIVE PAPERBACKS

FOR A FULL LIST OF PUBLICATIONS, VISIT:
www.dalkeyarchive.com